EMBODYING
Ambiguity

KRITIK: GERMAN LITERARY
THEORY AND CULTURAL STUDIES

Liliane Weissberg
Editor

*A complete listing of the books in this series
can be found at the back of this volume.*

EMBODYING
Ambiguity

Androgyny and Aesthetics
from WINCKELMANN to KELLER

CATRIONA MACLEOD

WAYNE STATE UNIVERSITY PRESS   Detroit

Library of Congress Cataloging-in-Publication Data

MacLeod, Catriona, 1963–
    Embodying ambiguity : androgyny and aesthetics from Winckelmann to
Keller / Catriona MacLeod.
        p.   cm. — (Kritik)
    Includes bibliographical references and index.
    ISBN 0-8143-2539-4 (alk. paper)
    1. German literature—18th century—History and criticism.
    2. German literature—19th century—History and criticism.
    3. Androgyny (Psychology) in literature.   4. Aesthetics,
German—18th century.   5. Aesthetics, German—19th century.
    6. Bildungsroman.   I. Title.   II. Series: Kritik (Detroit, Mich.)
PT313.M33   1998
830.9'353—dc21   97-47168

Designed by Betty Pilon

FOR NEIL

"... man sagt ja, die Wahrheit liege in der Mitte."
"Keineswegs!" erwiderte Montan: "in der Mitte bleibt das
Problem liegen, unerforschlich vielleicht, vielleicht auch
zugänglich, wenn man es darnach anfängt."

"... they say the truth lies in the middle."
"Not at all!" replied Montan: "The middle is where the
problem lies, unfathomable perhaps, but perhaps
also accessible, if you go after it."

Goethe, *Wilhelm Meisters Wanderjahre*

Contents

4

Collecting Statues   185

Acknowledgments

I would like to express my gratitude to the Mrs. Giles Whiting Foundation for invaluable support during the initial stages of this project. I am indebted to St. Hugh's College, Oxford, for awarding me a Randall-MacIver research fellowship, making it possible for me to revise and extend the book. The Frederick W. Hilles Publications Fund of Yale University also provided generous assistance.

Chapter 1 was adapted in part from my essay "The 'Third Sex' in an Age of Difference: Androgyny and Homosexuality in Winckelmann, Friedrich Schlegel and Kleist," in *Outing Goethe and His Age,* edited by Alice A. Kuzniar, with permission of the publishers, Stanford University Press. © 1996 by the Board of Trustees of the Leland Stanford Junior University. An earlier version of chapter 2 appeared in *Modern Language Notes* 103, no. 3: 389–46.

I am very grateful to my dissertation director, Dorrit Cohn, for her keen criticism, her guidance and encouragement. My thanks also go to Marjorie Garber, who was generous with her insights into "thirdness." I owe a special debt to Eric Downing for his always inspiring conversation as well as for his careful readings of the manuscript. His intellectual and personal support during all the phases of this project have been critical.

Further thanks go to my editors at Wayne State University Press, for their perspicuity and patience. Several others friends and colleagues encouraged me along the way, reading parts of my manuscript, offering me helpful suggestions and criticism, and sharpening my focus and ideas: Bettina Brandt, Jody Freeman, Abigail Gillman, Cyrus Hamlin, Alice Kuzniar, Ritchie Robertson, Anette Schwarz, Emery Snyder. To all of them, my warmest thanks. The students in my literature seminars at Yale supplied energy and new insights. Finally, and above all, I would like to thank my husband, Neil Garrioch.

Introduction: Theorizing Androgyny

To look at the androgyne is to look at how and why Western culture engenders fictions, narrates gender. The paradox of bourgeois myth, as Roland Barthes has argued so compellingly, is that it conspires to lend the vagaries of history the appearance of immutability, even of biological necessity: "Are there objects which are *inevitably* a source of suggestiveness, as Baudelaire suggested about Woman? Certainly not: one can conceive of very ancient myths, but there are no eternal ones; for it is human history which converts reality into speech, and it alone rules the life and the death of mythical language. Ancient or not, mythology can only have a historical foundation, for myth is a type of speech chosen by history: it cannot possibly evolve from the 'nature' of things."[1]

Aristophanes' playful recounting of the story of primordial union and its collapse into fragmentation, in Plato's *Symposium,* sets in motion a powerful cultural narrative about the origins of human sexuality. Significantly, Aristophanes himself lends credence to his argument—or "naturalizes" it, as Barthes would say—by grounding it within a mythological framework, the account of the divine interventions that modeled men and women as sexual beings. What is it about the myth of the androgyne that makes it such an addictive one for German artists and theorists of the late eighteenth and nineteenth centuries? Aristophanes' discourse on desire, as I show in this study, gains particular resonance in the German context of *Bildung,* itself a modern discourse on desire, formation, and discipline. And given that this particular bourgeois myth acquires central importance in an age that is bent on lending sexual difference the air of scientific necessity, it would seem particularly important to investigate textual fabrications of the androgyne, a figure that, promising wholeness, appears to contest binarism.

According to Aristophanes, human beings were originally of three sexes—male, female, and male-female—but because of their greed for divine power the gods resolved to split them in half, leaving us today in a perpetual quest for our lost halves. His account, importantly, is developmental in nature, falling into three distinct stages. The primordial human being was a spherical creature, bountifully equipped with two sets of hands, legs, faces, sexual organs, and so on. This comically polymorphous creature might be described as belonging to a fundamentally presexual, undifferentiated phase of human development. In the second stage of human history, following the divine punishment of differentiation, each creature was doomed to seek its lost half, in a quest to achieve human completion. (Aristophanes notes that this urge for completion could be fulfilled either through homosexual or heterosexual union.) The tragedy of this anatomical phase lay in the fact that the human genitalia were now positioned in such a way as to impede internal fertilization. In addition to this reproductive problem, as Aristophanes reveals, these human beings faced an even more fatal dilemma: now that they had been refashioned as sexual beings, and because of their obsessive quest for erotic fulfillment, they were barred from leading active, productive lives. "Now, since their natural form had been cut in two, each one longed for its own other half, and so they would throw their arms about each other, weaving themselves together, wanting to grow together. In that condition they would die from hunger and general idleness, because they would not do anything apart from each other."[2] In this phase of human development, then, the desire for sexual union meant certain death. Aristophanes then tells of the gods' mercy toward these sad and doomed human creatures: in order to make internal reproduction possible, Zeus, adopting the divine role of master surgeon or master sculptor, relocated the genitalia to the front of the humans' bodies. What this meant, on the one hand, was the possibility of social productivity, for both homosexual and heterosexual couples: "The purpose of this was so that, when a man embraced a woman, he would cast his seed and they would have children; but when male embraced male, they would at least have the satisfaction of intercourse, after which they could stop embracing, return to their jobs, and look after their other needs in life" (191C). On the other hand, the principal goal of sexual intercourse now became procreation, with human beings plunged into a new tragedy, that of sexual difference, of radical alterity. And for all the comic elements of the poet's narrative, his story is also undercut by the tragic awareness of the precarious nature of sexual union, which can at best offer a fleeting and enigmatic echo of original wholeness. Love, for Aristophanes, derives always from a primordial loss, and human beings find themselves embarked on a chain of supplemental love relationships that can only be substitutes for unobtainable wholeness.

Aristophanes' story of androgynous desire spells out the hopeless nostalgia behind the quest for plenitude, as well as its tantalizing promise of meaning, forever veiled:[3]

> No one would think it is the intimacy of sex—that mere sex is the reason each lover takes so great and deep a joy in being with the other. It's obvious that the soul of every lover longs for something else; his soul cannot say what it is, but like an oracle it has a sense of what it wants, and like an oracle it hides behind a riddle. (192C–D)

The myth of the primal being as a cosmic androgyne whose original unity disintegrates into a world of conflicting parts has persisted throughout Western philosophy, theology, psychology, and literature.[4] Following influential readings by Ricarda Huch and Albert Béguin that emphasized the centrality of the romantic androgyne as a harmonious figure alluding to prelapsarian unity, literary scholars have traditionally understood androgyny in a rather positive light, as a nostalgia for a lost psychic Eden or Platonic plenitude, thus, as I will show, tending to reproduce the structures imposed by the romantic version of the myth.[5] As I suggested, however, the androgynous myth seems to hold particular fascination for those historical moments when cultures are actively engaged in rethinking the most basic assumptions about gender and sexuality—whether that be the late eighteenth century, with its scientific and literary inscription and codification of difference, or the second half of the twentieth century, with the rise of the feminist movement and its ongoing debates over essentialism. It is no coincidence that Lou Andreas-Salomé, Luce Irigaray, and Julia Kristeva, among others, have made the Platonic account of androgyny the focal point of theoretical investigations of difference.[6] What I want to stress here is the continued intensity of the theoretical discussions surrounding androgyny and their significance for the varied positions staked out by modern feminism—an invitation, as I see it, to explore again the ambiguities of sex and gender that lie at the heart of classical German literature and aesthetics.

As at the close of the eighteenth century, with its emphasis on dualistic structures, androgyny—expressed as the desire for the expanded middle, where life is at its fullest and most beautiful—has seemed, in the eyes of certain gender theorists, to contain the potential to transcend or to subvert the reign of binaristic thought. The current theoretical debates about androgyny, which have succinctly been described by Kari Weil as "moving through claims to oneness, difference, and differance," were initiated by the reception of Virginia Woolf in Anglo-American academic feminism of the 1960s, and perhaps more specifically by the publication in 1964 of the book *Toward a Recognition of Androgyny,* Carolyn Heilbrun's enthusiastic recuperation of the androgynous ideal—in this case reformulated as a feminist myth promising both psychological and sociopolitical equality between the sexes.[7] In the pioneering essay *A Room of One's Own* (1929), Woolf herself paid tribute to the romantic conception of the androgynous creative genius that had been so famously evoked by Coleridge:

> I went on amateurishly to sketch a plan of the soul so that in each of us two powers preside, one male, one female; and in the man's brain the man predominates over the woman, and in the woman's brain the woman predominates over the man. The normal and comfortable state of being is that when the two live in harmony together, spiritually cooperating. If one is a man, still the woman part of the brain must have effect; and a woman also must have intercourse with the man in her. Coleridge perhaps meant this when he said that a great mind is androgynous. It is when this fusion takes place that the mind is fully fertilized and uses all its faculties.[8]

I turn briefly now to articulations of androgyny in German literary criticism and their convergence with early feminist concerns; more precisely, I want to draw the comparison between Woolf's influential appeal to androgyny and that of Ricarda Huch, the pioneering woman writer and scholar of German romanticism. Huch's important essay on women's literature, written thirty years before Woolf's *A Room of One's Own* but published posthumously, proposed a remarkably similar theory of androgynous art and genius.[9] Echoing eighteenth-century views of distinctive "masculine" and "feminine" aesthetic capabilities, Huch readily identified the "form-giving" spheres of architecture and sculpture as masculine, the more "spiritual" spheres of painting and music as feminine. But in the person of the artist one might also encounter what Huch called "eigentümliche[n] Mischungen, Versuche[n] der Natur, das mannweibliche Menschenideal hervorzubringen" (peculiar mixtures, nature's attempts to produce the androgynous human ideal). In another essay, on the nineteenth-century writer Annette von Droste-Hülshoff, Huch used this argument about the gender-neutral nature of aesthetic creativity to legitimate her exclusion of Droste-Hülshoff from a separate (and, one must surmise, implicitly inferior) category of "Frauen-literatur," or women's writing:

> Die Musen gehören zu den himmlischen Gestalten, die Mann und Weib nicht kennen; der einzige Maßstab für einen Künstler ist die Kunst, nicht Nationalität oder Geschlecht oder Konfession oder Stand. Geschlecht kann es schon deswegen nicht sein, weil jeder Dichter androgyn ist, es gibt keinen, der nicht Männliches und Weibliches in sich vereinigte.[10]

The muses belong to those divine beings who know neither male nor female: the only measure of an artist is art, not nationality or sex or religious denomination or class. Sex cannot be the criterion, for the simple reason that every poet is androgynous. There is no poet who does not unite within his person masculinity and femininity.

Where Woolf praised Shakespeare as the most perfect incarnation of such an androgynous genius, Huch venerated what she saw as the ambidextrous personality of Goethe. What she did not attempt, however, was to offer any suggestions about how this psychological "androgyny" might have translated itself into representation in Goethe's works (vol. 11, 508). She also paid tribute to the personalities and works of the German romantics, in particular to Friedrich Schlegel's novel *Lucinde,* a text that has since then been at the forefront of German debates on gender and literature, on androgyny and *Bildung.* Significantly for my arguments in this study, Huch's work on romanticism situated Schlegel's concept of androgyny alongside the mystical celebration of heterosexual union to be found in the writings of Novalis and Franz von Baader, thus eliding the corporeal and aesthetic effects of homoeroticism or bisexuality contained in the novel and mobilizing subsequent trends in hetero-textual interpretation. In a related move, Droste-Hülshoff's "mannish" personality, in Huch's complementary vision of androgyny, finds psychic wholeness in the symmetrical "girlishness" of her beloved Levin Schücking (vol. 6, 875).

Such reformulations of romantic plenitude proved powerfully seductive to Heilbrun, who expressed her own faith in androgyny as a transcendent psychological and aesthetic principle. (Similar expressions of enthusiasm are to be found in German literary scholarship of the 1970s, such as Richard Exner's paean to the "androgynous" nature of art and the artist, which takes as its starting point for an analysis of German texts a discussion of Woolf.)[11] But while Heilbrun's purely intellectual model of androgyny seemed to subvert sexual polarization, it also, as several critics noted, depended on heterosexual complementarity. What is more, most of the writers hailed by Heilbrun as "androgynous" were male, foremost among them Shakespeare, thus suggesting, as indeed had Woolf's and Huch's essays, the primacy of the "masculine" side of this androgynous equation. (Huch's essay on women's literature praised Goethe's supposed androgyny yet named no female writer.) It is also important to stress Heilbrun's implicit distancing of the term *androgyny* from *homosexuality* or *bisexuality,* her strategic avoidance of the ambiguous, eroticized body—this despite her tantalizing recognition that the ideal of androgyny arises in the novel during a historical period of polarization. As I will show in chapter 1, below, this deflection from the ambiguous body can be regarded as another uncanny repetition of eighteenth- and nineteenth-century discourses on androgyny.

Heilbrun's invocation of androgyny became a focal point for the emerging field of feminist literary theory. Charges of essentialism, that this was merely a seductive new (hetero)sexist myth, were, however, quick to follow the publication of her book. A special issue of the journal *Women's Studies* (significantly, only the second issue of the journal), based on a special session on androgyny at the 1973 annual meeting of the Modern Language Association, contained, along with an essay by Heilbrun and some more receptive voices, a chorus of denunciations and warnings.[12] What most critics found troubling about the revitalizing of this concept was a strange collapsing of categories. On the one hand, many feminists could and did embrace the unisex fluidity of the 1970s; on the other hand, and this was the difficulty, they detected the polar structures upon which such an androgynous ideal appeared to be premised, definable psychological categories of "masculine" and "feminine" that were aligned in a problematic fashion with the biological categories of "male" and "female." Androgyny, according to many of these commentators, was merely a camouflage for tried and tested patriarchal values and aesthetics. Barbara Gelpi and Cynthia Secor, for example, contended that androgynes are always feminized males and never masculine women; while Daniel Harris and Catherine Stimpson rightly observed that the myth of androgyny has often been used to express a codified cultural anxiety about homosexuals (the following chapters of this book will be opening up both of these provocative assertions for investigation).[13] Following on from this hotly contested debate, feminists began to criticize the dictatorship of binaries arguably at the heart of the myth and the problematic location of woman in the role of supplementary "other." In a more separatist vein of critical thought intent on carving out lost literary matrilineages, Elaine Showalter's *A Literature of Their Own,* once again turning to Virginia Woolf, repudiated her use of androgyny. For Showalter, Woolf's "flight into androgyny" represented sexual sublimation, a means of evading one's "painful femaleness," as well as a refusal to face up to the ideological implications of oppression.[14] It is indeed true, as I have indicated in the case of Huch, that when women writers of earlier generations appealed to a utopian androgynous understanding of creativity, this frequently involved the abjection of the female body. For example, a series of talks presented in 1957 by prominent German women writers on the theme of "Frauendichtung" (women's literature) presented the message that the androgynous nature of art had the power to liberate women from the baser corporeal realm of femininity.[15] As Kari Weil notes in her detailed analysis of the theoretical turns and twists in the history of androgyny in Anglo-American and French criticism, some leading voices in the women's movement would completely repudiate their initial enthusiasm for such a psychological ideal. Mary Daly, for example, having heralded androgyny as a transcendent model of "psychic wholeness" in her book *Beyond God the Father* (1973), savaged the ideal as a "semantic abomination" five years later in *Gyn/Ecology:*

> Feminist theorists have gone through frustrating attempts to describe our integrity by such terms as *androgyny*. Experience proved that this word, which we now recognize as expressing pseudowholeness in its combination of distorted gender descriptions, failed and betrayed our thought. The deceptive word was a trap, hard to avoid on an earlier stage of the Journey. When we heard the word echoed back by those who misinterpreted our thought we realized that combining the "halves" offered to consciousness by patriarchal language usually results in portraying something more like a hole than a whole.[16]

Kristeva, in a provocative reading of the (homo)erotics of Plato's *Symposium* and *Phaedrus,* also denounced the androgyne, as "the sliest masquerade of a liquidation of femininity."[17] In the literary sphere, Ingeborg Bachmann's experimental novel *Malina* (1971) can be read as a repudiation of the androgynous fiction of the whole, that is, of heterosexual supplementarity. Despite asserting at the beginning of her story "das ist nicht eine Frage des Geschlechts, der Art" (this isn't a question of sex or kind), the narrator continues by staging the relationship between herself and the shadowy Malina in supplemental terms relating both to sex and to narrative form:

> Mir scheint es dann, daß seine Ruhe davon herrührt, weil ich ein zu unwichtiges und bekanntes Ich für ihn bin, als hätte er mich ausgeschieden, einen Abfall, eine überflüssige Menschwerdung, als wäre ich nur aus seiner Rippe gemacht und ihm seit jeher entbehrlich, aber auch eine unvermeidliche dunkle Geschichte, die seine Geschichte begleitet, ergänzen will, die er aber von seiner klaren Geschichte absondert und abgrenzt.

> Then it seems to me that his calm comes from my ego being too familiar, too unimportant for him, as if he had rejected me as waste, a superfluous something-made-human, as if I were merely the dispensable product of his rib, but at the same time an unavoidable dark tale accompanying and hoping to supplement his own bright story, a tale which he, however, detaches and delimits.[18]

The novel turns on images of radical disunity: although she optimistically announces at the outset the healing of "die Schizothymie, das Schizoid der Welt, ihr wahnsinniger, sich weitender Spalt" (28) (the world's schizoid soul, its crazy, gaping split [14]), the narrator's struggle to cover over the abyss of difference ends in her disappearance in a crack in the wall. The impossible dialectic between male and female forces within the narrator's psyche degenerates into warfare, and finally into the swallowing up of the narrator herself.

If the confidence in androgyny as an equalizing, synthetic principle was quickly countered by the rise of such "gynocriticism" as Daly's, certain strands of French feminism and poststructuralism, with their theoretical reevaluations of sexual difference, contributed to what has been termed the emergent "third voice" in the debate.[19] Derrida, for example, spoke of the "desire for a sexuality without number"; Barthes spoke of an "amoral oscillation," of difference as "the very movement of dispersion, of friability, a shimmer . . . encroachments, overflows, leaks, skids, shifts, slips"—a need to pluralize both the sexes and the meanings of the opposition of the sexes.[20] Hélène Cixous, in her polemical essay of 1975, "The Laugh of the Medusa," rebuffed the fiction of a "total being" composed of two halves and celebrated instead a nomadic bisexuality, signaled by instability, multiplicity, and mutability.[21] With the new emphasis on the body by theorists such as Irigaray and Cixous, and on the blurring of borderlines between sexes and sexualities, now conceived of in all their multiplicity, beyond the number two, it appeared once more possible in the 1980s to speak in positive terms of androgyny. In this vein, Susan Suleiman, in her introduction to *The Female Body in Western Culture,* a collection of essays on the history of female representation, concluded with a hopeful gesture toward one of the most enduring (and problematic) fictions of gender—but coining kaleidoscopic new permutations on the word *androgyny, androgynandry* or *gynandrogyny.*[22] Rather than presenting a utopian vision of androgynous unity, of amalgamation, these writers on gender stressed the dislodging of stable meanings and identities.

Kari Weil's assessment of what she sees as the "third" phase of feminist criticism emphasizes its interest in contradiction, both in the rhetorical structures of irony, performance, and mimicry reclaimed as feminist strategies and in the political need to retain a concept of women as real subjects. The embodiment of postmodern feminist irony, according to this account, is the transgressive figure of the cyborg, introduced by Donna Haraway in her essay "A Manifesto for Cyborgs: Science, Technology, and Socialist Feminism in the 1980's."[23] A hybrid of male and female, technology and nature, human and animal, the cyborg is characteristic of a postmodern technological age and explicitly subversive of the classical desire for bodily integrity and wholeness. In this respect, it is revealing to compare it with the

Female Grotesque. (From *Abbildungen zu Johann Joachim Winckelmanns Sämtlichen Werken.* Donauöschingen: Verlag Deutscher Classiker, 1835. Courtesy of Avery Architectural and Fine Arts Library, Columbia University in the City of New York.)

grotesque body of the hermaphrodite in eighteenth-century culture, which over the course of the century increasingly became the object of medical scrutiny and taxonomy, as the uncanny double of the idealized, seamless whole of the androgyne. Significantly for my study, the grotesque has been characterized as a "species of confusion" where binary thinking collapses; despite its initial impression of unity, it discredits this unity because of its manifestly composite nature.[24] The rhetorically constructed cyborg is simply a mirror of late-twentieth-century reality. When late-night television talk shows parade before our increasingly habituated eyes seemingly endless throngs of androgynous rock stars, models, and actors, transvestites, intersexuals, and transsexuals, have we not all become (at least potentially) transsexuals, as Baudrillard has put it—with the interventions of the surgeon's knife quotidian postmodern allusions to Zeus's surgical strikes in the *Symposium*?[25] Nor is this simply a manufactured "third" sex: recent scientific work, notably by Anne Fausto-Sterling, has indicated the lability

of biological sex categories, questioning the often reassuring belief in two
real sexes and the utopian faith in a third.[26]

From Woolf to Wolf. Virginia Woolf's androgynous fictions have
proved a provocation and an inspiration to Anglo-American feminism,
and Christa Wolf, the most prominent German woman writer of postwar
years and herself an iconic figure for German feminism, has also rehearsed
the possibilities and impossibilities of romantic androgyny. In her utopian
narrative *Kein Ort. Nirgends* (1979), the account of an imagined encounter
between Karoline von Günderrode and Heinrich von Kleist in 1804, Wolf
presented a symmetrical dance of gender involving protagonists who themselves oscillate uneasily between polarities of "feminine" and "masculine"
and thus face alienation from a society predicated on binaries.[27] The fall
into difference, as Kleist observes with anguished insight, and echoing
Aristophanes, has caused a tragic split between man and woman (153).
For her part, Wolf's Günderrode, speaking in the voice of her time in a
hybrid work permeated by citation, signals the modern fragmentation of
men, torn between the public and the private spheres, and the desire for
plenitude experienced by women (137). Günderrode, first marked by the text
in decidedly androgynous, neuter terms as "Günderrödchen" (21), responds
in an interesting manner to the effeminate Kleist's remarks on difference:
it is the coexistence of mutually incompatible elements of "masculine" and
"feminine" within the psyches of each poet that is the true source of their
alienation. Thus, the focus seems to veer from a sense of difference as loss,
in Kleist's case, to a desire for absolute difference, for perfect symmetry
and complementarity, in Günderrode's. This theoretical move is intriguing:
Kleist and Günderrode, as historical citations, could be said to function as
proxies in the modern debates about androgyny. In a 1982 interview, Wolf
detected a critical antipathy toward what could be termed "the androgynous,"
what she described as fluid transitions ("fließende Übergänge"), and she went
on to express her personal discontent with rigid antinomies ("starre[n] Anti-
nomien").[28] Nevertheless, despite her tribute to blurred boundaries, Wolf's
line of thought depends on precisely these categories of "masculine" and
"feminine." The 1982 interview begins with a discussion of the systematic
exclusion of "the feminine" from industrialized societies, thus presupposing
a stable and knowable category of "the feminine" and arguably replicating
the binaristic structures inscribed at the close of the eighteenth century
with its invocation of the repressed feminine (880). Finally, what of the
utopian vision of "Berührung" (the touch) contained by Wolf's narrative,
which strikingly anticipates Irigaray's reading of the *Symposium* in her
Ethics of Sexual Difference? "Frau. Mann. Unbrauchbare Wörter. Wir, jeder

gefangen in seinem Geschlecht. Die Berührung, nach der es uns so unendlich verlangt, es gibt sie nicht" (159). (Woman. Man. Untenable words. We two, each imprisoned in his sex. That touching we desire so infinitely does not exist [108]). That fusion of male and female differences is at best an ephemeral dream, realizable only in the minds of the artificial and radically noncorporeal figures of Günderrode and Kleist. And, like Irigaray's project, it ultimately presents a curiously static and otherworldly image of the specular heterosexual couple. We seem to have been following an elliptical trajectory, returning again to the supplementary relationship of man and woman that marked the inscription of difference at the end of the eighteenth century. The hope of the touch, however glancing that touch may be, surely enacts the same desire as the dream of androgynous fusion; it is simply a more modest hope.

Cynthia Secor, one of the contributors to the 1974 *Women's Studies* issue on androgyny, voiced her objections to what she believed was a "static image of perfection, in eternity, an image which cannot take into account the rough going of historical process."[29] Barthes, of course, would agree with such a notion of myth as petrification; for him, the very goal of myths is to immobilize or embalm the world, imitating a fixed (and imaginary) universal order.[30] Appropriately, then, eighteenth- and nineteenth-century androgynes make their appearance on the textual stage in the most static form of all: as marble statues. As classical sculptures, they have the force of historical citations. But it is important to realize that they are also *constitutive* of history, playing, as they do, a critical role in the formation of body, of subjectivity, and of culture. *Bildung* implies both the making and the viewing of statues; for this reason, it is critical to ask serious questions about how and where power resides in the representation of ambiguous bodies. It is through looking at the ideal marble form that the fragmented modern viewer—always posited as male in the stories of *Bildung* that I examine—gains a sense of corporeal, psychological, and aesthetic unity. According to Lacan, a critical moment in the psychological development of an infant occurs when the child recognizes his image in a mirror—an image that appears stable, unified, fixed. Tellingly, Lacan stresses the Narcissistic dimension of the fantasy of wholeness by describing this version of the self as "the statue in which man projects himself."[31]

What I emphasize in this study is the strategic deployment of an-drogynous fictions in modern literary constructions of difference. Virginia Woolf, as I have shown, invoked androgyny in what has often been regarded as the first sustained work of feminist literary criticism; and one of the foundational scholarly projects of contemporary feminism has been the investigation, reformulation, and critique of Plato's account of androgyny and the fall into sexual difference. The debates about androgyny have themselves been rehearsed on multiple occasions and thus seem always to be repetitions of earlier androgynous fictions, hovering eternally, it would seem, between cultural complicity and critique. To indicate the citational force of androgyny, I will also demonstrate how readings of this myth can veer from an emphasis on stasis to a celebration of fluidity, and back again, depending on the cultural assumptions (and pedagogical impulses) brought to bear upon it. Remarkable about many poststructuralist approaches to sexuality and gender are the echoes of an earlier, nomadic androgynous subjectivity traced out on the body, which, as I argue, was repressed through a fixation on binary difference—or on what Alice Jardine aptly calls "the classically heterosexual couples of Western philosophy."[32] Aristophanes' androgyne has often been taken as a model of perfect, static balance, yet his account of human sexual development is in fact anything but symmetrical, depending as it does on a dizzying play of combination and recombination and permissive as it is of all the permutations of erotic union, heterosexual or homosexual. At the same time, Aristophanes' narrative does proceed along developmental lines, moving from an image of primordial, polymorphous unity to the fall into sexual difference. For this reason, it is important to delineate the full complexities of the Platonic myth and to reconsider the repeated evocation of ambiguous bodies in modern narratives of difference. The key shift in eighteenth-century literary treatments of androgyny is, I believe, that from a truly polymorphous bisexual model to an ideal of androgyny that regards heterosexual coupling as the norm and thus serves as the mythical cornerstone of an ideology of difference. This reading, it should be noted, itself reflects the general outline of Aristophanes' narrative. The androgyne, the embodiment of diffuseness and instability, merges, as I will show, with the iconic marble statue, the marker of neoclassical stability. The word *Bildung,* with its multiple connotations of forming, shaping, molding, education, cultivation, creation, and construction, is applied in the eighteenth century not only to artifacts such as sculptures but also to the body and mind of the newly disciplined human subject.[33] It is no accident, then, that the encounter with the marmoreal androgyne achieves central importance in German narratives connected with *Bildung,* preoccupied as they are with the dual questions of psychological maturation and bourgeois socialization; nor is it coincidental that both Freud and Lacan turn to Plato's *Symposium* as they map out their versions of human sexual development. Fictions of wholeness, as both Freud and Lacan demonstrate, are all the more powerful in that they are fictions.

Chapter 1 of this study traces a shift that can be detected in the late eighteenth century from the polymorphous, hermaphroditic ideal of androgyny proposed by Winckelmann to a model grounded in heterosexual complementarity central to the aesthetic programs of Wilhelm von Humboldt, Friedrich Schiller, and Friedrich Schlegel. Where Winckelmann's writings on sexually fluid sculptures take pleasure in the aesthetic and erotic effects of polymorphous bodiliness, later theorists who link androgyny, *Bildung,* and sculpture reassert static sexual polarities, thus averting the slide toward homoeroticism.[34] In chapter 2, the book turns to Goethe's classic novel of male maturation, *Wilhelm Meisters Lehrjahre.* In this narrative of bourgeois socialization, the dual-sexed androgyne, representative of the aesthetic realm, is the incarnation of a seductive but perilous phase in the hero's *Bildung,* a phase to be abandoned in favor of strict differentiation and marriage. Chapter 3 considers narratives by Eichendorff and Heine illustrating the late romantic tendency to repress androgynous indeterminacy and, in a parallel move, to transform living women, incarnations of the polymorphously perverse, into marble through the process of specularization. Finally, in chapter 4, I discuss two realist responses to the androgynous myth: Stifter's nostalgic citation of the marble statue, in *Der Nachsommer,* and Keller's parodic treatment of a commodified myth of unity, untenable in an age of atomization.

1

Toward an Androgynous Aesthetic

The "Middle Way" in an Age of Difference

That the eighteenth century is an age historically fixated on binary models of logic and scientific discourse is an argument advanced by, among others, Foucault. Such binaristic systems of signification, for Foucault absolutely central to the emergence of classicism, necessarily exclude the middle and can contain "no intermediary element."[1] Yet it is precisely the classical primacy of polarities that tends, as this chapter will indicate, to produce a desire for the middle and a demand for wholeness. The focus on mediation that permeates much of German thought in the eighteenth century also gives rise to what I will be identifying here as an androgynous aesthetic.

For German writers of the second half of the eighteenth century, Winckelmann's rediscovery of the classical world is critical. Winckelmann, the aesthetic pedagogue, also establishes the mystique of the androgyne, one of the most enduring sexual personae of German aesthetics and literature. It is hardly by mere chance that Winckelmann, the "prime ideologue of pedagogic eros,"[2] chooses to have himself depicted, in a portrait by Anton Maron executed during his time in Rome, with an engraving of Antinous emblematically placed across the leaves of his notebook. Antinous, the youthful favorite of the emperor Hadrian, had become the ideal neoclassical

Anton Maron, Johann Joachim Winckelmann. (Berlin: Bildarchiv Preußischer Kulturbesitz.)

embodiment of the androgyne.[3] The Antinous relief, created around A.D. 140 but rediscovered only in 1735, was the art sensation of its time, celebrated for its sensuality. Indeed, art historian Ellen Spickernagel argues that its sexual indeterminacy was the main cause of its wild success with contemporary viewers. The youthful figure is half-naked, and his robe, falling down in stiff folds, envelops the surface of the delicately modeled torso, seductive to the touch. By contrast, the profile is clearly delineated and severe. The fusion of clarity and delicacy, combined with the youth's melancholic expression, seemed to the art critics so successful that Antinous became the highest incarnation of the androgyne.[4]

It has become an academic commonplace to say of classical German aesthetics that it is underpinned by the notion of "the middle," or, in German, "Mitte," "Maß," "gemäßigt." Walter Bosshard, for example, gave his book on Winckelmann the subtitle *Ästhetik der Mitte,*[5] drawing on the neoclassical topos Winckelmann himself elucidates in the following passage. Beauty is an ideal "middle way": "Die Schönheit ist nichts anderes als das Mittel von zwei extremis. Wie eine Mittelstraße in allen Dingen das *Beste* ist, so ist sie auch das *Schönste.* Um das Mittel zu treffen, muß man die beiden extrema kennen." (Beauty is nothing other than the middle between two extremes. Just as the middle path is always the best, it is always the most beautiful. In order to find the middle, one must know the two extremes.)[6] Such a middle way also suggests a temporal location of "in-betweenness": a nostalgic vision of classical Greek perfection, a utopian call for an aesthetic state that could restore such wholeness. Moving both backward and forward in history, theorists like Winckelmann and Wilhelm von Humboldt, Friedrich Schiller, and Friedrich Schlegel recall and anticipate a mode of existence through art that is neither simply active nor simply passive, neither wholly "male" nor wholly "female," an ideal of androgynous beauty. For Winckelmann, as I will show, the classical Greek statue of the hermaphrodite becomes a cult object for contemplation, gaining life from the viewer's unresolvable struggle to resolve the statue's sexual indeterminacy. His is an artistic credo that draws its breath from ambivalence. In Schiller's *Über die ästhetische Erziehung des Menschen* (On the Aesthetic Education of Man) the key metaphor for the aesthetic state is the androgynous statue of the Juno Ludovisi—a tantalizing duality of maleness and femaleness, of divinity and humanity, of activity and passivity: "Indem der weibliche Gott unsre Anbetung heischt, entzündet das gottgleiche Weib unsre Liebe." (While the woman-god demands our veneration, the godlike woman kindles our love.)[7] For Schiller, as for Winckelmann, the central importance of this androgynous work of art lies in its ability to engage the viewer, as a whole person, in aesthetic play. This aesthetic play, which liberates us as fully integrated human beings, Schiller describes in the *Über die ästhetische Erziehung des Menschen* (vol. 20: 383) as the "mittlerer Zustand" (middle condition). In a similar vein, theologian Friedrich Schleiermacher, in a pedagogically minded women's "catechism" published in 1798 in the Schlegels' journal *Athenäum,* conceives of a utopian androgynous state recalling a form of "boundless" humanity that existed before the fall into difference, and in which the "Schranken des Geschlechts" (barriers of sex) would be overcome.[8]

Yet this appeal to a middle voice, to the paradoxical union of opposites that is the androgyne, becomes central at a time not only when difference, and specifically sexual difference, is a burning intellectual concern but also when it is being inscribed as a scientific fact of life. Not only are the sexes different, in the late eighteenth century, but they are different in every conceivable way, both morally and physically.[9] Schiller's *Über die ästhetische Erziehung des Menschen* was published, as it happened, in the same year and in the same journal as Wilhelm von Humboldt's pivotal and programmatic essays on sexual difference, "Über den Geschlechtsunterschied und dessen Einfluß auf die organische Natur" (On Sexual Difference and Its Influence on Organic Nature) and "Über die männliche und weibliche Form" (On Masculine and Feminine Form). Here, readers find delineated binary oppositions based on what Humboldt sees as the primary natural opposition, that between male and female. All the others—subject/object, movement/stasis, energy/matter—follow logically. Here, too, may be detected an attempt to overcome the newly established rule of difference. Once again, as in Schiller's works, a utopian moment of transcendence is located in the aesthetic realm, and the great artist, who is said to unite both male and female forms of creativity, has the ability to arouse in the viewer of art what the early scholar of androgyny Fritz Giese termed "eine wahre Synthese mit der gedachten Schönheit" (a genuine synthesis with imaginary beauty).[10] Synthesis of the sexes is suggested, along with synthesis with the object of contemplation. And yet the androgynous work of art remains characterized by its very diffuseness, ambiguity, and elusiveness, as in Friedrich Schlegel's novel of androgyny, *Lucinde,* which announces a scintillating aesthetic of "Verwirrung" (confusion).

It is surely no accident that every writer to focus on the figure of the androgyne, as well as every scholar who seeks to probe its enduring popularity, stumbles over definitions. The androgyne seduces at every turn, bewilders and frustrates at every turn. Yet it is used as the defining metaphor of a whole utopian aesthetic. As early as 1919, in the first major scholarly study of the romantic androgyne, Fritz Giese pointed to the considerable inconsistencies in eighteenth-century theorists' use of terms such as *hermaphrodite, eunuch,* and *androgyne.*[11] This confusion about clearly defining the androgynous body has persisted down to more recent scholarly works. For my purposes, I shall be arguing for hermaphroditism as biological fact, androgyny as poetic fiction.[12] If Winckelmann chooses the term *hermaphrodite,* however, what it really indicates is the plastic tradition in which he has been trained, since it is the term given to Greek statues of dual-sexed beings. What perhaps remains most revealing for current studies on androgyny is Giese's observation that Winckelmann seriously doubted the existence of real physical hermaphrodites, that is, human beings in whom both male and female genitalia are found.[13] The "true" hermaphrodite of Greek art depicts not an authentic human form but an unknown, and idealized, androgynous divinity.[14] So we can say, as Giese himself suggests, that the androgyne adopted by Winckelmann as an ideal of beauty must be, by its very nature, an aesthetic construction, self-consciously artificial.

It is also a linguistic construction. The word *androgyne* is a composite, suggesting in itself a forcible bringing together of polar opposites, an artful fusion. But it is an unruly word, one whose referentiality constantly eludes. Masquerading as the union of opposites, the word itself maintains separation, a concrete side-by-side of disparate elements, rather than enacting fusion. It can do no more than stage harmony. This point is emphasized by Freud in his essay "Über den Gegensinn der Urworte" ("The Antithetical Meaning of Primal Words") (1910): words that set together antithetical meanings attempt, in the manner of dreams, to combine opposites in an impossible unity.[15] The paradox becomes even more obvious in a language such as German, where the noun is coupled with a masculine article *(der Androgyn),* rather than the neuter article one might expect.[16] The problematic sexual hierarchy remaining in the concept here becomes visible. Perhaps the androgyne's elusive being is best expressed by an impossible linguistic sign—impossible in the sense that this composite signifier can at best allude to a forever deferred signified.[17]

Winckelmann: The Beautiful Boy as Aesthetic Icon

If the word *androgyne* is itself a composite, so, too, is the aesthetic for which it becomes a cipher: the neoclassicism of Winckelmann. Joel Black has convincingly made the link between Zeuxis's principle of *ars combinatoria,* related by Pliny, Cicero, and Dionysius of Halicarnassus, and Winckelmann's principle of "natural selection and artificial recombination."[18] Widely recounted in neoclassical theory, perhaps with the greatest force for future generations in Giovanni Pietro Bellori's *Le vite de' pittori, scultori et architetti moderne* (1672), Zeuxis's story may be briefly summarized. Having sought in vain a woman who would match up to his ideal of beauty and who could model for his Helen, the artist Zeuxis gathers in his studio the five most beautiful virgins of Croton, each of whom possesses at least one physical feature to perfection—shoulders, legs, breasts, and so on. By combining these individually perfect parts, Zeuxis is able to represent aesthetically a perfect feminine whole. Fragmentary traces of beauty sought after in nature are recombined in the hands of the master so that they—as a composite whole—transcend the deficiencies of nature.[19]

As Black shows, Winckelmann's aesthetics go a step farther, by suggesting that such a process of selection and recombination should not be restricted to the presentation of a single-sex ideal. For Winckelmann, as he describes it in his *Geschichte der Kunst des Altertums,* the Greek ideal of beauty "besteht darin, daß sie die Formen einer Jugend von längerer Dauer im weiblichen Geschlechte der Männlichkeit eines schönen Jünglings einverleibeten" (stems from the fact that it incorporated into the manliness of a beautiful boy the forms of enduring feminine youth [vol. 4: 75]). Greek sculptors have succeeded in creating an ideal form of indeterminate sexuality through their use of eunuchs as models, but this form "unterscheidet sich jedoch . . . allezeit sowohl von männlichen als von weiblichen Gewächsen, und ist eine mittlere Gestalt zwischen beiden" (differs, however, . . . as much from masculine as from feminine form, and is a middle entity between both [vol. 4: 73]). Yet the highest form of this combinatory art, the purest form of indeterminate beauty, has no models in nature, not even the most beautiful maidens of Croton. The eunuch, in Winckelmann's aesthetic hierarchy, is at best a beautiful but ephemeral shadow of the true androgynous ideal.[20] This ideal is represented by the Greeks in their sculptures of certain deities. Winckelmann writes, "die Alten gaben einigen derselben in mystischer Bedeutung beide Geschlechter in einem vermischet" (the ancients gave some of them, with mystical significance, both sexes in one [vol. 4: 75]), and he goes on:

> Die Kunst ging noch weiter, und vereinigte die Schönheiten und Eigenschaften beiderlei Geschlechter in den Bildern der *Hermaphroditen.* Die vielen *Hermaphroditen* in verschiedener Größe und Stellung zeigen, daß die Künstler in der aus beiden Geschlechtern vermischten Natur ein Bild hoher Schönheit auszudrücken gesuchet haben, und dieses Bild war *idealisch.* . . . *Hermaphroditen,* dergleichen die Kunst hervorgebracht hat, sind vermuthlich niemals erzeuget. Alle Figuren dieser Art haben eine jungfräuliche Brust, nebst den Zeugungsgliedern unsers Geschlechts, und im Übrigen das Gewächs in weiblicher Gestalt, so wie die Züge des Gesichts.

> Art went still further, and united the beauty and characteristics peculiar to each sex in the images of *hermaphrodites.* The many *hermaphrodites* of different size and posture show that artists intended to express in this entity comprised of both sexes an image of exalted beauty, and this image was *ideal.* . . . Hermaphrodites such as those produced by art have probably never

been conceived in reality. All figures of this kind have, in addition to the reproductive organs of our sex, virginal breasts, and their bodies and facial appearance are generally feminine. (vol. 4: 75–76)

Thus, the androgynous ideal of beauty is, from the outset, set apart from the natural world, above it, floating above time. It becomes the cipher for a mystical union of the sexes, for what Mircea Eliade, in his work on religious traditions of androgyny, has termed "the divine androgyne," accessible to human beings only in the form of a mystery or paradox.[21] The androgynous ideal, then, is an aesthetic construction, outside nature and beyond human understanding. More than this, suggests Black, the true physical hermaphrodite—a genuinely composite, hybrid being in whom the genitalia of both sexes are present—could not correspond to Winckelmann's seamlessly blended aesthetic ideal, "a delicate hermaphrodite of merely ambiguous sexuality."[22] Black continues:

> In attempts to represent the androgynous ideal, a new combination of parts does not result in the whole; some transformation—and beyond this, some transsubstantiation not unlike that featured in the ancient Eleusinian mysteries—is required in which a *part* of the body, unknown in nature and unrepresentable in art, must be called forth. . . . For in limiting ourselves to a composite form with multiple sex-features, a creature of multi-stable sexuality whose appearance would be dramatically unlike the restful beauty of Winckelmann's hermaphrodite, a grotesque and lecherous creature which would be the very

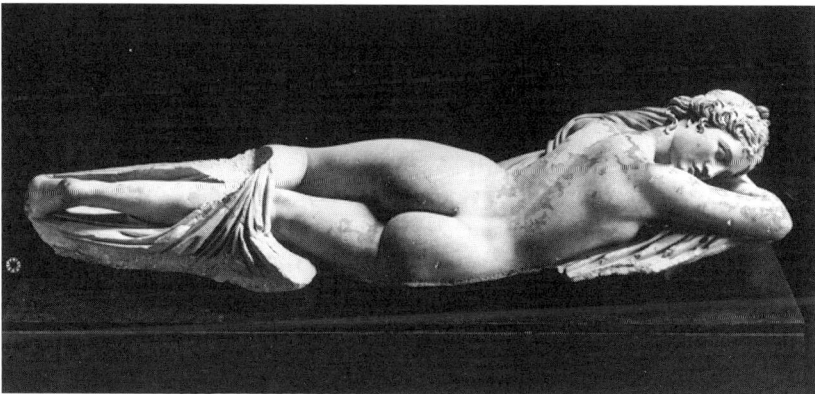

Hermaphrodite. (Rome: Museo Nazionale Romano delle Terme. Photo © Alinari /Art Resource, New York.)

opposite of Winckelmann's lovely faun—we would in effect be confronted by a monster.[23]

Indeed, the decorative popularity of the hermaphrodite in classical art, a vogue that began in the fourth century B.C., is in itself paradoxical, since everywhere in antiquity the birth of a real hermaphrodite was cause for horror. Since a hermaphrodite birth was a bad omen, presaging war, disaster, or plague, the infant was usually destroyed or abandoned. Such children were thought of as monstrous signs of parents' secret sins.

Already we have witnessed some of the uncanny doubleness that will mark the androgyne's future: monstrosity in the real world versus perfection in the aesthetic realm; overdetermination versus openness of form; instability versus peaceful harmony. This unsettling link between the beautiful and the grotesque will underpin the concept of the androgyne in its literary incarnations. Doubleness is inherent in the structure of the androgyne's name.

Doubleness is also a dominant feature of Winckelmann's writing. If the sculpture of the androgyne is characterized by its embracing of both masculine and feminine characteristics, Winckelmann's descriptions of such statues rely for effect primarily on the piling up of oppositional pairs and oxymorons, as well as on rhythmical symmetry. In his account of the Belvedere Apollo, we find a perfect example of Winckelmann's attempt to create a discourse that might itself hint at the androgynous ideal. The sculpture of Apollo displays "Verachtung" (disdain) and "Unmuth" (displeasure), but also "Friede," "Stille," and "Süßigkeit" (peace, tranquility, and sweetness). Winckelmann frequently juxtaposes, in perfect syntactical symmetry, complementary terms—"Natur und Kunst," "mit Majestät erfüllet und mit dem Donner gerüstet," "mit Bogen und Pfeile" (nature and art; filled with majesty and armed with thunder; with bow and arrow).[24] As Hans Zeller so exhaustively demonstrates—although without linking this carefully crafted style to the androgynous object of contemplation—Winckelmann's preferred sentence construction links two perfectly balanced clauses by means of a fulcrumlike *und:* "Zorn schnaubet aus seiner Nase und Verachtung wohnet auf seinen Lippen." (Rage snorts from his nostrils and disdain inhabits his lips.) Zeller also points to the marvelously complex linguistic balancing act achieved in certain sentences in which the first and second clauses act as perfect mirror reflections of each other around the *und* axis: "Über die Menschheit erhaben ist sein Gewachs, und sein Stand zeuget von der ihn erfüllenden Größe." (Above humanity towers his form, and his posture testifies to the greatness that fills him.)[25]

Winckelmann's language, however, is prone to problematic "double-ness" as is the androgyne itself. On the one hand, as Zeller observes, Win-ckelmann's language is rigorous, categorical, statuesque: "seine Sätze haben jene genau begrenzten Umrisse, und seine Aussagen eine Bestimmtheit von fast marmorner Härte, durch keine Einschränkung oder Bedingung, durch keinen Konjunktiv gemildert" (his sentences have just those clear contours, his pronouncements have an almost marmoreal certainty, a certainty that is not tempered by qualifications or contingencies or subjunctives).[26] Yet what this highly self-conscious literary style seeks to capture and express is, precisely, flux, instability, polymorphousness—not static binary oppositions. Is the point of intermingling, of polyvalence, located—just out of our grasp—somewhere around the fulcrum *und?* Significantly, Winckelmann ends his description of the Belvedere Apollo by admitting his inability to express in language the androgynous ideal, his failure to create a truly "androgynous" discourse:

> Wie ist es möglich es [mein Bild] zu malen und zu beschreiben. Die Kunst selbst müßte mir rathen, und die Hand leiten, die ersten Züge, welche ich hier entworfen habe, künftig auszuführen.
> Ich lege den Begriff, welchen ich von diesem Bilde gegeben habe, zu dessen Füßen, wie die Kränze derjenigen, die das Haupt der Gottheiten, welche sie krönen wollten, nicht erreichen konnten.

> How is it possible to draw and describe it [my image]. Art itself would have to advise me and guide my hand as it completes, in the future, the first lines that I have sketched here.
> I place the description I have given of this statue at its feet, like the wreaths of those who were unable to reach the heads of the gods to crown them.[27]

Winckelmann's first "sketch" of the Belvedere Apollo points to the impossibility of the androgynous discourse. His offering, placed at the feet of the gods, is related in a structure of opposition to the garlands with which the Greeks crowned the heads of their deities. Again we find ourselves circling around a mysterious, ineffable middle point, oscillating between a future, ideal representation of wholeness *(künftig)* and the inhabitants of ancient Greece, long dead.[28] From apparently crystalline, fixed binary structures to free-flowing undefinability—a certain tension becomes discernible.

Perhaps this is where we can locate, too, what one critic has described as Winckelmann's "elliptischer Umriß" (elliptical outline).[29] The line that describes the beautiful, writes Winckelmann, is neither straight nor curved; unexpressable in geometric terms, it evades human rationality:

Apollo Belvedere. (Vatican State: Museo Pio Clementino, Vatican Museums. Photo © Scala/Art Resource, New York.)

Die Linie, die das Schöne beschreibet, ist *elliptisch,* und in derselben ist das *Einfache* und eine *beständige Veränderung:* denn sie kann mit *keinem Zirkel* beschrieben werden und *verändert in allen Punkten ihre Richtung.* Dieses ist *leicht* gesaget, und schwer zu lernen: welche Linie, mehr oder weniger elliptisch, die verschiedenen Theile zur Schönheit formet, kann die *Algebra* nicht bestimmen.

The line describing the beautiful is *elliptical*—it displays both *simplicity* and *constant change,* for it cannot be described by *any pair of compasses* and *changes direction at any given point.* This is *easy* to say, but difficult to learn: *algebra* cannot predict which line, more or less elliptical, forms the different parts into beauty. (vol. 1: 207–8)

The ellipsis, for Winckelmann, is located somewhere between the straight line and the curved and yet is unlocatable, ungraspable by human reason. This aesthetic principle corresponds to another type of imagery that pervades his writings: water and waves; floating, hovering, suspension. Bosshard, in a section of his book devoted to aesthetic indeterminacy or *Unbestimmbarkeit,* sees the undefinability of art not merely as an abstract aesthetic concept but as concretized by Winckelmann in the formal demands he places on the artist. Thus, writes Bosshard of Winckelmann's aesthetics, the artist will avoid harsh, jarring moments, allowing different parts of the work to ebb and flow, wavelike. The artist, he continues, will avoid the hardness of the one-sidedly masculine and will allow hard masculinity and soft femininity to contribute in equal measure to each other and to the formation of shapes and contours—just as in softly formed, restlessly playful ocean waves one finds both form and formlessness.[30]

Thus, the Belvedere Hercules, for Winckelmann a pinnacle of artistic perfection, displays taut, well-defined muscles ("sägeformig," sawlike), but hard and virile as they appear, they are also soft and sensual, "wie das Wallen des ruhigen Meeres, fließend erhaben, und in einer sanften abwechselnden Schwebung" (like the surging of the peaceful ocean, sublime and flowing, in a gentle hovering motion [vol. 4: 140]).

So wie in einer anhebenden Bewegung des Meers die zuvor stille Fläche in einer neblichten Unruhe mit spielenden Wellen anwächset, wo eine von der andern verschlungen, und aus derselben wiederum hervorgewälzet wird: eben so sanft aufgeschwellet und schwebend gezogen fließet hier eine Muskel in die andere, und eine dritte, die sich zwischen ihnen erhebet, und ihre Bewegung zu verstärken scheinet, verlieret sich in jene, und unser Blick wird gleichsam mit verschlungen.

Just as, when the sea is rising, a previously still surface transforms itself, in misty turbulence, into playful waves, as each wave is swallowed up by another

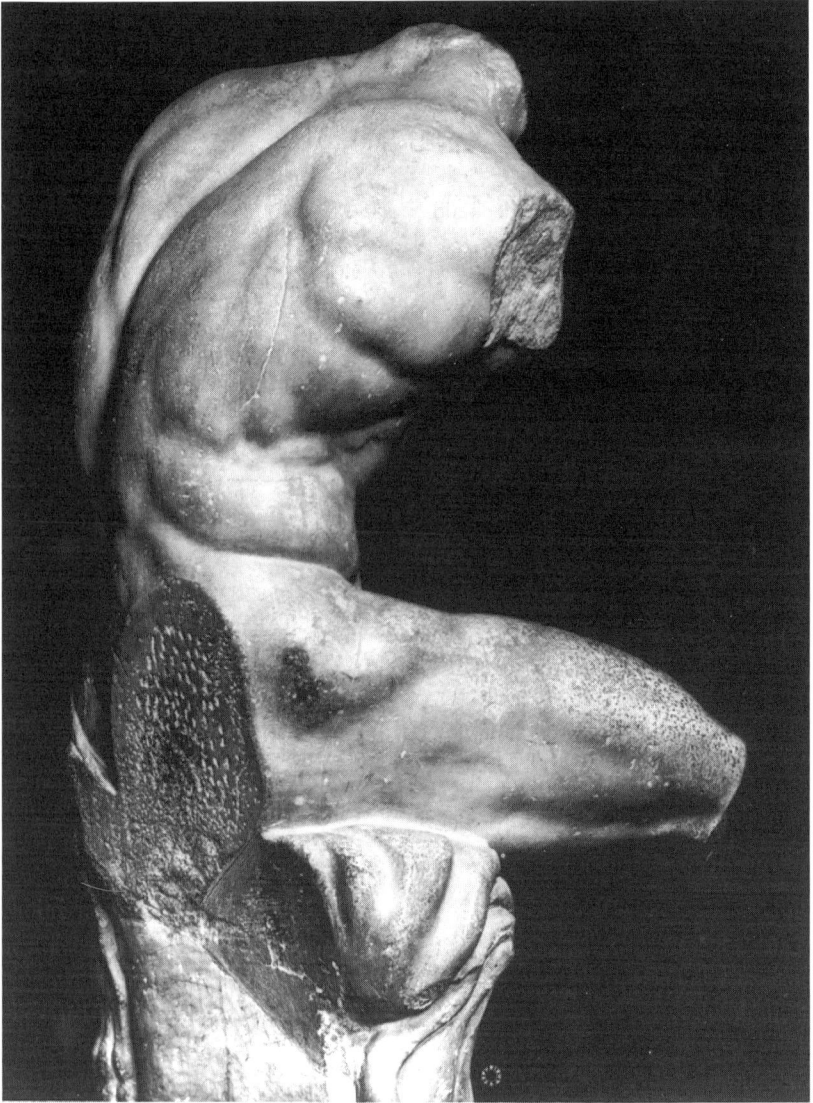

Torso Belvedere. (Vatican State: Vatican Museums. Photo © Alinari/Art Resource, New York.)

and then surges forth again: in just this fashion, softly swollen and hovering, one muscle here flows into the other, and a third, rising up between them and apparently strengthening their motion, is lost in the first two, and our gaze is engulfed with it. (vol. 1: 229)

As with so many of Winckelmann's descriptions, this view of the Belvedere Hercules depends on the harmonizing of seemingly unresolvable tensions: movement and stasis, hardness and softness, rigidity and fluidity, upward and downward, body and water, statue and viewer. It is as if we no longer know where each contour of the body begins and ends. Indeed, after gazing at the Hercules torso, this fragment that both suggests and demands completion, we can no longer discern where we end, as viewers, and where the statue begins.

Der Künstler bewundere in den Umrissen dieses Körpers die immerwährende Ausfließung einer Form in die andere, und die schwebenden Züge, die nach Art der Wellen sich heben und senken, und in einander verschlungen werden: er wird finden, daß sich niemand im Nachzeichnen der Richtigkeit versichern kann, indem der Schwung, dessen Richtung man nachzugehen glaubet, sich unvermerkt ablenkt, und durch einen andern Gang, welchen er nimmt, das Auge und die Hand irre machet.

Let the artist admire in the contours of this body the continuous flow of one form into another, and the hovering lines that rise and fall like waves and are engulfed in another: he will find that no one can be certain of reproducing this accurately in a drawing, since the curve he believes himself to be following imperceptibly changes direction, and bewilders both eye and hand with its new trajectory. (vol. 6: 98)

How can we explain this longing for this ocean, translated as an urge for form within formlessness, for differentiation within nondifferentiation? Klaus Theweleit, for one, has argued that the notion of flowing has a long and problematic history, that water is "the element in which desires flow."[31] He claims that if desire flows at all, in Western culture, it flows through women. Far more rare is an aimless flow of desire, a free-roaming desire for aesthetic freedom, which seems to be what we have observed in Winckelmann. However, the water imagery that pervades Winckelmann's writing is also significant for future representations of the androgyne, and the association of the androgyne with water does indeed go on to take a fatal turn, as I will show in chapter 2, below. By the time the androgyne has metamorphosed into a female androgyne, as in Goethe's *Wilhelm Meister* novels, it has become inextricably linked with water. Mignon, the doomed androgyne who fades from the *Lehrjahre* as a physical being, is mentioned in the *Wanderjahre* only in association with the Lago Maggiore. (Goethe's hero Wilhelm, having extricated himself from her influence, performs his final redemptive act at the end of the *Wanderjahre:* he saves his son Felix from drowning.)

Clearly, the relationship between viewer and statue in Winckelmann's writings is a desiring relationship. If, as Jean Baudrillard has suggested, "signs without referents, empty, senseless, absurd and elliptical signs" are those that most absorb the human imagination,[32] what can be more seductive than Winckelmann's aesthetic androgyne and its many descendants? The androgyne is an aesthetic construction, with no corollary in real life. Intangible, it seems tangible in the tantalizing contours of a marble statue. A word without referent, it comes to viewer and reader laden with contradictory meanings. Winckelmann attempts to grasp the elusive androgyne, the hard marble, by using water metaphors, themselves fluid and mutable. His aesthetic depends for its existence on the subjectivity of the viewer, who engages in free play with the sculpture, allowing himself to be seduced by its fleeting contours. (I am deliberately positing the viewer as male, following the structures set up by eighteenth- and nineteenth-century writings on statuary.) In one memorable passage from Winckelmann's "Abhandlung von der Fähigkeit der Empfindung des Schönen in der Kunst" (Treatise on the Ability to Feel Beauty in Art), the sensual nature of art is conjured up in the image of the marble Apollo being embraced by liquid plaster: "Das wahre Gefühl des Schönen gleichet einem flüssigen Gypse, welcher über den Kopf des Apollo gegossen wird, und denselben in allen Theilen berührt und umgibt." (The true feeling for beauty is like a fluid plaster that is being poured over the head of the Apollo and that touches and envelops it in every nook and cranny [vol. 1: 245].) The sculpture arouses in the viewer intense emotions that cause viewer and statue to become locked in a dialectical relationship of mutual metamorphosis. In the passage quoted above, the viewer appears to desire petrification, in order to achieve a state of perfect fusion or assimilation with the statue; in due course, the plaster must harden, encasing the marble. Elsewhere, the viewer animates the statue as a polymorphous sexual being. In a characteristic moment, Winckelmann rhetorically figures the confusion of conventional gender. The sex of a Telephus statue becomes dependent on the perspective of the observer at any given moment.[33] Winckelmann writes that he remains "zweifelhaft" (doubtful) about the figure's sex: "Das Gesicht dieses jungen Helden ist völlig *weiblich,* wenn man es von *unten herauf* betrachtet, und es scheinet sich etwas *Männliches* in dasselbe zu mischen, wenn man es von *oben herunter* ansiehet." (The face of this young hero is completely *feminine* when one looks at it *from below,* and it seems that something *masculine* is mixed in with it when one looks at it *from above* [vol. 4: 141].)[34] Such indeterminacy recurs throughout later literary confrontations with the androgyne, throwing the protagonists of works such as *Wilhelm Meisters Lehrjahre, Ahnung und Gegenwart,* and *Das Sinngedicht* into pronominal chaos; the most basic grammatical oppositions are rendered arbitrary, as the viewer is forced to decide between *er* and *sie* in situations that do not permit ready distinctions.[35] Whether the androgyne is male or female depends merely on the perspective adopted by the viewer at any given moment. The nomadic subjectivity of Winckelmann's androgynous aesthetic finds its mythological analogue in the craft of the legendary sculptor Daedalus, patron saint of the middle. That sculptor, creator of famously lifelike statues, also constructed the labyrinth for Minos, at the heart of which stood a hybrid, composite monster, the Minotaur.[36]

The importance of the classical marble statue cannot be underestimated in this relationship of desire, standing as it does at the very center of the debate on antiquity and modernity, subjectivity and objectivity, gender and aesthetics.[37] As I go on to trace the mutations of the androgynous ideal in German aesthetics and literature of the late eighteenth and early nineteenth centuries, I will consider many more alluring, sexually ambiguous statues—though in these later works, they will become more readily identifiable, in sexual terms, as female. The marble statue, focal point of discussions on aesthetics, also becomes central to cultural constructions of gender and difference. Theorizing the statue, as I will show, is a way of theorizing gender. From Schiller's Juno Ludovisi, to Eichendorff's *Marmorbild,* to Stifter's marmoreal Natalie, to Keller's bewildering sculptures in the *Sieben Legenden,* which seem at once pagan representations of Diana and Christian representations of Mary, the androgyne, consistently presented in statuary form, exerts its entrancing power over its viewers. The marble statue represents a movement eternally frozen in time, soft flesh become hard stone; indeed, the statue seems to exist in the midst of unresolved tensions, between presence and historical absence, eroticism and repression, animation and petrification. Like Pygmalion, Winckelmann notes in the penultimate paragraph of his description of the Belvedere Apollo, the viewer of the androgynous statue falls into raptures before the object of his gaze, and in turn his gaze imbues the statue with its own life. To cite one example of this dynamic, Winckelmann, while describing the Belvedere Apollo, a dead marble statue, slips in a description of a sensual living body with faintly perfumed hair—immediately before the Pygmalion allusion. It is important to emphasize Winckelmann's self-conscious twist on the Pygmalion myth: what is posited by Ovid's narrative of creation as the fusion of art and life, female and male, here takes on overtly homoerotic shades of desire. The reference to Branchos, one of Apollo's boy lovers—at the moment when Winckelmann has arrived at the statue's divinely sensual mouth—simply underlines the homoeroticism of the whole description.[38]

The statue is animated by the gaze of the viewer; the viewer falls before the statue as before a religious icon. Again, the androgyne is marked by doubleness, by a quasi-religious awe and by deep sexual desire. There are doubtless affinities between Winckelmann's ecstatic language and the vocabulary of German mysticism and Pietism;[39] the description of the Belvedere Apollo is full of religious vocabulary with distinctly erotic overtones, such as "Rührung" (emotion), "Wollust" (ecstasy), "Entzückung" (rapture), "außer sich" (beside oneself), "glückseelig" (blissful). Unlike the gaze of the mystic, however, Winckelmann's gaze is outer-directed, fixed as it is upon the voluptuous contours of the marble statue. Bosshard rightly perceives the significance of the eye in Winckelmann's aesthetic experience but shows how it functions differently from the inner-looking eye of the mystic: "Dem *myein,* dem Schließen der Augen und dem Einwärtswenden des Blicks, dem Begriff, um den alle Mystik kreist und der sie konstituiert, entspricht bei Winckelmann in der zentralen Stellung der genaue Gegenbegriff, das Öffnen der Augen und das Schauen der äußeren leibhaften Dinge." (The *myein,* the closing of the eyes and inward turning of the gaze, the concept that is at the heart of and that constitutes all mysticism, finds its parallel, in terms of its centrality in Winckelmann's work, in its absolute antithesis, the opening of the eyes and the perception of outer, concrete reality.)[40] Winckelmann's ideal is a physical presence engaging both optic and haptic modes of perception; his gaze is neither hard nor clinical. Rather, the gaze caresses, embraces the curves of the androgynous statue, becomes one with the sensual movement of the hand. We recall Winckelmann's description of the Belvedere Hercules' sinuous body and of how it seduces and bewilders "das Auge *und* die Hand" (my emphasis).[41]

The eroticism present in the relationship between viewer and statue is, like Winckelmann's aesthetic, an eroticism of indeterminacy. Winckelmann's most adored androgynes, as commentators have frequently noted, are modeled after adolescent boys, puberty being the critical moment of sexual indeterminacy and liminality. Indeed, Winckelmann seems to monitor the youthful male body closely for the distasteful signs of body hair, the harbinger of adulthood. As one critic has pointed out, at least fifty pages of the *Geschichte der Kunst des Altertums* are devoted to this subject. The most lovely hair, for Winckelmann, is the down on the adolescent's chin, an indication that the beard of manhood has not yet arrived, and he emphasizes the gorgeous softness of this hair and its signaling of the boy as "impubere."[42] Bosshard's characterization of Winckelmann's "Jüngling" emphasizes the androgynous openness of the pubescent boy: the youth occupies the middle position between feminine softness and masculine hardness and rigidity, between feminine passivity and masculine activity, between the contourlessness of the female and the clear outlines of the male.[43] Winckelmann himself describes this ideal of adolescent, androgynous beauty as follows:

> Der höchste Begrif jugendlicher Schönheit wurde den Figuren des *Bacchus* und *Apollo* zugeeignet. Diese Gottheiten zeigen uns, vermöge der ihnen von den Dichtern gegebenen Vereinigung beider Geschlechter, in ihren auf uns gekommenen Abbildungen eine vermischte und zweideutige Natur, welche sich durch die Völligkeit und stärkere Ausschweifung der Hüften und durch die zarten und rundlichen Glieder dem Körper der Verschnittenen und Weiber nähern.

> We receive the loftiest impression of youthful beauty in the figures of Bacchus and Apollo. These divinities reveal, in the depictions of them that come down to us, and due to the union of both sexes attributed to them by the poets, hybrid and ambiguous characteristics. Through the fullness and curviness of their hips and through their delicate, rounded limbs, they come close in nature to the bodies of castrati or women. (vol. 7: 111–12)

Furthermore, as Spickernagel notes in her commentary on Winckelmann's Medici Bacchus,[44] the adolescent god still revels—though fleetingly—in unalienated existence in nature, pursuing his desires undisturbed by consciousness. Dreamy and removed, the beautiful boy oscillates between masculine vigor and feminine languor. Winckelmann describes this sensual, supremely natural androgyne as a creature eternally poised between sleep and consciousness, between dream and reality, between childhood and adulthood, between femaleness and maleness:

> Das Bild . . . eines schon herangewachsenen Jünglings, welcher die Gränzen des Frühlings des Lebens betritt, wann die Regung der Wohllust wie die zarte Spize einer Pflanze zu keimen anfängt. Er scheinet daher in derselben Statue wie zwischen Schlummer und Wachen die ihm übrig gebliebenen Bilder eines fröhlichen Traumes, welchen er eben gehabt hat, nachsinnend zu sammlen, als wünsche er dieselben wirklich machen zu können. Seine Züge sind voll lüsterner Süßigkeit, aber dennoch tritt die fröhliche Seele nicht ganz in das Gesicht.

> The image . . . of an already full-grown youth, who approaches the threshold of the springtime of life, when sensuality begins to stir like the delicate bud of a plant. So in this statue he seems, between sleeping and waking, wistfully to

be recollecting the remaining images of a happy dream he has just dreamed, as if wishing he could make them real. His features are filled with voluptuous sweetness, but his joyful spirit does not manifest itself fully. (vol. 7: 112)

The association I have pointed to in Winckelmann's writings between the androgynous god and the realms of art and of nature perhaps yields some first clues about the unexpected shift, in Schiller, Goethe, and the romantics, to exclusive incarnations of androgyny in female figures.[45] Much feminist literary scholarship has, indeed, occupied itself with tracing the way in which female representation in Western literature has consistently been aligned both with nature and with art, and has identified the inscription of this constellation of categories in the late eighteenth century. As feminist criticism has shown, the longing for lost totality in an age of fragmentation and difference, the quest for a mode of existence that would not be alienated, is projected onto women, and in particular onto their representation in litera-ture.[46] Furthermore, the literary imagination transforms "the feminine" into a sensual, polymorphous cult object, mysteriously hinting at an undisturbed whole. And it is through the creation of the work of art, or through the experience of the work of art, that the male artist can approach the "natural" wholeness that comes to be symbolized in the late eighteenth century by "the feminine."[47]

The transition from Winckelmann's adolescent, androgynous boys—the delicate hermaphroditic muses—to the female androgyne muse of Goethe and the romantics is important to delineate. The beautiful boy is an adolescent hovering between a female past and a male future. An image of detachment from the real world, barely hovering around the frontiers of consciousness, an icon of ambiguity, the statue of the half-slumbering, half-waking androgyne easily merges with the women represented in Western literature of this period. If woman is the polymorphous Other, shifting between the poles of angel and monster, immersed in ineffable nature, and representing a stage along the trajectory of male development, then she easily accommodates the cult idol of neoclassicism. The androgynous muse, marker of primal wholeness, is marked by the dualism inherent in fictions of the feminine.

It is the eternal moment of liminality in the androgynous sculpture that leaves open for the viewer the possibility of *Bildung:* the extremes, as antitheses, do not cancel each other out in the middle; rather, they enter into the middle and are preserved intact. Thus, the middle contains all the extremes as possibilities, suggests the greatest potentiality.[48] This harmonizing of binaries, with its promise of growth, is, of course, one of the fundamental concepts of classical *Bildung*—as it is elaborated, for example, in Schiller's *Über die ästhetische Erziehung des Menschen* or in Goethe's theories of polarity. However, the stasis and lifeless fixity of the marble sculpture are a phase that must be overcome in real life through *Bildung*. The beautiful boy dreams, but there is no indication of intellectual maturation or engagement. His face is a blank page. In the case of the eunuch, so often the model for this incarnation of androgynous beauty, the problem of temporality is surgically averted; castration returns the eunuch to a state of pre- or nondifference. A real person could not remain at this stage of narcissistic self-absorption without mummification.[49]

Winckelmann's androgyne, then, is at the threshold of human development; it is also clear that his aesthetic androgyne fits into a hierarchy of life stages conceived of wholly from a male developmental perspective.[50] The androgynous boy, closely aligned with unconscious nature, represents the first stage of male development. This is followed by mature adulthood, represented by Mercury and Mars—heroism and energy incarnated. Jupiter, the most important god, symbolizes old age and wisdom. This vision of male maturation is clearly defined by the Greek "problem of the boy," as Michel Foucault terms it.[51] The careful attention paid to the type of sexual relationship between an older man and a boy, as he has argued, derives less from the fact that this was a dominant mode of sexual behavior in Greek society than from the boy's liminal status: unlike slaves and women, the boy would become a man and would enjoy the rights and privileges associated with this status. And since it would be unseemly for an adolescent to carry on his relationship with an older man into adulthood, part of what the boy could expect from his mentor was the correct education to render him a respected citizen. *Bildung*, then, is historically inscribed by Greek discourse as male. It is important to stress the fact that Aristophanes' famous speech on the origins of human sexuality not only embraces the possibility of male-male unions but is itself addressed to a group composed exclusively of men. And to return to Winckelmann's own conception of *Bildung*, the coalescence of aesthetic education and homoerotic friendship and sensuality becomes clear from his pedagogical 1763 essay "Von der Fähigkeit der Empfindung des Schönen in der Kunst." Publicly addressed to the young nobleman Friedrich von Berg, the treatise contains a recommended list of artworks to be viewed as part of a young man's program of art education (vol. 1: 235–73).[52]

Significantly, there is no parallel movement of *Bildung* to be found among the female goddesses catalogued in the *Geschichte der Kunst des Altertums* (History of Ancient Art); they do not undergo the same transition from nature to reason. Winckelmann, indeed, quotes from Aristotle's famous definition of women as defective men (vol. 4: 145–46). As they age, accord-

Amazon. (From *Abbildungen zu Johann Joachim
Winckelmanns Sämtlichen Werken.* Donauöschingen: Verlag
Deutscher Classiker, 1835. Courtesy of Avery Architectural
and Fine Arts Library, Columbia University in the City of
New York.)

ing to Winckelmann's developmental model, women's physical appearance changes but not their gender-determined personality. Venus, the goddess of beauty, appears for Winckelmann in two guises: as the "divine" and "earthly" Venus, she incarnates the duality of spiritual love and sexuality. But Venus is never portrayed in the stage of hesitation between male and female that is so characteristic of the male gods, such as Bacchus; her distinctly female orientation, writes Winckelmann, is always clear. While one might expect the mannish Athena and Diana to be mentioned by Winckelmann in the context of androgyny, this is in fact never the case. The Amazon, who will become a figure of eroticized indeterminacy in Goethe's *Wilhelm Meister,* and whom one might expect to join the ranks of sexually alluring androgynes, has for Winckelmann "nichts vom Frauencharakter mit erotischer Ausprägung" (nothing suggestive of an erotically charged female personality), as Fritz Giese observes.[53] For Winckelmann, the female deity remains excluded from the androgynous ideal. She is also excluded from progress, from the transition made by the male god from instinct to consciousness, from flesh to rationality. Winckelmann places Venus at the head of his hierarchy of female divinities, largely because she, like the male gods, is depicted in various developmental stages. But her development is presented in unambiguous terms; reproductive readiness is what we glimpse in the blossoming adolescent Venus, not androgyny:

> Die *mediceische Venus* zu Florenz ist einer Rose gleich, die nach einer schönen Morgenröthe beim Aufgang der Sonne aufbricht, und die aus dem Alter, welches, wie Früchte vor der völligen Reife, hart und herblich ist, in ein Alter tritt, in welchem sich die Gesäße zu erweitern und der Busen sich auszubreiten anfängt, wie selbst ihr Busen meldet, welcher schon ausgebreiteter ist, als an zarten Mädchens.

> The *Medici Venus* at Florence is like a rose blooming after a beautiful dawn, as the sun is rising, and that is making the transition from an age that is hard and acidic, like fruit before it has fully ripened, to an age where her hips become wider and her breasts begin to grow—as her breasts themselves announce, since they are already larger than those of delicate young girls. (vol. 4: 147)

Winckelmann's most enthusiastic classicizing admirers in Germany will go on to transform the genuinely bisexual androgyne of his theoretical works into a female androgyne, one who remains inextricably bound to nature and the unconscious and who is death-bound. What I see as most significant about the categories of "woman as artwork" (or, as I will be stressing, "woman as statue") and "woman as nature" is that both prove utterly inimical, if not antithetical to *Bildung.* Thus, on the one hand, female figures such as Ottilie in Goethe's *Wahlverwandtschaften* (Elective Affinities) and Anna in Keller's *Der grüne Heinrich* (Green Henry) are excluded from (male) progress by their reification as static, dead artworks; and an example of "the natural" such as Keller's Meretlein is similarly death-bound, barred from the successful socialization of the *Bildungsheld.*

One of the central questions I ask in this study is why it is the particular version of female androgyny that survives in the German narratives of *Bildung*. I propose that Aristophanes' own developmental account of androgyny, with its delineation of three distinct phases of human existence, provides an opening to this question. Winckelmann's dual-sexed statues, on the one hand, resemble the bisexual beings described in the *Symposium* as the primal androgynes. But in the structures of bourgeois socialization and sexual difference inscribed by the German *Bildungsroman,* the only productive model of androgyny is the one with which Aristophanes concludes his speech: the heterosexual, procreative version. The desiring relationship between a male viewer and an androgynous male statue yields to a completely heterosexual model, in which the statue becomes predicated as female, the viewer as male. The welter of oxymoronic attributes used of Winckelmann's androgyne will pass easily to the representation of women, who themselves characteristically embrace two seemingly irreversible, dualistic fates. Monsters and/or angels, female characters seem condemned to death or statufication. The metamorphosis of Winckelmann's beautiful boy androgyne into the female androgyne also has important implications for the notion of *Bildung* expressed in these narratives. Critics, as I have indicated, traditionally interpret Winckelmann's androgyne as eternally receptive to *Bildung* and also as fostering the harmonizing aesthetic potentialities of the viewer. The later androgynes, now posed in a heterosexual relationship based on difference and complementarity, tend, like other female characters, to be barred from development; instead, they facilitate the progress of the male hero of the *Bildungsroman,* static stages along the path of male development.

Wilhelm von Humboldt: Gendering Genius

The influence of Winckelmann's androgynous aesthetic ideal cannot be underestimated; it is at the heart of the aesthetic and literary enterprises of both classicism and romanticism. It is central, too, for Wilhelm von Humboldt's two pivotal essays on sexual difference, essays that preach biological necessity.[54] "Über den Geschlechtsunterschied" positions sexual difference as the cornerstone of the natural order, as the energizing force that alone defeats inertia:

Die Natur wäre ohne ihn [den Geschlechtsunterschied] nicht Natur, ihr Räder-
werk stände still, und sowohl der Zug, welcher alle Wesen verbindet, als der
Kampf, welcher jedes einzelne nöthigt, sich mit seiner, ihm eigenthümlichen
Energie zu waffnen, hörte auf, wenn an die Stelle dieses Unterschiedes eine
langweilige und erschlaffende Gleichheit träte.

Without it [sexual difference] nature would not be nature, its machinery would
stand still, and both the tension that unites all beings and the struggle that
necessitates each individual arming himself with his own form of energy
would cease, if a boring and enervating uniformity took the place of this
difference.[55]

But even this essay, a curiously bellicose celebration of polar oppositions,
contains a utopian call for transcendence through artistic androgyny. Giese
duly notes the importance of aesthetics in Humboldt's writings on gender,[56]
but I would go still further in my analysis of these essays. Not only are
the key binary concepts *zeugen* and *empfangen* (generation and conception)
declared as universally valid in the intellectual world as in the biological
world, but Humboldt sets about exploring and defining the physical world
in sensualistic aesthetic terms.[57] In "Über den Geschlechtsunterschied," he
even uses the analogy of artistic creativity as a way of facilitating the
reader's understanding of biological difference. The vocabulary of aesthetics
is explicitly sexual here—"Keim" (germ, embryo, or seed), "Sehnsucht"
(desire), "Zeugung" (procreation), and so on—and the description of artistic
creation is no less charged:

Die Kraft sammelt sich in sich selbst, nie fühlt sie sich reicher und größer,
nie lebhafter bewegt, nie rüstiger zur herrlichsten Thätigkeit. Selbst die Erinnerung an diese Stärke vermag noch, sie in der Folge begeisternd zu erwecken.
Aber in dieser Bewegung liegt der Keim einer unruhvollen Sehnsucht, die
zur Hervorbringung reizt. Sich, ihres Reichthums ungeachtet, so wie sie ist,
nicht genügend, ahndet sie etwas andres, mit dem vereint sie erst ein vollen-
detes Ganze bildet. Wird ihr Suchen hier mit glücklichem Finden gekrönt,
so strebt sie nach einer Vereinigung, welche jedes einzelne Daseyn vertilgt.
Es entsteht ein Wogen, ein Hin- und Herwanken, und jene Sehnsucht erreicht
eine schmerzliche Höhe. Die ganze Erwartung ist nun auf die Hervorbringung
gespannt, und das eigne Ich entäußert sich bis zu dem Grade, daß es sich selbst
gern für die neue Schöpfung hingeben möchte. Aus diesem höchsten Daseyn
springt das Daseyn hervor. Auf diesem einzigen Moment beruht die Erzeugung
auch des geistigen Products. Hat die Phantasie des Künstlers einmal das Bild
lebendig geboren, so ist das Meisterwerk vollendet.

Energy builds itself up—never does it feel so great and rich, never so vital,
never so well equipped for the most glorious endeavor. Even the memory of
this strength can stirringly arouse it again later. But in this impulse lies the

germ of a restless longing that arouses the desire for generation. Not sufficient
in itself, despite its riches, energy senses something outside itself—only when
united with that other can it form a perfect whole. If its search is rewarded here
with a happy find, then it strives for a union that will efface each individual
existence. There is a surging, a rocking to and fro, and desire reaches a painful
height. Expectations are now straining toward generation, and the individual I
yields itself up so that it would gladly sacrifice itself for the new creation. Out
of this most elevated form of being springs being. The generation of spiritual
products depends, too, on this elevated form of being. Once the imagination
of the artist has given birth to a living image, the masterpiece is complete.
(276–77)

It is this carefully elaborated image of artistic procreation, its eroticism
reminiscent of Winckelmann's writings on art, that is used to prepare the
reader for an explanation of sexual difference:

> Hier nun beginnt der Unterschied der Geschlechter. Die zeugende Kraft ist
> mehr zur Einwirkung, die empfangende mehr zur Rückwirkung gestimmt.
> Was von der erstern belebt wird, nennen wir *männlich,* was die letztere beseelt
> *weiblich.* Alles Männliche zeigt mehr Selbstthätigkeit, alles Weibliche mehr
> leidende Empfänglichkeit.

> This, then, is where sexual difference begins. The generative power is more
> suited to activate, the receptive power to be activated. What is given life by
> the former we call *masculine,* what imbues the latter with spirituality we call
> *feminine.* All that is masculine displays more independence, all that is feminine
> more suffering receptivity. (277)

While confirming sexual difference as a biological necessity, and a
desirable one at that, Humboldt views the androgynous union of polar
oppositions as the highest state to be attained by humanity. This androgynous
ideal is formulated at the opening of his essay "Über die männliche und
weibliche Form" (On Masculine and Feminine Form):

> die höchste und vollendete Schönheit erfordert nicht bloß Vereinigung, son-
> dern *das genaueste Gleichgewicht* der Form und des Stoffes, der Kunstmäßig-
> keit und der Freiheit, der geistigen und sinnlichen Einheit, und dieses erhält
> man nur, wenn man das Charakteristische beider Geschlechter in Gedanken
> zusammenschmelzt, und aus dem innigsten Bunde der reinen Männlichkeit
> und der reinen Weiblichkeit die Menschlichkeit bildet.

> the highest and perfect form of beauty demands not merely union, but *the most*
> *exact balance* of form and matter, of art and freedom, of spiritual and sensual
> unity, and this is only achieved when the characteristics of both sexes are
> melted together in thought, and humanity is fashioned from the most intimate
> union of pure masculinity and pure femininity. (296)

And if Humboldt lays the basis for his scientific inquiry with examples from the aesthetic realm, the key aesthetic figure is, for him as for
Winckelmann, the androgyne, in whom masculine "Form" and feminine
"Stoff" "umschlingen einander zu einem harmonischen Ganzen" (embrace
each other in a harmonious whole [279]). For Humboldt, however, it is the
artist, rather than the artwork, who stands as the androgynous ideal. Turning
to literary history for evidence of a distinctly masculine "Vernunft" (reason)
and a distinctly feminine "Phantasie," he identifies Virgil, Dante, Young, and
Aristotle as belonging to the former, "masculine," category, while Homer,
Ariosto, Thompson, and Plato are grouped together as "feminine."[58] Only
one author, and of course it is a Greek author, is pronounced a true genius, a
"geschlechtsloses Genie" (sexless genius): Sophocles (280). Like this artistic
genius, the viewer of art, too, must be androgynous:

> Wo sich der Mensch der Betrachtung des Schönen weiht, da muß er sich
> von aller Partheilichkeit lossagen, und geschlechtslos allein der Menschheit
> angehören. Nur in solchen glücklichen Momenten gelingt es ihm, sein Wesen
> zu dem höchsten Gleichgewichte zu stimmen, und die Kräfte, womit er der
> Natur und womit er der Gottheit verwandt ist, in Eins zu verschmelzen.

> When a human being devotes himself to studying beauty, then he must free
> himself from all bias and, sexless, belong to humanity alone. Only in such
> happy moments does he succeed in achieving the highest balance, and in
> fusing into one whole the powers that link him with nature and with the
> Godhead. (324)

However, Humboldt's vision of such androgynous perfection is tinged
by a recognition of its impossibility in real life. Again and again, he hints
at the ephemeral nature of his ideal: only Sophocles may be described as
a truly androgynous genius; the Greeks had to resort to idealized representations of certain divinities in order to express the concept of androgynous
perfection; in reality, no human being can ever perfectly unite masculinity and femininity. While celebrating a utopian relationship of reciprocity
between "Freiheit" and "Naturnotwendigkeit" (freedom and physical necessity), Humboldt concedes that reality cannot furnish the human imagination
with the evidence that a pure androgynous being exists, that sexual difference
may be transcended. There are only glimmers of androgynous harmony in
the real world:

> Indeß ist es dennoch unläugbar, daß zuweilen selbst in der Wirklichkeit, wenn
> gleich nur einzelne Züge einer Gestalt durchschimmern, die, als rein mensch-
> lich, zwischen der männlichen und weiblichen mitten inne steht, und weil jeder
> ein dunkles Bild davon in seiner Seele trägt, von niemand verkannt wird.

Yet it is undeniable that sometimes, even in reality, and however vaguely, traces of a purely human figure shimmer through, one that stands in the middle between masculinity and femininity, and it is recognized by everyone, since we all bear a murky image of it in our souls. (313)

Much of Humboldt's writing on androgyny recalls Winckelmann's ideas: the nostalgic recuperation of the Greeks; the stress on the aesthetic dimension of androgyny; the sensuality of the artistic experience; the evanescence of the androgynous ideal. Humboldt, indeed, grounds his speculative study of sexual difference on examples drawn from Greek art. Like Winckelmann, he lingers over classical statuary, and in particular over Greek representations of Bacchus:

> Reiche Fülle bezeichnet ihn; in fröhlichem Taumel durchzog er die Erde und bezwang entfernte und mächtige Völker mehr durch die üppige Macht seiner Natur, als durch die Anstrengung seines Willens. Seine Bildung ist noch zarter und jugendlicher, als die der übrigen Götter, seine Hüften sind weiblicher ausgeschweift, und der ganze Bau seiner Glieder ist voller und runder. Indeß er, mit der thätigen Kraft des Mannes gerüstet, gerade die Eigenthümlichkeiten des Geschlechts in seinem Charakter ausdrückt, nähert er sich dennoch der Gränze der Weiblichkeit.

> He is characterized by a rich plenitude; in a joyful frenzy he roamed across the world and conquered distant and mighty peoples more through his voluptuous natural powers than through an effort of his will. His form is even more delicate and youthful than that of the other gods, his hips are more feminine and curvaceous, and the whole structure of his limbs is fuller and rounder. Although he is equipped with the active powers of a man, and expresses these particular sexual traits in his personality, nevertheless he approaches the frontiers of femininity. (306)

And as we see here and in other key descriptions of the Greek ideal, Humboldt, like Winckelmann, saves his most rhapsodic prose for the celebration of male adolescence or "Jugend": "die, wenn die Bildung der *Kindheit* gewißermaaßen weiblicher ist, auf der schmalen Gränze zwischen beiden Geschlechtern steht" (which, even if the forms of *childhood* are to a certain degree more feminine, occupies the fine line between the two sexes [308]). That childhood is apostrophized here as "feminine" provides us with another revealing parallel to Winckelmann's observations. The pubescent boy, as portrayed in Humboldt's essays, hovers between a female, childish past and a male, adult future, eternally receptive to *Bildung*. If the androgynous male youth is characterized by openness, the moment of perfect beauty in the realm of female deities is not that of free-floating adolescence but rather the static self-sufficiency, the containment of the mature Juno (301). What becomes of those Greek goddesses who might seem to share in the idealized androgyny, in the sexual indeterminacy of a Bacchus? Any trace of femininity has been eradicated in Minerva, "Jupiters furchtbare Tochter" (Jupiter's terrible daughter), by wisdom, and the adolescent Diana, too, precisely because of her mannish tendencies, is "kein Ideal der Gattung" (not an ideal of her sex). Ultimately, it is women's lot to remain constrained by biology, while men go on to attain higher "Bildung" and "Menschlichkeit" (humanity)—as Humboldt puts it, "die größere Unabhängigkeit von dem Geschlechtsunter-schied gehört . . . unmittelbar mit zu dem Begriff der männlichen Bildung" (the greater independence from sexual difference is . . . a vital component of male *Bildung* [305]).

> Das weibliche Geschlecht hingegen muß gerade jede weibliche Eigenthüm-lichkeit mit schonender Sorgfalt zu erhalten bemüht seyn, um nicht jenen lebendigen Ausdruck seiner Gestalt selbst zu vernichten; und wenn ihm dieß Bemühen gänzlich mislingt; so sinkt es allein zu seiner Naturbestimmung und den Verrichtungen des äußern alltäglichen Lebens herab, oder geht zu Beschäftigungen über, die eigentlich nicht zu seinem Kreise gehören.

> The female sex, on the other hand, must take the utmost care to preserve precisely this feminine identity, so that it does not destroy the vital expression of its own form; and if this effort completely fails, it will sink into its natural functions and into the routines of everyday life, or it will take on occupations that are really not part of its sphere. (335)

Thus, "Über die männliche und weibliche Form" concludes with an exhortation to the female sex to remain within the bounds dictated by biological difference and to serve willingly in the cause of male completion, which Humboldt declares "die schöne Bestimmung dieses Geschlechts" (the beautiful destiny of this sex [335]). A similar move is staged with the figure of the genius, declared earlier to be androgynous in nature. Now, at the end of "Über die männliche und weibliche Form," Humboldt makes the link between masculine generative "Kraft" (energy) and the capacity of the artist to give life to or fertilize "todte Masse" (dead matter [328]). This association—between male sexual energy and artistic creativity on the one hand and between female receptivity and "dead matter" on the other—is illuminating, revealing as it does the inescapable rigidity of the binary system that Humboldt's androgynous ideal of genius would purport to overcome.[59]

A feminist critique of the androgynous ideal—that while it holds forth the liberating promise of sexual polymorphousness, it is posited on a scheme of unshakable binary oppositions—will be important for my consideration of both Schiller's and Schlegel's androgynous models for aesthetic and social liberation. Yet I should stress at this point that existing feminist critiques of androgyny are themselves often based on readings of the Platonic myth that do not allow for varying, even competing, aesthetic and philosophical constructions of androgyny. Winckelmann's nomadism is surely a markedly different version of androgyny from that of Humboldt. As I indicated in my discussion of Aristophanes' speech, that account of the origins of human sexuality signals a historical transition from a genuinely polymorphous primal being to a world that has collapsed into sexual differentiation. It is in the historical and aesthetic shift from nomadic fluidity to a world categorized rigidly according to difference that androgyny in the eighteenth century takes a turn toward petrification, and more specifically toward female petrification.

Schiller: Androgyny and the Aesthetic State

At the center of Schiller's aesthetic state stands a classical sculpture, the Juno Ludovisi. But *Über die ästhetische Erziehung des Menschen* is not the first work by Schiller to concern itself with classical statuary and its potential to foster harmonious spiritual and moral growth.[60] Inevitably, the model for Schiller's earliest writings on Greek antiquities is Winckelmann. He is present in every line of Schiller's "Brief eines reisenden Dänen" (Letter of a Traveling Dane, 1785), a rhapsodic description of the replicas of Greek sculptures to be seen in the celebrated collection at Mannheim. (Lessing, Herder, and Goethe had all been stimulated in their interest in Greek art by this collection.) Schiller's style in his early essay, with its predilection for oppositional structures, recaptures exactly the spirit of Winckelmann's Belvedere Apollo descriptions, discussed above. This is now Schiller's narrator, on the subject of the Vatican Apollo, but his vocabulary and rhetoric are Winckelmann's:

> Die reizendste Jünglingsfigur, die sich eben jetzt in den *Mann* verliert, Leich-tigkeit, Freiheit, Rundung und die reinste Harmonie aller Theile zu einem unnachahmlichen Ganzen, erklären ihn zu dem ersten der Sterblichen, Kopf und Hals verrathen den Gott. Diese himmlische Mischung von Freundlichkeit und Strenge, von Liebenswürdigkeit und Ernst, Majestät und Milde, kann keinen Sohn der Erde bezeichnen.

> The most charming youthful figure which is only now melting into *manhood,* the delicacy, freedom, curvaceousness and the purest harmony of parts in an inimitable whole, all these declare him to be the first among mortals; his head and neck reveal the god. This divine combination of friendliness and severity, of charm and gravity, of majesty and gentleness, could describe no earthly son. (vol. 20: 103)[61]

The youthful god—and again, as in Winckelmann, the stress is on the fleeting adolescent phase between femininity and masculinity—is presented as the divine union of polar oppositions, an expression of the innate harmony of the Greeks. This holy paradox may prove resistant to the faulty language of earthbound human beings. Yet the gaze of the viewer shares something of the generative powers of the sculptor; the sculptor transforms hard, unyielding stone into soft flesh, and the viewer, too, imbues the sculpture with movement and life: "Wer hat den starren, widerstrebenden Stein in so weiche, so geschmeidige Fleischmassen hingegossen?—Die Figur *ruht*. . . . Meine Phantasie leiht dem Kolossen Bewegung." (Who poured the rigid and resistant stone in such malleable masses of flesh?—The figure *rests*. . . . My imagination gives movement to the colossus [vol. 20: 102].) The Vatican Apollo over which Schiller's narrator lingers has the sinuous, bewildering contours of Winckelmann's androgynous sculptures; it appeals not only to the scrutinizing eye, the "forschendes Aug" (vol. 20: 103) of the critic, but also to human emotions and sensuality; as an icon of indeterminacy, it hovers before the viewer's eyes:

> Den geübtesten Zeichner wird es ermüden, die herrlichen Formen, die durch kontrastierende Schlangenlinien ineinanderschmelzen, *nur* für das Aug nach-zuahmen; denn der griechische Meister hat eben so delikat für das Gefühl gearbeitet; das Auge erkennt die *Schönheit,* das Gefühl die *Wahrheit.* Die letztere ist der ersteren untergeordnet, und obgleich kein Muskel vergessen ist, so hat doch der Künstler die feineren Nüancen dem Gesicht entzogen und der Berührung vorbehalten. Die Statue schwebt.

> Even the most experienced artist will be fatigued if he attempts to imitate, for the eye *only,* the marvelous forms that dissolve into one another with their contrasting, snakelike lines, for the Greek master worked just as delicately for the emotions: the eye perceives *beauty,* emotion perceives *truth.* The latter is subordinate to the former, and although no muscle has been forgotten, still the artist has withheld the finer nuances from the face and made them the preserve of our touch. The statue hovers. (vol. 20: 104)

Although this image of aesthetic perfection is not described explicitly as sexually ambiguous—at least not in this particular essay—it may resonate in the reader's mind as an allusion to Winckelmann's androgynous ideal. Later on in his letter, indeed, as he lists some of the other remarkable statues in the Mannheim collection, the narrator mentions an Antinous as among the finest, as well as the statue of a hermaphrodite (vol. 20: 104). With the naming of the key androgynous players of Winckelmann's repertoire, this is familiar terrain.

Still more insistently than Winckelmann, however, this narrator foregrounds the opposition, or historical difference, between Greek past and
German present, and that between the ideal world of art, cultivated by a
privileged aristocracy, and the sordid reality endured by so many. A "Tempel
der Kunst" (temple of art) may also be a "prahlerischer Palast" (gaudy palace)
that stands next door to a "sturzdrohende Schindelhütte" (dilapidated hut
[vol. 20: 101]). Paradoxically, it is in the fragment, in the broken torso of
Hercules, that the narrator glimpses a golden age of Greek wholeness, and a
possible solution, based on the aesthetic realm, for the modern world, which
has descended into fragmentation and alienation.[62] The statue functions,
characteristically, as an aesthetic object that would heal the wound between
(whole) past and (fragmented) present, between viewing subjectivity and
representation.

> Hier stehe ich vor dem berühmten Rumpfe, den man aus den Trümmern
> des alten Roms einst hervorgrub. In dieser zerschmetterten Steinmasse ligt
> unergründliche Betrachtung—Freund! . . . dieser *Rumpf* ligt da—uner-
> reicht—unvertilgbar—eine unwidersprechliche ewige Urkunde des göttlichen
> Griechenlands, eine Ausforderung dieses Volks an alle Völker der Erde.

> Here I stand before the celebrated torso that was once dug out from the
> ruins of ancient Rome. This shattered mass of stone invites unfathomable
> contemplation—friend! . . . this *torso* lies there—unattainable—indestruc-
> tible—an unchallengeable and eternal testimony to divine Greece, a provoca-
> tion thrown out by this people to all the peoples of the world. (vol. 20: 105)

The nature of this Greek challenge, "Ausforderung," to the modern
world is explored in Schiller's monumental work on aesthetics and *Bildung,*
Über die ästhetische Erziehung des Menschen in einer Reihe von Briefen,
published in 1795. Here again, the central challenge of Greece is given
metaphorical form in a classical sculpture, the Juno Ludovisi. The ideal of
a fully integrated human personality, one that comes into being through the
free play of the aesthetic realm, involves, too, a harmonizing of masculinity
and femininity. Indeed, Schiller's projected "Versöhnung" (reconciliation)
between sensuality and rationality is frequently expressed figuratively in
the sexual union of male and female, and, as in Humboldt's essays, the
language used to describe the aesthetic state is tinged with eroticism.[63] In
his "Anmut und Würde" (1793), in which Schiller describes the polarous
forces that both characterize and separate the sexes in an age of difference,
he also conjures up at one point the beauty of a physical form that would
both express and bring into harmony the gender-based qualities of "Anmut"
("feminine" grace) and "Würde" ("masculine" dignity).

Sind Anmuth und Würde, jene noch durch architektonische Schönheit, diese durch Kraft unterstützt, in derselben Person *vereinigt,* so ist der Ausdruck der Menschheit in ihr vollendet, und sie steht da, gerechtfertigt in der Geisterwelt und freygesprochen in der Erscheinung. Beyde Gesetzgebungen berühren einander hier so nahe, daß ihre Grenzen zusammenfließen. Mit gemildertem Glanze steigt in dem Lächeln des Mundes, in dem sanftbelebten Blick, in der heitern Stirne die *Vernunftfreyheit* auf, und mit erhabenem Abschied geht die *Naturnothwendigkeit* in der edeln Majestät des Angesichts unter. Nach diesem Ideal menschlicher Schönheit sind die Antiken gebildet, und man erkennt es in der göttlichen Gestalt einer Niobe, im belvederischen Apoll, in dem borghesischen geflügelten Genius, und in der Muse des Barberinischen Pallastes.

If grace and dignity, the former underlined by formal beauty, the latter by strength, are *united* in the same person, then the expression of humanity is perfected in that individual and stands there, justified in the mental world and possessed of manifest physical freedom. Both forms of law come so close to each other here that their borders dissolve. With a calm radiance, *mental freedom* appears in the smile, in the softly animated gaze, on the serene brow, and in a noble leave-taking *physical necessity* is submerged in the noble majesty of the face. The ancients are depicted according to this ideal of human beauty, as can be seen in the divine form of a Niobe, in the Belvedere Apollo, in the winged Borgia genius, and in the muse at the Barberini Palace. (vol. 20: 300–301)

In this work, more clearly than in the "Brief eines reisenden Dänen," it is precisely the androgynous quality of Greek statuary that is highlighted and then offered up as an aesthetic ideal. Again, though, the androgynous ideal of perfection, while it is described as the human being's "reifste Frucht" (ripest fruit), "ist bloß eine Idee, welcher gemäß zu werden er mit anhaltender Wachsamkeit streben, aber die er bei aller Anstrengung nie ganz erreichen kann" (is only an idea, for which he can strive with constant vigilance, but which with the greatest effort in the world he can never quite attain [vol. 20: 410]).

Unlike Winckelmann, however, Schiller locates the utopian moment of transcendence in sculptures representing both male and female deities, and it is the representation of the goddess, of the Juno Ludovisi, in *Über die ästhetische Erziehung des Menschen* that is central to his thought; she fulfills much the same iconic role as that of the androgynous Belvedere Apollo in Winckelmann's work.[64] Schiller's key metaphor for the aesthetic condition, the Juno Ludovisi appears at the end of letter XV, in a passage analogous to the section of "Anmut und Würde" discussed above. It is surely no coincidence that she stands, quite literally, at the center of Schiller's work, exactly at the symmetrical midpoint of the letters, the metaphor for androgynous unity and nonalienation, as well as for the reconciliation between the antagonistic "sinnlicher Trieb" (sensual drive) and "Formtrieb" (drive to form). One might indeed argue that metaphor, of itself, implies a dynamic interpretive position of doubleness, in which the reader is required to assess both meaning and context, as well as the dialectical relationship between the two.[65] In this passage, too, Schiller fully exploits his favorite rhetorical figure, chiasmus, again a stylistic element opening itself up to the play of dualisms.

"Immer näher komm ich dem Ziel, dem ich Sie auf einem wenig ermunternden Pfade entgegen führe" (I am drawing ever nearer the goal toward which I have been leading you by a not exactly encouraging path), promises Schiller at the opening of this fifteenth letter (vol. 20: 355).

> Es ist weder Anmuth, noch ist es Würde, was aus dem herrlichen Antlitz einer *Juno Ludovisi* zu uns spricht; es ist keines von beyden, weil es beides zugleich ist. Indem der weibliche Gott unsre Anbetung heischt, entzündet das gottgleiche Weib unsre Liebe; aber indem wir uns der himmlischen Holdseligkeit aufgelöst hingeben, schreckt die himmlische Selbstgenügsamkeit uns zurück. In sich selbst ruhet und wohnt die ganze Gestalt, eine völlig geschlossene Schöpfung, und als wenn sie jenseits des Raumes wäre, ohne Nachgeben, ohne Widerstand; da ist keine Kraft, die mit Kräften kämpfte, keine Blöße, wo die Zeitlichkeit einbrechen könnte. Durch jenes unwiderstehlich ergriffen und angezogen, durch dieses in der Ferne gehalten, befinden wir uns zugleich in dem Zustand der höchsten Ruhe und der höchsten Bewegung, und es entsteht jene wunderbare Rührung, für welche der Verstand keinen Begriff und die Sprache keinen Nahmen hat. (vol. 20: 359)

> It is not Grace, nor is it yet Dignity, which speaks to us from the superb countenance of a *Juno Ludovisi;* it is neither the one nor the other because it is both at once. While the woman-god demands our veneration, the god-like woman kindles our love; but even as we abandon ourselves in ecstasy to her heavenly grace, her celestial self-sufficiency makes us recoil in terror. The whole figure reposes and dwells in itself, a creation completely self-contained, and, as if existing beyond space, neither yielding nor resisting; here is no force to contend with force, no frailty where temporality might break in. Irresistibly moved and drawn by those former qualities, kept at a distance by these latter, we find ourselves at one and the same time in a state of utter repose and supreme agitation, and there results that wondrous stirring of the heart for which mind has no concept nor speech any name. (Wilkinson and Willoughby, 109)

The degree to which the Juno Ludovisi is marked by dualities is remarkable: she is neither active nor passive, forceful nor gentle; she demands the veneration of a god and kindles the sensual desire of a lover; she inspires both ecstasy and terror; she attracts the viewer while holding him at a distance. The viewer is left unable even to comprehend or to express in human terms what he sees before him. This experience of statue viewing, with its stress on the unbridgeable gap between viewing subjectivity and artwork, could not be more different from Winckelmann's utterly sensual evocation of mutual incorporation. Indeed, it is thanks to the marmoreal autonomy and impenetrability of the Juno statue that the viewer can successfully negotiate the competing drives within him. Successful *Bildung* is premised on difference. Here letter XV ends, and the next letter opens on a decidedly more sobering note:

> Aus der Wechselwirkung zwey entgegengesetzter Triebe, und aus der Verbindung zwey entgegengesetzter Principien haben wir das Schöne hervorgehen sehen, dessen höchstes Ideal also in dem möglichstvollkommensten Bunde und *Gleichgewicht* der Realität und der Form wird zu suchen seyn. Dieses Gleichgewicht bleibt aber immer nur Idee, die von der Wirklichkeit nie ganz erreicht werden kann. In der Wirklichkeit wird immer ein Uebergewicht des Einen Elements über das andere übrig bleiben, und das höchste, was die Erfahrung leistet, wird in einer *Schwankung* zwischen beyden Prinzipien bestehen, wo bald die Realität, bald die Form überwiegend ist. (vol. 20: 360)

> We have seen how beauty results from the reciprocal action of two opposed drives and from the uniting of two opposed principles. The highest ideal of beauty is, therefore, to be sought in the most perfect possible union and *equilibrium* of reality and form. This equilibrium, however, remains no more than an Idea, which can never be fully realized in actuality. For in actuality we shall always be left with a preponderance of the one element over the other, and the utmost that experience can achieve will consist of an *oscillation* between the two principles, in which now reality, now form, will predominate.[69] (Wilkinson and Willoughby, 111)

Schiller concedes that the best we can expect from reality is a flux between poles, rather than the harmonious rewards of the aesthetic state: "die Schönheit in der Erfahrung . . . wird ewig eine doppelte seyn, weil bey einer Schwankung das Gleichgewicht auf eine doppelte Art, nehmlich diesseits und jenseits, kann übertreten werden" (beauty in experience . . . will be eternally twofold, because oscillation can disturb the equilibrium in twofold fashion, inclining it now to the one side, now to the other [vol. 20: 360; Wilkinson and Willoughby, 111]). Significantly, a condition of flux, of constant slippage between polarities, is perceived here as an imperfect approximation of the androgynous ideal. But formally, too, *Über die ästhetische Erziehung des Menschen* denies the seductive symmetry that blossoms so briefly in the metaphor of the androgynous statue. As

Wilkinson and Willoughby show, the binary oppositions that dominate this
work perform a dizzying dance, patterns of achieved symmetry constantly
being broken down into new antitheses and recombining asymmetrically.[66]
    The image of androgynous perfection spills from the aesthetic treatises
into Schiller's poetic work, most notably in "Die Geschlechter" (The Sexes,
1797), a poem that should be read against the backdrop of contemporary gender theory.[67] The child, we are told, begins life as a naturally polymorphous,
dual-sexed being, a "doppelte Blume" (double flower) containing "zwei
liebliche Blumen," "Jungfrau und Jüngling" (two lovely flowers, girl and
boy). As Claudette Sartiliot has observed in her suggestive work on flowers
and textuality, the hermaphroditic morphology of flowers—the receptacle-
shaped corolla and the pistil with its long, erect style—has classically been
read as a symbolic subversion of traditional sexual opposition.[68] Only with
the onset of puberty, in Schiller's poem, does the child fall from this ideal
state of harmony into the fragmentation of sexual difference. This account of
primal androgyny and of the fall into difference corresponds perfectly with
the distinct phases of human development outlined by Aristophanes' speech
in the *Symposium*. In Schiller's delineation of the myth, nature is summoned
to restore androgynous perfection, now in the form of heterosexual union,
and the poem concludes with a return to the botanical image used in the
opening lines to define the original, nonalienated state:

> Siehe, da finden sie sich, es führet sie Amor zusammen,
> Und dem geflügelten Gott folgt der geflügelte Sieg.
> Göttliche Liebe, du bist's die der Menschheit Blumen vereinigt!
> Ewig getrennt, sind sie doch ewig verbunden durch dich.

> Behold, they find each other, Amor brings them together,
> And a winged victory follows the winged god.
> Divine Love, it is you who unites the flowers of humanity!
> Eternally separated, still they are eternally united by you.[69]

    This turn to a model of androgynous wholeness premised on struc-
tures of strict complementarity, as proposed by theorists such as Humboldt,
clearly posits sexual polymorphousness as the domain of infantile sexuality,
adulthood as the phase determined by difference, thus anticipating Freud's
developmental reading of the Platonic myth in the "Three Essays on the Theory of Sexuality" (1905).[70] Freud expresses this idea concisely at the end of
his later essay on "The Infantile Genital Organization" (1923): "Erst mit der
Vollendung der Entwicklung zur Zeit der Pubertät fällt die sexuelle Polarität
mit *männlich* und *weiblich* zusammen. Das Männliche faßt das Subjekt, die
Aktivität und den Besitz des Penis, das Weibliche setzt das Objekt und die

Passivität fort." (It is not until development has reached its completion at puberty that the sexual polarity coincides with *male* and *female*. Maleness combines [the factors of] subject, activity, and possession of the penis; femaleness takes over [those of] object and passivity.)[71] The state described by Freud as the "polymorphously perverse" is the initial phase of human psychological development in which we respond to others indiscriminately and without regard to genital identification. This is perhaps why, paradoxically as it might seem, Schiller's version of androgynous totality is accompanied by an often violent rejection of sexual indeterminacy, in particular when it is a question of female shape-shifting. (Women, after all, according to Freud, often retain the infantile "polymorphously perverse" disposition which children grow out of when guided by the correct form of *Bildung.*)[72]

Schiller was known to describe himself as something of a "hermaphrodite," a cross between poet and philosopher. In an August 31, 1794, letter to Goethe, he describes his own hybrid intellectual powers as "eine Zwitterart zwischen dem Begriff und der Anschauung, zwischen der Regel und der Empfindung, zwischen dem technischen Kopf und dem Genie" (a kind of hermaphrodite between ideas and contemplation, between rules and emotions, between the technical mind and the genius).[73] Given Schiller's self-identification with an androgynous aesthetic ideal, with the "thatenreiche[r] Stille" (deed-filled stillness) of the artistic genius,[74] it is illuminating to look at whether female creativity, too, may gain access to this privileged sphere. As Silvia Bovenschen has demonstrated, however, female artists of the late eighteenth century, in a systematic turn by male theorists, are barred from entering the domain of aesthetic production, that space where we might expect a creative give and take between the sexes.[75] Paradoxically, while Schiller can define himself, in positive terms, as partaking of an androgynous ideal, in this age of strictly enforced complementarity a woman who ventures into the aesthetic realm in a capacity other than that of muse will be denigrated as an androgyne.

In 1797, the year he composed the poem of radical androgyny "Die Geschlechter," Schiller penned the following lines to Goethe: "Ich muß mich doch wirklich darüber wundern, wie unsere Weiber jetzt, auf bloß dilettantischem Wege, eine gewisse Schreibgeschicklichkeit sich zu verschaffen wissen, die der Kunst nahe kommt." (I really am astonished at how our womenfolk are able now, in a purely dilettante fashion, to achieve a certain degree of talent in writing, talent that approaches art.)[76] In the fiercely parodic poem "Die berühmte Frau" (The Famous Woman), subtitled "Epistel eines Ehemanns an einen anderen" (Letter from One Husband to Another), we hear the woeful tale of the husband of the celebrated female writer Ninon de l'Enclos. This pitiable man demonstrates to a friend how fortunate the latter is to have an adulterous wife, as opposed to—what is infinitely worse—an intellectual one:

> Dich schmerzt, daß sich in Deine Rechte
> ein zweyter teilt?—Beneidenswerther Mann!
> Mein Weib gehört dem ganzen menschlichen Geschlechte.

> You feel hurt because another man
> shares your rights?—Enviable man!
> My wife belongs to the entire human race. (196)

By entering the public sphere of intellectual discourse, the woman writer makes herself into a "public woman" or whore, the poem suggests, a whore who is indeed inestimably more dangerous than the adulterous wife with whom she is compared. Ninon's body—here equated with her literary work—is offered up for public display and consumption:

> Ein Leipziger—daß Gott ihn strafen wollte!
> nimmt topographisch sie wie eine Vestung auf,
> und bietet Gegenden dem Publikum zum Kauf,
> wovon ich billig doch allein nur sprechen sollte.

> A man from Leipzig—may God punish him!
> takes down her topographical details as if she were a fortress,
> and offers for sale to the public
> certain areas about which only I should properly speak. (197)

Throughout this litany of complaints, we are reminded of the wife's true vocation. While she is engrossed in reading her reviews, she ignores the heart-rending wailing emanating from the nursery, and later her husband announces that he has been abandoned at home with seven "orphans" while she gads about the fashionable watering places of Europe. Ninon, far from approaching a harmonious "androgynous" state through her art, suffers a double attack. First, she becomes alienated from her "natural" role in the domestic sphere—that of wife and mother. Second, the poem makes it clear that in any case she can never scale the artistic heights attainable by male artists. Ninon, the darling of society, has no sensitive relationship with nature and can thus never express herself authentically: "Ihr ist der Frühling wonneleer." (For her the spring is devoid of joy.) What we are left with if gender boundaries are transgressed on the part of women is not a beautiful dual-sexed being but rather, as Bovenschen puts it, "eine groteske naturwidrige Fehlentwicklung" (a grotesque natural mutation).[77]

Indeed, Ninon de l'Enclos is castigated at the end of the poem precisely because she is androgynous, a "Zwitter" (hermaphrodite) or "Mittelding" (middle creature):

> Wen hab ich *nun?*—Beweinenswerther Tausch!
> Erwacht aus diesem Wonnerausch,
> was ist von diesem Engel mir geblieben?
> Ein *starker* Geist in einem *zarten* Leib,
> ein Zwitter zwischen Mann und Weib,
> gleich ungeschickt zum Herrschen und zum Lieben.
> Ein Kind mit eines Riesen Waffen,
> Ein Mittelding von Weisen und von Affen!

> What do I have now?—A lamentable exchange!
> As I awaken from this joyous dream,
> what is left of that angel?
> A strong spirit in a delicate body,
> a hermaphrodite cross between man and woman,
> equally unsuited to government and love.
> A child with the weapons of a giant,
> A middle creature between wise man and monkey! (200)

Here the negative aspects of the androgyne, already discernible in Winckelmann's writings on hermaphroditic statues, completely exclude more positive characteristics, and we are faced with a being that is ludicrously monstrous, freakish, grotesque, deformed, even bestial. This female androgyne, who has usurped for herself, to catastrophic effect, the male role of artist, may indeed be seen as a precursor of all those other female androgynes who inhabit narratives of *Bildung* produced during the late eighteenth and early nineteenth centuries.

What makes the grotesquely androgynous Ninon so radically different from the sexually ambiguous Juno Ludovisi, Schiller's metaphor for aesthetic perfection? The marble woman of the aesthetic realm, a passive object of contemplation and a playground of indeterminacy for the male viewer's "Spieltrieb" (play drive), is venerated as a cultural icon. But the female androgyne at once becomes monstrous if she steps off Juno's aesthetic pedestal and threatens to become an active player in the realm of art and *Bildung*. The binary-laden fiction of androgyny so prevalent in this period is determined, I argue, by its dominant literary fiction of receptive femininity. Eckermann reports, for instance, that Goethe identified the feminine as " 'das einzige Gefäß, was uns Neueren noch geblieben ist, um unsere Idealität hineinzugießen' " (the only vessel into which we moderns can still pour our ideals).[78]

On the one hand, the fiction of the androgyne emerges to fulfill a desire for wholeness, aesthetic completion. For the male artist, the myth of origin and of nonalienated existence is served both by the fiction of androgyny and by the fiction of femininity. Schiller's poem "Das weibliche Ideal" (The Feminine Ideal) declares, for example, that woman is "ewig nur Eines" (eternally One [287]), in words that echo descriptions of the androgynous ideal. Simultaneously, however, the sexes are slotted into rigid binaries that prohibit the androgynous flux and indeterminacy at the heart of Winckelmann's aesthetic. "Würde der Frauen" (The Dignity of Women), its alternating stanzas delineating the active, restless male destiny and the passive, domestic female sphere, illustrates the static nature of such a system:

> Ewig aus der Wahrheit Schranken
> Schweift des Mannes wilde Kraft,
> Und die irren Tritte wanken
> Auf dem Meer der Leidenschaft.
> Gierig greift er in die Ferne,
> Nimmer wird sein Herz gestillt,
> Rastlos durch entlegne Sterne
> Jagt er seines Traumes Bild.

> From the frontiers of truth
> Man's wild strength roams eternally,
> And his erring steps falter
> On the sea of passion.
> Lustfully he reaches for what is distant,
> His heart is never still,
> Restlessly through far-off stars
> He pursues the images that appear in his dreams. (Part 1, Vol. 1:240)

Man, having on his restless wanderings lost "die schöne Mitte, / Wo die Menschheit fröhlich weilt" (the beautiful center, / Where humanity tarries joyfully [243]), projects his desires onto an idealized version of femininity:

> Aber die Bilder, die ungewiß wanken
> Dort auf der Flut der bewegten Gedanken,
> In des Mannes verdüstertem Blick,
> Klar und getreu in dem sanfteren Weibe
> Zeigt sie der Seele krystallene Scheibe,
> Wirft sie der ruhige Spiegel zurück.

> But the images, hovering uncertainly
> On that flood of turbulent ideas,
> In the dark gaze of the man,
> Are shown to us clearly and faithfully in the gentler woman

By the crystal window of the soul,
And are reflected by the peaceful mirror. (241)

Reduced to a mirror of male desire, woman may serve both as a nostalgic image of origin, like the primal androgyne, and as a utopian promise of completion, following the supplementary logic of "androgynous" heterosexual union: "Aus der bezaubernden Einfalt der Züge / Leuchtet der Menschheit Vollendung und Wiege, / Herrschet des Kindes, des Engels Gewalt." (From the entrancing simplicity of her features / Shines the fulfillment and the cradle of humanity / Rules the power of the child, of the angel [243].) Aligned with the child and with the angel, this image of perfect femininity is also placed firmly within nature, perfectly domesticized, and excluded from *Bildung:*

In der Mutter bescheidener Hütte
Sind sie geblieben mit schamhafter Sitte,
Treue Töchter der frommen Natur.

With modest demeanor
They have remained in the simple huts of their mothers,
Loyal daughters of holy Nature. (240)

In the essay "Über die notwendigen Grenzen beim Gebrauch schöner Formen" (On the Limits Necessary in the Use of Beautiful Forms, 1795), Schiller strenuously denies that the female mind might share with its male counterpart the power of abstract thought. "Das andre Geschlecht kann und darf, seiner Natur und seiner Bestimmung nach, mit dem männlichen nie die *Wissenschaft,* aber durch das Medium der Darstellung kann es mit demselben die *Wahrheit* theilen." (The opposite sex, by virtue of its nature and destiny, can never and should never share with the male sex *artistic knowledge,* but through the medium of representation it can be privy to *truth* [vol. 21: 16].) Thus, women are destined to remain passive recipients of male knowledge—or, to use Schiller's own metaphor, infertile soil that constantly frustrates the efforts of toiling sowers:

Das Geschäft also, welches die Natur dem andern Geschlecht nicht bloß nachließ, sondern verbot, muß der Mann doppelt auf sich nehmen, wenn er anders dem Weibe in diesem wichtigen Punkt des Daseyns auf gleicher Stuffe begegnen will. Er wird also soviel, als er nur immer kann, aus dem Reich der Abstraktion, wo Er regiert, in das Reich der Einbildungskraft und Empfindung hinüber zu ziehen suchen, wo das Weib zugleich Muster und Richterinn ist. Er wird, da er in dem weiblichen Geiste keine dauerhaften Pflanzungen anlegen kann, so viele Blüthen und Früchte, als immer möglich ist, auf seinem eigenen

Feld zu erzielen suchen, um den schnell verwelkenden Vorrath auf dem andern desto öfter erneuern, und da, wo keine natürliche Ärnte reift, eine künstliche unterhalten zu können.

Thus, the man must doubly assume the task which nature did not assign to the other sex, and which it indeed forbade the other sex, so that he can meet the woman on an equal footing in this important sphere of existence. So he will attempt to move from the realm of abstraction, where he rules, to the realm of imagination and feeling, where the woman is both model and judge. Since he can lay out no permanent plantations in the female mind, he will try to cultivate as many blossoms and fruits as he can on his own field, so that he can frequently replenish the quickly fading crop on the other field, and sustain an artificial harvest where no natural harvest ripens. (vol. 21: 17)

Unlike men, who have the necessary capacities to go beyond mere passive observation of the beautiful and to penetrate "das Wahre" (truth), women cannot, implies Schiller, "tief eindringen, scharf unterscheiden, vielseitig verbinden und standhaft beharren" (penetrate deeply, distinguish sharply, make multiple connections, and show persistent determination [vol. 21: 20]). The hothouse flowers of speculation that bloom and fade so suddenly in their minds are, in fact, entirely the fruit of male endeavor. As in Humboldt's essays on sexual difference, it is the male intellect, we read, that gives life to resistant female matter.

The free flow and sexual indeterminacy of Winckelmann's androgynous ideal has in Schiller's writings become a matter of considerable anxiety. What results when women transgress the fixities of gender seems to be a perilous anarchy rather than a state of aesthetic harmony. Schiller's writing is dominated by contrasting metaphors of height and depth, of lofty abstraction and corrupting bestiality. Fear in the face of formlessness and indeterminacy is palpable, as in the ballad "Der Taucher" (The Diver) or here, in *Über die ästhetische Erziehung des Menschen:* "Nur wo die Masse schwer und gestaltlos herrscht, und zwischen unsichern Grenzen die trüben Umrisse wanken, hat die Furcht ihren Sitz." (Only where sheer mass, ponderous and inchoate, holds sway, its murky contours shifting within uncertain boundaries, can fear find its seat [vol. 20: 395; Wilkinson and Willoughby, 185]). Schiller's expression of terror before "uncertain boundaries" and "murky contours" we might imagine as equally applicable to the diffuse figure of the androgyne; "Masse," as we have seen, belongs with the "feminine" pole in Schiller's system. This collapsing of Winckelmann's bisexual androgyne into the category of the feminine produces a frighteningly uncontrollable image. As an apocalyptic vision of chaos, it obviously has important ideological implications: critics have pointed to Schiller's association of the human masses, nature, irrationality, and femininity, as in the historical work *Geschichte des Abfalls der vereinigten Niederlande von der spanischen Regierung* (The Defection of the Netherlands).[79] Sander L. Gilman, for example, while not referring specifically to Schiller's writings, has documented extensively such manifestations of unbridled sexuality, perversity, and madness, which he sees as central markers for difference, Otherness.[80]

In Schiller's nightmarish poetic vision of the French Revolution, "Das Lied von der Glocke" (The Song of the Bell), the horrors of political anarchy are rendered most palpable in the contrast between two types of femininity. In the intact prerevolutionary world, women safely occupy their place by the hearth:

> Und drinnen waltet
> Die züchtige Hausfrau,
> Die Mutter der Kinder,
> Und herrschet weise
> Im häuslichen Kreise,
> Und lehret die Mädchen, und wehret den Knaben,
> Und reget ohn' Ende
> Die fleissigen Hände,
> Und mehrt den Gewinn
> Mit ordnendem Sinn.

> And indoor rules
> The virtuous housewife,
> The mother of the children,
> Governing wisely
> In the domestic sphere,
> Teaching the girls, and keeping the boys in check,
> And she endlessly
> Keeps her hands busy,
> Increasing the profit
> With her sense of order. (230)

In direct opposition to this idyllic domestic scene are ghastly images of the godless and bestial revolutionary Furies:

> Freiheit und Gleichheit! hört man schallen,
> Der ruh'ge Bürger greift zur Wehr,
> Die Straßen füllen sich, die Hallen,
> Und Würgerbanden ziehn umher,
> Da werden Weiber zu Hyänen
> Und treiben mit Entsetzen Scherz,

Noch zuckend, mit des Panthers Zähnen,
Zerreissen sie des Feindes Herz.

Freedom and Equality! are heard resounding,
The peaceful citizen sets about defending himself,
The streets and the halls are filled,
And bands of cutthroats roam about,
Women turn into hyenas
And perpetrate horrifying jokes,
Still twitching, with the teeth of panthers,
They tear out the hearts of their enemies. (vol. 1: 237)

As Schiller paints it so vividly here, revolutionary change is accompanied by the most horrible sexual excess, the sexual excess of women. What is more, female sexuality, as it is depicted in this poem, may at any moment spill over the boundaries of clearly defined gender. The hyena, according to popular superstition, is a truly hermaphroditic beast possessing both male and female genitalia and changing sex each year.[81] Joan B. Landes, in her study of revolutionary France, shows that the representation of women was a burning issue of its day and describes powerful anxieties about women's proper speech, action, and dress. Which women were to be transmuted into icons of the Revolution, "the public women of the street and theaters, the austere female goddesses of the ancient [Roman] republic, or the privatized housewife-companions of the ideal republican family?"[82] Schiller's *Über die ästhetische Erziehung des Menschen,* of course, was written in response to and in reaction against the barbarous excesses of the Revolution once hailed by Schiller and so many of his German contemporaries, but the issue of "which women" is still of paramount importance. Salvation, from Schiller's perspective, is perhaps only possible through the twin projects of *Bildung* and art, both of which are the preserve of the bourgeois male. *Über die ästhetische Erziehung des Menschen,* I would suggest, seeks to dispel images of the hideous dual-sexed beasts of the Revolution by replacing them with another female icon, that of the awe-inspiring Juno Ludovisi, the petrified, passive muse.

F. Schlegel: Androgynous Chaos—Androgynous Stasis

If the neoclassical eighteenth century stands rapt before androgynous Greek sculpture, this obsession is shared by a writer of central importance for a whole young generation of romantics. Both the theoretical and poetic writings of Friedrich Schlegel are shot through with a vision of androgyny as an aesthetic ideal, a vision that undoubtedly owes much to Winckelmann, at least in its initial phases.[83] As an art critic, Schlegel shares the vocabulary of Winckelmann's aesthetics of indeterminacy and of his idealized "Mittelzustand" (middle state). Here, Schlegel characterizes the androgynous beauty he perceives in a Leonardo Madonna as representing a divine ideal of synthesis:

> Das Gesicht könnte fast ohne alle Veränderungen, oder doch mit wenigen, ganz kleinen und nichtsbedeutenden, auch einen sehr jugendlichen Christus vorstellen; so wie der Kopf des jugendlichen Heilands im Tempel von ihm, offenbar durch kleine Zufälligkeiten von dem Gesicht einer Madonna abweicht. Es hat also der Maler das Ideal des Göttlichen in der möglichsten Annäherung und Vereinigung ernster Weiblichkeit und jugendlicher Männlichkeit in den Formen und Zügen des Gesichts gesucht.

> The face of the blessed Virgin might, with little or no alteration, be taken for that of a youthful Christ, as that of the "Savior in the Temple," by the same master, seems equally fitted for a Madonna. The painter appears to have formed his ideal of the Divinity as combining in one form the closest possible union between serious womanhood and masculine adolescence.[84]

But the vocabulary of androgynous beauty in Schlegel's writings is more than stylistic embellishment, more than a modish and superficial allusion to Winckelmann's aesthetics. Schlegel is concerned above all with the radical aesthetic possibilities opened up by the indeterminate figure of the androgyne. Here, in his emphasis on indeterminacy and chaos, he would seem to break completely with the integrational androgynous model of Schiller, an ideal of plenitude and harmony. Schlegel's novel *Lucinde,* published in 1799, is the quintessential novel of androgyny, not simply for thematic reasons—though, of course, its hero and heroine, Julius and Lucinde, revel in dizzying sexual role-playing and their love relationship is represented as a perfect androgynous union—but because the novel's whole structure is set in motion by notions of aesthetic indeterminacy and erotic chaos. The spiraling "system" of the novel is laid out in its opening pages, in a letter from Julius to Lucinde.[85] While Julius ostensibly begins his letter in conventional narratorial mode, by announcing his desire to lay bare his past history and the reasons for his present state of bliss, he willfully breaks the narrative thread and declares his intention: "daß ich gleich anfangs das was wir Ordnung nennen vernichte, weit von ihr entferne und mir das Recht einer reizenden Verwirrung deutlich zueigne und durch die Tat behaupte" (to destroy at the very outset all that part we call "order," remove it, and claim explicitly and affirm actually the right to a charming confusion).[86] Offering the justification that the raw material for the novel, "unser Leben und Lieben" (our life and love), is "so unaufhaltsam progressiv und so unbiegsam systematisch" (so systematic and so progressive) that any novel mirroring it formally would be unbearably dull and uniform, Julius asserts his "unbezweifeltes Verwirrungsrecht" (incontestable right to confusion). His novel will both recreate and enhance "das schönste Chaos von erhabnen Harmonien und interessanten Genüssen" (the most beautiful chaos of sublime harmonies and fascinating pleasures [vol. 5: 9; Firchow, 45]). The opening section of the novel ends with a telling vignette: from among the many notes composed to Lucinde that are scattered all over his room, we see Julius selecting his favorite pages and inserting them, it seems randomly, into the body of his novel. The resulting work does indeed appear anarchic and hybrid: letters are interspersed with dialogues, an idyll, dreams, allegories, and fantasies, and it is known that Schlegel's plans for continuation also stressed the inclusion of poetry.[87] We would probably do best, however, to employ an oxymoron ourselves and call the novel an ordered chaos; that Schlegel in fact carefully contrived its overall symmetry is clear from the novel's structure, its central confessional narrative surrounded on both sides by six "arabesques."[88] The aesthetic coincidence of androgynous symmetry and androgynous chaos will become clearer toward the end of my discussion of Schlegel.

Such a genuinely hybrid form, one that perfectly illustrates Schlegel's famous definition of romantic poetry in the Athenaeum Fragment 116 as "eine progressive Universalpoesie" (a progressive, universal poetry), appears to be a radical departure from the integrational androgynous aesthetic delineated by Schiller. Yet many of Schlegel's theoretical pronouncements on art, themselves paradoxes, are expressed in oxymora that recall Schiller's description of the Juno Ludovisi. In his review of Goethe's novel *Wilhelm Meister,* for example, Schlegel praises the novel's "gebildete Willkür" (crafted willfulness [vol. 2: 134]); and in the "Gespräch über die Poesie" (Dialogue on Poetry), he declares, paradoxically, that his ideal consists of a combination of chaos *and* symmetry: "künstlich geordnete Verwirrung, diese reizende Symmetrie von Widersprüchen" (this artfully ordered confusion, that charming symmetry of contradictions [vol. 2: 318]).[89]

When the reader turns to the thematics of *Lucinde* itself, the artful staging of sexual/textual chaos becomes evident. In the last of the six framing episodes preceding the "Lehrjahre der Männlichkeit" (Apprenticeship for Manhood), entitled "Treue und Scherz" (Fidelity and Playfulness), the two lovers appear for the first time and engage in a playful dialogue that culminates in their sexual union. Their bantering debate on the theme of fidelity and jealousy, the exchange of words and thoughts, clearly heightens the eroticism of the scene, and the way in which they self-consciously adopt sparring conversational roles echoes the sexual role-playing of the "Dithyrambische Fantasie" (Dithyrambic Fantasy). If at the end of "Treue und Scherz" the reader finds the sexes mingled in the totality of an androgynous union, it is apt that this relationship be described in oxymoronic form: their desire is represented as spiritual, their apotheosis is eroticized.

In the "Allegorie von der Frechheit" (Allegory of Impudence), a section of the novel that resists and frustrates the reader's struggle for unambiguous meaning perhaps more than any other in this multilayered work, the androgyne appears in person on the novel stage. The section opens with a ghastly hallucinatory experience in which Julius sees before him a monstrous creature that eludes all zoological classifications—but when he kicks this strange mutant onto its back, it becomes clear that it is only a common frog. The meaning of this hybrid apparition is revealed to Julius by a handsome young man who introduces himself as "der Witz" (Wit): it represents public opinion. In order to demonstrate to Julius that poets should shun the vile creature, "der Witz" presents the allegorical spectacle of "einige Jünglinge am Scheidewege" (some youths at the crossroads), who represent, he claims, "die echten Romane, vier an der Zahl" (the genuine Novels, four in number [vol. 5: 16; Firchow, 53]). One is described as a stalwart knight, sunk in prayer; one is a melancholic, ethereal boy dressed in classical Greek robes; one is a worldly and sociable young cosmopolitan. The first youth to be introduced is, however, the most capricious and mutable in form, and his fleeting appearances in the text punctuate and destabilize the more orderly, unified descriptions of the other youths:

> ein schöner Jüngling flog kaum bekleidet über die grüne Ebne. Schon war er fern und ich sah nur noch eben, daß er sich auf ein Roß schwang und davon eilte als wollte er den lauen Abendwind überflügeln und seiner Langsamkeit spotten.

> a beautiful, almost naked youth running across the green plain. He was already far away and I could barely see him swing himself onto a horse and gallop away as if trying to overtake the mild evening breeze and mock its slowness. (vol. 5: 16; Firchow, 53)

This mercurial figure seems to outstrip the winds as he gallops off into the distance, barely clothed. However, when he next appears, after the description of the pious knight, his mood is more contemplative: "Der Jüngling, der zuvor so schnell war, lag nun ganz ruhig am Abhange und sonnte sich in den letzten Strahlen." (The boy who'd been so quick before was now lying quietly on the slope and bathing himself in the last rays of the sun.) Barely able to keep up with him, and with the staccato syntax of his narrative mirroring the youth's volatile movements, Julius next sees him plunging into the river, that natural environment for androgynous desires: "[D]ann sprang er auf, entkleidete sich, stürzte in den Strom und spielte mit den Wellen, tauchte unter, kam wieder hervor und warf sich von neuem in die Flut." (Then he jumped up, undressed, plunged into the river and played with the waves, dived under the water, came up again, and again plunged into the river [vol. 5: 16; Firchow, 54].) Cutting short Julius's description of the Grecophile youth, the androgynous boy marches into our field of vision again, this time in a new costume:

> Jener ernste[90] sinnliche Jüngling war unterdessen der einsamen Leibesübungen überdrüssig geworden und eilte mit leichten Schritten gerade auf uns zu. Er war nun ganz bekleidet, fast wie ein Schäfer, aber sehr bunt und sonderbar. Er hätte so auf einer Maskerade erscheinen können, auch spielten die Finger seiner Linken mit den Fäden, an denen eine Maske hing. Man hätte den fantastischen Knaben eben so gut für ein mutwilliges Mädchen halten mögen, das sich aus Laune verkleidet.

> Meanwhile the first youth—the sensuous one—had grown tired of his solitary gymnastics, and was hurrying with easy steps straight toward us. Now he was completely clothed, almost like a shepherd, but very colorfully and strangely. He could have gone to a masquerade like that, and in fact his fingers were playing with the laces of a mask. This fantastic boy could just as well have been mistaken for a spirited girl who had disguised herself on a whim. (vol. 5: 17; Firchow, 54)

What is the reader to make of this curious figure? Announced as he is as an allegorical figure, he demands clear interpretation, yet as an androgynous and capricious adolescent boy, he is immediately bewildering, teasing. A figure of artifice, he is presented with a mask in one hand, dressed in the extravagant carnivalesque attire of a rococo shepherd. The text signals the polymorphous disposition of the youth by comparing his costume with a girl's whimsical cross-dressing. More than this, the reader is informed that the paradoxically serious yet fantastical youth is an allegory for some type of novel—but precisely which kind of novel he represents is not made clear in the text. In a March 1799 letter to Caroline Böhmer, however, Schlegel reveals that one of the four youths—the androgynous boy—stands for his own *Lucinde,* while the three others represent plans for future novels.[91] Thus, Schlegel conjures up his own novel as a player on the stage of that same novel, signaling the multiple layers present within *Lucinde.*[92] And more than this, Schlegel suggests, the form of androgynous desire and textuality that his novel incarnates is set in motion by a powerful element of homoeroticism.

The allegorical crossroads, or "Scheideweg," forces the four youths to choose between maidens who represent conventional feminine virtues such as "Sittlichkeit" (Morality), "Bescheidenheit" (Modesty), "Delikatesse" (Delicacy), and so on, and a female figure who stands apart from them, "Frechheit" (Impudence). Significantly, Julius's vision ends with the androgynous boy rejecting public opinion and leaving arm in arm with Lady Impudence, who has delivered a scathing attack on the hypocritical mask of morality worn by the virtuous maidens. Finally, Julius's companion on this bewildering allegorical journey, "der Witz," calls upon him to reveal the chaos of nature in a new kind of novel:

> Bilde, erfinde, verwandle und erhalte die Welt und ihre ewigen Gestalten im steten Wechsel neuer Trennungen und Vermählungen. Verhülle und binde den Geist im Buchstaben. Der echte Buchstabe ist allmächtig und der eigentliche Zauberstab. Er ist es, mit dem die unwiderstehliche Willkür der hohen Zauber-in Fantasie das erhabene Chaos der vollen Natur berührt, und das unendliche Wort ans Licht ruft, welches ein Ebenbild und Spiegel des göttlichen Geistes ist, und welches die Sterblichen Universum nennen.

> Create, discover, transform, and retain the world and its eternal forms in the perpetual variation of new marriages and divorces. Veil and bind the spirit in the letter. The real letter is all-powerful; it's the true magic wand. It is the letter with which the irresistible will of that great magician, Fantasy, touches the sublime chaos of all-encompassing nature, touches it and calls the infinite word to light, the word that is an image and a mirror of the divine spirit, and that mortals call the universe. (vol. 5: 20; Firchow, 58)

Again, this aesthetic principle of constant flux, of incessant combination and recombination, recalls the volatile personality of the allegorical androgynous boy, and the games of sexual shape-shifting that are described by Julius as an allegory of true humanity:

> Aber weißt du wohl, das dieses süße Spiel für mich noch ganz andre Reize hat als seine eignen? Es ist auch nicht bloß die Wollust der Ermattung oder das Vorgefühl der Rache. Ich sehe hier eine wunderbare sinnreich bedeutende Allegorie auf die Vollendung des Männlichen und Weiblichen zur vollen ganzen Menschheit.

> But are you aware that this sweet game still has quite other attractions for me than its own—and not simply the voluptuousness of exhaustion or the anticipation of revenge? I see here a wonderful, deeply meaningful allegory of the development of man and woman to a full and complete humanity. (vol. 5: 12; Firchow, 49)

Later, at the end of the "Lehrjahre der Männlichkeit," Julius returns again with fascination to the androgynous boy—the reason the boy pleased him so much was his obvious artificiality, his artful weaving of art and life:

> Es war nicht ohne Grund, daß der fantastische Knabe, der mir am meisten gefiel unter den vier unsterblichen Romanen, die ich im Traum sah, mit der Maske spielt. Auch in dem was reine Darstellung und Tatsache scheint, hat sich die Allegorie eingeschlichen, und unter die schöne Wahrheit bedeutende Lügen gemischt.

> It's not without a reason that the fantastical boy whom I liked best of the four immortal Novels who appeared to me in the dream was playing with a mask. Allegory has crept even into what seems pure description and fact, and has mixed meaningful lies with beautiful truths. (vol. 5: 59; Firchow, 104)

Critics have readily identified Schlegel's guiding aesthetic strategy as the arabesque.[93] I believe that it is crucial to understand, too, the link between an "androgynous" aesthetic and the romantic arabesque. Androgyny, in Schlegel's novel, is more than a thematic concern summed up in the love union between Julius and Lucinde. If readers take into account the teasing adolescent who represents, allegorically, this dizzying novel, they can begin to see androgyny as a central formal principle, fundamentally connected with Julius's "Verwirrungsrecht" (right to confusion). It is in this figure, too, that one can trace the path followed by the composite aesthetic ideal since Winckelmann.[94] As Joel Black has argued, the composite "Zeuxian" whole envisioned by neoclassical theorists such as Winckelmann, which also informs the ideal of androgynous completion and plenitude in the writings of Humboldt and Schiller, is radically revised by the romantics, who locate ideal beauty beyond the sphere of representability. Thus, the strategy of the composite is replaced by a fragmentary—or, as Black terms it, synecdochic[95]—aesthetic, in which ideal wholeness can only be hinted at, represented by a part. As is well known, Schlegel expresses his wariness of the illusion of wholeness, and his celebration of the fragment, in the famous Athenaeum Fragment 116. Positing romantic poetry as an aesthetic of the indeterminate middle sphere—"doch kann sie auch am meisten . . . auf den Flügeln der poetischen Reflexion in der Mitte schweben" (yet it too can soar . . . on the wings of poetic reflection, midway between the work and the artist)—Schlegel defies neoclassical closure: "Die romantische Dichtart ist noch im Werden; ja das ist ihr eigentliches Wesen, daß sie ewig nur werden, nie vollendet sein kann." (The Romantic type of poetry is still becoming; indeed its peculiar essence is that it is always becoming and that it can never be completed [vol. 2: 182–83; Behler and Struc, 140–41]). Gender indeterminacy, it might be argued, is one of the characteristics of this fluid middle space.

Schlegel's seminal "Gespräch über die Poesie" (1800) contains an important and revealing allusion to Winckelmann. The conversation containing the reference deserves to be quoted at some length:

ANDREA. Ich bitte die alten Götter in Ehren zu halten.

LOTHARIO. Und ich bitte sich an die Eleusinischen Mysterien zu erinnern. Ich wünschte, ich hätte meine Gedanken darüber zu Papiere gebracht, um sie Euch in der Ordnung und Ausführlichkeit vorlegen zu können, welche die Würde und Wichtigkeit des Gegenstandes erfordert. Nur durch die Spuren von den Mysterien habe ich den Sinn der alten Götter verstehn lernen. Ich vermute, daß die Ansicht der Natur die da herrrschte, den jetzigen Forschern, wenn sie schon reif dazu sind, ein großes Licht anzünden würde. Die kühnste und kräftigste, ja ich möchte fast sagen die wildeste und wütendste Darstellung des Realismus ist die beste. Erinnern Sie mich wenigstens daran, Ludoviko, daß ich Ihnen bei Gelegenheit das orphische Fragment bekannt mache, welches von dem doppelten Geschlecht des Zeus anfängt.

MARCUS. Ich erinnre mich einer Andeutung im Winckelmann, aus der ich vermuten möchte, daß er dieses Fragment ebenso hoch geachtet wie Sie.

ANDREA. I beg you to honor the old gods.

LOTHARIO. And I ask you to remember the Eleusinian mysteries. I wish I had put my thoughts about it on paper, so that I could present them to you in the order and detail befitting the dignity and importance of the subject. Only through the extant mysteries have I come to understand the meaning of the ancient gods. I would like to think that the view of nature prevalent there would illuminate many things for present-day scholars, if they were ready for it. The most daring and powerful, indeed I am tempted to say the wildest and most enraged expression of realism is the best. Remind me, Ludovico, at least to show you the Orphic fragment which starts with the bisexuality of Zeus.

MARCUS. I remember a hint in Winckelmann from which I would assume that he values this fragment as much as you do. (vol. 2: 326; Behler and Struc, 91)

The key to deciphering this allusion to an obscure Orphic fragment pointing to the dual sexuality of Zeus perhaps lies, as Black has suggested, in a recognition that the Orphic passage is itself a fragment. Only through the fragmentary trace is one capable of penetrating the ancient mysteries and that most obscure enigma of Zeus's sexuality. Zeus's sexual polymorphousness is centered in the mystery of wholeness, which may be detected in all androgynous myths, but this ideal plenitude can only be realized through the natural human condition of partiality and deficiency. As Black puts it: "In our natural lives as individual men or women we are each but a part, positioned in an implicit synecdochic relationship with an ideal polymorphous sexuality,

a condition of androgynous wholeness from which we are now separate
and a-part."[96] Only in the fragment can we retrieve a sense of Platonic
wholeness and penetrate what Schlegel calls "eine mystische Wissenschaft
vom Ganzen" (a mystic discipline of the whole [vol. 2: 325; Behler and
Struc, 90]). But the Platonic myth, it is important to note, is viewed here
through the lens of radical difference.

Like Winckelmann, like Humboldt and Schiller, Schlegel here turns
to the Greek past for evidence of androgynous wholeness; for Schlegel,
however, a radical goal of his writings on antiquity is to force his readers to recognize and to reconsider their own historically produced sexual
limitations. The notion that the sexuality of the Greeks predates the fall
into polarities already determines his earlier studies on classical antiquity,
notably the essay "Über Diotima" (On Diotima). Much of its vocabulary
of Greek wholeness is by now familiar to us. Classical Greek education
makes possible "eine Fülle in freier Einheit" (a plenitude in free unity
[vol. 1: 78]), for example, and the figure of Diotima, who also appears
in Plato's *Symposium,* is praised as "ein Bild vollendeter Menschheit" (an
image of perfected humanity [vol. 1: 71, 115; the phrase is used at both
the beginning and the end of the essay, in a framing gesture]). Turning to
the Greeks for examples of "complete" individuals, Schlegel also seeks to
bring to light the female achievement untold in Greek history. In Plato's
Diotima, Schlegel finds evidence for both—here is a woman of intellectual
accomplishment, a woman who also seems unrestricted by conventional sex
roles, and who represents, rather than a perfect example of her sex, a higher
form of humanity that has transcended sexual difference. Like Schiller's
divine image of perfection, the Juno Ludovisi, Diotima seems to embrace
the characteristics of both sexes: "Ihre reichhaltigen Gedanken über das
Verlangen und das Schöne sind eben so umfassend als scharfsinnig, eben
so bestimmt als zart." (Her deep thoughts about desire and beauty are as
comprehensive as they are astute, as definite as they are sensitive [vol. 1:
71].) And Diotima's androgynous nature is insisted upon again by Schlegel
in his conclusion to the essay:

> Plato . . . hat mit wenigen Meisterzügen eine Frau verewigt, . . . die sein
> zartes Gefühl und die hohen Ideen der Vernunft gleich sehr befriedigte:—
> Diotima, in welcher sich die Anmuth einer Aspasia, die Seele einer Sappho, mit
> hoher Selbständigkeit vermählt, deren heiliges Gemüth ein Bild vollendeter
> Menschheit darstellt.

> Plato . . . has in a few masterful strokes immortalized a woman, . . . who
> satisfied in equal measure his delicate feelings and his lofty conceptions of

reason:—Diotima, in whom are united the grace of an Aspasia, the soul of a Sappho, along with a high degree of independence, and whose holy person represents the image of perfect humanity. (vol. 1: 115)

The androgynous Diotima is also implicitly linked with Schlegel's notion of the fragment. Radically questioning accepted notions about women's history in the classical world, Schlegel presents his own pioneering vision through the metaphor of artistic reconstruction. Although lacunae will inevitably remain in this fragmentary history, the task itself opens up suggestive possibilities:

> So wie es oft nicht unmöglich ist, aus den kleinsten Bruchstücken einer zerstückelten Statue, und bei beträchtlichen Lücken, das Ganze des Bildes wiederherzustellen; so zeigt sich auch hier ein Leitfaden, das Verlorne zu ergänzen, das Zerstückte wieder zusammenzusetzen, und die Hoffnung zu einer nicht ganz unvollständigen Geschichte der Griechischen Weiblichkeit.

> Just as it is often possible to restore, even with considerable lacunae, the wholeness of a ruined statue from its tiniest fragments, so a connecting thread may be discerned here that enables us to supplement what is lost, to piece together what is fragmented, and we see a hope that we might achieve a not altogether incomplete history of Greek womanhood. (vol. 1: 72)

Despite the difference in emphasis, Schlegel's suggestive image for finding potential completion in the fragmented "torso" of history recalls something of Winckelmann's position as viewer of androgynous Greek sculpture.[97] But while Winckelmann seeks to recreate and express a harmonious, nonalienated whole, one senses with Schlegel that the fragment has an appeal all of its own.

If, as I argue, an androgynous aesthetic is inextricably bound with radical romantic theories of the fragment, it is also revealing to consider shifting attitudes toward the androgynous icon itself. Schlegel's allusion to Winckelmann in the "Gespräch über die Poesie" is suggestive of these changes. When, in the passage quoted above, Lothario declares, "Ich möchte fast sagen die wildeste und wütendste Darstellung des Realismus ist die beste" (I am tempted to say the wildest and most enraged expression of realism is the best [vol. 2: 326; Firchow, 91]), this dynamic, raging "realism" immediately reminds him of the Orphic fragment cited by Winckelmann. Again, the Greek artist Zeuxis comes to mind, whose famed superrealism Black persuasively links to Schlegel's concept of turbulent Dionysian realism, affirmed throughout the "Gespräch über die Poesie." This "realism" is expressed fully in the arabesque, an "organic" form belonging exclusively neither to nature nor to art, an open-ended, intoxicating, vegetative form.[98] This association of the arabesque with vegetative forms also implicitly links it with femininity, a point I will elaborate later. Viewers or readers of arabesques are constantly teased, constantly on the verge of recognition, but the anticipated glimpse of the complete whole, of a torso that has finally acquired a head and arms, is withheld. I noted above Winckelmann's own ambivalence toward the androgyne, his idealization of androgynous representations in art and his unease at the notion that such creatures could exist in real life. In Schlegel's aesthetics, as in romanticism in general, the beautiful itself comes uncannily close to the grotesque, and the grotesque is present in the sinuous curves of the arabesque, of the androgyne. Conceived in its immediate physical totality—as a fragment or compilation of fragments—the representation of the androgynous ideal, far removed from the harmonizing figures admired by Winckelmann and Schiller, may take the form of a grotesque beast, more monster than god. For the romantics, who feel the erotic thrill of angelic and demonic female figures, such an androgyne, "wild und wütend" (wild and enraged), surely proves irresistible. In his notebooks, Schlegel observes that for him "die höchste Wollust liegt in d[er] Idee vom *Hermaphroditen*" (the highest ecstasy is to be found in the idea of the *hermaphrodite* [vol. 16: 195]).[99] Yet fascination is often mingled with horror—as Georges Bataille puts it, "eroticism springs from an alternation of fascination and horror, of affirmation and denial."[100] Schlegel's early essay "Über die weiblichen Charaktere in den griechischen Dichtern" (On the Female Characters in Greek Poetry) on the one hand expresses admiration at the androgynous, integrated personality of Sophocles' Antigone. Yet the women described in Aristophanes' comedy as usurping male power and dress arouse conflicting emotions of ferocious desire and repulsion reminiscent of Schiller's "Lied von der Glocke":

> die Sitten der Weiber, die er aufführt, . . . das Kolorit des Ganzen geben ein nur zu vollständiges Gemälde weiblicher Zügellosigkeit. Der bloße Inhalt einiger Stücke mag errathen lassen, was unsre Sprache nicht genau ausführen darf. In einem derselben rottieren sich alle Weiber einer Stadt zusammen, unzufrieden über den schon lange geführten Krieg, verschwören sich zu einer heroischen Enthaltsamkeit und zwingen ihre Männer Frieden zu schließen, durch das große Mittel, durch welches kluge Frauen sinnliche Männer zu beherrschen pflegen. In der weiblichen Volksversammlung bemächtigen sich die Weiber, als Männer verkleidet, durch List des Marktplatzes und der Regierung, dekretieren die Herrschaft der Weiber und Gehorsam der Männer, Freiheit und Gleichheit auch in der Liebe, Gemeinschaft der Güter und der Männer; durch ein andres Dekret erhalten Häßlichkeit und Alter (vermuthlich die Majorität) gleiche Rechte auf die Liebe und den Besitz der Männer, als Schönheit und Jugend.

Durch diese grenzenlose Zügellosigkeit und Sinnlichkeit . . . mußte auch
die üppigste Kraft sehr bald sich selbst schwächen.

the morals of the women that he presents, . . . the atmosphere of the whole
thing, create an all too complete picture of female anarchy. Just the content of
a few dramas will hint at what our language dares not detail in full. In one of
them, all the women of a city gang together, discontented at the war that has
been raging so long, pledge themselves to heroic abstinence, and force their
menfolk to conclude a peace treaty by means of that great strategy used by
clever women to master sensual men. In their female assembly the women,
dressed as men, take over by cunning the marketplace and the government,
decree female control and male obedience, freedom and equality—in love
also, common ownership of property and men; in another decree ugly and
old women (presumably the majority) obtain the same rights to love and to
ownership of men as the young and beautiful.
    As a result of this boundless anarchy and sensuality . . . even the most vital
of powers would be bound to weaken. (vol. 1, 64–65)

What are the implications of such an ambivalent androgynous aesthetic
ideal for Schlegel's concept of *Bildung?* When Schlegel observes, in the essays "Über die Diotima" and "Über die Philosophie. An Dorothea" (On Philosophy. To Dorothea), that only "selbständige Weiblichkeit" (independent
femininity) and "sanfte Männlichkeit" (gentle masculinity) are beautiful, in
the same breath he declares that these "hybrid" models of femininity and
masculinity also represent the only truly moral human state. Like Schiller,
then, Schlegel turns to the androgyne as a metaphor for an aesthetic state that
engages the whole human personality, both ethical and aesthetic impulses.
The androgyne is both "gut" and "schön" (good and beautiful).
    This ethical valorization of the androgynous model also has important
implications for Schlegel's representation of and attitude toward sexual
difference. He has often been hailed for his emancipatory statements on
behalf of women, for his exhortations that they pull themselves up "aus
dem großen Weltmeere der Vorurteile und der Gemeinheit in die Höhe" (to
the heights, from the great ocean of prejudice and mediocrity [vol. 8: 43]).
In his earlier essays on Greek literature and history, as well as in *Lucinde,*
his novel of *Bildung,* he would seem to propose a Greek-inspired bisexual
model of androgyny as a new strategy for women (and men) of his day.
In Sophocles' Antigone, he sees an ideal woman, one possessed of male
and female characteristics—"alle Kräfte sind in ihr vollendet und unter sich
eins" (in her all powers are perfected and harmonious [vol. 1: 58])—and
Diotima, as I noted earlier, is represented as an androgynous being. In "Über
die Diotima," written in part as a response to Humboldt's standard catalog

of sexual stereotypes, "Über die männliche und weibliche Form," Schlegel refuses what he sees as an unquestioning and misleading appropriation of Greek history in order to back up modern assumptions regarding sexual difference.[101] His reference to the Greek historian Xenophon powerfully illustrates the contingency, indeed reversibility, of the kinds of sexual stereotypes that underpin Humboldt's anthropological speculations:

> War sie auch so kurz, so gab es doch eine Zeit, wo man behaupten konnte, daß Lakonische Frauen männliche Kraft und Selbständigkeit, Lakonische Jünglinge aber weibliche Bescheidenheit, Schamhaftigkeit und Sanftmut besaßen.

> No matter how brief it was, there was a time when one could state that Laconian women possessed male strength and independence, while Laconian youths possessed female modesty, demureness, and gentleness. (vol. 1: 91)

At only one point in his essay does he himself fall into a polarizing characterization of male and female, and even then he swiftly inserts a cautionary "vielleicht":

> Man nimmt . . . in den Begriff der reinen Weiblichkeit—der *vielleicht* [my emphasis] nur zwei Bestandteile: Innigkeit und Zartheit, wie der Begriff der Männlichkeit: Umfang und Bestimmtheit, hat—zu viel Merkmale auf, Merkmale die aus der Erfahrung geschöpft sind, und nur einer übertriebenen Weiblichkeit zukommen: *Beharrlichkeit* und *Einfachheit,* als einen Vorzug des Geschlechts. Man versteht darunter nichts anders als die absolute Charakterlosigkeit, die das Gesetz ihrer Sitten von einem fremden Wesen empfängt; und die von Außen *gegebne* Einheit ist hier freilich vollendeter als die selbstthätige von innen mühsam erkämpfte Beharrlichkeit des Mannes. Aber eben der herrschsüchtige Ungestüm des Mannes, und die selbstlose Hingegebenheit des Weibes ist schon übertrieben und häßlich.

> Too many characteristics are incorporated in the concept of pure femininity—which *perhaps* [my emphasis] only has two components: depth and delicacy, just as the concept of masculinity comprises breadth and certainty. These characteristics are drawn from experience, and only apply to an exaggerated femininity: *steadfastness* and *simplicity,* as the distinguishing feature of the sex. This can be understood as nothing other than absolute characterlessness, which receives the principles governing its nature from an external source; and the unity *bestowed* externally is here admittedly more perfect than the innate steadfastness of the man, striven for from within. But just this domineering impetuousness of the man and this selfless devotion of the woman are already exaggerated and ugly. (vol. 1: 93)

Schlegel demands: "Was ist häßlicher als die überladne Weiblichkeit, was ist ekelhafter als die übertriebne Männlichkeit, die in unsern Sitten, in unsern Meinungen, ja auch in unsrer bessern Kunst herrscht?" (What is uglier than overloaded femininity, what is more repulsive than exaggerated masculinity, which reigns in our morals, in our opinions, indeed even in our better art? [vol. 1: 92]) Rigid adherence to the binaries of feminine and masculine is both aesthetically distasteful ("häßlich") and morally repulsive ("ekelhaft"). In "Über die Philosophie. An Dorothea," addressed to his future wife, Dorothea Veit, Schlegel goes on to uncover the societal origins of sexual difference, disclaiming biology as the sole root of role division. Although he uses the term *androgyny* neither in the Diotima essay nor in this later work, he does refer cryptically to the Platonic myth of the androgyne, as "eine alte Sage" (an old legend):

> Der eigne Sinn, die eigne Kraft und der eigne Wille eines Menschen ist das Menschlichste, das Ursprünglichste, das Heiligste in ihm. Ob er zu dieser oder jener Gattung gehöre, das ist unbedeutender und zufälliger; die Geschlechtsverschiedenheit ist nur eine Äußerlichkeit des menschlichen Daseins und am Ende doch nichts weiter als eine recht gute Einrichtung der Natur, die man freilich nicht willkürlich vertilgen oder verkehren, aber allerdings der Vernunft unterordnen, und nach ihren höhern Gesetzen bilden darf. In der Tat sind die Männlichkeit und die Weiblichkeit, so wie sie gewöhnlich genommen und getrieben werden, die gefährlichsten Hindernisse der Menschlichkeit, welche nach einer alten Sage in der Mitte einheimisch ist und doch nur ein harmonisches Ganzes sein kann, welches keine Absonderung leidet.

> The true meaning, the true strength, and the true will of a human being are the most human, the most natural, and the most holy things about him. Whether he belongs to this sex or to another is less important and more coincidental; sexual difference is only an external factor of human existence, and in the end it is no more than an excellent natural arrangement, which, of course, one should not willfully destroy or overturn, but which one should subordinate to reason and which one can mold according to reason's higher principles. Indeed, masculinity and femininity, as they are generally understood and propagated, are the most dangerous impediments to humanity, which according to an old legend resides in the middle and can still only be a harmonious whole that tolerates no division. (vol. 8: 45)

Citing his own remark, in "Über die Diotima," that "nur sanfte Männlichkeit, nur selbständige Weiblichkeit" (only gentle masculinity, only independent femininity) can be "die rechte, die wahre und schöne" (right, true, and beautiful), Schlegel continues by radically asserting the right of each individual "sich nach Lust und Liebe in dem ganzen Bezirke der Menschheit frei zu bewegen" (to move freely according to his or her own preference, along the whole spectrum of humanity [vol. 8: 45]). Such a notion of free-flowing desire, of genuinely polymorphous sexuality, might indeed be viewed as a revolutionary assault on the models of strict sexual complementarity established by both Humboldt and Schiller. But it remains to be seen whether this radical new concept of androgyny is what informs Schlegel's view of the sexes in his novel *Lucinde,* which was published in 1799, the same year as "Über die Philosophie. An Dorothea." Certainly many readers were morally offended by the free eroticism of the relationship at the center of this novel, by passages in which the hero, Julius, describes the sexual acrobatics of his lovemaking with Lucinde. Here, the game is in ever new forms of combination and recombination, an erotic version of *ars combinatoria:*

> Eine [Situation] unter allen ist die witzigste und die schönste: wenn wir die Rollen vertauschen und mit kindischer Lust wetteifern, wer den andern täuschender nachäffen kann, ob dir die schonende Heftigkeit des Mannes besser gelingt, oder mir die hinziehende Hingebung des Weibes. Aber weißt du wohl, daß dieses süße Spiel für mich noch ganz andre Reize hat als seine eignen? Es ist auch nicht bloß die Wollust der Ermattung oder das Vorgefühl der Rache. Ich sehe hier eine wunderbare sinnreich bedeutende Allegorie auf die Vollendung des Männlichen und Weiblichen zur vollen ganzen Menschheit. Es liegt viel darin, und was darin liegt, steht gewiß nicht so schnell auf wie ich, wenn ich dir unterliege.

> One [situation] above all is the wittiest and most beautiful: when we exchange roles and in childish high spirits compete to see who can mimic the other more convincingly, whether you are better at imitating the protective intensity of the man, or I the appealing devotion of the woman. But are you aware that this sweet game still has quite other attractions for me than its own—and not simply the voluptuousness of exhaustion or the anticipation of revenge? I see here a wonderful, deeply meaningful allegory of the development of man and woman to full and complete humanity. There is much in it—and what is in it certainly doesn't rise up as quickly as I do when I am overcome by you. (vol. 5: 12; Firchow, 49)

At the same time, as Achim Aurnhammer has pointed out, Schlegel appropriates the botanical analogy that we saw in Schiller's poem "Die Geschlechter" as a marker of primal undividedness.[102] One fragment declares: "Auch als Hermaphrodit ist d[ie] Pflanze das höchste." (As a hermaphrodite, too, the plant is supreme [vol. 18: 153].) According to *Lucinde,* societal and economic pressures, rather than biology, lie behind sexual difference, "denn der Fleiß und der Nutzen sind die Todesengel mit dem feurigen Schwert, welche dem Menschen die Rückkehr ins Paradies verwehren" (because industry and utility are the angels of death who, with fiery swords, prevent man's return to paradise [vol. 5: 27; Firchow, 65]). Androgyny, as

Schlegel sees it exemplified in the plant world, frees us from the shackles of sexual difference, in an ethical sense and, importantly, in an aesthetic sense. What is more, the concept of pure androgynous vegetation would seem antithetical to the classical notion of *Bildung,* with its concomitant sexual maturation—and differentiation:

> Um alles in Eins zu fassen: je göttlicher ein Mensch oder ein Werk des Menschen ist, je ähnlicher werden sie der Pflanze; diese ist unter allen Formen der Natur die sittlichste, und die schönste. Und also wäre ja das höchste vollendetste Leben nichts als ein *reines Vegetieren.*

> In a word: the more divine a man or a work of man is, the more it resembles a plant; of all the forms of nature, this form is the most moral and the most beautiful. And so the highest, most perfect mode of life would actually be nothing more than *pure vegetating.* (vol. 5: 27; Firchow, 66)

This ideal of passive vegetation, which translates itself into art as "Größe in Ruhe" (greatness in repose [vol. 5: 26; Firchow, 65]),[103] also recalls the luxuriant organic forms of the arabesque:

> So erzeugte sich der erste Keim zu dem wundersamen Gewächs von Willkür und Liebe. Und frei wie es entsprossen ist, dacht' ich, soll es auch üppig wachsen und verwildern, und nie will ich aus niedriger Ordnungsliebe und Sparsamkeit die lebendige Fülle von überflüssigen Blättern und Ranken beschneiden.

> That is how the first germ of that wonderful plant of love and caprice was conceived. And as freely as it sprouted, I thought, should it also grow and run wild; and never, from a base love of order and frugality, will I prune its living fullness of superfluous leaves and branches. (vol. 5: 26; Firchow, 64)

What may have been even more offensive than heterosexual play to contemporary audiences, however, is the homoerotic suggestiveness of *Lucinde,* embodied in the impudent allegorical boy androgyne. One anonymous satire that appeared soon after the publication of *Lucinde* accused Schlegel of having mingled "der Sauheit Funken mit der Griechheit Dämpfen" (sparks of swinishness with the steaminess of the Greeks), an overt allusion to homosexuality or "Greek love."[104] I want to suggest, however, that Schlegel covertly reformulates the androgynous myth in this novel in terms of exclusively heterosexual love. Despite the references to botanical hermaphroditism, it is important to signal the particular—heterosexual—phase of the Platonic myth of androgyny that underpins the teleology of Schlegel's *Lucinde.* Where the essay on Diotima tells of the giddying power of each human being to move freely within the whole spectrum of sexual possibilities, *Lucinde* actually places us within a model initiated by bisexual mobility but culminating in strict heterosexual complementarity.

The homoerotic subtext is particularly marked in the section of the novel "Allegorie von der Frechheit," discussed above; that it forms an integral part of the process of *Bildung* is evident from its role in the novel's central narrative of erotic apprenticeship, the "Lehrjahre der Männlichkeit." Indeed, the moral outrage that greeted the publication of Schlegel's novel may be more explicable if we turn our attention to this homoerotic subplot and away from the heterosexual union with which the narrative ends, which is, after all, the conventional conclusion of the *Bildungsroman* as a genre. Julius himself has the indeterminate marmoreal beauty and the rounded contours of Winckelmann's sculptures (vol. 5: 55; Firchow, 100). Beyond this, the novel reveals that Julius's early, and troubled, erotic encounters with women are punctuated with intense, passionate friendships with men— significantly, it is the latter form of relationship that is described as "divine" (vol. 5: 45; Firchow, 88). With one male friend, Julius "fand mehr als weib- liche Schonung und Zartheit bei erhabenem Verstande und fest gebildetem Charakter" (he found more than feminine consideration and delicacy of feeling combined with a sublime intelligence and a firm, cultivated character [vol. 5: 45; Firchow, 88]). With another, however, "war sein Verhältnis verstimmt und fast gemein geworden. Es war ganz geistig gewesen, und so hätte es auch bleiben sollen" (friendship had become strained and almost coarse. It had been completely spiritual at first and should have remained so [vol. 5: 46; Firchow, 90]). Yet these tumultuous relationships, which lead Julius to a mental state bordering on madness, are ultimately unsatisfactory because of their transitory, irrational, and unsociable nature; as the novel makes clear, true happiness is to be found in a relationship of domesticized heterosexual complementarity. The tension between these competing sexual- ities is obliquely suggested in "Treue und Scherz" (Fidelity and Playfulness), which immediately precedes the "Lehrjahre der Männlichkeit." Lucinde, unusually resistant to Julius's amorous advances, begs him to remove from her immediate proximity a bouquet of cloyingly scented hyacinths (vol. 5: 30; Firchow, 70). The word used to describe the scent of the flowers, "Betäubung" (with its connotations of deadening, numbing, rendering in- sensible), is telling. These hyacinths, an allusion to one of Apollo's boy lovers, hint at Lucinde's awareness of Julius's ambiguous sexuality and at its double-edged effects: erotic mobility and erotic paralysis. One of the final sections of the novel, at first glance an irritating and digressive letter to a male friend, Antonio, in fact ironically signals the irretrievable breakdown of a male-male intimacy as the affair with Lucinde reaches its apotheosis and heterosexual union is reaffirmed. The irony is further intensified, I would argue, when Julius chooses this epistolary forum in order to express his ideal of friendship, in overtly androgynous terms: "[e]ine wunderbare Symmetrie . . . diese schone Mystik" (a wonderful symmetry . . . this beautiful mysticism [vol. 5: 77; Firchow, 125).[105] A powerful subtext in Schlegel's *Lucinde,* then, is its depiction of male homoeroticism as a seductive phase in the hero's erotic and aesthetic *Bildung,* a phase that is domesticated in favor of the relationship with a woman, and a woman who is also, and importantly, a mother. In doing so, the novel performs its own reading of the developmental account of homosexuality and heterosexuality traced out by Aristophanes in the *Symposium,* a text well known to Schlegel and one with which he was particularly preoccupied as he came to write *Lucinde.*[106]

In Schlegel's novel, the restorative powers of heterosexual androgynous union bring about a love that encompasses "Freundschaft, schöner Umgang, Sinnlichkeit und auch Leidenschaft" (friendship, pleasant society, sensuality, and passion, too [vol. 5: 35; Firchow, 76]), thus effacing the tragic consequences of a state of dualism between mind and body. Oxymora expressing this reconciliation are scattered throughout *Lucinde:* "geistige Wollust" (spiritual voluptuousness), "sinnliche Seligkeit" (sensual beatitude), and so on (vol. 5: 7; Firchow, 44). Androgynous union of the sexes also demolishes the fatal barrier between subject and world, subject and object: "Nur in der Antwort seines Du kann jedes Ich seine unendliche Einheit ganz fühlen." (Only in the answer of its "you" can every "I" wholly feel its boundless unity [vol. 5: 61; Firchow, 106].) Schlegel refers consciously to the Platonic myth of the androgyne, hailing love as the unifying force that brings together the lost halves of humanity: "[es ist] die Liebe . . . die uns erst zu wahren vollständigen Menschen macht" (it is love that first makes us true and complete human beings [vol. 5: 64; Firchow, 110]). If in Schlegel's essay "Über die Diotima" we read of the dizzying powers of each human being to move freely within the whole spectrum of sexuality, *Lucinde* nevertheless places us again within a model of strict heterosexual complementarity, thereby upholding the rule of biological difference. It has been suggested that Schlegel rather nervously begins to accentuate sexual binaries in order to efface the suggestion of homosexual union present in the Platonic model. It seems more likely, however, that Schlegel is consciously juxtaposing two versions of androgynous desire, fully aware of their sexual implications. Schlegel is perhaps also capitulating to the expectations of his readers by following romantic philosopher Franz von Baader's Neoplatonic androgynous model, which superimposes on Aristophanes' story an orthodox Catholic concept of marriage as heterosexual androgynous union, as a return to prelapsarian undividedness.[107] This perception of the sexes as antipodal forces is already in evidence in Schlegel's "Über die Philosophie. An Dorothea." Although his language recalls an earlier, perhaps more radical concept of androgyny, wholeness no longer requires a neutralization of sexual characteristics—indeed, Schlegel can reassure Dorothea that her interest in such a masculine field of endeavor as philosophy will not damage her femininity.[108]

Schelling's *Von der Weltseele* (Of the World Spirit, 1798) may have influenced Schlegel's revised philosophical notion of androgyny. For the *Naturphilosoph* Schelling, the entire natural world is a living organism pulsating with polarities. Progress arises from the harmonious union of self-renewing oppositions, oppositions that are defined in sexual terms. In accepting this view that a chaos of opposing natural forces provides the momentum for union, and thus for progress, Schlegel inevitably commits himself to maintaining sexual difference as a biological fact.[109] As cautious as he is in his early works when it comes to accepting conventional sexual stereotypes, he later begins viewing the sexes in terms of strictly polarous forces, often using plant and mineral analogies. Significantly for a consideration of the androgynous aesthetic ideal, allied in *Lucinde* with a state of plantlike, polymorphous vegetation, Schlegel in his notes and aphorisms propagates essentializing binaries, identifying women with plants, men with minerals: "Die *weibliche Gestalt* ist ganz Blüthe und Frucht—der Blumen und Fruchtkelch herrscht in ihrem Leibe. Die eckigere Organisation d[es] Mannes ist viell[eicht] mehr Miner[alisch]." (The *female form* is all blossom and fruit—flower and calyx dominate her body. The more angular organization of the male is perhaps more mineral [vol. 18: 144].) Implicit in this distinction between the sexes is the passivity of women, their rootedness in nature and their unconscious state of being: "Das Weib nähert sich auch durch s[eine] mindere Locomotivität d[er] Pflanze." (The woman comes closer to the plant, too, in her lesser locomotiveness [vol. 18: 145].) "Das Unbewußtsein des Animal[ischen] ist den Weibern nothwendig." (Animal unconsciousness is necessary to women [vol. 16: 232].) The form of art with which women are associated, moreover, is also linked with plants and children: "die formlose und bewußtlose Poesie, die sich in der Pflanze regt, im Lichte strahlt, im Kinde lächelt, in der Blüte der Jugend schimmert, in der liebenden Brust der Frauen glüht" (the formless and unconscious poetry that stirs in the plant, that shines in the light, smiles in the child, shimmers in the bloom of youth, glows in the loving bosom of a woman).[110] The curious thing here is the blurring between the two models of androgyny considered in this chapter, between androgyny

as an infantile state of polymorphous sexuality and indeterminacy, pre-
Bildung, and androgyny as the next phase in psychological maturation,
when strictly differentiated human beings seek to recreate lost totality in
heterosexual union. Women, for Schlegel, may become identifiable with both
androgynous ideals—botanically, psychologically, aesthetically. On the one
hand, like the dual-sexed, prerational androgyne, like the fluid androgynous
aesthetic, woman is mystery and indeterminacy personified. As Schlegel
puts it: "Mysterien sind weiblich; sie verhüllen sich gern, aber sie wollen
doch gesehen und erraten sein." (Mysteries are feminine; they like to veil
themselves, but they still want to be seen and uncovered [vol. 2: 149].)
This characterization of the feminine anticipates Nietzsche's metaphorical
definition of woman, in *Die Fröhliche Wissenschaft* (The Gay Science), as
"ein geisterhaftes, stilles, schauendes, gleitendes Mittelwesen" (a spirit-like
intermediate being: quietly observing, gliding, floating), best viewed from
a distance.[111] On the other hand, the final rigidity of an androgynous model
that might seem to offer free flow is clearly visible in the section of *Lucinde*
entitled "Eine Reflexion" (A Reflection). Here, Schlegel broadens the vision
of androgynous union symbolically, glorifying nature as an entity fueled by
the combination and recombination of sexual dualities. Here, too, Julius
finally posits woman as the mysterious and unknowable Other, a dangerous
and unknowable supplement that falls outside the parameters of *Bildung*
and that can be mastered only by an aestheticizing move.[112] Opposed to
the indeterminate and static plantlike feminine principle is the clearly male
principle of determinacy, an active and energizing natural force. There is not
much to separate this from the polarizing androgynous model proposed by
Wilhelm von Humboldt, male "Energie" and female "Materie":

> Das Unbestimmte ist geheimnisreicher, aber das Bestimmte hat mehr Zauber-
> kraft. Die reizende Verwirrung des Unbestimmten ist romantischer, aber
> die erhabene Bildung des Bestimmten ist genialischer. Die Schönheit des
> Unbestimmten ist vergänglich wie das Leben der Blumen und wie die ewige
> Jugend sterblicher Gefühle; die Energie des Bestimmten ist vorübergehend
> wie das echte Ungewitter und die echte Begeisterung. . . .
>   Das Bestimmte und das Unbestimmte und die ganze Fülle ihrer bestimmten
> und unbestimmten Beziehungen; das ist das Eine und Ganze, das ist das Wun-
> derlichste und doch das Einfachste, das Einfachste und doch das Höchste. Das
> Universum selbst ist nur ein Spielwerk des Bestimmten und des Unbestimmten
> und das wirkliche Bestimmen des Bestimmbaren ist eine allegorische Miniatur
> auf das Leben und Weben der ewig strömenden Schöpfung.

The indefinite is more mysterious, but the definite has greater magical power.
The charming confusion of the indefinite is more romantic, but the noble

refinement of the definite is more like genius. The beauty of the indefinite is
perishable, like the life of flowers and the eternal youth of human feelings;
the energy of the definite is fleeting like a genuine thunderstorm and genuine
inspiration. . . .

The definite and the indefinite and the whole wealth of their definite and
indefinite relations: that is the one and the all, the strangest and yet the
simplest, the simplest and yet the best. The universe itself is only a plaything
of the definite and the indefinite; and the real definition of the definable is an
allegorical miniature of the warp and woof of everflowing creation. (vol. 5:
72–74; Firchow, 120)

Through the model of heterosexual androgynous union, Julius seeks to
recapture his own lost wholeness. Paradoxically, however, as feminist critics
have observed, though Lucinde is in theory only one half of this androgynous
whole, she herself is idealized by Julius as the representative of the whole
world of organic nature from which he, as a rational and fragmented modern
man, feels alienated. As I have been arguing, this dissymmetric collapsing
of categories may derive from a blurring of two different implications of the
androgynous myth. Central to the novel, too, is the fact that Lucinde is a
mother as well as a lover, thus inextricably bound with "Mother" Earth. In
her, Julius perceives a mysterious and infinite wholeness, remarkably close
to the harmony glimpsed in the androgynous ideal itself: "du fühlst alles
ganz und unendlich, du weißt von keinen Absonderungen, dein Wesen ist
Eins und unteilbar" (you feel completely and infinitely; you know of no
separations, your being is one and indivisible [vol. 5: 11; Firchow, 47]).

What the reader learns of Lucinde as an individual is that she functions
as a blank mirror to Julius's desiring narcissistic gaze: "in diesem Spiegel . . .
sehe ich mich ganz und harmonisch" (only here [in such a mirror] do I
see myself complete and harmonious [vol. 5: 10; Firchow, 46]). Although
the novel reveals that she, too, is an artist, as a woman she is excluded
from progress, and thus she does not create her own version of Julius's
Bildungsroman. There is no equivalent, for Lucinde, of Julius's "Lehrjahre
der Männlichkeit." Her landscape paintings are those of a dilettante, Julius
opines; their contours are vague and indeterminate; she lacks the patience
and stamina for oils; her art is completely dominated by emotion. While
Lucinde's art is described only through the lens of Julius's novel, in Lucinde's
proximity Julius's art gains new vibrancy: "Wie seine Kunst sich vollendete
und ihm von selbst in ihr gelang, was er zuvor durch kein Streben und
Arbeiten erringen konnte: so ward ihm auch sein Leben zum Kunstwerk."
(Just as his artistic ability developed and he was able to achieve with ease
what he had been unable to accomplish with all his powers of exertion and

hard work before, so too his life now came to be a work of art for him [vol. 5: 57; Firchow, 102].) An idealized fulcrum around which Julius moves in his quest for the perfection of the androgynous ideal, Lucinde allegedly already possesses this natural harmony. But as one feminist critic has noted, Julius matures as an artist, progressing with the novel we are reading, while Lucinde retires to a role of doting domesticity.[113] Women remain excluded from the forward movement of *Bildung,* associated as they are with the organic, unconscious existence of the hermaphroditic plant. As Schlegel puts it in one of his fragments: "Vielleicht ist die sogenannte *Bildsamkeit* d[es] menschl[ichen] Leibes durchaus mineralisch. Das lange Wachstum hingegen ist ein Aehnlichkeit mit d[en] Pflanzen." (Perhaps the so-called *malleability* of the human body is absolutely mineral. Slower growth, on the other hand, is closer to the plant world [vol. 18: 147].) The dynamic impulse to art belongs to the male sphere: "Es ist eine unauflösl[iche] Gleichung zwisch[en] Männlichk[eit] und Weiblichk[eit]. Jeder *Mann* ist genialisch; Harmonie ist das Wesen des Weibes / Jeder Mann hat einen Daemon—jede Frau eine Ehe in sich." (There is an ineradicable equation between male and female. Every *man* is a genius; harmony is the essence of a woman's being. Every man has a demon, every woman has a marriage within her [vol. 16: 219].) So Schlegel's *Lucinde,* often viewed as an emancipatory work of literature precisely because of its apparent questioning of gender stereotypes, sets up a female muse not so very different from Schiller's vision of ideal femininity. Each muse has her own fatal double: the graceful Juno Ludovisi is contrasted with the monstrous female artist Ninon de l'Enclos, and Lucinde herself may be viewed as a mirror image of the languorous, statuesque beauty who holds Julius enthralled in the "Lehrjahre der Männlichkeit" and who is famed for her "seltne Gewandheit und unerschöpfliche Mannichfaltigkeit in allen verführerischen Künsten der Sinnlichkeit" (the rare skill and inexhaustible variety of her sensuality [vol. 5: 41; Firchow, 84]). The courtesan, described at the center of the novel in her eternally fixed boudoir pose, is simply the marmoreal twin of the strangely lifeless Lucinde:

> Ihr Boudoir war einfach und ohne alle gewöhnlichen Meublen, nur von allen Seiten große, kostbare Spiegel und wo noch Raum übrig blieb, einige gute Kopien von den wollüstigen Gemälden des Correggio und Tizian, desgleichen einige schöne Originale von frischen, vollen Blumen- und Fruchtstücken; statt der Lambris die lebendigsten und fröhlichsten Darstellungen in Basrelief aus Gips nach der Antike; statt der Stühle echte orientalische Teppiche und einige Gruppen aus Marmor in halber Lebensgröße: ein gieriger Faun, der eine Nymphe, die im Fliehen schon gefallen ist, eben völlig überwinden wird;

eine Venus, die mit aufgehobenem Gewande lächelnd über den wollüstigen Rücken auf die Hüften schaut und andre ähnliche Darstellungen. Hier saß sie oft auf türkische Sitte Tage lang allein und die Hände müßig im Schoß.

Her boudoir was simple and without the usual items of furniture; only on all sides of the room there were large, expensive mirrors, and, where there was any space left, some good copies of the most voluptuous paintings of Correggio and Titian, as well as a few beautiful original still lifes of flowers and fruit. Instead of panelling, there were some extremely lively and delightful figures done in bas-relief in plaster of paris, in the classical style. Instead of chairs, there were genuine Persian rugs and a few groups of marble statues reduced to half-size: a lustful satyr about to overcome a nymph already fallen in flight; a Venus raising her gown and looking across her voluptuous back at her hips; and more statues of the same kind. In this room she often remained alone for days on end, sitting in the Turkish way with her hands resting idly in her lap. (vol. 5: 42; Firchow, 84)

Rather than turning inert marble to life, the classical aesthetic move that Julius suggests is possible in his allusion to Pygmalion in the concluding sentence of the section "Metamorphosen" (vol. 5: 61; Firchow, 106), this androgynous desire actually enacts female petrification. (What is more, the coupling of the Pygmalion reference with the homoerotically charged allusion to Ganymede, a male lover of Zeus, indicates the tension between two modes of statue viewing.) Sigrid Weigel's comments on the fate of Lucinde in this novel can be taken quite literally: "Sie [die Frau] erstarrt auf dem Sockel der Bewunderung zur Statue, zur künstlichen Natur." (She is petrified as a statue, as artificial nature, on the pedestal of love.)[114] This marmoreal stasis, terrifying to the male viewer, has its implications, too, for the aesthetic of chaos proposed by Schlegel's novel. As the attentive reader will recall, Julius expressed his desire to create "eine reizende Verwirrung" (a charming confusion) precisely as an antidote or cure to one potential literary outcome of his love story, "eine *unerträgliche Einheit* und Einerleiheit" *(insufferably unified* and monotonous [Firchow, 45; my emphasis]). Androgyny, as this passage would have it, may function precisely as the *antithesis* to "reizende Verwirrung," to a nomadic sexuality and a nomadic aesthetic. Nowhere is the blurring of two readings of androgyny more apparent in Schlegel's work. The message here seems to be: androgynous union avoids petrification only if endlessly deferred.[115]

Why this ambivalent shading to erotic union? Freud, in *Jenseits des Lustprinzips* (Beyond the Pleasure Principle) (1920), once again creatively rereads Aristophanes' account of androgyny, referring to a hypothesis, "die aber von so phantastischer Art ist—gewiß eher ein Mythus als eine wissenschaftliche Erklärung—daß ich nicht wagen würde, sie hier anzuführen, wenn sie nicht gerade die eine Bedingung erfüllen würde, nach deren Erfüllung wir streben. Sie leitet nämlich einen Trieb ab *von dem Bedürfnis nach Wiederherstellung eines früheren Zustandes"* (but it is of so fantastic a kind—a myth rather than a scientific explanation—that I should not venture to produce it here, were it not that it fulfils precisely the one condition whose fulfilment we desire. For it traces the origin of an instinct to *a need to restore an earlier state of things).*[116] This allusion to the Platonic myth is used to illustrate Freud's conclusion that the goal of the sexual instinct is to restore a primal state of nondifferentiation—androgyny, or death. Indeed, eros functions in an almost machinelike way to combine and recombine organic substances into ever larger unities. That love is, however, inextricably bound with the death drive Freud demonstrates with another literary reference, this time to Tasso's epic *Gerusalemme liberata* (Jerusalem Delivered), a work that is also of central importance to Goethe's *Wilhelm Meisters Lehrjahre* (see chapter 2, below). (Indeed, Freud seems to be reading Tasso via Goethe, quoting from *Wilhelm Meister* almost verbatim; see *Artemis-Gedenkausgabe,* vol. 7: 29.) As an example of the compulsion to kill the object of one's desires, Freud cites Tancred's murder of the cross-dressing Clorinda.[117] The androgynous (female) body is the dreamlike incarnation of a desire for primal wholeness, which so often in fictions of androgyny collapses into a desire for death. Man can only embrace the androgynous muse as an aestheticized, fetishized object, since to embrace her physically would lead to his own absorption or extinction.[118] The experience of the androgyne, which I see as becoming increasingly interchangeable with the experience of the feminine, becomes a central fiction of male *Bildung* for Goethe as well as for the romantics. In the following chapters, I will show how these two fictions are inextricably bound up with each other in some of the most important narratives of *Bildung* of the eighteenth and nineteenth centuries. Seductive and repulsive, by turns domesticated and threatening, the androgynous female body becomes the locus for textual and sexual theorizing. Sexuality and textuality, as Barbara Johnson points out, are indeed inescapably bound:

> If human beings were not divided into two biological sexes, there would probably be no need for literature. And if literature could truly say what the relations between the sexes are, we would doubtless not need much of it then, either. . . . It is not the life of sexuality that literature cannot capture; it is literature that inhabits the very heart of what makes sexuality problematic for us speaking animals. Literature is not only a thwarted investigator but also an incorrigible perpetrator of the problem of sexuality.[119]

These perceptive comments seem to me to express precisely the relationship between literary texts and their fictions of androgyny. On the one hand, the texts that I have been examining express the urge to investigate the conditions of difference, and the idealizing impulse to suspend its effects; on the other hand, what they reveal is literature's entanglement in the very system it seeks to evade, in a fantasy of unity.

2

Pedagogy and Androgyny in Wilhelm Meisters Lehrjahre

Laertes: "deswegen geht sich's so angenehm mit Weibern um, die
sich niemals in ihrer natürlichen Gestalt sehen lassen." (That's why
women are so agreeable, for at first they never show their true colors.)

GOETHE, *Wilhelm Meisters Lehrjahre.*[1]

"Es sind Beispiele und Veranlassungen zu der Theorie der Weiblichkeit,
die in jener großen Lebenskunstlehre nicht fehlen durfte." (These are
examples of, and the inspiration for, a theory of femininity, which should
not be found lacking among those great artistic guidelines for life.)

F. SCHLEGEL, "Über Goethes Meister."[2]

In an 1835 essay, Karl August Varnhagen von Ense reflected on a curious aspect of Goethe's novel *Wilhelm Meisters Lehrjahre,* published forty
years previously. Why, he wondered, had no critical attention been paid
to the strange transvestite women who dominate the text?[3] They remain
an arresting, even troubling feature of this novel. From the first page of
Wilhelm Meisters Lehrjahre, the reader is cast into a deeply perplexing
world of sexual ambiguity. Within the framework of the classical *Bildungsroman,* typically the account of male maturation, Goethe presents
a huge supporting cast of women, many of whom are marked with the
signature of transvestism, of gender transgression. That such sexual indeterminacy is bound to generate almost boundless confusion is suggested
by the following prefatory remarks by Freud in his lecture on femininity:
"Männlich oder weiblich ist die erste Unterscheidung, die Sie machen,
wenn Sie mit einem anderen menschlichen Wesen zusammentreffen, und
Sie sind gewöhnt, diese Unterscheidung mit unbedenklicher Sicherheit zu
machen." (When you meet a human being, the first distinction you make
is "male or female?" and you are accustomed to make the distinction with
unhesitating certainty.)[4] At the most basic level, we find ourselves caught,
whenever we encounter new characters in the novel, and like Wilhelm
Meister himself, in an interpretative snare. What unnerves human beings

more than having to puzzle out the sex of the person standing before them? The novel's permutations on the theme of gender confusion are suggestive and wide-ranging, from theatrical travesty to androgyny to the Amazonian clan centered around Natalie. Indeed, one of the few female characters in this novel who never presents the reader with such decision-making problems is Philine, the anarchic coquette, whom Laertes, setting her apart from the rest of her dissimulating sex, describes as "keine Heuchlerin" (in no wise hypocritical), but the fact that it is this female who is apostrophized as the "wahre Eva" (real Eve), the original woman, invites critical exploration (106; Blackall, 55).

Varnhagen von Ense, a nineteenth-century reader, proceeded to explain the female transvestites of this novel empirically, through the lens of fashion history: English trends in men's clothing, which had begun to efface class distinctions in male dress toward the end of the eighteenth century, became the rage for modish women, too, blurring gender difference as well as class difference. Fashion journals of the eighteenth century do indeed furnish evidence of such transvestite trends in clothing for women. An illustration from a 1790 issue of the *Journal des Dames,* for example, shows a young woman in an elegant riding costume modeled after English men's fashions and adopted for city wear: she sports black breeches, cravat, waistcoat, and redingote and flourishes a cane and a mannish black hat in her left hand.[5] In 1792, the *Journal des Luxus und der Moden* noted reprovingly that revolutionary fashions had transformed Frenchwomen into genuine "Androgynen,"[6] and a few years later, in 1796, a correspondent for the same magazine commented on the trend for women to imitate men "in Tracht, Manieren und Beschäftigung soviel als möglich" (as much as possible in costume, manners, and occupation).[7]

However, to explain away the female cross-dressing that is such a dominant feature of *Wilhelm Meister* as a simple reflection of contemporary women's fashions is to ignore the genuinely perturbing effects of such transvestism in the world of the novel. This is no superficial detail of interest only to historians of style. The novel inevitably places in the foreground many of the concerns and paradoxes of the contemporary debate on gender and difference which I explored in chapter 1, above, on the aesthetics of androgyny.[8] Female masquerade is initiated as a central element in the theatrical experience that permeates the novel; but more than this, it is crucial for the developmental journey embarked upon by the naive young merchant's son. Here, as in the theoretical writings of Winckelmann, Humboldt, Schiller, and Schlegel, I will be exploring the intersection of sexual polymorphousness, pedagogy, and aesthetics.

In the first paragraph of the novel, Barbara, the servant of Wilhelm's mistress, Mariane, impatiently awaits the return of the actress, described as her "schöne Gebieterin" (pretty mistress). Mariane strides into the novel in the dashing costume of a young officer—theater enters real life, and, what is more, with our first glimpse of Mariane, theatrical masquerade begins to exert its power on every level of the literary text. This opening moment of Goethe's novel—of the classical *Bildungsroman* tradition, it may be argued—is more than skillful stage setting. The transvestite figure who had become such a pivotal element of the Renaissance drama now steps, quite literally, onto the stage of what Bakhtin persuasively termed the most hybrid of genres.[9] (*Wilhelm Meisters Lehrjahre*, of course, is marked by its intertwining of the strands of theater, notably Shakespeare's *Hamlet*, with those of the novel.) To read Mariane's male costume most obviously, then, it belongs in the world of travesty, or theatrical cross-dressing. Mignon, too, first appears on the textual stage of the novel in male clothing, but it is male clothing that marks her as a member of the theatrical world: "Ein kurzes seidnes Westchen mit geschlitzten spanischen Ärmeln, knappe lange Beinkleider mit Puffen standen dem Kinde gar artig." (The child was neatly dressed in a short silk bodice with slashed Spanish sleeves and puffed-out long slim trousers [97; Blackall, 50].) (It is worthy of mention, too, that the "actresses" of Goethe's novel are generally characterized by their costume, as in the description of Mignon, rather than by their bodily appearance. The parallels with character descriptions in dramatic texts are striking.) Other women are also seen to participate in such theatrical transvestism. The impresario Serlo intends, for example, to give the role of either Rosencrantz or Guildenstern to a woman, to generate added audience interest in his production of *Hamlet* (322; Blackall, 181). And the playful Baronesse reveals a fondness for carnivalesque male disguise, which in her case permits her to cross over the boundaries between classes as well as between sexes: "sie liebte die Verkleidungen und kam, um die Gesellschaft zu überraschen, bald als Bauernmädchen, bald als Page, bald als Jägerbursche zum Vorschein." (She liked to dress up and was always appearing, in order to surprise everybody, as a peasant girl, or a page boy, or a huntsman [201; Blackall, 110].)

It has been argued that this initial ambiguity of dress functions principally to contribute to the carnivalesque, rococo sexual ambivalence that marks the appearance at court of Wilhelm's troupe.[10] But I see more than careful stage setting at work, more than the painting in of a persuasively realistic backdrop. It is important to point out the multidimensionality of such theatrical figures as Mariane and Mignon, who reveal so much more depth and complexity than the easily recognizable standard types characteristic of

comedy.[11] The transvestism prevalent in the theater also serves as more than
a simple foil to the stolid bourgeois values of Werner and the mercantile
paternal realm. The world of actors and actresses is one of marginality, of
transgression of entrenched societal boundaries, of permissiveness. Indeed,
during the troupe's interlude at court, their orgiastic annihilation of what
little order they set out with is characterized by costuming and disguise,
as well as by erotic encounters that cross class boundaries and proprieties
(174; Blackall, 94). It is important to bear in mind that Wilhelm's journey
toward maturity also culminates in a "mixed," hybrid marriage of bourgeois
and aristocrat that becomes the fuel for intense intellectual controversy.
Critics have argued that playful cross-dressing of the type that dominates
the actors' milieu may be one way of registering, in a socially permissible
way, dissatisfaction with societally imposed structures of class and gender.[12]
Transvestism in *Wilhelm Meisters Lehrjahre,* as I will show, signals disruptions that ripple through an entire belief system, disruptions of class, of
gender, and of genre. As Terry Castle has observed in her important work on
masquerade in eighteenth-century England, this was a period that saw a deep
correspondence between clothing and language: "not only was language
the 'dress' of thought—that lucid covering in which the mind decorously
clothed its ideas—but clothing was in turn a kind of discourse. Dress spoke
symbolically of the human being beneath the folds. It reinscribed a person's
sex, age, rank, occupation—all the distinctive features of the self."[13] And
yet, because the meanings read into clothing are always culturally inscribed,
this system of signification can be endlessly subverted, as can the linguistic
code itself. Indeed, clothing, as Castle argues, serves the eighteenth century
as a master trope for instability and deceitfulness. Masquerade costume—
and, as I would argue, the exotic theatrical dress of Mariane's circle—goes
a step further, as a self-conscious demystification of an information code
responsible for constructions of gender.

Goethe himself, in the *Italienische Reise* (Italian Journey) (vol. 11:
533–67), expresses his fascination with a contemporary cultural phenomenon characterized by transvestism: the fantastic spectacle of the Roman
carnival. In this orgiastic setting, class differences and age differences
are effaced, as are gender distinctions. He witnesses one scene, complete
with mock labor pains and crowned with the successful delivery of a
"newborn," in which a man impersonates a pregnant woman. Both sexes
engage in playful and provocative cross-dressing, and Goethe confesses
that transvestite women have about them a rather erotic allure: "man muß
bekennen, daß es ihnen gelingt, in dieser Zwittergestalt oft höchst reizend
zu sein" (it must be admitted that they often succeed in looking extremely

charming in this hybrid form [541; Heitner, 395]). He also observes that the
revelers indulge in sexual gaming based on the masking and unmasking of
sexual identity: "jeder ist neugierig, unter den vielen männlichen Gestalten,
die dort zu sitzen scheinen, die weiblichen herauszusuchen und vielleicht in
einem niedlichen Offizier den Gegenstand seiner Sehnsucht zu *entdecken"*
(everyone is curious to pick out which are the female among the many
seemingly masculine figures sitting there, perhaps to *discover* the object
of his longing in a dainty officer [550; Heitner, 402; my emphasis]). It
is precisely this moment of uncertainty regarding gender that generates
eroticism and desire. That such cross-dressing may also go beyond flirtatious
play becomes clear in another essay drawn on Goethe's experiences in Italy,
on the subject of transvestism on the Roman stage. Noting that the prohibition
on female actors still holds fast in Rome, Goethe goes on to argue for the
creative possibilities opened up by this apparent artistic limitation. Cross-
dressing, he argues, may serve the important function of drawing attention
to the art and artifice that lie behind the theatrical experience:

> ich fühlte ein mir noch unbekanntes Vergnügen und bemerkte, daß es viele
> andre mit mir teilten. Ich dachte der Ursache nach und glaube sie darin gefun-
> den zu haben: daß bei einer solchen Vorstellung der Begriff der Nachahmung,
> der Gedanke an Kunst immer lebhaft blieb, und durch das geschickte Spiel
> nur eine Art von selbstbewußter Illusion hervorgebracht wurde.

> I felt a pleasure that I had not felt before and noticed that many others shared it.
> Wondering about the reason for this, I think that I have found the answer in the
> fact that in these performances the art of imitation, the thought of art, remained
> keen throughout and that by means of skillful play only a kind of self-conscious
> illusion was produced. ("Frauenrollen," vol. 14: 11; Ragusa, 99)

Transvestism, as Judith Butler has observed, reveals the imitative,
performative nature of gender itself, in the contingent link between "imitation" and "original." The recognition of this contingency, Butler argues,
adds to the giddying pleasure of the performance and presents viewers with
the dramatization of cultural mechanisms: "This perpetual displacement
constitutes a fluidity of identities that suggests an openness to resignification
and recontextualization; parodic proliferation deprives hegemonic culture
and its critics of the claim to naturalized or essentialist gender identities."[14]
But cross-dressing may have other aesthetic consequences. Rather than
simply reproducing the external features of the other sex, the transvestite
can perhaps gain access to a "third sex" that transcends divisions between
male and female. In other words, transvestism, in its self-reflexive artfulness
and artificiality, may open up an androgynous space of possibility beyond

the binary of male and female. Marjorie Garber, indeed, sees in this aesthetic position of "thirdness" an analogue to the Lacanian symbolic and asserts that "transvestite theater *is* the Symbolic on the stage."[15] Goethe's comments on cross-dressing in the Roman theater would seem to support this line of thought. He likens this heightened state attained through impersonation to the operation of art in general, which can never be reduced to simple mimesis:

> Ebenso entsteht ein doppelter Reiz daher, daß diese Personen keine Frauenzim-
> mer sind, sondern Frauenzimmer vorstellen. Der Jüngling hat die Eigenheiten
> des weiblichen Geschlechts in ihrem Wesen und Betragen studiert; er kennt sie
> und bringt sie als Künstler wieder hervor; er spielt nicht sich selbst, sondern
> eine dritte und eigentlich fremde Natur. Wir lernen diese dadurch nur desto
> besser kennen, weil sie jemand beobachtet, jemand überdacht hat, und uns
> nicht die Sache, sondern das Resultat der Sache vorgestellt wird.
>   Da sich nun alle Kunst hierdurch vorzüglich von der einfachen Nachah-
> mung unterscheidet, so ist natürlich, daß wir bei einer solchen Vorstellung
> eine eigne Art von Vergnügen empfinden.

> A double attraction arises likewise from the fact that these actors are not
> women but portray women. The young man has studied the characteristics of
> the female sex in its essence and bearing; he has learned to know them and
> to give them life as an artist; he does not portray himself but a third nature
> actually foreign to him. We come to know this nature even better because
> someone else has observed it, reflected on it, and presents us not with the
> thing itself but with the result of the thing.
>   Since all art is distinguished from simple imitation primarily in this respect,
> it follows naturally that we feel a special pleasure in such a representation.
> (vol. 14: 11; Ragusa, 99)

These theoretical statements on transvestism uncover new connections between the heterogeneous sexual shape-shifters in Goethe's novel. Cross-dressing may be a way for a character to gain access to what Goethe terms a "third nature," rather than a phenomenon distinct from and unrelated to the androgynous aesthetic proposed by writers such as Friedrich Schlegel. Curiously, however, while Goethe's revealing comments on theatrical travesty are based on male cross-dressing, *Wilhelm Meisters Lehrjahre* is predominantly populated by women who impersonate men. And since so many female characters in the novel bear the transvestite signature, this would seem to suggest that these masquerading women enjoy privileged access to an aesthetic, androgynous state. (One male, Friedrich, shares their sexual polymorphousness; I will return to this remarkable point later in my discussion.) The carnivalesque world of female theatrical transvestism seems to make possible a radical new aesthetic position, one that transcends biological sex. Indeed, the claim has been made that the sexually ambivalent female characters of *Wilhelm Meisters Lehrjahre* have the power to efface, as a consequence of their aesthetic nature, the fragmentation or "Zersplitterung" that plagues the male hero.[16] A central question in my consideration of Goethe's novel concerns the direction taken by this "androgynous" *Bildung*. Who precisely is gaining access to *Bildung?* Certainly not the female androgyne. As I stress, in opposition to Garber's notion of symbolic "thirdness," the androgyne, with its dyadic oscillation between masculinity and femininity, properly belongs to the pre-oedipal sphere of the imaginary and indeed cannot survive in the triangulated world of *Bildung* and socialization.[17] Freud, as noted in chapter 1, above, linked the initial phase of infantile sexuality with the "polymorphously perverse," adulthood with the acceptance of difference.

These theoretical considerations serve to shed more light on Mariane's appearance in the opening chapter. The first words used to describe Barbara's "schöne Gebieterin" already hint at a sexual ambivalence that may run deeper than theatrical travesty. When the reader first sees Mariane, she is no longer masquerading as an army officer solely because this is part of her theatrical profession. She self-consciously returns to her lodgings in costume and counters Barbara's cajoling reminders of Norberg and his "feminizing" gift of a flimsy white nightgown with physical violence:

> Der Alten fehlte es nicht an Gegenvorstellungen und Gründen; doch da sie in fernerem Wortwechsel heftig und bitter ward, sprang Mariane auf sie los und faßte sie bei der Brust. Die Alte lachte überlaut. Ich werde sorgen müssen, rief sie aus, daß sie wieder bald in lange Kleider kommt, wenn ich meines Lebens sicher sein will. Fort, zieht Euch aus! . . . es ist eine unbequeme Tracht, und für Euch gefährlich, wie ich merke. Die Achselbänder begeistern Euch.

> The old woman had counterarguments enough. But when the exchange began to get violent and bitter, Mariane jumped up and grabbed her. The old woman only laughed uproariously and said, "If I am to be sure of my life, I have to see to it that you are soon in a long dress again. Go and change! . . . It's an uncomfortable costume, and dangerous for you, I see. The epaulettes have gone to your head." (10; Blackall, 2)

Transvestite costume is perceived by Barbara as dangerously infectious and threatening; but for Mariane the officer's uniform is a means of authentic self-representation rather than an actor's disguise: "Wenn Norberg zurückkehrt, bin ich wieder sein, bin ich dein, mache mit mir, was du willst, aber dahin will ich mein sein." ("When Norberg comes back, I'll be his again, I'll be yours—do with me what you will. But until then, I want to be myself" [10; Blackall, 1].) Mariane refuses to comply with Barbara's command that she change into women's clothing, and it is in officer's dress that she greets Wilhelm. Her deliberate rejection of the trappings of femininity, while merely adding to Wilhelm's amorous fervor, does nothing but repel and infuriate her wealthy bourgeois suitor, Norberg, who urges her to put aside somber male costume. It is this clothing, Norberg implies, that lends Mariane subversive and threatening powers of prophecy and wisdom: "Höre, tu mir nicht wieder die schwarzgrünbraune Jacke an, du siehst drin aus wie die Hexe von Endor. Hab' ich dir nicht das weiße Negligé darum geschickt, daß ich ein weißes Schäfchen in meinen Armen haben will?" ("And listen, don't wear that black, green and brown jacket. It makes you look like the Witch of Endor. Didn't I send you that white negligé, so that I could hold a white lamb in my arms?" [79; Blackall, 40].)

Wilhelm, by contrast, literally embraces the theatrical world of costume, travesty, and sexual ambivalence. Mariane herself almost occupies second place in the arms of her lover, after the male garments she is wearing: "mit welchem Entzücken umschlang er die rote Uniform! drückte er das weiße Atlaswestchen an seine Brust!" (How passionately he embraced that red uniform and the white satin vest [11; Blackall, 2].) The clothing of his beloved acquires fetishistic powers; in touching these garments, Wilhelm is somehow cloaked by the absent body of Mariane herself:

> Wie oft ist mir's geschehen, daß ich abwesend von ihr, in Gedanken an sie verloren, ein Buch, ein Kleid oder sonst etwas berührte, und glaubte ihre Hand zu fühlen, so ganz war ich mit ihrer Gegenwart *umkleidet*. . . . Er fühlte nach dem Halstuch, das er von ihr mitgenommen hatte, es war vergessen, es steckte im vorigen Kleide. Seine Lippen lechzten, seine Glieder zitterten vor Verlangen.

> "How often has it happened that, being away from her, or lost in thoughts of her, I touched a book or some garment, and thought it was her hand I felt, so *absorbed* was I in her presence. . . ." He tried to find the scarf that he had taken from her room, but he had left it in his other suit. His lips were burning and his limbs quivering with desire. (77; Blackall, 39; my emphasis)

The romantic liaison with the transvestite Mariane also represents for Wilhelm an emotionally charged encounter with the aesthetic domain. Both she and the theater are repeatedly apostrophized as "reizend" (charming, but with the connotation of sexual allure), and Wilhelm's first glimpse of the actress is enhanced by the flattering stage light illuminating her face. The theatrical world is mysterious, confusing in its verisimilitude. Caught up in the disarray of an actor's world, Wilhelm understands something of its artificiality as he surveys "die Trümmer eines augenblicklichen, leichten und

falschen Putzes" (the remains of some momentary false adornment). Yet the
chaos of the dressing room and the giddying sensuality that prevails have
their own appeal: "so fand er zuletzt in dieser verworrenen Wirtschaft einen
Reiz, den er in seiner stattlichen Prunkordnung niemals empfunden hatte"
(he discovered a certain charm in this household of disorder such as he had
never experienced in the splendor of his own room [63; Blackall, 31]). Like
the hero of Schlegel's *Lucinde,* Wilhelm surrenders himself fully to sexual
confusion. The results, however, prove devastating.

In Book VII, Barbara reveals the true facts of what happened on the
fateful night when Wilhelm believed Mariane to be in the company of his
rival. Wilhelm learns that Mariane had in fact resisted both Norberg and
Barbara, for both of whom her male disguise had proved so threatening,
and, significantly, Barbara tells him how Mariane had dressed to receive
him the following day:

> Ich fand sie zu meiner Verwunderung in ihrer Offizierstracht, sie sah unglaub-
> lich heiter und reizend aus. Verdien' ich nicht, sagte sie, heute in Mannstracht
> zu erscheinen? Habe ich mich nicht brav gehalten? Mein Geliebter soll mich
> heute wie das erste Mal sehen, ich will ihn so zärtlich und mit mehr Freiheit
> an mein Herz drücken, als damals: denn bin ich jetzt nicht viel mehr die Seine
> als damals, da mich ein edler Entschluß noch nicht frei gemacht hatte? . . .
> Diese Szene bereite ich ihm, bereite ich mir zu.

> "To my surprise I found her in her officer's costume, looking charming and
> radiant. 'Don't I deserve to appear in men's clothing today? Haven't I been
> bold? I want my lover to see me as he did that first evening, and I will hug him
> as warmly and with even more abandon than I did then. For now I am much
> more his than I was when I had not yet broken loose in a noble decision. . . .
> This is a scene which I am arranging for us both. . . .' " (516; Blackall, 294)

Contrary to the opinions of Norberg and Barbara, it is possible for
Mariane to dress as a man while at the same time exhibiting beauty and
"Heiterkeit" (grace), qualities so commonly attributed both to women and
to the aesthetic ideal, most notably in the works of Schiller.[18] Mariane
deliberately makes use of the language of artistic convention and, like the
transvestite Roman actor described by Goethe, self-consciously presents
herself as an actor in a "Szene." Paradoxically, her male disguise is no simple
impersonation but rather a mark of authenticity. This triumphant assertion
of "thirdness" might lead the reader to interpret the theatrical travesty at
the beginning of *Wilhelm Meisters Lehrjahre* as the first tentative step in a
progression toward a utopian vision of androgyny. But the transvestite Mariane cannot be sustained in the world of the novel as an androgynous being,

and indeed by the time we hear of her proud scenario of self, she is already dead. Earlier, Wilhelm's apparently interminable account of his childhood had lulled her into a deep sleep (31, 35; Blackall, 13, 15). But the soporific story has more sinister overtones. As Mariane dozes, Wilhelm relates the horrible fate of Tasso's hero Tancred, who mistakenly kills the woman he loves, having failed to recognize her in her transvestite costume (29; Blackall, 12). Wilhelm Meister's narrative of *Bildung,* too, has deathly effects upon the female muse.[19] In the opening chapters, Mariane slips into the languid reverie of a Winckelmannian statue; and in another important scene, she has become no more than an evanescent dream image, flowing and dissolving into the formlessness characteristic of Winckelmann's hermaphroditic ideal. The fluid, indeterminate androgynous condition inspires both erotic desire and utter terror in the male hero:

> dein Bild schwebte mir vor; ich sah dich auf einem schönen Hügel, die Sonne beschien den ganzen Platz; wie reizend kamst du mir vor! Aber es währte nicht lange, so sah ich dein Bild hinuntergleiten, immer hinuntergleiten; ich streckte meine Arme nach dir aus, sie reichten nicht durch die Ferne. Immer sank dein Bild und näherte sich einem großen See, der am Fuße des Hügels weit ausgebreitet lag, eher ein Sumpf als ein See. Auf einmal gab dir ein Mann die Hand; er schien dich hinaufführen zu wollen, aber leitete dich seitwärts, und schien dich nach sich zu ziehen. Ich rief, da ich dich nicht erreichen konnte, ich hoffte dich zu warnen. Wollte ich gehen, so hinderte mich das Wasser, und sogar mein Schreien erstickte in der beklemmten Brust.

> "your image hovered before me and I saw you standing on a beautiful hilltop in the sunlight. How charming you looked! But it didn't last long: your image floated down from the hill, down and down, and I stretched out my arms to you, yet couldn't reach you. You were slipping towards a big lake at the foot of the hill, more of a swamp than a lake, when suddenly some man took your hand. He seemed to be wanting to lead you back up, but in fact led you off to the side, trying to drag you towards him. I called out, since I myself couldn't reach you, to warn you. When I tried to move, the ground held me fast, and when I could move, the water blocked me and even my cries were stifled in my anxious breast." (47; Blackall, 22)

At the opening of Book II, Wilhelm consigns the contents of a "reliquary" to the flames; this casket contains "sacred" souvenirs of Mariane, along with his own youthful writings. The concrete objects of her daily life are to be destroyed, as Wilhelm extricates himself from this phase of his *Bildung.* Miraculously, however, two of Mariane's trinkets—a floral scarf and a strand of pearls—escape incineration and circulate throughout the text from one female character to the next, from one androgynous muse to the other, functioning as textual emblems of female absence. Costume serves as a tangible link between many of the women who appear in *Wilhelm Meisters Lehrjahre*. To name only a few striking examples, both the Baronesse and Therese are described as wearing huntsman's clothing, and Mariane's delicate white negligé is replicated in Philine's rather grubby version of the same garment. The migration of the negligé to the ultra-feminine Philine suggests that Mariane, Wilhelm's first love object, combines the feminine oedipal role (later to be displaced onto Natalie) with the androgynous position, since Mignon gains possession of her scarf.

For Wilhelm, the novel stresses, these female garments attain fetishistic status. Fetishism, according to Freud, signals a concern with the loss of the phallic mother, a disavowal of woman's castration: the fetish is intended as a substitute for the mother's penis, a guarantor of lost wholeness. To put this in more general terms, as Lacan and Granoff have done in their essay on fetishism, the fetish functions as a denial of sexual difference. Loss, then, is not necessarily to be equated with the "castrated" female body of the Freudian model but is rather the loss of the perfectly plenitudinous body as such. It is not surprising that fetishism plays such an important role in Wilhelm Meister's transition from the polymorphous condition of childhood to triangulation and heterosexual socialization: as Lacan and Granoff put it, "oscillation . . . constitutes the very nature of the critical moment. To realize the difference of the sexes is to put an end to play, to accept the three-sided relationship."[20] Thus, fetishism, which promises to restore the ideal perfection of originary plenitude, may be read through the prism of Freud, Lacan, and Granoff as a phenomenon closely related to the female transvestism and androgyny present in Goethe's novel. At the opening of Book II, as noted above, Wilhelm ceremoniously burns the contents of a "Reliquienkästchen" that held trinkets and clothing belonging to Mariane. Yet by Book IV, Wilhelm himself appears in exotic theatrical garb, wearing Mariane's silk scarf around his neck. And Natalie's coat—or, rather, her uncle's coat, marker of the patriarchal *Turmgesellschaft* (Society of the Tower)—attains similar status: "Mit der größten Sorgfalt für dieses Gewand war das lebhafteste Verlangen verbunden, sich damit zu bekleiden. Sobald er aufstand, warf er es über, und befürchtete den ganzen Tag, es möchte durch einen Flecken, oder auf sonst eine Weise beschädigt werden." (The care he took of this garment he combined with a passionate desire to wear it; and whenever he got up from his bed, he hung it over his shoulder, fearing all day long that he might get a spot on it, or in some way damage it [252; Blackall, 139].) The fetish, then, functions as a "memorial" to a lost object, simultaneously replacing the object and declaring its irrevocable loss.

Fittingly for the supplemental economy and metonymic structure of this novel, female characters are repeatedly represented as themselves interchangeable, fillers of "Lücken" or lacunae within Wilhelm's psyche.[21] As Luce Irigaray puts it, woman's value resides only in her exchangeability.[22] Not only are these women in Goethe's novel sexually ambiguous, and thus highly problematic in an interpretative sense, but they also fade physically from the text. They are ephemeral, nebulous beings, and only their clothing remains tangible.

As Mariane fades from the novel as a living entity at the end of Book I, Mignon comes to occupy her role.[23] That these two figures are intimately connected is suggested by the fact that Mignon comes to wear the pearls belonging to Mariane which alone have survived the flames—but Mignon winds this string of pearls around her hat as she readies herself for the dangers of the forest, and she carries a hunting knife in her hand, thus intensifying the sexual ambiguity we already recognize as Mariane's signature and legacy (237; Blackall, 131). (Later, we discover that Mignon is also in possession of Mariane's scarf [382; Blackall, 215].) The pearls resonate with symbolic significance: commonly associated with the representationally ambivalent Aphrodite, goddess of love and of war, they later serve as a tangible link connecting the transvestite Mariane, the androgyne Mignon, and the Amazonian family of the "schöne Seele" (Beautiful Soul), who have inherited a similar pearl necklace from their aunt.[24] In Wilhelm's memories of his dreamlike encounter with the Gräfin, he seems also to enter into an erotic relationship with the pearls she wears around her neck: "die schöne Gräfin erschien ihm als Kind mit den Perlen ihrer Tante um den Hals; auch er war diesen Perlen so nahe gewesen, als ihre zarten liebevollen Lippen sich zu den seinigen neigten." (He could picture the charming countess as the child with her aunt's pearls around her neck. And he had been so near these pearls when her delicate, loving lips had pressed themselves on his [557; Blackall, 318].) As I will be showing, however, these legacies of garments and jewelry from one woman to the other frequently prove to be fatal exchanges.

In the deeply ambivalent figure of Mignon is to be found the most radical image of androgyny in Goethe's work. As noted above, Mignon's initial appearance, in exotic male costume, places her, like Mariane, in the theatrical world of travesty, of professional transvestism, and her strange ritual greeting also has the air of an overstated stage gesture (104; Blackall, 54). Mignon is first presented by the narrator in strictly neuter terms, as "ein junges Geschöpf," "das Kind" (a young creature, the child [97; Blackall, 50]). In fact, the narrator only switches to the use of the feminine pronoun *sie* when it seems that Wilhelm himself has established mentally the gender of the child. In other contexts, pronouns shift apparently at random: "Auch hatte Wilhelm bemerkt, daß *es* für jeden eine besondere Art von Gruß hatte. Ihn grüßte *sie,* seit einiger Zeit, mit über die Brust geschlagenen Armen." (Wilhelm also noticed that she [*it* would be the accurate translation] had a different greeting for everyone. For some time now *she* had been greeting him with arms folded on her breast [117; Blackall, 61; my emphasis]). Indeed, in earlier scenes narrated in the *Theatralische Sendung* (Theatrical Mission), the sexual/textual confusion is still more extreme. Not only is Mignon referred to, apparently at random, as *sie* or *es* (for "das Kind"), but the androgynous creature can also attract masculine pronouns: "Mignon, *der* sich hinter Wilhelms Stuhl ganz ruhig hingestellt hatte, antwortete." (Mignon, who had quietly gone to stand behind Wilhelm's chair, replied [*Artemis-Gendenkausgabe,* vol. 8: 671].) The following passage from the *Theatralische Sendung* perfectly illustrates the grammatical chaos so prevalent in that earlier work:

> Mignon trat herein mit einem Kästchen unter dem Arme. Was bringst du mir, rief Wilhelm *ihr* entgegen. Mignon hatte die rechte Hand auf das Herz gelegt und machte, indem *er* den rechten Fuß hinter den linken brachte und beinah mit dem Knie die Erde berührte, eine Art von spanischem Kompliment mit der größten Ernsthaftigkeit. Eine gleiche Verbeugung folgte mitten in der Stube, und endlich, als *er* gegen Wilhelmen herankam, kniete *er* ganz auf das rechte Knie nieder, stellte die Schachtel auf den Boden, faßte Wilhelms Fuß und küßte sie mit großem Eifer, doch ohne eine anscheinende Bewegung des Herzens, ohne einen Ausdruck von Rührung oder Zärtlichkeit. Wilhelm, der nicht wußte, was er daraus machen sollte, wollte *sie* aufheben.

> Mignon came in with a casket under *her* arm. "What is this you are bringing me?" Wilhelm called out to *her.* Mignon had placed *her* right hand on *her* heart, and placing the right foot behind the left, and almost touching the ground with the knee, *he* performed a kind of Spanish curtsey, with the greatest gravity. In the middle of the room *he* made another bow of this kind, and when *he* finally reached Wilhelm *he* kneeled down completely on *his* right knee, placed the box on the ground, and took hold of Wilhelm's foot and kissed it with great ardor, but all without any signs of emotion, without any expression of tender feelings. Wilhelm, who didn't know what to make of this, wanted to lift *her* up. (vol. 8: 672; my emphasis)

Part of this sexual confusion, of course, derives from Mignon's name, of French origins, which is marked as a masculine adjective.[25] On every level, from Mignon's name to her outlandish dress to what has aptly been called the narrator's "pronominal sleight of hand,"[26] we find ourselves as readers caught in the same interpretative snare as Wilhelm:

Er sah die Gestalt mit Verwunderung an, und konnte nicht mit sich einig
werden, ob er sie für einen Knaben oder für ein Mädchen erklären sollte.
Doch entschied er sich bald für das letzte, und hielt sie auf, da sie bei ihm
vorbei kam, bot ihr einen guten Tag und fragte sie, wem sie angehöre.

He looked at the figure with amazement, uncertain whether it was a boy or
girl. But he finally decided in favor of the latter and stopped her as she was
rushing past, wished her goodday, and asked to whom she belonged. (vol. 7:
97; Blackall, 50)

But if the gender label Wilhelm finally decides upon is female, it is
this sex with which Mignon refuses to identify. Wilhelm promises her a new
suit of clothes, and she enters his room at daybreak the following morning
accompanied by a tailor: "Sie brachte graues Tuch und blauen Taffet, und
erklärte nach ihrer Art, daß sie ein neues Westchen und Schifferhosen, wie
sie solche an den Knaben in der Stadt gesehen, mit blauen Aufschlägen
und Bändern haben wolle." (She brought with her some gray cloth and blue
taffeta, saying, in her own peculiar way, that she wanted a new jacket and
sailor pants, such as she had seen on boys in the town, with blue ribbons and
lapels [124; Blackall, 65].) The novel reveals that as a small child, Mignon
enjoyed exchanging clothes with her male friends (629; Blackall, 359), and
now she vehemently resists the efforts of successive guardians to dress her
as a girl (e.g., 222, 361; Blackall, 122, 204), declaring, "Ich bin ein Knabe,
ich will kein Mädchen sein!" ("I am a boy, I don't want to be a girl"). Mignon
actually joins in the skirmish with bandits, and her denial of her biological
sex is sufficiently strong that she remains silent about the wound she has been
dealt lest the truth of her sex be discovered by the doctor (253; Blackall, 140).
Mignon's transvestism, even more obviously than Mariane's, goes beyond
theatrical cross-dressing, beyond a childish desire to behave as a tomboy,
and can be read as emblematic of her desire for a transcendent position of
"thirdness." Mignon bears multiple marks of the androgyne. On the rare
occasions when she has not lapsed into muteness, she speaks a strange
hybrid language containing elements of French, Italian, and German—a
literal example, perhaps, of Bakhtinian "polyglossia" (117; Blackall, 61).
Like Winckelmann's hermaphrodite sculptures permanently poised between
childhood and adulthood, Mignon longs to remain in this polymorphous
state: as she pleads in the final line of her angelic song, "Macht mich auf
ewig wieder jung!" ("Now make me young for ever more" [554; Blackall,
316]). The danger presented by adulthood, as Aristophanes suggests in
his account of androgyny in Plato's *Symposium*, is that sexual maturity
brings differentiation and thus fragmentation (189E–193D). Volatile and

unpredictable in her movements, Mignon resists all fixity and constantly bewilders the gaze of the viewer: "Es ging die Treppe weder auf noch ab, sondern sprang; es stieg auf den Geländern der Gänge weg, und eh man sich's versah, saß es oben auf dem Schranke." (She never walked up or down stairs, she always ran. She climbed up on to banisters, and before one knew it, there she was on top of a closet [117; Blackall, 61].) Surprised by the child's sudden and unexpected fascination with maps, Wilhelm quickly realizes, however, that Mignon's scholarly interest is strictly limited: herself a living contradiction, she cares only about the geographical poles: "eigentlich schien sie bei den Ländern kein besonderes Interesse zu haben, als ob sie kalt oder warm seien. Von den Weltpolen, von dem schrecklichen Eise daselbst, und von der zunehmenden Wärme, je mehr man sich von ihnen entfernte, wußte sie sehr gut Rechenschaft zu geben." (She was really only interested in whether various countries were cold or warm. She gave a vivid description of the poles and the terrible ice there, and how the warmth increased the further one got away from them [304; Blackall, 169].)

Her very parentage, several critics have noted, was destined to produce such a dual-sexed being, for the novel tells us that she is the product of an incestuous union.[27] The love of brother for sister, Mignon's father suggests, is the nearest approximation on earth to a state of androgynous unity, the issue of one womb being of the same flesh and blood. Augustin, defending his love for his sister Sperata, justifies it as a natural phenomenon:

> Fragt nicht den Widerhall eurer Kreuzgänge, nicht euer vermodertes Pergament, nicht eure verschränkten Grillen und Verordnungen, fragt die Natur und euer Herz, sie wird euch lehren, vor was ihr zu schaudern habt. . . . Seht die Lilien an: entspringt nicht Gatte und Gattin auf einem Stengel? Verbindet beide nicht die Blume, die beide gebar, und ist die Lilie nicht das Bild der Unschuld, und ihre geschwisterliche Vereinigung nicht fruchtbar?

> "Don't listen to the echoes of your cloisters, don't consult your musty parchments, your crotchety and quirky regulations: ask Nature and your hearts. Nature will tell you what you have to tremble at. . . . Consider the lilies: Do not husband and wife grow on one and the same stem? Does not the blossom they bear unite them? And is not the lily the image of innocence? Is not its sibling union fruitful?" (625; Blackall, 357)

As the novel is at pains to inform us, Mignon is the fruit of this transgressive and monstrous love between brother and sister, an androgyne thrown up as the mark of society's ultimate taboo. Significantly, when she makes her appearance onstage as a sexless angel, she carries in her hand what Augustin identifies as the botanical emblem of the androgyne: a single white lily (553; Blackall, 315).[28] Her incestuous origins ripple throughout the novel, as the relationship between this androgynous child and Wilhelm oscillates uneasily between that of daughter and father and that of lover and lover:

> Mein Kind! rief er aus, indem er sie aufhob und fest umarmte, mein Kind, was ist dir?—Die Zuckung dauerte fort, die vom Herzen sich in den schlotternden Gliedern mitteilte; sie hing nur in seinen Armen. Er schloß sie an sein Herz, und benetzte sie mit seinen Tränen. Auf einmal schien sie wieder angespannt, wie eins, das den höchsten körperlichen Schmerz erträgt; und bald mit einer neuen Heftigkeit wurden alle ihre Glieder wieder lebendig, und sie warf sich ihm, wie ein Ressort, das zuschlägt, um den Hals, indem in ihrem Innersten wie ein gewaltiger Riß geschah, und in dem Augenblick floß ein Strom von Tränen aus ihren geschlossenen Augen in seinen Busen.

> "My child," he said, lifting her up and gripping her with his arms, "what is it?" But the convulsions persisted, spreading from the heart into her dangling limbs. She was just hanging in his arms. He clasped her to his heart and covered her with tears. Suddenly she seemed taut again, like someone experiencing great bodily pain. All her limbs became alive again, and with renewed strength she threw herself around his neck, like a lock that springs shut, while a deep cleft opened up inside her and a flood of tears poured from her closed eyes on to his breast. (153; Blackall, 82)

The pathological embraces of Mignon and Wilhelm, culminating in this orgasmic moment, are also described in terms of an actual physical fusion, one that goes beyond the momentary union of the sexual act and echoes the heterosexual version of the Platonic androgyne found in Schlegel's *Lucinde:* "Er sehnte sich, dieses verlassene Wesen . . . seinem Herzen einzuverleiben." (He wanted to take this abandoned creature to his bosom [124; Blackall, 65].) However, Wilhelm's erotic union with this second androgynous female again seems inevitably to lead to her physical dissolution:[29]

> Sie weinte, und keine Zunge spricht die Gewalt dieser Tränen aus. Ihre langen Haare waren aufgegangen, und hingen von der Weinenden nieder, und ihr ganzes Wesen schien in einen Bach von Tränen unaufhaltsam dahin zu *schmelzen.* Ihre starren Glieder wurden gelinde, es ergoß sich ihr Innerstes, und in der Verirrung des Augenblickes fürchtete Wilhelm, sie werde in seinen Armen *zerschmelzen,* und er nichts von ihr übrig behalten.

> She wept tears such as no tongue can describe. Her long hair hung loosely around her as she wept, and her whole being seemed to be *dissolving* into a steady flood of tears. Her rigid limbs unfroze, her whole inner self poured

itself out, and in the confusion of the moment Wilhelm feared that she might
melt away in his arms so that nothing of her would remain. (153; Blackall, 82;
my emphasis)

This erotically charged scene, in which Wilhelm declares himself to
be Mignon's adoptive father, culminates in Mignon and Wilhelm addressing
each other as "Mein Vater!" (my father) and "Mein Kind!" (my child).
Moments later, the Harfner, who is later revealed to be Mignon's father,
makes a powerful entrance; thus, confronted with the dissolution produced
by androgynous desire, the novel powerfully forges the restabilizing links
between androgyny and incestuous desire.

Even more deeply than Mariane, this androgynous love object is bound
up with the aesthetic realm. The identification with the aesthetic domain has
been understood as being, at least in part, a response to Winckelmann's
theory of androgynous indeterminacy.[30] As noted above in the discussion of
Mignon's bewildering first appearance on the stage of the novel, the reader's
perspective, as well as that of Wilhelm, is involved in the deciphering of her
sex. Mignon engages her viewers in a kaleidoscopic process of seeing; the
perspective of Wilhelm, who finally arrives at the decision that this creature
is female, contradicts the firm belief of the doctor, "der sie bisher immer
für einen Knaben gehalten hatte" (who all this time had taken her for a boy
[253; Blackall, 140]). The androgyne is profoundly enigmatic, apostrophized
repeatedly as "das wunderbare Kind," "das Rätsel" (the strange girl, our
mystery [104; Blackall, 54]), or "geheimnisvoll" (veil[ing] some secret
[105; Blackall, 54]). Wilhelm, the narrator reports, "machte sich vielerlei
Gedanken über diese Gestalt, und konnte sich bei ihr nichts Bestimmtes
denken" (went home full of thoughts about this strange creature and unable to make up his mind about her [117; Blackall, 61]). Similarly, the
oxymoron "rastlose Stille" (a suppressed state of unrest [281; Blackall,
156]), used to describe Mignon's fluid position of "in-betweenness," recalls
Winckelmann's androgynous aesthetic ideal, expressed most eloquently in
the dualistic structures of his writings on the Belvedere Apollo.

Mignon is consistently more articulate in song than in free speech,
and it is in the form of her aesthetic productions that the reader learns most
about her origins and motivations, as, for example, in "Kennst du das Land?"
(Know You the Land?), a song permeated by images of incest and sexual
taboo. She can scarcely exist, in fact, outside the realm of art, artificiality,
"Schein." The novel first displays her in theatrical costume, and her funeral
is an elaborately staged dramatic performance. Indeed, it is possible to view
Mignon as a work of art in human form, particularly in the light of Wilhelm

and Jarno's lengthy discussion of Shakespeare. Significantly, Shakespeare's genius is itself described as a harmonious union of polarities: of "Stärke und Zartheit," "Gewalt und Ruhe" (forcefulness and tenderness, violence and control [205; Blackall, 112]). Shakespeare's characters, says Wilhelm, seem both artificial and human, both mysterious and decipherable. They function with harmony and ease, yet their artistic form, the mechanisms by which they are animated, are at all times visible:

> Seine Menschen scheinen natürliche Menschen zu sein, und sie sind es doch nicht. Diese geheimnisvollsten und zusammengesetztesten Geschöpfe der Natur handeln vor uns in seinen Stücken, als wenn sie Uhren wären, deren Zifferblatt und Gehäuse man von Kristall gebildet hätte, sie zeigen nach ihrer Bestimmung den Lauf der Stunden an, und man kann zugleich das Räder- und Federwerk erkennen, das sie treibt.

> His personages seem to be ordinary men and women, and yet they are not. Mysterious composite creatures of nature act out their lives before us in his plays, like clocks with faces and movements of crystal, showing the passage of time in accordance with their regulated progression; at the same time one can perceive the springs and wheels that make them go. (205; Blackall, 112)

On the one hand, Mignon, too, is a living child of flesh and blood. Yet the description of her strange, mechanical "Eiertanz" (egg dance) also points forward to the later discussion of Shakespeare's artistic creations:

> sie verband sich die Augen, gab das Zeichen, und fing zugleich mit der Musik, wie ein aufgezogenes Räderwerk, ihre Bewegungen an, indem sie Takt und Melodie mit dem Schlage der Kastagnetten begleitete. . . . Unaufhaltsam, wie ein Uhrwerk, lief sie ihren Weg.

> She blindfolded herself, gave a sign for the music to begin, and started to move like a wound-up mechanism, beating the time of the melody with the clap of her castanets. . . . She pursued her course relentlessly like clockwork. (123; Blackall, 64)

Later, as Mignon dances for Wilhelm and the other actors, the narrator calls her a "Holzpuppe" (puppet [350; Blackall, 197]), recalling the marionettes that first drew Wilhelm as a child into this aesthetic realm. The crazed Sperata, moreover, believing her child to have been lost at sea, engages in a strange *ars combinatoria:* she collects animal bones washed up on the shore and attempts to reconstruct her daughter, as if she were a work of art:

> Sie nahm an . . . , daß es nur darauf ankomme, die Gebeine des Kindes wiederzufinden, um sie nach Rom zu bringen, so würde das Kind auf den

Stufen des großen Altars der Petruskirche wieder, mit seiner schönen frischen Haut umgeben, vor dem Volke dastehn. . . . [E]ine unglaubliche Wonne verbreitete sich über die arme Kranke, als die Teile sich nach und nach zusammen fanden, und man diejenigen bezeichnen konnte, die noch fehlten. Sie hatte mit großer Sorgfalt jeden Teil, wo er hingehörte, mit Fäden und Bändern befestigt; sie hatte, wie man die Körper der Heiligen zu ehren pflegt, mit Seide und Stickerei die Zwischenräume ausgfüllt.

She assumed . . . that what she had to do now was to find the bones and take them to Rome; then the child would appear before the people, in its fresh white skin, on the steps of the high altar of St. Peter's. . . . [A] great joy spread over the poor woman's face when the parts gradually fitted together and she was told which were still lacking. She had fastened every part where it belonged with ribbon and thread, and had filled in the gaps with silk and embroidery as is done to honor the remains of saints. (630, 632; Blackall, 360, 361)

Like Mariane, however, Mignon is only seen to attain a state of perfect aesthetic harmony as she dematerializes from the novelistic world. Barbara, mindful of bourgeois respectability, warns Mariane of the perils of travesty. Schiller, the first critic of Goethe's novel, expresses similar distaste for the hermaphroditic traits of Mignon. Mignon, he observes, is a "Mißgeburt der Natur" (freak of nature), a creature who does not fit into the harmonious and beautiful "Planetensystem" (planetary system) of the end of the novel.[31] And it is her very androgyny, the perverse sexuality of this child who must remain forever "halb entwickelt" (half developed [562; Blackall, 321]), that makes her into a freak. Paradoxically, Schiller suggests, it is only through her death, in which her anomalous sexuality ceases to be of importance, that she gains access to a utopian state of androgyny. The physically fading androgynous child, it would appear, is no longer disturbing or threatening:

Mignon hat gerade vor dieser Katastrophe angefangen, weiblicher, weicher zu erscheinen und dadurch mehr durch sich selbst zu interessieren; die abstoßende Fremdheit dieser Natur hatte nachgelassen, mit der nachlassenden Kraft hatte sich jene Heftigkeit in etwas verloren, die von ihr abschreckte.

Just before this catastrophe, Mignon had begun to appear softer, more feminine, and so she began to be of more intrinsic interest; the repulsive foreignness of her personality had begun to wane, and with the waning of her strength she had lost some of that vehemence that had proved repellent to readers.[32]

Schiller's view echoes, almost uncannily, that of Jarno, who warns Wilhelm in no uncertain terms of the "albernes zwitterhaftes Geschöpf" (silly androgynous creature) who holds such fascination for the young man (207;

Like no other literary figure,
Mignon becomes the
object of visual fixation
throughout the nineteenth century.
In the illustrations that follow,
what is particularly striking
is the increasingly feminized portrayal
of the androgynous body.

Eduard Mörike, Mignon. (Marbach: Schiller-Nationalmuseum/Deutsches Literatur-
archiv.)

Gustav Leybold, after Ludwig Ferdinand Schnorr von Carolsfeld, Mignon's
Death. (Stiftung Weimarer Klassik: Herzogin Anna Amalia Bibliothek.)

Johann Gottfried Schadow, Marianne Schlegel as Mignon, 1802. (Berlin: Kupfer-stichkabinett, Staatliche Museen zu Berlin–Preußischer Kulturbesitz.)

Wilhelm von Schadow, Mignon, ca. 1826. (Leipzig: Museum der bildenden Künste.)

Ary Scheffer, Mignon Longing for Heaven, 1838. (From L. Vitet, *Oeuvre de Ary Scheffer.* Paris: Goupil, 1860. Courtesy of Yale Collection of German Literature, Beinecke Library.)

Ary Scheffer, Mignon Longing for Her Homeland, 1838. (From
L. Vitet, *Oeuvre de Ary Scheffer.* Paris: Goupil, 1860. Courtesy of
Yale Collection of German Literature, Beinecke Library.)

Ary Scheffer, Mignon and Her Father, 1838. (From L. Vitet, *Oeuvre de Ary Scheffer.* Paris: Goupil, 1860. Courtesy of Yale Collection of German Literature, Beinecke Library.)

Mignon. (From Frederick Pecht, *Goethe Gallery.* New York: D. Appleton, 1870.
Courtesy of Yale Collection of German Literature, Beinecke Library.)

Blackall, 113). The strong emotion expressed in these statements by Jarno and Schiller is noteworthy. How are these expressions of "Ekel und Verdruß," of fear and scathing ridicule, to be understood? And how is it possible to reconcile the words of Schiller and Jarno with Schiller's own integrational model of aesthetic *Bildung,* which finds its most perfect expression in the sculpture of the Juno Ludovisi, itself representationally ambiguous?

The answer is complex. On the one hand, the transvestite Mariane and the androgynous Mignon provide Wilhelm with the aesthetic and erotic experiences that form an important part of his program of *Bildung.* I will argue that the androgynous ideal, when it comes into contact with an authoritarian purveyor of *Bildung* such as the *Turmgesellschaft,* may be manipulated or distorted as a pedagogical tool. On the other hand, when it comes to the physical incarnations of this ideal in the novel, androgynous female characters such as Mariane and Mignon, they remain excluded from the possibility of growth and are denied access to the symbolic order, the world of the *Turmgesellschaft.* Mignon, for example, seems remarkably impervious to conventional education; we are told that her handwriting, despite all her efforts, remains illegible (144; Blackall, 77) and that she is incapable of processing, in the normal manner, information gleaned from books: "sie fing nun an, dasjenige, was sie wußte, teils herauszusagen, teils nach ihrer Art die wunderlichsten Fragen zu tun. Man konnte auch hier wieder bemerken, daß bei einer großen Anstrengung sie nur schwer und mühsam begriff" (she began to recite what she had learnt and in her own special way asked the strangest questions. Once again it became apparent that, for all her energy, her comprehension was slow and laborious [281; Blackall, 156]). Significantly, various members of the Society of the Tower, the *Turmgesellschaft,* turn their pedagogical attention to Mignon; it is Natalie who attempts to have Mignon dress in a manner befitting her sex, and another plan for Mignon's education involves sending the child to Therese's disciplined household. However, Mignon remains, to the end, resistant to *Bildung,* protesting, "Ich bin gebildet genug" ("I am educated enough" [525; Blackall, 299]).

If the androgynous ideal promises endless possibilities, endless openness, in the figure of Mignon we find instead the perpetuation of rigid binaries, exclusion from progress. In fact, the *Turmgesellschaft* actively impedes a move toward "thirdness": at Mignon's elaborate, aestheticized funeral, organized by this society of pedagogues, we find a careful ritualization of dualisms. In the alternating, incantatory responses of the children's choir and the four angelic young boys, Mignon is celebrated, in turn, as male and female:

KNABEN. Ach! wie ungern brachten wir *ihn* her! Ach! und *er* soll hier bleiben! laßt uns auch bleiben, laßt uns weinen, weinen an *seinem* Sarge! . . . Ach! die Flügel heben *sie* nicht; im leichten Spiele flattert das Gewand nicht mehr; als wir mit Rosen kränzten *ihr* Haupt, blickte *sie* hold und freundlich nach uns.

BOYS. Sadly we brought him here, here shall he stay. We too will stay, weep and mourn, shed our tears above his corpse. [Blackall, interestingly, chooses to alter Goethe's pronouns, presumably in the interests of consistency. I regard this as a deliberate narrative strategy on Goethe's part.] . . . They lift her not, those mighty wings. Her garments float no more in easy play. Her head we crowned with roses, sweet and friendly was her gaze. (616; Blackall, 352; my emphasis)

While Winckelmann's hermaphroditic ideal of indeterminacy results in the animation of the work of art, here the opposite move is staged: the kinetic androgyne of flesh and blood having faded away, her corpse is mummified, rendered statuelike, preserved in a state of liminal adolescence.[33] In other words, the narrative of male *Bildung* results in the enervation of this female androgyne and her transformation into an inanimate work of art, in this case her own funeral ornament. The metonymic dynamic of the novel here gives way to the making of a metaphor: the androgyne becomes a statue. Mignon is entombed within a marble sarcophagus, her body fixed by the embalmer's skills in the artificial appearance of eternal youth. With this scientific intervention, the dangerous mutability of organic decomposition, as well as her mobile sexuality, is arrested. (As if to underscore this fatal metamorphosis, we learn that the "Saal der Vergangenheit," the Hall of the Past, in which Mignon is buried, is guarded by two Egyptian sphinxes, emblems of mysterious, petrified femininity.) Having received her final oedipal wounds, Mignon is literally unveiled to the mourners by the Abbé. The surprising gesture reveals the inscription of Mignon's dead body into the symbolic order of the *Turmgesellschaft:* "Er streifte . . . ihren rechten Arm auf, und ein Kruzifix, von verschiedenen Buchstaben und Zeichen begleitet, sah man bläulich auf der weißen Haut." (The Abbé lifted the sleeve from her right arm, and there on her white arm they saw a bluish crucifix, together with various letters and signs [618; Blackall, 353].) Here, the *Turmgesellschaft* also dictates how her death is to be read: as a didactic lesson on repentance and redemption. The Abbé displays Mignon as his own pedagogical and aesthetic construct:

> Aber wenn die Kunst den scheidenden Geist nicht zu fesseln vermochte, so hat sie alle ihre Mittel angewandt, den Körper zu erhalten und ihn der Vergänglichkeit zu entziehen. Eine balsamische Masse ist durch alle Adern

gedrungen, und färbt nun an der Stelle des Bluts die so früh verblichenen Wangen. Treten Sie näher, meine Freunde, und sehen Sie das Wunder der Kunst und Sorgfalt!

"But if art could not give permanence to her spirit, it could employ every skill to preserve her body and save it from decay. Balsam has been introduced into all her veins and, instead of blood, this colors those cheeks that faded so early. Draw near, my friends, and observe the wonders of art, the sum of solicitude!" (617; Blackall, 353)

With this melodramatic gesture, that of a freak-show impresario, the *Bildungsroman,* whose goal is the education of desire, declares itself as the agent of Mignon's death. The Abbé refers to Mignon here, in a striking turn of phrase, as a "Fremdling" (stranger [617; Blackall, 353]). As a "Fremdkörper," a foreign body in the novel that must submit to corporeal discipline, the perversely sexual child has a fate that is sealed from the beginning.

I would also like to stress in this context the notion of Mignon's funeral as a theatrical production staged by the *Turmgesellschaft.* Mignon is identified from the beginning with the theatrical realm, but it is important to note that this is pre-bourgeois "Vortheater," the nomadic world of circus. (On a psychological level, this should be linked, of course, with Mignon's polymorphous, infantile sexuality.) Mignon, unlike the successfully integrated members of society who make up the ranks of the *Turmgesellschaft,* is unable to distinguish art from reality—hence, for example, her confusion as she feverishly attempts to remove stage makeup from her face:

Sie stellte sich oft an ein Gefäß mit Wasser, und wusch ihr Gesicht mit so großer Emsigkeit und Heftigkeit, daß sie sich fast die Backen aufrieb, bis Laertes durch Fragen und Necken erfuhr, daß sie die Schminke von ihren Wangen auf alle Weise los zu werden suche, und über dem Eifer, womit sie es tat, die Röte, die sie durchs Reiben hervorgebracht hatte, für die hartnäckigste Schminke halte.

She would often take a vessel of water and wash her face so vigorously and thoroughly that she almost rubbed her cheeks raw. Laertes teased her about this, but found out that she was trying to get rid of the paint on her cheeks and thought that the red patches she had caused by her vigorous rubbing, were particularly stubborn paint. (114; Blackall, 59)

In the hands of the *Turmgesellschaft,* however, theater is no longer a world in which desires roam freely but rather a mechanism for controlling desire and for channeling it into the appropriate—oedipal—directions.[34] As

it is described in Wilhelm's account of his childhood, in fact, bourgeois
theater becomes a forum for boys to learn how to be boys, for girls to
learn how to be girls, with the polymorphous play of transvestism as a
developmental stage to be passed through on the way to the acquisition
of "correct" gender roles: "Erst spielten wir die wenigen Stücke durch,
in welchen nur Mannspersonen auftreten; dann verkleideten wir einige
aus unserm Mittel, und zogen zuletzt die Schwestern mit ins Spiel. . . .
Knaben und Mädchen waren in diesen Spielen nicht lange beisammen, als
die Natur sich zu regen, und die Gesellschaft sich in verschiedene kleine
Liebesgeschichten zu teilen anfing." ("First we performed the few plays that
had only male characters. After that some of us dressed up as women, using
what costumes we had. And finally we persuaded our sisters to join in. . . . It
was not long before natural instincts began to stir in boys and girls, and the
company divided up into little love-affairs" [33; Blackall, 14].) On a later
occasion, the novel explicitly reveals a transvestite female being yoked in the
service of the *Turmgesellschaft*. Thus, the cross-dressing Baronesse, Jarno's
mistress, participates in the theatrical oedipalization of Wilhelm; it is she who
sets Wilhelm up in his catastrophic masquerade as the Gräfin's husband.
In Mignon's case, the contradiction between biological sex and clothing
apparently remains until Mignon is in Natalie's care and is persuaded to
act the part of an angel, a role that necessitates her wearing a long white
dress, as well as the prerequisite pair of wings. Here, the Christmas play has
been harnessed in the service of the *Turmgesellschaft's* pedagogical goals, in
order to impart to an audience of children the all-important lessons of correct
gender. Yet Mignon's cooperation in the charade has its subversive potential.
As in Goethe's discussion of cross-dressing on the Roman stage, a theatrical
charade acts as a revelation of higher truth rather than as a concealment.
Mignon refuses to lay aside her angelic garb after the play is over, just as she
previously protested against relinquishing her exotic male costume. But in
keeping the long white dress, she is not acknowledging her female sex; rather,
she borrows the appearance of what she believes she is to become, an angel:

> So laßt mich scheinen, bis ich werde;
> Zieht mir das weiße Kleid nicht aus!
> Ich eile von der schönen Erde
> Hinab in jenes feste Haus.

> So let me seem till I become:
> Take not this garment white from me!
> I hasten from the joys of earth
> Down to that house so fast and firm. (553; Blackall, 316)

What is more, she believes that when she is an angel, the question of sex will become irrelevant; the polarities of male and female will be suspended:

> Und jene himmlischen Gestalten
> Sie fragen nicht nach Mann und Weib,
> Und keine Kleider, keine Falten
> Umgeben den verklärten Leib.

> For all those glorious heavenly forms,
> They do not ask for man or wife,
> No garments long or draperies fine
> Surround the body now transformed. (554; Blackall, 316)

Here the figure of the angel becomes a stylized and radical image of androgyny.[35] But in order to retain her sexual polymorphousness, Mignon finds herself death-bound. In a connected move, it is also the Abbé who relates, at third hand, the story of Mignon's origins. For this representative of the *Turmgesellschaft,* power resides in telling (hi)stories, "Vorgeschichten," as well as in staging dramas. Mignon, as a living creature unable to communicate her own history, is once again appropriated aesthetically by the *Turmgesellschaft;* after her elaborately theatrical funeral, which has transformed her into a statue as well as into a sign (the crucifix), she is turned into narrative. That she can be given meaning at all is predicated on her immobilization in death. The content of the Abbé's narrative is itself revealing, in that it casts the child's story as an incest plot, the only form in which the androgynous Mignon can be rendered intelligible by these purveyors of bourgeois socialization. Explaining desire in the "safe" familial terms of the oedipal drama is a way of containing the (unspeakable) story of androgyny. Significantly, the Abbé also reports that the Marchese, following her disappearance, literally substituted a more suitable body for the missing Mignon, when he and his family provided a despairing Sperata with the skeleton of another child; it is this strategically placed "double" that Sperata is able to aestheticize. When Mignon has been fixed as a work of art—and in the *Wanderjahre,* she exists only as an artist's fantasy—Wilhelm is able to follow a more conventional path toward *Bildung.* Turning his attentions away from the aesthetic realm, Wilhelm now assumes his paternal responsibilities toward a son who is very much of flesh and blood. Tellingly, it is the *Turmgesellschaft* that hands over Felix to his father, and Wilhelm accepts from this source of patriarchal power the assignation of paternity that he has previously denied. The father-son relationship will dominate the further course of Wilhelm's *Bildung*—and it is surely no accident that the culminating moment of this process comes when Wilhelm saves Felix from drowning, from the watery element in which androgynous desires flow:

> Mignon im langen weißen Frauengewande, teils mit lokkigen, teils aufgebundenen, reichen, braunen Haaren, saß, hatte Felix auf dem Schoße und drückte ihn an ihr Herz; sie sah völlig aus wie ein abgeschiedener Geist, und der Knabe wie das Leben selbst; es schien, als wenn Himmel und Erde sich umarmten.

> Mignon, in a long white dress, her thick brown hair hanging loose and partly arranged, was seated with Felix on her lap, pressing him to her breast. She looked like a departed spirit, and the boy like life itself; it seemed as though heaven and earth were here conjoined. (564; Blackall, 322)

Indeed, Felix is to become the ultimate replacement object for all of the androgynous women who have passed through Wilhelm's life:

> Komm, lieber Knabe! . . . sei und bleibe du mir alles! Du warst mir zum *Ersatz* deiner geliebten Mutter gegeben, du solltest mir die zweite Mutter *ersetzen,* die ich dir bestimmt hatte, und nun hast du noch die größere *Lücke auszufüllen.*

> "Come, dear boy, . . . may you be and remain everything for me. You were given to me *in place of* your dear mother, you shall *replace* that second mother I had intended for you; now you have a larger *gap to fill.*" (610; Blackall, 349; my emphasis)

This exclusion of the dual-sexed Mignon from the social sphere, or from any satisfactory human relationships, may result from the particular model of androgyny expressed. Mignon longs for a state of "thirdness" that resembles most closely the first phase of Aristophanes' androgynous model: a primordial, sexless creature. Mignon, however, represents a self-absorbed, even autistic version of androgyny, a polymorphous creature whose fate in the hands of the *Turmgesellschaft* can only be death. Lothario confides to Wilhelm, for example, that Mignon is consuming herself: "die arme Mignon scheint sich zu verzehren." (Poor Mignon seems to be wasting away [546; Blackall, 311].) Such a solipsistic, profoundly antisocial being can find no place within the pedagogic realm of the *Turmgesellschaft* and can serve this society at best as an educational tool.[36]

I turn now to a constellation of figures related both to the theatrical female transvestite and to the androgyne: the powerful Amazonian tribe that has the ingenuous Wilhelm Meister in its grips throughout his journey of *Bildung.*[37] The Amazon is, on the one hand, the dream vision that haunts Wilhelm on each station of his developmental journey. But she also appears in various incarnations throughout the novel, from the "schöne Seele" (Beautiful Soul) in her youth to Therese and Natalie. The first Amazon of the novel, if we take the chronology of Wilhelm's life, is of course a fictional construct, the exotic Ethiopian princess from Tasso's *Gerusalemme liberata*.[38] From the beginning, the Amazon of *Wilhelm Meisters Lehrjahre* is experienced by Wilhelm aesthetically and erotically: "es waren . . . Stellen, die ich auswendig wußte, deren Bilder mich umschwebten. Besonders fesselte mich Chlorinde mit ihrem ganzen Tun und Lassen" (there were passages in it that I soon knew by heart and whose images haunted me. Especially Clorinda, in all that she did, fascinated me [28; Blackhall, 11]). What haunts Wilhelm throughout the novel seems to be a harmonious union of sexual polarities, "die Mannweiblichkeit," "die ruhige Fülle ihres Daseins" (her almost masculine femininity, the serenefulness of her being [28; Blackall, 11]). This androgynous plenitude would seem at odds with the martial aggression characteristic of the mythological Amazon.[39]

On the one hand, Goethe's novel presents women who passionately seek to break away from rigid gender dichotomies, to enact transsexual fantasies. These figures are all in some sense marginal, among them the desperate and bitter Aurelie; the resolutely practical Therese, who is characterized as a "real" Amazon (473; Blackall, 269); the "schöne Seele," disciplined as a young woman for her unwomanly conduct. Both Mariane and Mignon, of course, display quintessentially Amazonian tendencies, by dressing as men and refusing to accept female norms of behavior. But the woman most powerfully linked with Wilhelm's childhood vision—Natalie, the beautiful Amazon or "schöne Amazonin"—bears scant resemblance to a transgressive female warrior. The male costume in which Wilhelm first sees her is, in fact, not her preferred form of dress; Natalie has donned her uncle's heavy cloak for purely utilitarian reasons, to protect her from the cold (244; Blackall, 135). The subversive image of the Amazon is transmuted, rendered symbolic, in order to facilitate the *Turmgesellschaft's* project of *Bildung*. While Therese is "wahr" (real), Natalie is the "schöne Amazonin" who slips into her place, and, indeed, into the place of all the other women, as the true incarnation of Wilhelm's vision, and as the *Turmgesellschaft's* chosen partner for him:

> Er sah die schöne Amazone reitend aus den Büschen hervorkommen, sie näherte sich ihm, stieg ab, ging hin und wieder, und bemühte sich um seinetwillen. Er sah das umhüllende Kleid von ihren Schultern fallen; ihr Gesicht, ihre Gestalt glänzend verschwinden. Alle seine Jugendträume knüpften sich an dieses Bild. Er glaubte nunmehr die edle heldenmütige Chlorinde mit eignen Augen gesehen zu haben.

> He saw the lovely Amazon riding out of the bushes, saw her coming toward him, get off her horse, walk up and down, and occupy herself with his needs.

He saw the coat falling from her shoulders, her face and figure disappearing
in a blaze of light. All his youthful visions returned to his mind and associated
themselves with this image. He now thought he had seen the heroic Clorinda
with his own eyes. (252; Blackall, 139)

Before turning to a closer examination of this idealized Amazon,
however, it is illuminating to consider those other women who seem to
subvert stereotypical gender roles and, most importantly, their fate in the
novel. Both Mariane and Mignon, as discussed above, exist at the end of
the novel only as transcendent, aestheticized beings. Unlike so many of
the female characters in *Wilhelm Meisters Lehrjahre,* the actress Aurelie
is not seen to dress in Amazonian uniform. Yet Schiller identifies her,
too, as an Amazon, as a female who is doomed precisely because of—
as Schiller puts it—her "Unnatur" (freakishness), her "Mannweiblichkeit"
(masculine femininity).[40] As an actress, Aurelie notably channels all her
transgressive energies into the role of the mannish Gräfin Orsina, in Lessing's
Emilia Galotti, a woman who famously flouts gender expectations (379–80;
Blackall, 214). Aurelie's life, as a woman and now as an actress, consists
of desperately playing out one unauthentic role after another: "welche
entsetzliche Arbeit ist es, sich mit Gewalt von sich selbst zu enfernen!"
(what a terrible effort it is to separate oneself forcibly from oneself [300;
Blackall, 167]). At the climax of her frenzy, Aurelie seizes her phallic dagger,
her "treue[r] Freund" (trusty friend [275; Blackall, 152]), and viciously
slashes Wilhelm's hand (301; Blackall, 168). What Aurelie describes as
the "marking" of a man, or female inscription of the male body, stands
as a direct challenge to the conventional fate of women in the text—from
the wound imprinted on the Gräfin's breast by her husband's diamond-
studded portrait (374; Blackall, 211) to the sudden appearance of Mignon's
tattoo. An important link may be made between Aurelie's aggressive act,
prefigured in her violent tussle with Serlo in an earlier episode, and Tasso's
Amazonian Chlorinde, who wounds Tancred in the fatal duel.[41] Nevertheless,
Aurelie, like the other "Mißgeburten der Natur," fades physically from the
novel, becomes mute, and is finally carried off by a sudden fever. Yet she,
too, appears to be softened in the hours before her death, by a written
communication from the *Turmgesellschaft,* the "Bekenntnisse einer schönen
Seele" (Confessions of a Beautiful Soul). She is no longer the virago of old:
"Das heftige und trotzige Wesen unsrer armen Freundin ward auf einmal
gelinder." (The poor woman's violence and pity suddenly all calmed down
[380; Blackall, 215].) But ultimately, says Lothario, her former lover, the
mannish Aurelie has no place within the *Turmgesellschaft* because: "sie war

nicht liebenswürdig, wenn sie liebte, und das ist das größte Unglück, das
einem Weibe begegnen kann." (She was not lovable when she loved, and
that is the worst misfortune that can befall a woman [503; Blackall, 286].)
Aurelie can only approach the *Turmgesellschaft* as a peripheral figure; she
can never enter it. One more virago is excluded from the happy denouement
of the novel.

The world of the *Turmgesellschaft* is itself occupied by a powerful
Amazonian clan, but this is a tribe whose members differ radically from the
breastless female warriors of myth. The ancestor of all of these women
is the "schöne Seele" herself. As a child, Natalie's analytically minded
aunt is drawn to books and natural science, rather than to the domestic arts
encouraged by her mother:

> Meiner Mutter und dieser Wißbegierde hatte ich es zu danken, daß ich bei
> dem heftigen Hang zu Büchern doch kochen lernte; aber dabei war ewas
> zu sehen. Ein Huhn, ein Ferkel aufzuschneiden, war für mich ein Fest. Dem
> Vater brachte ich die Eingeweide, und er redete mit mir darüber, wie mit einem
> jungen Studenten, und pflegte mich oft mit inniger Freude seinen mißratenen
> Sohn zu nennen.

> I have to thank my mother, and my own curiosity, for learning to cook as
> well as reading books. There was always something worth looking at in the
> kitchen, and cutting up a chicken or a suckling pig was a real occasion for me.
> I would bring my father the innards, and he would talk to me about them as
> if I were a young student. He often took pleasure in calling me his errant son.
> (387; Blackall, 218)

Her deep-rooted affinity for the world of learning is, however, crushed
by her engagement to Narciß, a superficial young courtier who despises
intellectual women yet also attempts to impose on her his own vision of
Bildung: "er machte es wie alle Männer, spottete über gelehrte Frauen und
bildete unaufhörlich an mir." (His attitude was that of men in general. He
made fun of learned women and yet kept trying to educate me all the time
[403; Blackall, 227].) The image of theatrical masquerade, so frequently
employed in connection with Mariane, Mignon, the Baronesse, and Aurelie,
also appears in the writing of the "schöne Seele." Like Aurelie, she is forced
to play a role that is not hers, to dress in "das Gewand der Torheit" (the
robe of folly [407; Blackall, 229]): "Ich erkannte auf einmal, daß es nur
eine Glasglocke sei, die mich in den luftleeren Raum sperrte; nur noch so
viel Kraft sie entzwei zu schlagen, und du bist gerettet! Gedacht gewagt.
Ich zog die Maske ab." (I realized that it was a glass cover enclosing
me in an airless space, and if only I could summon up enough strength

to shatter it, then I would be free [408; Blackall, 230].) She proclaims to her family, "mit männlichem Trotz" (with almost manly defiance), that from this point on she plans to live her life in full independence (408; Blackall, 230). The chosen path of the "schöne Seele" is religion, and, as a member of a religious order, a "Stiftsdame," she is no longer occupied with questions of gender or sexuality: "Es war als wenn meine Seele ohne Gesellschaft des Körpers dächte; sie sah den Körper selbst als ein ihr fremdes Wesen an, wie man etwa ein Kleid ansieht . . . der Körper wird wie ein Kleid zerreißen, aber Ich, das wohlbekannte Ich, Ich bin." (It was as if my soul were thinking without my body, looking on the body as something apart from itself, like some garment or other . . . the body will be rent like a garment, but I, the well-known I, I am [447; Blackall, 252].) The "schöne Seele" begins life as an Amazonian woman, but by the end of her career she is repeatedly described as a transcendent, saintly being, radically divorced from the social sphere of the *Turmgesellschaft*. The form of androgyny that persists in the narrative of the "schöne Seele" is the mystical Pietistic notion of union between the human soul as bride and Christ as bridegroom.

The parallels with Mignon's path are striking, but Goethe's aestheticizing of this female character is even more extreme. Significantly, the "schöne Seele" is never even a physical presence in the novel but, rather, a disembodied voice that does not appear to have the human trappings of a name. Furthermore, it is a posthumous voice. As one critic has put it, "Woman's exclusively spiritual development is a death warrant."[42] The only tangible evidence we have of her as a physical entity is her portrait, which announces the strong familial resemblance between the "schöne Seele" and the other Amazons of the *Turmgesellschaft*. (Significantly, we once more find a female character captured in the fixity of a work of art.) But since she had actively been barred from playing any role in the education of her sister's children, the Stiftsdame's influence is reduced to that of educational tool in the hands of the *Turmgesellschaft*. It is no accident that the *Turmgesellschaft* places a story of failed androgynous development in the hands of the mannish Aurelie, as a catalyst for "correct" female *Bildung*. Power, in this novel, derives from the strategic (dis)placement of female narratives— Mariane's, Mignon's, the "schöne Seele's." Even the positioning of the Stiftsdame's history within Wilhelm Meister's—the creation, one might say, of an "androgynous" or hybrid narrative—marks its supplementarity within the structure of the *Bildungsroman*.[43] I shall return to the question of androgyny and supplementarity below, in connection with Natalie and her status as supplement.

The Stiftsdame, then, does not come to the end of her career as a defiant female warrior; rather, she points to a world in which all physicality yields to spirituality. Significant in this discussion of the Stiftsdame, as well as of her nieces, Natalie and the Gräfin, is an 1806 review written by Goethe of Friederike Unger's novel *Bekenntnisse einer schönen Seele von ihr selbst erzählt* (Confessions of a Beautiful Soul Related by Herself). While conceding that this novel might justifiably lay claim to such a title, Goethe concludes: "Wir hätten aber doch dieses Werk lieber 'Bekenntnisse einer Amazone' überschrieben." (We would have preferred to entitle this work "Confessions of an Amazon.") The two terms, it would seem, are mutually exclusive:

> Denn es zeigt sich uns wirklich eine Männin. . . . Und wie jene aus dem Haupt des Zeus entsprungene Athene eine strenge Erzjungfrau war und blieb, so zeigt sich auch in dieser Hirngeburt eines verständigen Mannes ein strenges, obgleich nicht ungefälliges Wesen, eine Jungfrau, eine Virago im besten Sinne, die wir schätzen und ehren, ohne eben von ihr angezogen zu sein.

> For we are presented here with a genuine virago. And just as Athena, who sprang from the head of Zeus, was and remained a severe virgin, so this fantasy of an intelligent author reveals itself as a severe, though not displeasing creature, a virgin, a virago in the best sense of the word, whom we can appreciate and venerate, though without being attracted to her.[44]

So what of the perplexing array of epithets presented by Goethe's own novel—the "schöne Seele," the "wahre Amazone," and the "schöne Amazone"? Book VI of *Wilhelm Meisters Lehrjahre* is the only one to bear a title, and that is "Bekenntnisse einer schönen Seele." Yet both Goethe and Schiller seem anxious to qualify the term "schöne Seele" as it first appears. In a July 1796 letter, Schiller comments: "Ich wünschte, daß die Stiftsdame ihr [Natalie] das Prädicat einer schönen Seele nicht weggenommen hätte, denn nur Natalie ist eigentlich eine rein ästhetische Natur." (I wish that the Stiftsdame had not deprived her [Natalie] of the title of Beautiful Soul, for only Natalie has a purely aesthetic nature.)[45] Goethe responds that it is indeed Natalie to whom this title will justly be applied—Schiller should wait to read the end of the novel.[46] The Stiftsdame does not qualify for "schöne Seele" status, then. And Therese, despite being described as the "wahre Amazone," seems, as I will show, more to resemble the admirable if uncharismatic "Männin" of Goethe's review. Schiller comments acerbically: "Theresen verspreche ich wenig Gönner." (I foresee few admirers for Therese.)[47]

Jarno, one of the most outspoken representatives of the patriarchal *Turmgesellschaft,* is the person to call Therese "die wahre Amazone": "sie beschämt hundert Männer, und ich möchte sie eine wahre Amazone nennen, wenn andere nur als artige Hermaphroditen in dieser zweideutigen Kleidung herum gehen." ("She would put a hundred men to shame, and I would call her a real Amazon, whereas others who go around like her in ambiguous clothing are nothing but dainty hermaphrodites" [473; Blackall, 269].) Wilhelm, at this point, has not yet encountered Therese, but Jarno's words, another manipulative narrative detour by the *Turmgesellschaft,* encourage him to believe that he is, at long last, to meet the woman of his dreams. This is not to be: "In Theresen, die ihn und Lydien an der Kutsche empfangen hatte, fand er seine Amazone nicht, es war ein anderes, ein himmelweit von ihr unterschiedenes Wesen." (It was Therese who had welcomed him and Lydie as they got out of the carriage, but she turned out not to be his Amazon: she was a totally different person [475; Blackall, 270].) Therese is not Wilhelm's Amazon, but this is precisely because she is, according to stereotypes, the "wahre Amazone." She is actively engaged in fields of endeavor normally regarded as the exclusive domain of men. And, like so many of the women in this novel, she dresses as a man, in "zweideutige Kleidung" (ambiguous clothing). As in his first encounter with Mignon, Wilhelm is bewildered about the sexual identity of the person he meets (479; Blackall, 273). Therese asks Wilhelm to excuse what she explicitly calls a "Maskerade" but adds that she is sorry her costume is no more than that, at least on this occasion. Cross-dressing here has little to do with the theatrical world of illusion and artifice, and indeed Therese recalls her childhood bemusement at actors who dressed up as people they patently were not. Her male dress is not a form of theatrical impersonation but rather an expression of her true personality, like the arduous physical work that she undertakes on the estate with such undisputed efficiency. This transvestite woman becomes another in Wilhelm's long chain of love objects, being displaced only by the "schöne Amazone." Indeed, Therese herself has the perspicacity to remark on this chain of substitution: "Achtet man mich so wenig, daß man glaubt, es sei so was Leichtes diesen mit jenem aus dem Stegreife wieder umzutauschen?" ("Have they so little respect for me that they believe it is so easy to exchange one for the other again, on the spur of the moment?" [577; Blackall, 330].) But precisely her resolute practicality, her literalness, summed up in her adoption of male clothing, marks her as an unsuitable partner for Wilhelm.

Natalie and her sister, the Gräfin, are of a different breed. Both are explicitly linked with the spirituality of the "schöne Seele" by a remarkable familial resemblance. Wilhelm mistakenly identifies a portrait of the "schöne Seele" as that of Natalie (555; Blackall, 317). Images of the Gräfin and Natalie flow interchangeably before Wilhelm's eyes, and he describes them as identical twins while still unaware of their kinship (257; Blackall, 142). This incredible similarity extends further than mere facial appearance; perhaps there is nothing so unusual, after all, about sisters who physically resemble each other. Handwriting offers more miraculous evidence: that of the sisters is almost identical.

The Gräfin, the delicate, graceful, and thoroughly mundane precursor of her sister in the novel, curiously enough also brings to Wilhelm's mind both Amazonian and androgynous images. An allegorical play is to be performed in honor of her husband, and at the Graf's suggestion that Minerva, the goddess of wisdom and war, play a central role, Wilhelm feels himself "auf eine sehr angenehme Weise gezwungen" (pleasantly compelled) to comply with the artistic scheme (181; Blackall, 98). A lengthy debate and an extensive library search ensue over the vexing question of the appropriate costume for the actress who is to play Minerva. Finally, it occurs to the Graf to ask which goddess Wilhelm has in mind: Minerva, the Roman goddess of war, or Pallas Athena, her Greek counterpart, the goddess of art. Wilhelm responds by pointing to the dual nature of the deity: she appears in the guise of a powerful warrior, but her ultimate accomplishment is peace and harmony, what Schiller might term the aesthetic state:[48]

> Sollte es nicht am Schicklichsten sein, . . . wenn man hierüber sich nicht bestimmt ausdrückte, und sie, eben weil sie in der Mythologie eine doppelte Person spielt, auch hier in doppelter Qualität erscheinen ließe. Sie meldet einen Krieger an, aber nur um das Volk zu beruhigen, sie preist einen Helden, indem sie seine Menschlichkeit erhebt, sie überwindet die Gewalttätigkeit und stellt die Freude und Ruhe unter dem Volke wieder her.

> "Wouldn't it be best . . . not to be specific on that point?" Wilhelm suggested. "Why not present her in the double character which she had in mythology? She announces the arrival of a fighter, but only to bring peace to the populace. She praises a hero for his humaneness. She forcibly restrains force and thereby restores peace and quiet." (183; Blackall, 99)

There are obvious parallels between this mythological model, with its strong suggestions of an androgynous aesthetic ideal, and the description of the "schöne Amazone." The goddess of war is actually a harbinger of humanity, peace, and harmony, in whom male and female elements are united. Dazzled by the elegance and beauty of Natalie's sister, Wilhelm almost instinctively draws the analogy between this living woman and Minerva, the virgin goddess of wisdom and warfare, who was born, already fully armed, from the head of Jupiter. Again, the botanical image underlines the androgyny of this figure: "Wenn Minerva ganz gerüstet aus dem Haupte des Jupiter entsprang, so scheinet diese Göttin in ihrem vollen Putze aus irgendeiner Blume mit leichtem Fuße hervorgetreten zu sein." ("For if Minerva rose fully armed from the head of Jupiter, this goddess seems to have emerged light-footed from some flower in all her finery" [213; Blackall, 117].) As suggested above, the positive image of androgyny or "Mannweiblichkeit" is an aestheticized image. In Goethe's 1806 review, cited above, he describes an Athena whom one can respect and admire, "ohne eben von ihr angezogen zu werden" (without being attracted to her). Here, where any resemblance to a bellicose Amazon has been highly abstracted, in the analogy between the excessively "feminine" Gräfin and the allegorical representation of Minerva, a female character can be both "manly" and seductive.

The character who exemplifies most perfectly such an impulse toward the idealizing and mythologizing of sexually ambiguous female characters is, of course, the "schöne Amazone," described by Schiller as "eine rein ästhetische Natur" (of a purely aesthetic nature).[49] In the final pages of the novel, Lothario declares that it is his sister who merits the title "schöne Seele," more even than his spiritual aunt (651; Blackall, 372). The indeterminacy of Natalie's appearance arouses dual emotions in her viewer, suggesting an aesthetic ideal of androgynous indeterminacy, of endless fluidity: "bestimmte und unbestimmte Gegenstände wechselten in seiner Seele und erregten ein endloses Verlangen" (definite and indefinite images floated before his mind and aroused desires that had no limit [258; Blackall, 143]). The "schöne Amazone" is also oddly interchangeable with other androgynous female images:

> Die Erinnerung an die liebenswürdige Gräfin war ihm unendlich süß. Er rief sich ihr Bild nur allzugern wieder ins Gedächtnis. Aber nun trat die Gestalt der edlen Amazone gleich dazwischen, eine Erscheinung verwandelte sich in die andere, ohne daß er im Stande gewesen wäre, diese oder jene fest zu halten.

> The memory of the beautiful countess was one of extreme sweetness: he took constant pleasure in recalling her image. But now the person of the noble Amazon had interposed itself, and the two images became one, so that he was quite unable to keep hold of the one and let go of the other. (257; Blackall, 142)

> nur die Bilder Mignons und Nataliens schwebten wie Schatten vor seiner Einbildungskraft.

> Only the forms of Mignon and Natalie hovered like shadows before his imagination. (584; Blackall, 334)

Natalie in fact scarcely exists as a physical, corporeal being. She is repeatedly described in aesthetic rather than physical terms, as a "Bild" (image) or, like Mignon, as an "Erscheinung" (apparition) or "Engel" (angel). In Book VIII, Wilhelm goes so far as to describe her as the ghost of an image, fainter even than a "Bild" itself: "Schließest du die Augen, so wird sie dich dir darstellen; öffnest du sie, so wird sie vor allen Gegenständen hinschweben, wie die Erscheinung, die ein blendendes Bild im Auge zurück läßt." ("If I close my eyes, she will appear before me; if I open them, she will dominate everything like the effect produced by a blinding image in the eye" [609; Blackall, 348].) No description of her appearance is to be found, apart from rather vague, idealizing adjectives such as "schön," "heilig," "sanft," "still," "liebenswürdig," "edel" (lovely, saintly, gentle, calm, compassionate, noble [242–45; Blackall, 134–35]). Indeed, in Wilhelm's visions of the Amazon, her body literally seems to dissolve away before his eyes:

> In diesem Augenblicke, da er den Mund öffnen und einige Worte des Dankes stammeln wollte, wirkte der lebhafte Eindruck ihrer Gegenwart so sonderbar auf seine schon angegriffenen Sinne, daß es ihm auf einmal vorkam, als sei ihr Haupt mit Strahlen umgeben, und über ihr ganzes Bild verbreite sich nach und nach ein glänzendes Licht. . . . Die Heilige verschwand vor den Augen des Hinsinkenden.

> When he opened his mouth to murmur some words of thanks, the vivid impression of her presence had the strangest effect on his impaired senses. Her head seemed to be surrounded by shafts of light and there was a glow spreading across her whole appearance. . . . So the saint disappeared from his fainting sight. (244; Blackall, 135)

> Das Kleid fiel von ihren Schultern; ihr Gesicht, ihre Gestalt fing an zu glänzen und sie verschwand.

> Her coat slipped from her shoulders, her face, indeed her whole body, shone, and then she disappeared. (315; Blackall, 176)

Natalie's is not, however, the confusing sexuality of so many of the other female characters of the novel. She is immediately introduced as a "Dame" (243; Blackall, 134), and as soon as the man's cloak, borrowed from her uncle, slips from her shoulders, any trace of ambiguity is removed. Once Natalie has departed from the forest, that wild uncivilized space, we find her in a safe domestic setting in which her female sex is unambiguous, in the orbit of the *Turmgesellschaft.*

In the transition from Mignon to Natalie, the most important transvestite women of this novel, Wilhelm makes the move from a mobile, bisexual

model of androgyny to a heterosexual ideal of androgynous completion
through union with the opposite sex.[50] Natalie retains only the vestigial
marks of sexual ambiguity. This developmental model helps to clarify why
she can be known, throughout, as an Amazon, while retiring to a domestic
life considered by the *Turmgesellschaft* a model of perfect femininity; the
androgyne, in the domesticated form of Natalie, is simply incorporated into
the oedipal structures of Wilhelm's *Bildung*. The novel itself suggests that
a heterosexual model of androgynous wholeness is at play by the time
of Wilhelm's betrothal, with Friedrich's lighthearted remarks to his sister
Natalie containing more than a grain of truth: "Ich glaube, du heiratest
nicht eher, als bis einmal irgendwo eine Braut fehlt, und du gibst dich
alsdann nach deiner gewohnten Gutherzigkeit als Supplement irgendeiner
Existenz hin." ("I don't believe you will marry until some bride or other
is missing, and you, with your customary generosity, will provide yourself
as a supplement to someone's existence" [606; Blackall, 346].) Friedrich
Schlegel takes this statement further and calls Natalie the "Supplement des
Romans" (supplement of the novel).[51] Both strategic uses of the word may
be productively read alongside Derrida's discussion of supplementarity, in
particular as it relates to human sexuality.[52] For Derrida, the supplement
functions as an addition to an already complete entity and at the same
time as a compensation for a deficiency in what is supposedly already
complete. Premised on an original lack, desire also functions through an
endless chain of contingent supplements, producing a mirage of the thing
deferred. As Derrida proposes, childhood is the first manifestation of the
lack that calls for substitution, and education is regulated by supplementarity. With Natalie's marriage to Wilhelm, his endless pursuit of perversely
sexual love objects seems finally to be over, apparently culminating in
mature adult sexuality, a harmonious union of the sexes. But this model
of androgynous harmony is predicated on sexual difference, on the upholding of polarities, and on the denial of polymorphousness and fluidity. For
both Therese and Natalie, their situation at the end of the novel is hardly
what one might expect of Amazons. The "wahre Amazone," Therese, is
portrayed as the perfect housekeeper. Paradoxically as it might seem for
an Amazon, Therese is most powerfully attracted to Lothario during his
excursus on the proper place for women in society. After a conversation
in which several of the neighboring ladies protest against the roles assigned to women—"Tändelpuppen oder Haushälterinnen" (playthings or
housekeepers)—Lothario's speech unwittingly reveals some of the problems
inherent in the "supplemental" androgynous model. Women, according
to his ideal, remain confined to the domestic sphere and excluded from

progress, while extending to their husbands the promise of wholeness (486–87; Blackall, 277).

The situation for Natalie is scarcely different. She repeatedly meets Wilhelm's gaze as an aesthetic being, as a statuesque work of art, and by the conclusion of the novel she has been both aestheticized and oedipalized, as the woman in the painting of the "kranker Königssohn" (sick prince). Yet she herself is excluded from participation in the aesthetic sphere; unconcerned with art or nature, all of her energies are concentrated toward compensatory, "supplementary" activities:

> Die Reize der leblosen Natur, für die so viele Menschen äußerst empfänglich sind, hatten keine Wirkung auf mich, beinah noch weniger die Reize der Kunst; meine angenehmste Empfindung war und ist es noch, wenn sich mir ein Mangel, ein Bedürfnis in der Welt darstellte, sogleich im Geiste einen Ersatz, ein Mittel, eine Hülfe aufzufinden.

> "The delights of inanimate nature, so meaningful to others, left me unmoved, and art appealed to me even less. My greatest delight was, and still is, to be presented with some deficiency, some need in others, and be able to think of some way of repairing or alleviating it." (565; Blackall, 322)

Natalie submits fully to the patriarchal order of the *Turmgesellschaft*—from her deferential attitude toward her uncle, in Book IV, to her acceptance of what is essentially an arranged marriage. Her betrothal is not even sealed with a kiss, and at the end of the novel she continues a chaste career as a correspondence bride; Wilhelm's trajectory appears to swerve away from its own teleological conclusion. The image of the Amazon, in Natalie's case as well as Therese's, is drained of eroticism in order to make it containable within the program of the *Turmgesellschaft*. (Tellingly, Natalie's appearance in the novel occurs at the moment when Wilhelm has just received his oedipal wounds, in his masquerade as the Graf, and in the *Hamlet* performance.) It is also Natalie who continues the pedagogical mission of the *Turmgesellschaft* by attempting to dress Mignon in female clothing, and her vocation is in bringing up deprived children. Both the "schöne Seele" and the Gräfin retreat from sexual desire to a life of spirituality. Nor is there any place in this orderly, patriarchal world for a woman of dubious morals and of Philine's considerable and subversive vitality,[53] or for the "Mißgeburt der Natur" (freak of nature), the perversely sexual Mignon.

The move away from nomadic androgynous desire toward androgynous supplementarity can also be traced in Wilhelm's erotic history. Wilhelm's first objects of desire in the novel are, of course, the sexually ambiguous Mariane and the androgyne Mignon. As Wilhelm shares with Mariane his delight in the marionettes from the biblical David drama, Mariane's amorous identification of the smooth-chinned Jonathan puppet with her lover is one early hint of Wilhelm's own mobile sexuality (16; Blackall, 5).[54] Philine's seductive strategies, in the early chapters of Book II, prove oddly discomforting to Wilhelm, who during this phase of the novel is experiencing a confusing erotic attraction to Mignon. Wilhelm's relationship with Mignon, which the novel so insistently explains in oedipal (heterosexual) terms, surely has strong undercurrents of bisexual desire, her name itself being a code word for a male homosexual prostitute in the eighteenth century.[55] And finally, in the *Wanderjahre,* Wilhelm reveals—in a letter to his fiancée Natalie—the story of his youthful passion for a fisher-boy. Again, water is presented as the seductive realm of homoerotic desire: the boy bathes in the river while Wilhelm looks on in a state of confused arousal and is finally persuaded to plunge into the water himself.[56] The boy's tragic death by drowning is preceded by a symbolically charged scene in which Wilhelm strolls through a flower garden in the company of an attractive blond woman; the novel reveals that the hyacinth blooms have already faded, suggesting the passing away of homoerotic desire. (There are clear parallels between this moment and the passage in *Lucinde* about the disturbing effects of hyacinth scent on the heroine.) The scene culminates in Wilhelm's futile attempts to breathe life into the marmoreal corpse of the boy—yet another fatal inversion of the Pygmalion myth.

One other important figure remains to be examined in this study of pedagogy and androgyny, and that is the wayward brother of Natalie, Lothario, and the Gräfin: Friedrich. Friedrich is the only male in *Wilhelm Meisters Lehrjahre* who consistently exhibits androgynous tendencies, the only male, other than Wilhelm, who is associated with transvestism. (Wilhelm had been persuaded by Philine to don her "Pudermantel" or smock before she curled his hair [100; Blackall, 50].) Friedrich is introduced, in vocabulary reminiscent of Winckelmann's exquisite hermaphrodite sculptures, as an eternal adolescent, a *"Mittelding* zwischen Kind und Jüngling" (*half* boy and *half* man [149; Blackall, 80; my emphasis]). Natalie describes him as "los" and "locker" (frivolous and carefree), and he passes through the world of the novel in mercurial fashion, ever likely to materialize from behind a bush (559; Blackall, 319). Later, Friedrich and Philine, a subversive and "zweideutige[s] Paar" (dubious pair [365; Blackall, 206]), stage an elaborate charade that leads Wilhelm to believe he is in the presence of Mariane:

> Beide [Serlo und Wilhelm] waren im Hereintreten sehr verwundert, als sie
> Philinen in dem zweiten Zimmer in den Armen eines jungen Offiziers sahen,

der eine rote Uniform und weiße Unterkleider an hatte, dessen abgewendetes
Gesicht sie aber nicht sehen konnten.

They [Serlo and Wilhelm] were both amazed to find Philine in the inner room,
in the arms of a young officer in a red uniform and white undergarments,
whose face they could not see because it was turned away from them. (362;
Blackall, 204)

Philine replies, tantalizingly:

daß es nur eine gute Freundin ist, die sich einige Tage unbekannt bei mir
aufhalten will. Sie sollen ihre Schicksale künftig erfahren, ja vielleicht das
interessante Mädchen selbst kennen lernen. . . . Wilhelm stand versteinert da;
denn gleich beim ersten Anblick hatte ihn die rote Uniform an den so sehr
geliebten Rock Marianens erinnert; es war ihre Gestalt, es waren ihre blonden
Haare, nur schien ihm der gegenwärtige Offizier etwas größer zu sein. Um des
Himmels willen! rief er aus, lassen Sie uns mehr von Ihrer Freundin wissen,
lassen Sie uns das verkleidete Mädchen sehen.

"that it's only a girl friend of mine who is staying for a few days with
me incognito. You shall hear all about her later and you may well find her
extremely interesting. . . ." Wilhelm stood transfixed to the spot, for the red
uniform had immediately reminded him of his beloved Mariane—the same
figure, the same blond hair, though this officer seemed somewhat taller. "For
Heaven's sake," he cried, "do let us know more about your friend, let us see
this dressed-up girl." (362; Blackall, 204)

The twist in this curious tableau is that while Friedrich is not actually
cross-dressing, he bears the signature of transvestism, plays with its subversive potential. Wilhelm, for one, is fully persuaded that the person embracing
Philine is none other than his beloved female transvestite, Mariane.

Friedrich is the despair of his family. Natalie expresses her fears to
Wilhelm that her capricious brother will, unlike his more educable siblings,
fall victim to the pedagogical experiments of the *Turmgesellschaft:* "Was
aus Bruder Friedrich werden soll, läßt sich gar nicht denken; ich fürchte, er
wird das Opfer dieser pädagogischen Versuche werden." ("And what is to
become of my brother Friedrich, I haven't the least idea. I'm afraid that he
may well be the victim of these pedagogical experiments" [559; Blackall,
319].) Certainly, if we consider the fate of the androgynous women in this
novel, Natalie has good reason to fear for Friedrich's future. These female
androgynes fail to survive the project of *Bildung,* lingering on in the text
only as idealized images, garments without occupants, disembodied voices,
vanishing bodies. But Friedrich's playfulness not only permits him to subvert
Wilhelm's amorous expectations, it also enables him to survive *Bildung,*

indeed to deconstruct its totalizing claims. His is a parodistical notion of *Bildung,* one that opposes his own "composite" androgynous personality with the ideals of organic development advocated by the *Turmgesellschaft.* Friedrich's own speech, for example, is cobbled together from randomly selected citations, and his alternative to the *Bildung* of the *Turmgesellschaft,* a hilarious autodidactic project, proceeds in similar haphazard fashion:

> Endlich hatte Philine den herrlichen Einfall, die sämtlichen Bücher auf einem großen Tisch aufzuschlagen, wir setzten uns gegeneinander und lasen gegen-einander, und immer nur stellenweise, aus einem Buch wie aus dem an-dern. . . . Wir variieren diese Art uns zu unterrichten auf gar vielerlei Weise. Manchmal lesen wir nach einer alten verdorbenen Sanduhr, die in einigen Minuten ausgelaufen ist. Schnell dreht sie das andere herum, und fängt aus einem Buche zu lesen an, und kaum ist wieder der Sand im untern Glase, so beginnt das andere schon wieder seinen Spruch, und so studieren wir wirklich auf wahrhaft akademische Weise, nur daß wir kürzere Stunden haben, und unsere Studien äußerst mannigfaltig sind.

> "Then Philine lit upon the splendid idea of piling all the books on the table and opening them up. We sat across from each other and read to each other, always bits and pieces, from one book and then from another. . . . We varied our means of instructing ourselves, sometimes reading against an hourglass that would run out in a few minutes, then be reversed by Philine as she began to read from another book, and when the sand reached the bottom glass, I would begin my piece. And so we studied away in true academic fashion, except that our lessons were shorter and our studies more varied." (598–99; Blackall, 342)

Not only does Friedrich subvert the serious pedagogical enterprise that propels the novel, but it is he who theatrically brings together the threads of this complex narrative of *Bildung.* To transpose the motif of theatrical transvestism to the level of narrative structure, the novel as a whole may be described as a work of disguise and uncovering, with the final chapters, orchestrated by Friedrich, functioning as an ironically grandiloquent unmasking, both of plot and of pedagogy.

Friedrich's manipulation of his sexual polymorphousness is not within the powers of the androgynous women in this novel, as shown above. In *Wilhelm Meisters Lehrjahre,* the female androgyne suffers one of two fates. It may, like Mariane and Mignon, simply fade physically from the text, as a transfigured and nebulous being, leaving the male hero with his experience of enlightenment. Or, as with Natalie and her sister, the trappings of androgyny may become so abstracted that the female characters can continue to lead the lives expected of them in the patriarchal *Turmgesellschaft* without any apparent contradiction. Wilhelm's path of maturation is strewn with these female victims, all of whom remain excluded from *Bildung.* Female androgynes, in this world of *Bildung,* ultimately only serve male completion, whether they are refashioned as suitably feminine marriage material or their narratives of self are appropriated for pedagogical use. *Wilhelm Meisters Lehrjahre* imposes on a multiplicity of sexual desire the teleological narrative of heterosexuality. It is to this end that the novel makes the shift to a heterosexual model of androgyny in which Natalie functions as a supplement to Wilhelm, displacing a genuinely dual-sexed being like Mignon who can find no place within the oedipal bourgeois family.[57] William Larrett, in the last sentence of his article on the Amazons of *Wilhelm Meisters Lehrjahre,* unwittingly points to the problem of the female androgyne: "Behind Wilhelm's love and seeking out of Natalie, the beautiful Amazon, there lies Man's quest for wholeness."[58]

3

Disciplining the Androgynous Body

Twilight Zones: Eichendorff and Female Transvestism

Manches bleibt in Nacht verloren—
Hüte dich, bleib wach und munter!

Much remains obscured by the night—
Beware! Stay awake and vigilant!

<small>EICHENDORFF, *Ahnung und Gegenwart*[1]</small>

"das Kostüm [ist] niemals willkürlich oder
zufällig" (costume is never arbitrary or incidental)

<small>EICHENDORFF, *Der Adel und die Revolution*[2]</small>

The German romantic novel is a literary space teeming with transvestites, or, more accurately speaking, with female transvestites. Much of the fascination with female cross-dressing must be ascribed to the enormous influence of Goethe's *Wilhelm Meisters Lehrjahre*, which, as outlined in chapter 2, above, returns repeatedly to problems of gender and genre slippage. Where Goethe's novel may be read as a response to circulating eighteenth-century discourses on androgyny, aesthetics, and *Bildung*, many of the romantic authors who take *Wilhelm Meister* as their cue seem primarily to be interested in the most superficial manifestation of the gender/aesthetics debate: the thrill of the transvestite female body. But of course it is precisely the imitative nature of cross-dressing, its expressly citational function, that makes it the perfect analogue to a literature bent on quotation—transvestism *as* citation. In Brentano's *Godwi,* two central female characters, Flametta and the Gräfin von Godwi, engage in cross-dressing; Tieck's *Franz Sternbald* features the eroticized masquerading of the Gräfin Adelheid; Arnim's novel *Gräfin Dolores* includes scenes of theatrical transvestism; and Dorothea Schlegel's *Florentin* presents a heroine who embarks on forbidden forest adventures dressed in male clothing.[3] In this respect, the works of Joseph von Eichendorff can be read as exemplary of one of the central preoccupations of German romanticism. Yet there is a peculiarly obsessive quality to Eichendorff's literary treatment of transvestism and masquerade that makes his works a privileged source for theoretical investigation. Indeed, the very names of his heroes and heroines seem dizzyingly interchangeable, to the point where gender distinctions, too, are blurred: Fortunato, Fortunat, Fiametta, Florentine, Florio, Flora, Romana, Rosa, Romano.[4] Eichendorff's comedy *Die Freier* (The Suitors), very probably inspired by Shakespeare's gender-bending plays *Twelfth Night* and *As You Like It,* is propelled forward by scenes of female cross-dressing and mistaken identity. Gräfin Diana in the story *Die Entführung* (The Abduction) is described as an alluring Amazonian beauty who slips in and out of male dress. In *Das Schloß Dürande* (Castle Dürande), Gabriele wears male clothing during the storming of the castle in her attempt to save her lover's life. The mercurial huntsman Florentin in the narrative *Viel Lärmen um Nichts* (Much Ado about Nothing) reveals himself finally in his true guise, that of a woman, the beautiful Aurora. In *Aus dem Leben eines Taugenichts* (Memoirs of a Good-for-Nothing), the wastrel hero discovers, much to his bewilderment, that one of the highwaymen he encountered on his picaresque adventures is none other than a cross-dressing young noblewoman, Flora. In *Eine Meerfahrt* (A Sea Voyage), the savage Caribbean queen bedecks herself triumphantly with a necklace made from the teeth of slain Spanish adventurers, and her niece appropriates the clothing of her conquistador lover. Eichendorff's *Bildungsroman Ahnung und Gegenwart*[5] is strewn with eroticized scenes of female transvestism, and the hero of the novel is accompanied on his path toward maturation by an androgynous child who bears an uncanny resemblance to Goethe's Mignon. The novella *Das Marmorbild* (The Marble Statue) finds its conclusion in a dramatic unveiling of "correct" female gender.[6] I will show that Eichendorff's narratives of male *Bildung* are, indeed, generated by such female masking and unmasking, which come to function as a key structural, as well as thematic, principle.

As I argued in the case of *Wilhelm Meisters Lehrjahre,* transvestism must be read as more than a modish novelistic motif, more than a literal borrowing from theatrical comedy or the *Trivialroman.*[7] While the prominence of tropes of "Verkleidung" and masquerade throughout Eichendorff's work has been well documented by scholars such as John Fisher and Otto Eberhardt, their accounts tend not to differentiate between disguise, in all its various manifestations, and the particular case of transvestism. Eberhardt, for example, who proposes a strictly religious interpretation for "Verkleidung" in Eichendorff's works, arguing that it represents allegorically the mystical veiling of divine truth, does not pause to consider the complex interplay of transvestism and gender. Nor, significantly, do Fisher and Eberhardt hesitate over the fact that cross-dressing in Eichendorff's texts, as in Goethe's *Wilhelm Meisters Lehrjahre,* is almost exclusively presented as a feminine strategy. (And yet it is Eberhardt who reminds us of Eichendorff's lifelong love of theatrical masquerade, and who notes that as a boy the writer had himself experimented with playing female roles, while commenting almost as an aside that the transvestism in Eichendorff's works is generally of the female-to-male variety.)[8] Again, as with Goethe's essay on theatrical cross-dressing, considered in chapter 2, above, transvestism is transposed from the stage world of the boy actor into that of narrative and female masquerade. Readers are confronted with a slippage of categories, both of gender and of genre. Does this mean, then, that the transvestite effects in Eichendorff's narratives should be read as liberatory, subversive gestures toward a transcendent position of aesthetic "thirdness," as Goethe suggested might be the case for theatrical cross-dressing?

When in *Aus dem Leben eines Taugenichts* the Taugenichts finds himself in the confusing company of two sexually ambiguous highwaymen, his complete loss of orientation is expressed in terms of a dizzying play of binary oppositions.

> So zogen wir eigentlich recht närrisch in die mondhelle Nacht hinein. . . . Dabei das einförmige Pferdegerappel und das Wirren und Schwirren der Reiter hinter mir, die unaufhörlich in einer fremden Sprache miteinander plauderten, und das helle Mondlicht und die langen Schatten der Baumstämme, die wechselnd über die beiden Reiter wegflogen, daß sie mir bald schwarz, bald hell, bald klein, bald wieder riesengroß vorkamen. Mir verwirrten sich ordentlich die Gedanken.

> Thus we rode into the moonlit night, quite crazily. . . . Behind me the rhythmical galloping of the horses; and the babble and gabble of the riders, who

were chattering incessantly in a foreign language; and the bright moonlight
and the long shadows alternately casting themselves over the two riders, so
that they seemed first dark, then fair, small and then again gigantic in size. I
was in a state of utter confusion. *(Neue Gesamtausgabe,* vol. 2: 377)

For Eichendorff as for Shakespeare, the forest provides the perfect
backdrop to comedic transvestite adventures.[9] A liminal setting, set apart
from city and culture, it bewilders the traveler with dappled, erratic effects
of light and shadow. Apparently immutable binaries of male and female, day
and night, are destabilized. Dawn and twilight, of course, are the privileged
temporal settings of Eichendorff's lyrics and narratives, times of flux and
indeterminacy when contours dissolve. Into this space of indeterminacy and
fluidity wander all of Eichendorff's male heroes. In the forest, Friedrich, in
Ahnung und Gegenwart, variously encounters the flirtatious young Marie,
her mistress Rosa, Julie, and the dangerously seductive Romana, all dressed
as huntsmen. The transvestite Aurora, in *Viel Lärmen um Nichts,* lures
Romano, Leontin, and Faber deep into the forest. Gabriele, in *Das Schloß
Dürande,* torn between the rigid categories of social class, expresses her
longing "[sich] einmal bei Nacht [zu] verwirren recht im tiefsten Wald" (to
lose herself one night deep in the forest [vol. 2: 817]). In the lush tropical
jungle of a Caribbean island, the setting of *Eine Meerfahrt,* categories such
as East/West, Christianity/paganism, civilization/nature, victor/vanquished,
male/female are called into question, and it is this disruption of simple
binaries, it may be argued, that finds symbolic form in the transvestism
of the native woman Alma.[10] Transvestism, in this story, is the marker of
rampant category confusion. Don Diego's recollections of the savage queen,
for example, stress a never-ending oscillation between binaries: "sie selber
war wie das Gebirge, in launenhaftem Wechsel bald scharf gezackt, bald
sammetgrün, jetzt hell und glühend bis in den fernsten, tiefsten Grund, dann
alles wieder grauenhaft verdunkelt" (she herself was like the mountain range,
moody and changeable: one minute rough and jagged, the next velvety green,
one minute bright and glowing even in the furthest, deepest valley, then the
next minute horribly dark again [vol. 2: 797]).
  Uncertainty, the blurring of binary oppositions of gender, intensifies or
even serves to generate sexual desire in Eichendorff's narratives. In several
key encounters in *Ahnung und Gegenwart,* for example, the erotic allure
of a female transvestite is heightened by her ambiguous clothing. In one
early scene, Friedrich witnesses a breakdown in sexual proprieties apparently
provoked by Marie's transvestite costume:

  Die kleine Marie nämlich, die am Morgen mit dem Jäger auf der Wiese
  gesungen, hatte sich als Jägerbursche angezogen. . . . Leontin fing sie auf

und setzte sie vor sich auf seinen Schoß. Er strich ihr die Haare aus den munteren Augen und gab ihr aus seinem Glase zu trinken. Sie trank viel und wurde bald ungewöhnlich beredt, daß sich alle über ihre liebenswürdige Lebhaftigkeit freuten. Leontin fing an, von ihrer Schlafkammer zu sprechen und andere leichtfertige Reden vorzubringen, und als er sie endlich auch küßte, umklammerte sie mit beiden Armen seinen Hals.

For little Marie, who had been singing with the huntsman on the meadow that morning, had dressed up as a hunter. . . . Leontin picked her up and set her on his knee. He brushed her hair out of her mischievous eyes and offered her his glass. She slaked her thirst and was soon so uncommonly talkative that everyone was delighted at her charming vivaciousness. Leontin began dropping comments about her bedroom and the like, and when he finally kissed her as well, she threw her arms about his neck. (vol. 2: 33)

Only a few pages later, the narrator, alluding to Marie's awakening sexuality, which seems to be causally linked with her male costume, observes her as she darts through the forest, locus of gender gaming, "wie ein reizender Kobold" (like a charming imp [35]). Significantly, too, the adolescent Marie is described as hovering between childhood and adulthood. Like Erwin, and of course also like Goethe's Mignon, the shape-shifter occupies the most sexually polymorphous of life phases, *boy*hood. Later in the novel, Friedrich, seeing Rosa for the first time in the male costume of a huntsman, suddenly seems mesmerized by her new and dazzling beauty (199). Rosa's adoption of huntsman's costume is additionally, of course, overlaid with the erotic symbolism of the hunt, though it is she who becomes the prey, that very night, of the seductive strategies of the Prince.[11] Julie, too, the novel reports, looks "überaus reizend" (utterly charming) in her guise as a huntsman (289). Cross-dressing is a doubly erotic practice. Not only does it enhance, or even generate, a woman's erotic appeal in the eyes of male admirers, but it would seem that transvestism is an inherently arousing experience for the woman herself. While sex researcher Robert J. Stoller's ground-breaking study of transvestism resolutely denies the very existence of such a creature as a female transvestite, claiming that women do not fetishize male garments, Eichendorff's novel would seem a persuasive literary counterproof to that hypothesis.[12] Rudolf's story of his and Angelina's bohemian existence in Rome speaks both of the allure of male costume for the female wearer and of its infectious effects on female behavior. Having first adopted male dress for pragmatic reasons, in order to pass unrecognized on the illicit journey, Angelina learns to relish the transgressive potential of gender play, of her "Spiel der Sinnlichkeit" (game of sensuality):

"Wir führten einen gar wunderlichen, ziemlich unordentlichen Haushalt mit-einander, denn Angelina gewöhnte sich sehr bald an das freie, sorglose

Künstlerwesen. Sie hatte, gleich als wir ans Land stiegen, Mannskleider anlegen müssen, um nicht erkannt zu werden, und ich gab sie so für meinen Vetter
aus. Die Tracht, in der sie mich nun auch frei auf allen Spaziergängen beglei-
tete, stand ihr sehr niedlich, sie sah oft aus wie Correggios Bogenschütz. . . .
Indes entging es mir nicht, daß Angelina anfing, mit der Mädchentracht nach
und nach auch ihr mädchenhaftes, bei aller Liebe verschämtes Wesen abzule-
gen, sie wurde in Worten und Gebärden kecker, und ihre sonst so schüchternen
Augen schweiften lüstern rechts und links. Ja, es geschah wohl manchmal,
wenn ich sie unter lustige Gesellen mitnahm, mit denen wir in einem Garten
oft die Nacht durchschwärmten, daß sie sich berauschte, wo sie dann mit den
furchtsam dreisten Mienen und glänzend schmachtenden Augen ein ungemein
reizendes Spiel der Sinnlichkeit gab."

"We kept house together in quite a strange and chaotic fashion, since Angelina
had quickly become accustomed to the carefree artistic life. As soon as we
landed she had had to don men's clothing so as to pass unrecognized, and I
introduced her as my cousin. In this costume she was able to accompany me
freely whenever I went out, and it made her look so sweet, like Correggio's
archer. . . . Nevertheless, it didn't escape my attention that when Angelina put
to one side her girl's clothing she also began to lose her girlish character, her
blushing demureness—her actions and words became bolder, and her eyes,
normally so timid, roved around lasciviously. Yes, sometimes when I took
her out with my fun-loving friends for one of our nights on the town, she got
drunk, and then, with her fearfully bold demeanor and her shining, languishing
eyes, she presented an incredibly alluring game of sensuality." (271)

It would appear that desire is generated in the male viewers as a direct
result of Angelina's sexual ambiguity; she, too, takes on the appearance of
an androgynous cherub and engages in a giddying gender performance. In it,
seemingly polar and gender-specific traits, "furchtsam dreiste Mienen" (her
fearfully bold demeanor) and "glänzend schmachtende Augen" (her shining,
languid eyes), oscillate in one person, producing a seductive spectacle of
polymorphous sensuality.[13]

Perhaps the most intriguing example of such sexual shape-shifting
in *Ahnung und Gegenwart* is the androgynous child Erwin, who—rather
logically—is revealed as the daughter of yet another transvestite female,
Angelina. That Eichendorff was borrowing another major element from
Goethe's *Wilhelm Meister* was soon pointed out by his friend Loeben, who
expressed some dissatisfaction with the literary results: "Erwin ist eine
Mignon, interessiert aber nicht wie dieser." (Erwin is a Mignon, but not
as interesting).[14] Certainly, many aspects of Erwin's story and personality
seem to owe their existence to sustained literary citation. Aptly enough for a
romantic descendant of Goethe's androgyne, she is a sartorial quotation. With
her dark curling hair and fiery black eyes, her appearance echoes Mignon's,

and even her exotic theatrical costume, a blue Spanish doublet, duplicates
that of her literary cousin (77). Like Goethe's Mignon, the child is linked
with the imaginary realm, expressing herself fully only in song; Leontin
characterizes her, for example, as "eine wunderbare Laute aus alter Zeit, die
jetzt niemand mehr zu spielen verstehe" (a wonderful lute from days gone by,
which no one knows how to play any longer [36]).[15] She arrives at Friedrich's
side in mysterious circumstances and declares, like Mignon, eternal devotion
to her new master. Like the self-enclosed, almost autistic Mignon, Erwin is
the personification of enigma: "Er war allen unbegreiflich . . . er [mischte]
sich in keine Geschäfte oder Lust der anderen, erschien zerstreut, immer
fremd, verschlossen und fast hart, so lieblich weich auch seine helle Stimme
klang." (He was a mystery to all of them . . . he never joined in the affairs or
diversions of the others, always appeared distracted, eternally alien, reserved,
and almost hard, however gentle and soft his silvery voice seemed to be [35].)
An androgynous being, she is volatile, kinetic, oscillating endlessly between
male and female. As she urges Friedrich to quit the city for the liminal realm
of the forest, Erwin's embraces display the erotic fever of Mignon's highly
charged encounter with Wilhelm:

> Friedrich küßte den begeisterten Knaben auf die Stirn. Da fiel er ihm um den
> Hals und küßte ihn heftig, mit beiden Armen ihn fest umklammernd. Voll
> Erstaunen machte sich Friedrich nur mit Mühe aus seinen Armen los, es war
> etwas ungewöhnlich Verändertes in seinem Gesichte, eine seltsame Lust in
> seinen Küssen, seine Lippen brannten, das Herz schlug fast hörbar, er hatte
> ihn noch niemals so gesehen.

> Friedrich kissed the emotional boy on the forehead. Then the boy embraced
> him and kissed him ardently, holding him fast in his arms. Friedrich, caught
> completely unawares, struggled out of his arms. There was something different
> in his face, a strange desire in his kisses, his lips were burning, he could almost
> hear his heart beating, he had never seen him like this. (174)

With the progression of the novel, Erwin, like Mignon, seems to
consume herself, "sich zu verzehren" (175). If Mignon manages to conceal
her true sex even from the surgeon who tends her wounds, Erwin, too,
displays an almost pathological fear of doctors, an anxiety similarly related
to the clinical uncovering of "authentic" gender (178). The reader learns
that Julie, like Natalie in the *Lehrjahre,* attempts to mold her charge into the
correct gender role. Tellingly, this pedagogical venture relies on marking
Erwin with a properly feminine name and clothing, blocking access to the
perilous imaginary realm and "baptizing" her in the symbolic order, or, as the
narrator puts it, in "gemeingültige Prosa" (ordinary prose). As I have been

stressing throughout, however, the androgyne, with its dyadic oscillation
between masculinity and femininity, properly belongs to the pre-oedipal
sphere of the imaginary and indeed cannot survive in the triangulated world
of *Bildung* and socialization.[16] The novel emphasizes that the child Erwin has
a horror of being confined within the four walls of a human habitation, and
also that—like Mignon—she proves resistant to conventional *Bildung* (176).
It comes as no surprise, then, that the results of pedagogical intervention, as
in Mignon's case, are fatal:

> "Julie bot alles auf, sie zu retten. Sie nannte sie Erwine, gab ihr Frauen-
> zimmerkleider, suchte überhaupt alles erinnernde Phantastische aus ihrer
> Lebensweise zu entfernen und taufte sie so, nach dem gewöhnlichen Verfahren
> in solchen Fällen, in gemeingültige Prosa. Das Mädchen wurde dadurch auch
> stiller, aber es war eine wahre Grabesstille, von der sie sich nur manchmal in
> Gesange wieder zu erholen schien."

> "Julie tried everything she could to save her. She called her Erwine, gave her
> women's clothing, attempted to banish anything reminiscent of the fantastic
> from her life, and therefore baptized her, in the standard way for such cases,
> in ordinary prose. The girl did become calmer as a result, but it was truly a
> sepulchral calm, from which she only seemed to emerge occasionally, through
> song." (244)

It is also in the figure of Erwin, as in Goethe's Mignon, that the
reader may locate the most obvious intersection between transvestism and
androgyny.[17] Both adolescents are linked, through botanical metaphors, to
androgynous flowers. Mignon carries a white lily in her hands during her
staging of self as an androgynous angel, and her father uses precisely the
dual-sexed nature of this flower as a biblical analogy justifying incestuous
union.[18] *(Ahnung und Gegenwart,* while not foregrounding a story of incestuous origins, does eventually uncover such forbidden desires: Rudolf reveals
to a deeply shaken Friedrich that Erwin is none other than his daughter, and
thus Friedrich's niece [276].) In the case of Erwin, the botanical connection
is so carefully set up by the novel as to seem almost overdetermined, as for
example in the following description of her physical appearance. At least one
critic has viewed Erwin, as she is represented in this scene, as the human
incarnation of the focal romantic metaphor of androgyny, Novalis's blue
flower, or "blaue Blume":[19]

> Eine Art von spanischem Wams nämlich, himmelblau mit goldenen Kettchen,
> umschloß den schlanken Körper des Knaben. Den weißen Hals trug er bloß, ein
> zierlicher Kragen umgab den schönen Kopf, der mit seinen dunklen Locken
> und schwarzen Augen wie eine Blume über dem bunten Schmucke ruhte.

The boy's slim body was sheathed in a kind of Spanish doublet, sky-blue with gold chains. His pale neck was bare, and his beautiful face was framed by a delicate collar, so that his head, with its dark ringlets and black eyes, was poised like a flower above the exotic apparel. (77)

While Novalis's novel *Heinrich von Ofterdingen* is shot through with the mystical and alchemical tradition of androgynous flower imagery, it is Klingsohr's Märchen that most vividly illustrates the botanical analogy: cradled within a floating blossom, Eros and his beloved Freya embrace, and in this paradisiacal state of heterosexual union they, in turn, resemble a single androgynous flower.[20] Like *Wilhelm Meisters Lehrjahre, Ahnung und Gegenwart,* however, presents an androgyne bound for death. The image of Erwin as an androgynous flower resonates tragically when, after her death, the narrator comments on her resemblance to "eine abgebrochene Blume" (an uprooted flower [243]).

The intriguing common denominator of these scenes of androgyny and/or transvestism is, I stress once again, that each seems to be the exclusive domain of Eichendorff's female characters. Marjorie Garber, however, in her book on cross-dressing, cogently makes a case for investigating the transvestite body *as such,* independently of gender:

> It is curious to note how many literary and cultural critics have recently studied the phenomenon of cross-dressing in literature from the Renaissance to high modernism. The appeal of cross-dressing is clearly related to its status as a sign of the constructedness of gender categories. But the tendency on the part of many critics has been to look *through* rather than *at* the cross-dresser, to turn away from a close encounter with the transvestite, and to want instead to subsume that figure within one of the two traditional genders. To elide and erase— or to *appropriate* the transvestite for particular political and critical aims.

Citing Sandra Gilbert and Susan Gubar, who in their work on modernism describe transvestism as an aptly feminine aesthetic strategy, and playing their findings against Stephen Greenblatt's emphasis on the cross-dressing "boy" of Renaissance drama, Garber's critique begins with a refusal to allow the transvestite to slip into one or the other of the simple gender binarisms. The "thirdness" of transvestism is not *a* sex, she argues, but rather "a mode of articulation, a way of describing a space of possibility."[21] Yet to look at, rather than through, Eichendorff's transvestites is precisely to be confronted with "gendered" transvestism, with an activity encoded by all of Eichendorff's texts as feminine. In *Ahnung und Gegenwart,* as the *Historisch-Kritische Ausgabe* notes (vol. 3: 391), all of the principal female characters engage in cross-dressing on at least one occasion; not one of the male characters does. To be sure, the reader will occasionally encounter a stray male in Eichendorff's works who is associated with transvestism. Like the capricious Friedrich in Goethe's *Wilhelm Meisters Lehrjahre,* the only character in that novel to survive gender gaming unscathed, Eichendorff's Taugenichts generates a pantomime of mistaken gender identity. Significantly, however, neither boy actually engages in cross-dressing; the twist in the male transvestite plot is that they are *mistakenly* read as cross-dressers and, to confuse matters still further, as *female* cross-dressers. In other words, transvestism, in the narratives I am considering, is posited as a one-sidedly feminine strategy. The unsuspecting Taugenichts finds himself misread as the transvestite young noblewoman Flora, and he is even subjected to a passionate barrage of "Idio und cuore und amore und furore!" by a would-be lover. In this scene, the illegibility of gender that provokes the suitor's declarations is neatly paralleled by the comic linguistic impenetrability of the speech; the woefully undereducated Taugenichts, in his turn, understands no Italian. Yet what on the face of it seems like a lighthearted interlude can quickly turn sinister, and the Taugenichts relates his experience of mistaken gender identity as sexually disorienting and threatening: "Als er aber am Ende gar anfing, auf beiden Knien schnell und immer näher auf mich zuzurutschen, da wurde mir auf einmal ganz grauslich." (When he ended up actually falling to his knees and slithering up closer and closer to me, I was overcome by a sudden dread [vol. 2: 398].)

If for Eichendorff transvestism is a peculiarly feminine pursuit, it is also an unsettling, even terrifying phenomenon for the male character who comes into contact with it. In his recollections of artistic life in Halle and Heidelberg, Eichendorff reproduces almost verbatim a passage from *Ahnung und Gegenwart* describing a scene of shallow salon life which he considers of some critical import: "dieses Treiben [ist] insofern von literarhistorischer Wichtigkeit, als dasselbe den schmählichen Verfall der Romantik vorzüglich verschuldet hat" (this spectacle is of literary-historical significance in that it successfully hastened the ignominious decline of romanticism).[22] Tellingly, the centerpiece of this "degraded" social scene is the performance of a dance by a cross-dressing little girl who seems to be a perfect replica of Goethe's Mignon. Once again, the transvestite appears as a marker of what Garber terms category crisis, in this case a category crisis pertaining to romanticism itself:

> Es hatte sich unterdes ein niedliches, etwa zehnjähriges Mädchen eingefunden, die in einer reizenden Kleidung mit langen Beinkleidern und kurzem schleiernen Röckchen darüber, keck im Zimmer herumsprang. Es war die Tochter vom

Hause. Ein Herr aus der Gesellschaft reichte ihr ein Tamburin, das in einer Ecke auf dem Fußboden gelegen hatte. Alle schlossen bald einen Kreis um sie, und das zierliche Mädchen tanzte mit einer wirklich bewunderungswürdigen Anmut und Geschicklichkeit, während sie das Tamburin auf mannigfache Weise schwang und berührte und ein niedliches italienisches Liedchen dazu sang. Jeder war begeistert, erschöpfte sich in Lobsprüchen und wünschte der Mutter Glück, die sehr zufrieden lächelte. Nur Friedrich schwieg still. Denn einmal war ihm schon die moderne Knabentracht bei Mädchen zuwider, ganz abscheulich aber war ihm diese gottlose Art, unschuldige Kinder durch Eitelkeit zu dressieren. Er fühlte vielmehr eine tiefes Mitleid mit der schönen kleinen Bajadere.

Meanwhile a pretty little girl, about ten years old, had arrived, and she jumped about the room in a charming costume consisting of long trousers with a short diaphanous skirt worn over them. She was the daughter of our hosts. A gentleman in the party handed her a tambourine that had been lying on the floor in a corner of the room. Everyone gathered in a circle around her, and the elfin child danced with a truly wonderful grace and agility, all the time shaking and beating the tambourine with all manner of variations, and singing a pretty little Italian song. All of the audience were charmed, exhausted themselves in complimentary speeches, and congratulated the mother, who wore a contented smile. Only Friedrich was silent. He found the modern fashion for girls to wear boy's clothing detestable enough, but what he found even more loathsome was this ungodly tendency to train innocent children by indulging their vanity. He felt rather sorry for the beautiful little *bayadère*.[23]

The transvestite typically arouses fluctuating emotional responses. As in the case of the other fictional cross-dressers I have examined, the male viewer perceives this transvestite child as "niedlich" (pretty) and "reizend" (charming), but also as pitiful and repulsive. Clearly, the girl has—in Friedrich's eyes, at least—become the victim of defective feminine *Bildung*. Her modishly transvestite dress renders her, most disturbingly of all, excessively sexual, a "Bajadere." The critical moment I identify in this passage is in the association between *dress* and *dressieren* (compare the English *dressage*). Both words, significantly, have common roots in the Old French *drecier,* from the Latin *dirigere,* "to direct."[24] Dressing the child in the clothing appropriate for the opposite sex is tantamount to willful *mis*direction, or to a perversion of "normal" female *Bildung*. That there is a crucial link between costume and *Bildung* is a point repeatedly made by Eichendorff's novel *Ahnung und Gegenwart.* Rudolf's response to Angelina's scandalous transvestism indicates the perils of such behavior: " 'Weiber ertragen solche kühnere Lebensweise nicht.' " ("Women can't take this bolder way of life" [272].) Similarly, in *Die Entführung,* the reader learns that Diana's transgressive masculine behavior is directly attributable to a faulty education: "Schon als Kind elternlos und auf dem abgelegenen Schlosse ihres Vormunds ganz männlich erzogen, soll sie diesen in allen Reiter- und Jagdkünsten sehr bald übertroffen haben." (Even when she was a child, an orphan living in her guardian's remote castle and receiving the education of a boy, she is said to have been quick to outstrip him in riding and hunting skills [vol. 2: 861].)

In *Ahnung und Gegenwart,* it is Romana, both "anziehend und zurück- stoßend" (alluring and repulsive [vol. 2: 135]), who poses the greatest threat, because of her own cross-dressing but also, and importantly, because of her seductive, possibly lesbian influence on her friend Rosa, whose transvestite inclinations she encourages. The novel circles around intimate scenes between the two women, often set in Rosa's dressing room. Romana's transvestism, like Angelina's, is the marker of a perversely transgressive personality. Unlike the Amazons of Goethe's *Wilhelm Meisters Lehrjahre,* Romana is presented as a truly polymorphous being, uniting both an excess of female sexuality and a markedly masculine temperament.[25] Friedrich, for example, is struck in equal measure by her ravishing beauty and by "die fast unweibliche Kühnheit ihrer Gedanken" (the almost unfeminine boldness of her thinking [158]). Her first appearance in the novel is revealing. Romana lures into her clutches Rosa, who, dressed in a fashionably "Amazonian" riding habit, has been traveling in the company of Friedrich and Leontin, her brother: "Zuletzt bat sie [Romana] dieselbe, mit ihr zu fahren. Rosa wollte anfangs nicht, aber die fremde Dame streichelte und küßte sie und schob sie endlich halb mit Gewalt in den Wagen." (In the end she [Romana] invited her to travel with her. To begin with, Rosa was reluctant to do so, but the unknown lady caressed and kissed her, and then bundled her almost violently into the carriage [61].) Leontin instantly recognizes this stranger as Romana: " 'Eine junge, reiche Witwe, . . . die nicht weiß, was sie mit ihrer Schönheit und ihrem Geiste anfangen soll, eine Freundin meiner Schwester, weil sie mit ihr spielen kann, wie sie will, eine tollgewordene Genialität, die in die Männlichkeit hineinpfuscht.' " ("A wealthy young widow . . . who doesn't know what to do with her beauty and her intellect, a friend of my sister, because she can wind her around her little finger, a genius who has confounded herself with the masculine world and gone mad" [62].) In other words, what makes this female transvestite particularly suspect is precisely her encroachment into the properly male domain of *Bildung;* she resists male attempts to educate her, while undertaking the project of *Bildung* on another female character, Rosa. Romana's masculine attributes also render her extremely threatening in the eyes of the male characters in Eichendorff's novel. Not only does she appropriate men's clothing, but on several occasions the reader witnesses her brandishing a "Flinte," or flintlock gun. Once she turns it against Friedrich (223); ultimately, she uses it against herself, and the novel reports that she dies with "das Gewehr, wie ihren letzten Freund, noch fest in der Hand" (the gun still clutched in her hand, as if it were her best friend [224]). Given the common nineteenth-century slang usage of *Flinte,* Friedrich is surely being presented with an image of terrifying phallic potency, with Romana as the incarnation of the castrating woman.[26]

Romana's incursions into the world of "Genialität" and poetry also threaten "natural" gender binarisms, certainly as Eichendorff himself viewed them.[27] She consciously situates herself in a literary genealogy of female subversives, citing Tasso's belligerent sorceress Armida, from *Gerusalemme liberata,* as her progenitrix (205). As an individual who oscillates apparently at will between gender polarities, the polymorphous Romana's association with the imaginary realm follows the logic of the androgyne. Significantly, however, even Romana's attempts to domesticate her desires, to provide for herself, however belatedly, a suitable feminine *Bildung,* fail precisely because they are composed of literary fictions: "Sie mochte sich stellen, wie sie wollte, sie konnte . . . ihre ganze Bekehrungsgeschichte wie ein wohlgeschriebenes Gedicht, Vers vor Vers, inwendig vorauslesen, und der Teufel saß gegenüber und lachte ihr dabei immerfort ins Gesicht." (She could play any role she wanted, she could . . . recite at will, verse by verse, the whole story of her conversion, like a well-wrought poem, and the devil was sitting opposite her the whole time laughing in her face [188].) Even her repentant letters to society intimates are misinterpreted by them as literary sketches for an edifying novel. The themes of Romana's songs are in themselves transgressive, mirroring the transgressive nature of poetry making. Her song "Frische Fahrt" (Joyful Journey), for example, expresses her powerful longing, as a young woman, to escape from the limiting confines of her mother's carefully cultivated garden. What attracts her is forest wilderness, "das Wirren bunt und bunter" (gay confusion), in which, as I showed above, all boundaries seem to dissolve, most notably those of gender. In this setting, too, the contours of Romana's own identity seem endlessly fluid: " 'Und ich mag mich nicht bewahren!' " ("And I will not preserve myself!" [124].)[28] Importantly, Romana's vain struggle to reform is coupled with gestures that seek to reimpose domestic boundaries: the doors and windows of her castle, which have stood permanently open, she now orders shut (188).

From the vantage point of 1847, Eichendorff was to reflect with considerable acerbity on the salon culture that had flourished in the romantic period and that had owed so much to the contributions of literary women.

But Eichendorff in this late essay identifies the decadence that he believed had overcome the movement, incarnated in *Erlebtes* in the figure of the cross-dressing girl, with any form of feminine poetic endeavor. Once again, female transvestism represents both aesthetic and political crisis: "Es ist die Zeit der *Massen,* die sich die Formeln abgemerkt und nun ihrerseits die Sturm- oder Drang-Periode der Genies nachmachen. Und in diesem Bildungsfieber, das epidemisch alle ergriffen, ist denn auch die Poesie, mehr als jemals, unter die Weiber gekommen." (This is the era of the *masses,* who have learned the formulas and who now imitate for themselves the Storm and Stress period of genius. And with this feverish self-cultivation that has gripped everyone in an epidemic, poetry has got among women.)[29] Arguing the familiar late-eighteenth-century theory of strict gender complementarity, Eichendorff—echoing, among others, Schiller's earlier anxiety about androgyny—observes that "ein Mannweib ist überall ebenso lächerlich als ein weibischer Mann" (a mannish woman is everywhere as laughable as an effeminate man).[30] He concludes that poetry is a pursuit utterly unsuitable for women, whose "natural" domain is the domestic sphere: "so steht eine dichtende Frau allerdings schon an den äußersten Grenzen ihres natürlichen Berufes" (so a woman who writes poetry is already at the extreme limit of her natural vocation).[31] As an example of such an unnaturally androgynous creature, he chooses Bettina Brentano, "eine . . . anomale Erscheinung" (an anomaly), whose poetic works he finds deeply deficient: "Denn wo sie in ernsten, und namentlich in religiösen oder politischen Dingen, den Männern ins Handwerk pfuscht, ist sie durchaus ungenügend, weil unklar und phantastisch." (For where she has confounded herself with affairs proper to men, namely with religious or political matters, she's quite inadequate, because of her lack of clarity and her fancifulness.)[32] Tellingly, the *Historisch-Kritische Ausgabe* identifies the mannish Bettina Brentano as the model for Romana.[33] Whatever his exact sources may have been, it is certainly obvious that Eichendorff once again identifies the transvestite female body as the site of a category crisis, of an aesthetic crisis involving the very nature of romanticism. Theorizing gender becomes a way of talking about aesthetic theory. Romana's name already links her with a certain kind of decadent "Romantik," with a pagan, anarchic version of romanticism that stands in direct contrast to Friedrich's—and Eichendorff's own—Catholic aesthetic.[34] Eichendorff's principal target here is doubtless the Grecophile Friedrich Schlegel, who in his celebrated novel of androgyny, *Lucinde,* presented a scintillating example of aesthetic and sexual chaos. In the opening pages, the hero, Julius, willfully interrupts his own narrative to announce: "daß ich gleich anfangs das was wir Ordnung nennen vernichte . . . und mir das Recht einer reizenden

Verwirrung deutlich zueigne und durch die Tat behaupte." (No purpose, however, is more purposeful for myself and for this work . . . than to destroy at the very outset all that part that we call "order," remove it, and claim explicitly and affirm actually the right to a charming confusion.)[35] Significantly, *Ahnung und Gegenwart* reveals the core identity of the transvestite Romana as an "entsetzliche Lücke" (hideous lacuna), the very center of her being as "Lügenhaftigkeit" (mendacity [187]). Transvestism, for Eichendorff, marks an unsettling shifting of meaning, even the complete destabilization or absence of meaning; at the same time, Romana's unbridled "Phantastarei" (fantasy [187]) signals a historical rupture, that of moral and aesthetic crisis.[36]

If transvestism is the scandalous outcome of defective female *Bildung,* paradoxically it also has everything to do with the successful progress of Eichendorff's *Bildungshelden* toward maturation, from blindness to insight.[37] The heroes of Eichendorff's narratives find themselves engaged in a struggle to decipher the universe, and the decoding of gender and costume that is such a compulsion in this fictional universe provides the focus for the larger hermeneutical task. Inevitably, however, the world refuses to yield easily to interpretative efforts; category confusion reigns in the chaos of the natural world, as I have shown, but also in the hypercivilized domain of the court, where Eichendorff's hero is confronted with a sophisticated language of masquerade that he finds impenetrable and disturbing.[38] Friedrich's personal experience of masquerade, in *Ahnung und Gegenwart,* is worth looking at in some detail. In this passage, Friedrich himself has just been coerced into donning carnivalesque disguise, and he enters the masked ball desperate to find Rosa:

> Er ging ins Haus hinein, versah sich mit einem Domino und einer Larve, und hoffte seine Rosa noch heute in dem Getümmel herauszufinden. Geblendet trat er aus der stillen Nacht in den plötzlichen Schwall von Tönen, Lichtern und Stimmen, der wie ein Zaubermeer mit rastlos beweglichen, klingenden Wogen über ihm zusammenschlug. Zwei große, hohe Säle, nur leicht voneinander geschieden, eröffneten die unermeßlichste Aussicht. Er stellte sich in das Bogentor zwischen beide, wo die doppelten Musikchöre aus beiden Sälen verworren ineinanderklangen. Zu beiden Seiten toste der seltsame, lustige Markt, fröhliche, reizende und ernste Bilder des Lebens zogen wechselnd vorüber, Girlanden von Lampen schmückten die Wände, unzählige Spiegel dazwischen spielten das Leben ins Unendliche, so daß man die Gestalten mit ihrem Widerspiel verwechselte, und das Auge verwirrt in der grenzenlosen Ferne dieser Aussicht, sich verlor. Ihn schauderte mitten unter diesen Larven. Er stürzte sich selber mit in das Gewimmel, wo es am dichtesten war.

> He entered the building, donned a domino cloak and a mask, and set out with the hope that he would still find his Rosa that day somewhere in the crowd.

Dazzled, he stepped from the peaceful night into a sudden flood of noises, lights, and voices, which engulfed him like an enchanted ocean in its restless, agitated, booming waves. An immense panorama was opened up by two almost identical rooms, large and high-ceilinged. He stood in the archway between the two spaces, where the twin orchestras from the two ballrooms competed with each other in utter confusion. On each side of him the party raged, uproarious and bizarre; images passed in quick succession, carefree, then charming, then solemn; the walls were festooned with lanterns; innumerable mirrors created endless reflections of life, so that human forms became confused with their images in the glass and the eye lost itself, bewildered by the boundless panorama. He shuddered at the sight of the masks. He hurled himself into the densest point of the milling human mass. (113)

Dualities underpin the structure of this passage: there are two almost identical halls, two competing orchestras, the text stresses doubleness with its litany of "zwei," "beide," "doppelt" (two, both, twin). Friedrich finds himself in an unsettling and precarious position of absolute inbetweenness, occupying as he does the arched doorway located exactly between the two ballrooms. Gradually, however, the binary oppositions upon which the text has insisted crumble into a state of absolute chaos, and reality and simulation are dizzyingly conflated in the play of mirrors and reflections. Friedrich's failure to recognize Rosa among the throng of masked revelers is closely connected, I would argue, with his chronic inability to make legible the language of transvestism, a language that disrupts, and thereby also denies, easy binaries.

If we turn once again to his relationship with the androgynous Erwin, the stress on Friedrich's utter blindness to the truth is apparent. In this respect, Eichendorff's novelistic treatment of Erwin differs emphatically from Goethe's structuring of the sexually ambiguous Mignon. In Goethe's novel, Mignon is presented throughout as sexually fluid, from her initial confusing appearance before Wilhelm's gaze to the narrator's strategic, shifting use of masculine, feminine, and neuter pronouns. Even in the angelic performance staged by the pedagogically minded Natalie, Mignon eludes the "correct" feminine role that the performance is supposed to "engender," and plays her own utopian vision of self, a transcendent, sexless being. At the same time, however, and paradoxically as it may seem, neither Wilhelm Meister nor the reader ever lingers more than momentarily over Mignon's, or over the other transvestite women's, "correct" biological gender. It might be argued that the confusion present in Goethe's novel lies exactly in the gap between biology and self-construction. In *Ahnung und Gegenwart,* by contrast, Friedrich all too successfully represses Erwin's sexual ambiguity, apparently never for a single instant questioning the male gender of his pageboy. (This despite the fact that he first sees Erwin in her "authentic" role as a girl.) Toward the end of the novel, it is true, Friedrich quite literally uncovers the truth, but only after Erwin has suffered a deadly seizure:

> Friedrich, außer sich, stürzte über ihn her und öffnete schnell sein Wams, denn es war dieselbe phantastische Kleidung, die der Knabe sonst auf dem Schlosse des Herrn v. A. getragen hatte. Wie sehr erschrak und erstaunte er, als ihm da der schönste Mädchenbusen entgegenschwoll, noch warm, aber nicht mehr schlagend.—Er blieb wie eingewurzelt auf seinen Knien und starrte dem Mädchen in das stille Gesicht, als hätte er es noch nie vorher gesehn.

> The distraught Friedrich rushed to his aid and quickly undid his doublet—for it was the same fantastic costume that the boy had previously worn at the castle of Herr von A. He was overcome with alarm and amazement when he saw beneath him the most gorgeous, blooming female bosom, still warm—but the heart had stopped beating. Unable to rise to his feet, he stared into the girl's serene face as if seeing it for the first time. (242)

It is this shocking revelation that seems to trigger, for the first time in the novel, a confusing pronominal uncertainty. But if this critical scene is considered more carefully, the reader might detect that the narrator's shifting use of pronouns is actually structured quite logically, beginning as it does with a pronoun reflecting Erwin's adopted male gender, continuing with a neuter noun, and concluding with a pronoun that corresponds to biological truth: "In stummer Geschäftigkeit, ohne sich wechselseitig zu erklären, waren alle nur bemüht, *ihn* ins Leben zurückzurufen—aber alles blieb vergebens, *das schöne, seltsame Mädchen* war tot. Julie hatte *sie* trostlos vor sich auf dem Schoße liegen." (With a quiet zealousness, and without explaining their actions to one another, they all endeavored to bring *him* back to life—but all was in vain, for the *strange beautiful girl* was dead. The inconsolable Julie held *her* on her lap [242; my emphasis].) Significantly, too, Julie's pedagogical efforts to instill correct feminine behavior into the child, and the awareness of Friedrich's friends of Erwin's true sex, are revealed to Friedrich—and to the reader—only after her death. A few pages on from the death scene, the narrator suddenly, and without commentary, redesignates "Erwin" as "Erwine" (247). And yet the slipperiness of the transvestite continues to subvert stable categories; just when the text seems to have assigned to the child an appropriate feminine version of her name, her self-production as a male reasserts itself, and she is referred to once again as "Erwin" (263). I would stress here Friedrich's utter entrapment as a viewer in the simulacra generated by transvestite performance, even what Foucault might term his "will to nonknowledge" regarding the truth of sex and of his own desire,[39] but also our own and very real entanglement, as readers, in the narrative's play of appearance and reality, "Schein" and "Sein." During his forest adventures with the mysterious pair of huntsmen, for example, Friedrich remains oblivious to their real sex. Introduced as "Jägerburschen" (huntsmen [180]), Rosa and Romana encounter Leontin and Friedrich at nightfall, the time of day when contours are naturally dissolving, "so daß sie einander nicht wohl erkennen konnten" (so that they could barely recognize one another [183]). At this point, the novel begins to scatter tantalizing clues to the huntsmen's true identity: "Die Bäume hingen voll heller Tropfen, der enge Fußsteig war durch den Regen äußerst glatt geworden. Die beiden Jäger gingen sehr vorsichtig und furchtsam, hielten sich an alle Sträucher und glitten mehrere Male bald Friedrich, bald Leontin in die Arme." (The trees glittered with raindrops, and the narrow footpath had become extremely slippery because of the rain. The two huntsmen walked with extreme care and caution, clinging on to branches as they went, and more than once they slithered into Friedrich's or Leontin's arms [183].) Is this gingerly descent—a deliberately clichéd representation of feminine behavior, as one critic has suggested—an immediate giveaway of their gender? Or do the dripping branches evoke forbidden erotic desire, the spectral possibility of sexual union between the disguised women?[40] Friedrich and Leontin certainly remain impervious to the hints, even when Romana breaks into Leontin's song and takes on the role of the Lorelei, the personification of feminine evil: "O flieh! du weißt nicht, wer ich bin." ("Flee, for you know not who I am!" [184].) Still later, we hear that the two huntsmen are physically appealing to Friedrich and Leontin, albeit in a boyish sense: "Sie waren gar lieblich anzusehen, schienen beide noch Knaben." (They were utterly charming in appearance, both still boys [186].) And, finally, Leontin comes comically close to discovering the truth when he asks Rosa to play a tune on her horn: "er [Rosa] versicherte aber, daß er es nicht könne. Leontin lachte ihn aus, was sie für Jäger wären." (But he [Rosa] protested that he didn't know how. Leontin teased him, asking him what kind of huntsmen that made them [186].) Whatever our suspicions may be by this point, it is left to Erwin, herself a cross-dresser, to identify conclusively another transvestite, when a flash of lightning illuminates Rosa's face for a split second and Erwin flees in horror; but still the novel leaves Friedrich and Leontin oblivious to the truth.

Earlier in this discussion of gender illegibility, I posited the progress of Eichendorff's heroes as one from blindness to insight. Now I would like to revise that claim somewhat, in order to stress the revelatory nature of Eichendorff's narrative endings: it is not so much that the hero achieves insight as a result of his own intellectual and emotional growth but rather that the narrative orchestrates an experience of disclosure, imposes a final, and authoritarian, pedagogical turn. These are less narratives of *Bildung* than they are narratives of Christian "Erlösung," of epiphany and redemption. Indeed, this has been described as a process of "*Entbilden*"—both in the sense of anti-*Bildung* and in the sense that Eichendorff's heroes proceed through a bewildering world of images ("Bilder") to a divine, transcendent image or "Ur-Bild."[41] The literary use of transvestism and androgyny, as I have been arguing, need not automatically be a radical gesture. Here in Eichendorff's works, rather, the formal unveiling of transvestism may be read as a deeply conservative tactic, as the key strategic move for an ideologue of political and religious restoration. Making the ambiguous body legible serves, in fact, to confirm the most conservative conviction that gender identity should correspond with biological fact. Nor is it an accident that the uncovering of correct gender may coincide also with the uncovering of correct class; the Taugenichts's reassuring discovery of Flora's female identity is coupled with the miraculous revelation that the "schöne Gräfin," the unattainable aristocratic woman of his dreams, actually shares his own humble origins and is thus an eminently suitable marriage partner.[42] With such a dual disclosure, then, an idyll of restoration is complete: "und es war alles, alles gut" (and everything ended happily ever after [434]). Similarly, the political and social chaos of the French Revolution is inscribed by Eichendorff on the body of the female transvestite Gabriele in *Das Schloß Dürande*. Gabriele cross-dresses in order to overcome the barriers of social class that have separated her from her aristocratic lover. In the case of this novella, however, disclosure of gender—as well as of class—comes too late to avert tragedy, both for the aristocracy and for the peasantry, and the narrative ends with an admonition to the reader against boundary transgression: "Du aber hüte dich, das wilde Tier zu wecken in der Brust, daß es nicht plötzlich ausbricht und dich selbst zerreißt." (Beware of arousing the wild animal in your breast, so that it doesn't break loose and tear you to pieces [*Neue Gesamtausgabe*, vol. 2: 849].)

As I have been arguing, Eichendorff's narratives tend to proceed from a deliberate blurring of binaries, figured in the transvestite female, to a flourishing gesture that reveals the "truth" of the relationship between costume and the body underneath. It is an attempt, after the event, to impose rigidity and clarity on the sexual/textual chaos described by early romantic writers such as Friedrich Schlegel. Eichendorff's heroes emerge from a bewildering twilight state of liminality into the clear light of day, and experience an epiphany directly related to this final illumination of gender. As I showed earlier, the shadowy forest world provides the setting for many

heroic peregrinations, but it is important to highlight the contrast between
the trompe l'oeil effects experienced in that realm and the light that floods
Eichendorff's narrative endings. Friedrich's final monologue in *Ahnung
und Gegenwart* calls for an end to apocalyptic category confusion: "Mir
scheint unsre Zeit dieser weiten, ungewissen Dämmerung zu gleichen! Licht
und Schatten ringen noch ungeschieden in wunderbaren Massen gewaltig
miteinander." (To me, the age we live in is like this boundless, uncertain
twilight. Fantastic masses of light and dark are still furiously wrestling with
one another, inseparable [vol. 2: 302].) Significantly, the return to clarity is
linked in Friedrich's speech with a stripping away of masks. Also in *Ahnung
und Gegenwart,* Angelina's song of wandering in the murky depths of the
forest has clearly tragic implications:

> "Es lockt so tief, es lockt so fein
> Durchs dunkelgrüne Haus,
> Der Jäger irrt und irrt allein,
> Findt nimmermehr heraus."

> "He is lured so deep, with such cunning,
> Into the dark green canopy,
> The hunter errs, and errs alone,
> And never finds his way out." (273)

Compare this with the magnificent sunrise that closes the novel, or with
the reassuring rays of light that accompany the revelation of Bianka's true
gender in *Das Marmorbild.* Moments later, in that novella, Bianka and Florio
ride off together to greet the morning sun: "Der zierliche Knabe . . . hatte
unterdes auch, wie Blumen vor den ersten Morgenstrahlen, das Köpfchen
erhoben. —Da erkannte Florio mit Erstaunen Fräulein Bianka. . . . Eine
seltsame Verblendung hatte bisher seine Augen wie mit einem Zaubernebel
umfangen. (Meanwhile the delicate boy had lifted his head like a flower at
the first rays of morning sun. That was when an astonished Florio recognized
Miss Bianka. Until that moment a strange blindness had enveloped his eyes,
like a magical mist [vol. 2: 345].)

Das Marmorbild provides an instructive example of Eichendorff's
narrative motion from category blurring to category reconstruction. Critical
readings have themselves repeatedly stressed binary structures, dividing up
the entire inventory of the novella, its characters, settings, and plot sequences,
strictly according to the antithesis between the sensual, pagan Venus statue
and the virginal, Christian Bianka.[43] Following the lead of recent discourse-
oriented scholarship, however, I would prefer to emphasize instead the

structural fluidity of these seemingly inviolable binary oppositions.[44] Eichendorff's novella insists from the outset on evoking an atmosphere of precarious indeterminacy. If *Das Marmorbild* culminates in a glorious sunrise, in
"klare Luft" (clear air [346]), and celebrates the morning as "kerngesund"
(wholesome [319]), it opens, tellingly, with Florio's twilight wanderings
through the streets of Lucca. Florio finds himself carried along by a stream
of promenading townspeople, in a bewildering, eroticized scene of trompe
l'oeil dominated by effects of "schimmern," "Bewegung," "schweben,"
"funkeln," "ewig wechselnde Bilder," "Verwirrung" (shimmering, movement, hovering, sparkling, endlessly shifting images, confusion [308–11]).
The sinister Donati, who makes his first appearance long after sunset, is
sinister precisely because of his volatility, his polymorphousness:

> "Gott sei Dank," rief Fortunato aus, "daß ihn die Nacht wieder verschlungen
> hat! Kam er mir doch wahrhaftig vor, wie einer von den falben, ungestalten
> Nachtschmetterlingen, die, wie aus einem phantastischem Traume entflogen,
> durch die Dämmerung schwirren und mit ihrem langen Katzenbarte und
> gräßlich großen Augen ordentlich ein Gesicht haben wollen."

> "Thank God!" cried Fortunato, "that he's been swallowed up by the night
> again. He really did remind me of one of those dun, deformed moths that
> buzzes through the gloaming as if the product of some fantastic dream, and
> that looks as though it has a real human face, with its long whiskers and huge,
> gruesome eyes." (315)

It is important to note, however, that Fortunato, too, "der klare Sänger"
(the pure singer [326]) whom critics have conventionally opposed antithet-
ically to the diabolical Donati, himself stages a masquerade; but it is to
pedagogical effect, since Florio finds himself plunged by it into an interpretative struggle to distinguish the two women who hold such erotic powers
over him. The impact on Florio is predictably bewildering, indeed uncanny,
as he discovers himself to be incapable of perceptual decision making:

> viele waren maskiert und gaben unwillkürlich durch ihre wunderliche Er-
> scheinung dem anmutigen Spiele oft plötzlich eine tiefe, fast schauerliche Be-
> deutung. . . . Verwundert durchstrich nun der letztere [Florio] die rauschende
> Menge. Was er heimlich gehofft, fand er nirgends, und er machte sich beinah
> Vorwürfe, dem fröhlichen Fortunato so leichtsinnig auf dieses Meer von Lust
> gefolgt zu sein. . . . Sorglos umspülten indes die losen Wellen, schmeich-
> lerisch neckend, den Gedankenvollen und tauschten ihm unmerklich die
> Gedanken aus. . . . Die vielen Lichter warfen einen zauberischen Schein zwi-
> schen das zitternde Laub. Die hin und her schweifenden Masken mit ihren
> veränderten, grellen Stimmen und wunderbarem Aufzuge nahmen sich hier
> in der ungwissen Beleuchtung noch viel seltsamer und fast gespenstisch aus.

Many were masked, and their fantastic appearance, without their realizing it, occasionally lent the charming entertainment a sudden, deeper, and almost eerie significance. . . . The latter [Florio] now roamed through the swarms of people in astonishment. Nowhere did he find what he had secretly hoped for, and he almost reproached himself for having followed the merry Fortunato so carelessly into this sea of pleasure. . . . Seductively and teasingly, the volatile waves lapped about the pensive Florio, imperceptibly changing his thoughts. . . . Here in the uncertain light, the many lanterns cast a bewitching light though trembling leaves; and the roaming masks, with their altered, piercing voices and their fantastic get-up, looked still weirder, even ghoulish. (327–28)

Das Marmorbild deliberately frustrates binary-making desires, blurring past and present, nature and artifice, night and day. It does this most thoroughly in its mystification of the opposition between Bianka and Venus. Quite aside from the arguable iconic convertibility of Virgin and Venus images in Western art,[45] the text itself refuses simple polar categories, generating instead a dizzying experience of indeterminacy. Fortunato's masked ball perfectly illustrates this category slippage, with the figure of the feminine "Doppelbild" (328) oscillating endlessly under the viewer's gaze between Virgin and Venus. The identity of this Greek beauty remains a complete enigma to Florio: at one point she is described as "niedlich" (sweet [328]), but during a later encounter she seems puzzlingly "größer, schlanker und edler als vorhin" (taller, slimmer, and more regal than before [331]). One scene might lead the reader to conclude that the classical "schöne Najade" (beautiful naiad) is none other than the incarnation of Venus, and yet this same image frustrates any attempt at interpretation: "Sie hatte die Larve abgenommen und spielte gedankenvoll mit einer Rose in dem schimmernden Wasserspiegel. Schmeichlerisch schweifte der Mondschein über den blendendweißen Nacken auf und nieder, ihr Gesicht konnte er nicht sehen, denn sie hatte ihm den Rücken zugekehrt." (She had removed her mask, and pensively brushed the shimmering surface of the water with a rose. The flattering moonlight roamed across her gleaming white neck, but he could not see her face, for she had turned her back on him [329].) Moments later, and incongruously if this is the predatory Venus, the "schönes Bildchen" (lovely little picture) flees in terror, "wie ein aufgescheuchtes Reh" (like a startled deer [329]). At the same time, if we determine that the timid girl with the modest downturned gaze is none other than Bianka, what do we make of the fact that the mysterious beauty leaps onto a snowy steed and gallops away dramatically into the night? Tellingly, the utterly bewildering experience of the masked ball is prefigured by Florio's glimpse of two vaguely familiar women: "Doch konnte er vor den im Mondesglanze zitternden Blättern und Blüten nichts genau unterscheiden." (But because of the leaves and blossoms trembling in the moonlight, he could distinguish nothing [325].) What is more, even at those moments when we can apparently feel sure about the identity of the female character before us, a certain semantic "contagion" may be observed at play. The adjective "weiß" (white) is insistently applied to both women, suggesting at the same time marmoreal sensuality and virginal purity; Venus is alluded to on several occasions as the goddess of spring, but Bianka, too, is described as "recht wie ein fröhliches Bild des Frühlings anzuschauen" (just like a joyful image of spring [309]); Bianka appears in Greek dress at the masquerade. The flower symbolism surrounding the two female characters suffers its own strange slippage: the rose, clearly an attribute of the erotic Venus figure, is also linked with the chaste Bianka; it is she who hands Florio the flower during the masked ball. But Bianka is herself capable of the sensuality we might expect from the Greek goddess:

> Sie erkannte ihn [Florio] sogleich wieder und saß still und schüchtern da, aber die langen furchtsamen Augenwimpern hüteten nur schlecht die dunkelglühenden Blicke . . . er hatte so herzlich bewegt gesungen und neigte sich nun mit den schönen bittenden Augen so dringend herüber, daß sie es willig geschehen ließ, als er sie schnell auf die roten, heißen Lippen küßte.

> Sitting there, quiet and timid, she recognized him [Florio] immediately, but her long, demure eyelashes did a poor job of concealing her ardent gaze. . . . He had sung so passionately, and his beautiful yearning eyes drew so insistently to hers that she willingly acquiesced when he planted a kiss on her burning red lips. (310)

Such category confusion throughout the novella ultimately yields, however, to a restoration of stability. It can be argued that Fortunato functions pedagogically as an orchestrator both of disorientation and of enlightenment, since his presence also seems to precipitate the critical moment when Bianka's gender is revealed. More than this, immediately before the reassuring revelation of correct gender, Fortunato sings a song that reestablishes a clear binary opposition between the now vanquished pagan Venus and the triumphant Virgin Mary (343). We can also infer that Florio's joyful final song, a poem whose theme is divine "Erkennen" (recognition), is the same hymn sung by Fortunato in order to open Florio's eyes to the perilous wiles of the Venus statue. Salvation and power have everything to do with the discriminative powers of the gaze. As Foucault has suggested, the persistent need in post-Enlightenment discourse to uncover the "true" sex is linked to a desire for totalizing systems. Foucault goes on to describe brilliantly the

nineteenth-century surveillance of sexuality, linking it with a sensualization
of power itself:

> The medical examination, the psychiatric investigation, the pedagogical re-
> port, and family controls may have the over-all and apparent objective of
> saying no to all wayward or unproductive sexualities, but the fact is that
> they function as mechanisms with a double impetus: pleasure and power. The
> pleasure that comes of exercising a power that questions, monitors, watches,
> spies, searches out, palpates, brings to light; and on the other hand, the pleasure
> that kindles at having to evade this power, flee from it, fool it, or travesty
> it. The power that lets itself be invaded by the pleasure it is pursuing; and
> opposite it, power asserting itself in the pleasure of showing off, scandalizing,
> or resisting.[46]

Certainly, the power that emerges at the end of Eichendorff's *Das
Marmorbild* is a power located in the gaze, preoccupied with the constant
slippage between enlightenment and evasion, a power that can find erotic
pleasure in the transvestite body while at the same time seeking relentlessly
to expose the truth of the naked body. But the thrills of sexual ambiguity are
perilous for the object of the gaze: Eichendorff's narrative endings, which
so often strive to reestablish a symmetrical geometry of gender, also serve to
negate eroticism. Goethe's *Wilhelm Meister,* as I showed in chapter 2, above,
follows a similar pattern in its treatment of transvestite female characters, but
whereas that novel culminates in a domestication of desire, Eichendorff's
narratives rather refuse the modern process of bourgeois socialization and
rely instead on sublimating eroticism through the religious experience. One
of the final ironies of *Das Marmorbild* is that the marble Venus statue is
more a creature of flesh and blood than the living woman, Bianka. Any
trace of pagan carnality hinted at in Bianka's earlier passionate embrace of
Florio is canceled out by our final glimpse of an asexual, childlike heroine
"wie ein heiteres Engelsbild" (like a radiant angel [346]). This structure of
sublimation repeats itself throughout Eichendorff's works. In *Ahnung und
Gegenwart,* of course, Friedrich evades the amorphousness generated by the
dual perils of transvestism and poetry in his new career as a monk. Upon the
androgynous Erwin's death, the novel declares that the child resembles an
angel. Of the transgressive, Amazonian Diana in *Die Entführung,* we hear
that she ultimately relinquishes the world, becomes the mother superior of
a convent, and is revered by the community "fast wie eine Heilige" (almost
as if she were a saint [*Neue Gesamtausgabe,* vol. 2: 888]). It is important,
in this connection, to note the biblical prohibition against cross-dressing,
contained in Deuteronomy 22:5: "The woman shall not wear that which
pertaineth unto a man, neither shall a man put on a woman's garment; for all

that do so are abomination unto the Lord thy God." Christianity excludes the transvestite, in Eichendorff's fictional world. In the story *Eine Meerfahrt,* to cite one of the clearest examples of this moral interdiction, Alvarez is reluctant to let Alma, the heathen, visit a Christian hermit, precisely because of her transvestite dress (vol. 2: 789).

What Eichendorff's narrative endings articulate, then, is the need to contain the scandalous female cross-dresser, to negate the erotic potential of transvestism. Eichendorff's strategy is intriguingly double-edged: while the reader is placed in the precarious position of the *male* hero vis-à-vis female transvestism, we know that several of his early works, among them *Das Marmorbild,* were placed for publication in a magazine intended for a *female* audience, the *Frauentaschenbuch* edited by Friedrich de la Motte Fouqué.[47] The pedagogical objective of these works is only emphasized by their intended audience: women readers who are confronted with the spectacle of gender (re)stabilization, the restoration of the powers of the male gaze.[48] This fantasy of costume control has, of course, everything to do with monitoring a threatening form of sexuality. If transvestism is presented as a peculiarly feminine and as a peculiarly dangerous strategy, this, I believe, derives from Eichendorff's vision of women as inherently polymorphous and therefore imperiling beings. One has only to recall the wild replication of female figures in *Das Marmorbild:* Florio has a dream in which the image of Bianka proliferates uncontrollably in the form of fatally attractive sirens (vol. 2: 316); in Venus's pleasure garden, beautiful girls seem to burgeon from among the flowers (335); most horrifying of all, Venus herself awakens to life from inert marble. Female characters are figures of organic excess, figures that deny boundaries. Perhaps this explains why Eichendorff's works repeatedly seek to confine these potentially uncontainable female figures within the relative "safety" of binary classifications, dividing women neatly into bad and good, pagan and Christian: Venus and Bianka in *Das Marmorbild,* Diana and Leontine in *Die Entführung,* Flora and the "schöne gnädige Frau" in *Aus dem Leben eines Taugenichts.*[49] For all of these reasons, Eichendorff's narratives stress the reestablishment of stable gender identity and, in a related gesture, the fixing of polymorphous females in statue form.

This latter narrative strategy, which we have already seen at work in Goethe's *Wilhelm Meisters Lehrjahre,* is thus the exact opposite of Winckelmann's aesthetic of androgynous fluidity. There, the hermaphroditic marble sculpture is animated by the gaze of the viewer, who is aroused precisely by the erotic indeterminacy of the statue. In Eichendorff's works, by contrast, the labile female transvestite becomes the object of male anxiety; and this anxiety repeatedly finds expression in the image of an animated marble

statue. In *Viel Lärmen um Nichts,* to offer an example of this move, encounters with the mercurial, androgynous Florentin—who is in reality a
cross-dressing woman—provoke the hero's ghastly nightmare of statuary
stirring into life: "es war, als streckten und dehnten sich hinter ihm die
erwachten Marmorbilder, und ein widerliches Lachen schallte durch die
Luft" (it was as though the marble statues behind him had awoken and
were stretching themselves, and a sinister laugh resounded in the air [vol.
2: 461]). Significantly, upon waking from this dream, Romano glimpses a
marmoreal Florentin (Aurora) whose locks hang down before his face just
like those of the ghoulish statues in Romano's vision: "Er schien an einem
Bache sich zu waschen, seine dunklen Locken verschatteten sein Gesicht, der
Mondschein spielte wie liebestrunken über den schönen entblößten Nacken
und die Schultern des Jünglings." (He appeared to be bathing in a stream,
his dark locks obscured his face, and the moonlight, as if infatuated with
him, caressed the youth's beautiful bare neck and shoulders [461].)

Romano's anxiety, like that of so many of Eichendorff's heroes, is
aroused by a Pygmalion-like erotic encounter with ambiguous marble statuary, but in this fictional world the encounter emerges as more deathly than
charmed. In place of the "edle Einfalt" (noble simplicity) of Winckelmann's
classicism, what these characters encounter is a burgeoning, vegetative
version of Greek antiquity, a return of the repressed. The only solution
for Eichendorff's heroes, it would seem, is to transform the threatening,
polymorphous woman into inert, aestheticized matter. To return for a moment
to *Ahnung und Gegenwart,* it can escape no reader's attention that each
of the female protagonists in this novel comes to a tragic end. Echoing
Goethe's *Wilhelm Meisters Lehrjahre,* Eichendorff has Rosa fall asleep during Friedrich's telling of his personal history, a hint of the female petrification
that will recur throughout the novel (vol. 2: 56). Although Julie is still cross-
dressing as she and Leontin set off for America, we are told that at her
wedding she relinquishes her male clothing and that in her white dress
she takes on the appearance of an artwork, a "schönes, altdeutsches Bild"
(beautiful antique German painting [289]). Thus, the transvestite female is
snugly defined, reintegrated into tradition, into another kind of narrative,
that of history. (Tellingly, Bianka, in *Das Marmorbild,* adopts male dress
precisely in order to evade history: "um ungehinderter reisen zu können
und zugleich alles Vergangene gleichsam von sich abzustreifen, hatte sie
Knabentracht anlegen müssen" (in order to be able to travel unhindered and
at the same time to divest herself of her past, she had had to don boy's
clothing [vol. 2: 345]). When Friedrich encounters Romana for the last time,
she is described as "versteinert wie eine Bildsäule" (petrified like a stone

column [vol. 2: 222]). And in the last scene in the novel, Rosa loses consciousness when she sees Friedrich dressed as a monk—the most potent and fatal version of the apotropaic veiled phallus. The terrifying indeterminacy generated by female transvestism—indeed by femininity itself—is resolved by Eichendorff's narratives in death and petrification, in a restoration of the hardest and least permeable contours of all, those of white marble.

From Pygmalion to Perseus: Narrative and Mortification in Heine's *Florentinische Nächte*

I will next elaborate what I see as a significant paradigm shift from Pygmalion to Perseus, the overturning of Medusean feminine powers through an appropriation of the Gorgon's own weapon of petrification. Heine's narrative *Florentinische Nächte* (Florentine Nights), a work that cites both Goethe and Eichendorff, explicitly foregrounds this mythical turn.

In June 1835, Heine accepted an invitation extended by Princess Christina Belgiojoso to her country estate near Saint-Germain, La Jonchère, and it was in this peaceful setting that he was able to complete a work already begun more than ten years earlier, the *Florentinische Nächte*. His hostess there was no ordinary woman. Described by Mario Praz as the incarnation of a certain type of perilous, "Medusean" beauty which haunted the romantic imagination, Princess Belgiojoso had dark secrets: in a search of her villa at Locata in 1848, the Austrian police were to discover, hidden in one of her closets, the embalmed corpse of her young secretary and lover, Gaetano Stelzi.[50] In a letter the same year, the princess tells of her necrophilic motivations: "I brought him here to a tomb inside the house itself, so that Mrs. Parker and I have the sad satisfaction of adorning him with flowers and of maintaining the place more as a chamber than as a sepulchre."[51]

Contemporary accounts of Princess Belgiojoso forcefully recall the principal female character of Heine's *Florentinische Nächte,* the beautiful, moribund Maria. Madame d'Agoult, for example, an acquaintance of the princess, reminisces in her memoirs of 1877 on her sinister, spectral appearance: "Pale, thin, bony, fiery-eyed, she played on her ghostly, phantomlike image. She willingly substantiated certain rumors which, more for *effect* than anything else, placed in her hands the poison cup or dagger of Italian treachery at the court of the Borgias."[52] Both women, the Princess Belgiojosa and the fictional Maria of Heine's story, seem to possess the predatory sexuality of a Medusa, her paralyzing eyes, the ability to transform her male admirers into dead matter. Awakening from a fitful sleep in the opening scene of the *Florentinische Nächte,* the dying Maria presents the horrible spectacle of such a Medusean figure: "An was dachten Sie eben, Maximilian, wiederholte sie nochmals und erhob sich so hastig in die Höhe, daß die langen Locken, wie aufgeschreckte Goldschlangen, ihr Haupt umringelten." ("What were you thinking just now, Maximilian?" she repeated, raising herself suddenly, so that her long locks shook around her like snakes of gold.)[53] The Medusa's head, with its terrifying serpentine coiffure, may be read as symbolic of the *vagina dentata,* of woman both as castrated, in that she is decapitated, and castrating, in her marmoreal impenetrability.[54] Freud, in his influential essay "Das Medusenhaupt," interprets the head of the Medusa as "genitalized," an upward displacement of the female sexual organs, with the mouth standing for the *vagina dentata,* the snakes for pubic hair. The myth of the Medusa, as Freud would have it, represents in allegorical form the dread experienced by a male child as he discovers woman's lack of a penis, and thus the possibility that he, too, may suffer castration:

> Kopfabschneiden = Kastrieren. Der Schreck der Meduse ist also Kastrations-schreck, der an einen Anblick geknüpft ist. Aus zahlreichen Analysen kennen wir diesen Anlaß, er ergibt sich, wenn der Knabe, der bisher nicht an die Drohung glauben wollte, ein weibliches Genitale erblickt. Wahrscheinlich ein erwachsenes, von Haaren umsäumtes, im Grunde das der Mutter.

> To decapitate = to castrate. The terror of Medusa is thus a terror of castration that is linked to the sight of something. Numerous analyses have made us familiar with the occasion for this: it occurs when a boy, who has hitherto been unwilling to believe the threat of castration, catches sight of the female genitals, probably those of an adult, surrounded by hair, and especially those of his mother.[55]

Certainly mothers, in Maximilian's narrative, are related to Medusa figures: the marble statue belongs to the forbidden maternal realm; Maximilian becomes fixated on Renaissance Madonnas; Maria shares her name with the Virgin Mary. But it is the male viewer, the voyeur, who receives the mark of castration. Freud's emphasis on the male gaze—dread is bound up with the viewer's "Anblick," with "erblicken"—I will be linking with the privileged role of vision in Heine's text, where it is experienced throughout as an ambivalent force, empowering or endangering, like eroticism itself. The sight of the Medusa stiffens the male spectator in terror, petrifies him, while at the same time providing him with an arousing erotic experience: Freud makes the claim that "das Starrwerden bedeutet die Erektion, also in der ursprünglichen Situation den Trost des Beschauers" (becoming stiff means an erection. Thus in the original situation it offers consolation to the spectator).[56]

Later in the *Florentinische Nächte,* this time during Maximilian's narrative, another man, the gifted young composer Bellini, falls prey to the paralyzing charms of a beautiful vamp. If the logic of displacement at work in Freud's "Medusenhaupt" is applied to this scene from Heine's narrative, the predatory sexuality of this seductress may be seen as closely related to that of the Medusa. This phallic woman, too, shares the castrating powers of Princess Belgiojoso and Maria, gleefully destroying the young artist's carefully coiffed blond curls with his own cane—an unambiguous phallic symbol if there ever was one, described as a diminutive "spanisches Röhrchen, womit er seiner schwachen Rhetorik manchmal zu Hülfe kommen wollte" ("the cane with which he attempted at times to reinforce his weak rhetoric" [573; Carter, 35]). Maximilian, who has faced the life-threatening effects of his own Medusa, at this moment feels a sudden affinity with the doomed Bellini.

The woman who brings about Bellini's death smiles the deadly smile of a Mona Lisa, her complexion pale, marmoreal. Praz has commented on the frequent literary association between the paralyzing gaze of the Medusa and the enigmatic smile of the Mona Lisa, both women performing as key players in the well-stocked romantic repertoire of "femmes fatales."[57] In Heine's *Florentinische Nächte,* however, the Medusa and the related figure of the Mona Lisa, prevalently represented as agents of male petrification, themselves undergo a significant and ultimately fatal mutation, one that calls into question the very nature and intent of Maximilian's act of narration. Notice the twist in Heine's version of the Medusa story: as myth has it, the Gorgon with the serpentine hairdo has the power to freeze the male spectator into stone, but in the *Florentinische Nächte* a stunning inversion is staged, and it is the male viewer who lives to tell the tale, while the Medusa herself is petrified in the form of a marble statue. Survival is, indeed, posited quite literally on "telling the tale," for what Heine's *Florentinische Nächte* throws into relief are the therapeutic and/or fatal powers of narration. The male hero, Maximilian, positions himself mythically in the role of Perseus: Perseus, as we recall, succeeds, with the help of his reflective shield, both in avoiding the direct gaze of Medusa and in turning that perilous gaze back upon the monstrous female, thus enabling him to decapitate her. What is more, having dispatched the Gorgon, Perseus inherits her powers of petrification; after slaying her, he pins her head to his shield as an apotropaic emblem, to petrify his enemies. Barbara Johnson has suggested the following equation: if woman presents herself to the male gaze as lack ("castration"), then her death becomes the lack plus a lack—a convoluted kind of restoration.[58] As I will be showing here, the mirror that

Maximilian turns against the Medusean Maria is the mirror of art, more precisely of narration.

The fatal effects of narration become clear as soon as the reader turns to the opening of the *Florentinische Nächte*. Maximilian enters Maria's sickroom just as her doctor is about to leave. It is the doctor who prescribes storytelling for its curative effects, stressing that "nur geistige Bewegung ist ihr heilsam" ("a little mental stimulation, however, may do her good" [558; Carter, 9]). But, perhaps more ominously, the doctor approves of Maximilian's stories principally because of their tranquilizing powers over both the female invalid's movements and her speech. Already in the opening moments of Heine's work, narrative is bound up with petrification: "Ich brauche Ihnen nicht zu empfehlen, sie durch kein Geräusch zu wecken; und wenn sie erwacht, darf sie bei Leibe nicht reden. Sie muß ruhig liegen, darf sich nicht rühren, nicht im mindesten bewegen, darf nicht reden. . . . Bitte, erzählen Sie ihr wieder allerlei närrische Geschichten, so das sie ruhig zuhören muß." ("I need hardly remind you not to make a sound; when she wakes on no account may she talk. She is to lie quietly without moving, she must not say a word. . . . Tell her more of those fantastic tales of yours which she hears with such rapt attention" [558; Carter, 9].) Ironically, while we might initially believe ourselves to be in a situation like that of the *Arabian Nights,* where the act of storytelling has the subversive power to sustain life, Maximilian's rather chilling first words suggest the very opposite narrative intent: telling his tale will merely accentuate, or even hasten, the process of mortification: "Seien Sie unbesorgt, Doktor, erwiderte Maximilian mit einem wehmütigen Lächeln. Ich habe mich schon ganz zum Schwätzen ausgebildet und lasse sie nicht zu Worte kommen. Und ich will ihr schon genug phantastisches Zeug erzählen, so viel Sie nur begehren. . . . Aber wie lange wird sie noch leben können?" ("Never fear, doctor," said Maximilian with a melancholy smile. "I have now trained myself to be a chatterbox and I won't let her get a word in. I'll tell her as much fantastic stuff as you could wish for. . . . But how long do you give her?" [558; Carter, 10].)

As Maximilian gazes at the sleeping invalid, suggestive images press into his consciousness. Maria's white muslin nightgown flowing over a green silk-covered sofa uncannily kindles memories of a white marble statue lying on green grass. It is precisely at this moment, with its ironic play on the romantic motif of involuntary memory, that Maria jolts into life, her hair coiling snakelike around her head. Maximilian's reactions determine the subsequent fatal course of events: after pinning the invalid down, quite literally, to her sofa, silencing her speech, and putting a stop to her movements, he embarks upon his own narrative of development, a story strewn with statues, murderous desires, and female phantoms. As I have been arguing, this deadly structure of desire indeed seems to underpin most classic narratives of *Bildung,* from Goethe's *Wilhelm Meisters Lehrjahre* to the narratives of Eichendorff.

The *Urszene* related by Maximilian mirrors parodistically Eichendorff's famous tale of seduction by a Medusean marble statue, *Das Marmorbild.*[59] Moonlight, a ruined castle, a garden overgrown with rampant vegetation, a callow young hero, a beautiful Venus statue that is at the same time repulsive and alluring—all of these elements are drawn from Heine's romantic precursor. But Maximilian's erotic encounter with the statue differs significantly from that of Eichendorff's hero, Florio: where Florio recoils at the last instant from sexual contact with the pagan Venus statue, and instead finds peaceful fulfillment in his relationship with the virginal Christian Bianka, Maximilian yields to the powerful eroticism of the moment and kisses the statue:

> Im grünen Grase lag die schöne Göttin ebenfalls regungslos, aber kein steinerner Tod, sondern nur ein stiller Schlaf schien ihre lieblichen Glieder gefesselt zu halten, und als ich ihr näherte, fürchtete ich schier, daß ich sie durch das geringste Geräusch aus ihrem Schlummer erwecken könnte. Ich hielt den Atem zurück als ich mich über sie hinbeugte, um die schönen Gesichtszüge zu betrachten; eine schauerliche Beängstigung stieß mich aber von ihr ab, eine knabenhafte Lüsternheit zog mich wieder zu ihr hin, mein Herz pochte, als wollte ich eine Mordtat begehen, und endlich küßte ich die schöne Göttin, mit einer Inbrunst, mit einer Zärtlichkeit, mit einer Verzweiflung, wie ich nie mehr geküßt habe in diesem Leben. Auch nie habe ich diese grauenhaft süße Empfindung vergessen können, die meine Seele durchflutete, als die beseligende Kälte jener Marmorlippen meinen Mund berührte.

> "In the green grass the lovely goddess lay motionless, but it was not the petrifaction of death, but rather a marmoreal sleep which seemed to hold her lovely limbs in bond. As I approached I feared that my least movement might wake her from her slumber. I held my breath as I bent over her to gaze at the exquisite features; a shuddering fear repelled me, but adolescent passion drew me back, my heart beat as if I were about to commit a murder; and at last I kissed the lovely goddess with such desire and tenderness and desperation as I have never again known in my life. Nor have I ever forgotten the sweet and awful sensation which filled my soul when the blissful coolness of those marble lips touched my own." (562; Carter, 17)

This passage, so central to the *Florentinische Nächte,* I see as a powerful rereading and indeed reversal of the Pygmalion myth which dominates literature and aesthetics of the eighteenth century. Literary works and aesthetics of the Enlightenment and of classicism are filled with references to Pygmalion, whose love for a beautiful statue imbues the marble with life.[60] Eichendorff's romantic hero, as I have shown, already experiences a more perilous erotic relationship with a classical marble statue. Heine's postromantic hero, rather than adopting the Pygmalion persona, positions himself instead in the role of Perseus, thus foregrounding the more sinister, indeed lethal, aspects of the relationship between artist and artwork. Kissing the statue was no life-giving act, Maximilian recalls in his macabre bedtime story, but rather a murder, or "Mordtat." What he had feared above all was precisely the ghastly possibility enacted in the Pygmalion legend, the possibility that the statue might awaken from her deathly stasis. Maximilian's kiss, however, far from bringing the marble Venus to life, was a vampiric transaction, her chilly last gasp animating his body: "Auch nie habe ich diese grauenhaft süße Empfindung vergessen können, die meine Seele durchflutete, als die beseligende Kälte jener Marmorlippen meinen Mund berührte." ("Nor have I forgotten the sweet and awful sensation which filled my soul when the blissful coolness of those marble lips touched my own.") This precisely reverses the scenario of a poem written by Heine for the preface to the third edition of the *Buch der Lieder* (Book of Songs); there, the poet's kiss animates a marble sphinx, but with horrifying results.[61] The statue, we are told, vampirically sucks away the breath of the poet, almost to the point of his extinction (vol. 1: 15).

Maximilian, in the *Florentinische Nächte,* is not slow to turn the mirror of his deathly narrative upon the moribund Medusa lying before him on her green sofa: "Und sehen Sie, Maria, als ich eben vor Ihnen stand und ich Sie, in Ihrem weißen Musselinkleide, auf dem grünen Sofa liegen sah, da mahnte mich Ihr Anblick an das weiße Marmorbild im grünen Grase. Hätten Sie länger geschlafen, meine Lippen würden nicht widerstanden haben." ("And so you see, Maria, when I was just now standing there and saw you in your white muslin frock lying on the green sofa, it reminded me of the marble statue in the green grass. Had you slept longer, my lips could not have refrained" [562; Carter, 17].) Maria's reaction is highly ambiguous: "Max! Max! schrie das Weib aus der Tiefe ihrer Seele—Entsetzlich! Sie wissen, daß ein Kuß von ihrem Munde . . ." ("Max! Max!" cried the woman from the depth of her soul, "how appalling! You know that a kiss from your mouth . . ." [562; Carter, 17].) Thanks to Maximilian's characteristic interruption, the reader does not hear Maria complete her train of thought. Is she suggesting, as his narrative does, that his kiss will hasten her death? Or, equally plausibly, is this a thinly veiled threat—is the tubercular woman implying that her kiss would fatally infect Maximilian? And if the latter is the case, is she ironically turning the Pygmalion myth itself against Maximilian, a myth that focuses on the life-giving powers of the lips?

Following the bizarre predatory encounter with the Venus sculpture, Maximilian now tells Maria, he developed a strange passion for marble statues; he indulged in a flirtation with a Renaissance painting of the Madonna; and he even, climactically, fell in love with dead or imagined women. (It is revealing that Maximilan abandons one of these "women," the painted Madonna, for a marble Greek nymph.) Maximilian seems to relish the erotic potential of a woman in a state of guaranteed and absolute passivity—death.

What of the words that Maria, the still living woman, exchanges with Maximilian? Maria's comments, I argue, perceptively uncover the mechanisms of desire in Maximilian's narrative, laying bare his obsessions. She correctly points to his fundamental indifference to music, for example, and suggests that he visits the opera purely in order to indulge his scopophilia, his erotic pleasure in gazing at the statuelike Italian beauties who throng the opera house. It is vision, I would emphasize, that *makes* statues of these women, that makes them "legible" and thus assimilable into his narration. Telling as Maria's observations are, the principal aim of Maximilian's narrative is precisely to eliminate any possibility of dialogue: the anecdotes he relates become suffocating in length, his reactions to Maria's interruptions increasingly menacing:

> Und das ist die ganze Geschichte? schrie auf einmal Maria, indem sie sich leidenschaftlich emporrichtete.
>
> Maximilian aber drückte sie wieder sanft nieder, legte bedeutungsvoll den Zeigefinger auf seinen Mund und flüsterte: Still! still! nur kein Wort gesprochen, liegen Sie wieder hübsch ruhig, und ich werde Ihnen den Schwanz der Geschichte erzählen. Nur bei Leibe unterbrechen Sie mich nicht.

> "And is that all the story?" cried Maria passionately, starting up.
>
> Maximilian pressed her down gently, significantly placed his finger on his lips and whispered: "Be quiet, don't say a word! Lie down nicely and I will tell you the conclusion of the story. Only don't interrupt me!" (596; Carter, 76)

In the case of Bellini, too, Maximilian is seen adopting the Medusean role of the "Jettatore," that is, of one who has the power to cast the evil eye upon his victim. Bellini, as I mentioned, apparently becomes the prey of a deadly vamp. Yet Maximilian's own recollections of the composer suggest another possible explanation for his premature demise: that it is Maximilian's repeated and malicious taunts about the short life expectancy of geniuses that have taken their toll, another indication that, as Teresa de Lauretis has

suggested, sadism may operate as the generative force of narration.[62] The ca-
daverous violinist Paganini, on the other hand, seems almost miraculously to
evade the clutches of death, a zombie-like, automaton-like, vampiric figure:

> Hat er diese Komplemente einem Automaten abgelernt oder einem Hunde?
> Ist dieser bittende Blick der eines Todkranken, oder lauert dahinter der Spott
> eines schlauen Geizhalses? Ist das ein Lebender der im Verscheiden begriffen
> ist und der das Publikum in der Kunstarena, wie ein sterbender Fechter, mit
> seinen Zukkungen ergötzen soll? Oder ist es ein Toter, der aus dem Grabe
> gestiegen, ein Vampir mit der Violine, der uns, wo nicht das Blut aus dem
> Herzen, doch auf jeden Fall das Geld aus den Taschen saugt?

> "Had he learnt this manner of bowing from an automaton or from a dog? Was
> this the entreating look of a man sick to death, or was it to hide the mockery
> of a crafty miser? Was it a live man on the point of dying, who had to make
> sport for the public in the arena of the arts like a gladiator about to die, with
> convulsive movements? Or was it a corpse that had risen from the grave, a
> vampire with a violin, who, though he might not suck the blood out of our
> hearts, did at least extract the money from our pockets?" (577–78; Carter, 42)

The vampiric tendencies of the artist were already apparent in Maximilian's recollections of his erotic encounter with the Venus statue. Significantly, the rapturous climax of the first half of the violin concert coincides,
in Maximilian's imagination at least, with Paganini's murder of a beautiful
young female singer. Art requires female sacrifice.[63] For Maximilian, the
most vivid image of the performance is that presented by Paganini, as his
hood falls, "und die lockigen Haare, im Winde dahinflatternd, umringelten
sein Haupt wie schwarze Schlangen" ("and ringlets of his hair fluttering in
the wind formed round his head a halo of black serpents" [582; Carter, 49]).
Paganini, it seems clear, has, like Maximilian, usurped for himself Medusean
powers of metamorphosis and control over life and death; indeed, in this
incarnation he has taken on the appearance of a Medusa. The choice of the
artist, then, seems to be either to petrify or be petrified. And the apotropaic
Medusean display is what protects the artist from his own deathly powers.
According to the mythical account, Pegasus, the winged horse of poetry, is
born from the blood of the slain Medusa.[64]

Maria, meanwhile, sleeps, and we have no clear idea how much of
Maximilian's disturbing story she has heard. Narrative has exerted its fatal
grip, and the living woman has become mummified, completely static. It is
the doctor, having quietly entered the room during the narrative, who has to
point out to Maximilian that Maria has fallen into a deathly sleep, that she
has already taken on the characteristics of a plaster death mask. Maximilian,

far from showing distress at the doctor's pessimistic prognosis, openly longs for her extinction, expressing the desire to possess such a relic of Maria's final mortification: "Sie wird auch als Leiche noch sehr schön sein." ("Even as a corpse she will still be very beautiful" [584; Carter, 54].) But the doctor, an enlightened if resigned spirit, pointedly remarks on the deathliness of such masks, if not of all art, and it is he who leads Maximilian out of the sickroom, away from the fascinating moribund female body.

The doctor's remarks at the end of this first evening of storytelling are surely also a diagnosis of the demise of the era that Heine called the *Kunstperiode* or "Age of Art," a demystification of the cult of form.[65] In his *Romantische Schule* (Romantic School), Heine had memorably characterized the works of Goethe, the colossus of the *Kunstperiode,* as marble statues, sensual but frigid, seductive but sterile.[66] The artist who positions himself in the role of Pygmalion is exposed as leading an ultimately fruitless existence, since the union between him and his beloved statue can produce no children—such offspring representing for Heine "Taten," or actions in the political sphere:[67]

> Sie [Goethes Werke] zieren unser teueres Vaterland, wie schöne Statuen einen Garten zieren, aber es sind Statuen. Man kann sich darin verlieben, aber sie sind unfruchtbar. . . . Die Tat ist das Kind des Wortes, und die Goetheschen schönen Worte sind kinderlos. Das ist der Fluch alles dessen was bloß durch die Kunst entstanden ist. Die Statue, die der Pygmalion verfertigt, war ein schönes Weib, sogar der Meister verliebte sich darin, sie wurde lebendig unter seinen Küssen, aber so viel wir wissen hat sie nie Kinder bekommen.

> They [Goethe's works] adorn our dear fatherland as beautiful statues adorn a garden, but they are, after all, statues. You can fall in love with them, but they are sterile. . . . A deed is the child of the word, and Goethe's beautiful words are childless. This is the curse on everything that has originated in art alone. The statue that Pygmalion made was a beautiful woman, even the artist fell in love with her, she came to life from his kisses, but as far as we know she never had children. (*Die Romantische Schule,* vol. 3: 395)[68]

Significantly, Heine later expressed his deepest political resignation and despair in his account of a disillusioned farewell to the Venus de Milo in 1848. Heine describes himself as lying in tears at her feet, only to come to two devastating realizations: that she, a dead marble statue with no arms, cannot come to his aid, and, perhaps more tragically, that he has lost the poetic power of a Pygmalion to bring her to life.[69] His visit to the sculpture exhibitions at the Louvre prompted Heine to reflect on Goethe's beautiful but deathly works in terms that echo the words of Maria's doctor in the *Florentinische Nächte:*

Da standen sie, mit den stummen weißen Augen, in dem marmornen Lächeln
eine geheime Melancholie, eine trübe Erinnerung vielleicht an Ägypten,
das Totenland, dem sie entsprossen, oder leidende Sehnsucht nach dem
Leben, woraus sie jetzt durch andere Gottheiten fortgedrängt sind, oder
auch Schmerz über ihre tote Unsterblichkeit:—sie schienen des Wortes zu
harren, das sie wieder dem Leben zurückgäbe, das sie aus ihrer kalten,
starren Regungslosigkeit erlöse. Sonderbar! diese Antiken mahnten mich an
die Goetheschen Dichtungen, die ebenso vollendet, ebenso herrlich, ebenso
ruhig sind, und ebenfalls mit Wehmut zu fühlen scheinen, daß ihre Starrheit
und Kälte sie von unserem jetzigen bewegt warmen Leben abscheidet, daß
sie nicht mit uns leiden und jauchzen können, daß sie keine Menschen sind,
sondern unglückliche Mischlinge von Gottheit und Stein.

There they stood with their blank white eyes, a secret melancholy in their
marble smiles, perhaps a sad recollection of Egypt, the land of the dead, from
which they came, or painful longing for life, from which they have now been
crowded out by other deities, or even sorrow at their lifeless immortality:—
they seem to await the word that will bring them back to life, that will release
them from their cold, rigid immovability. Strange! These antiquities reminded
me of Goethe's works, which are just as perfect, just as magnificent, just as
serene, and also seem to feel with melancholy that their rigidity and coldness
separate them from the stir and warmth of modern life, that they cannot suffer
and rejoice with us, that they are not human, but unfortunate half-breeds of
divinity and stone. (*Die Romantische Schule,* 395–96; Mustard, 36)

Maria's transformation into a frigid marble statue, in the course of
Maximilian's story, pushes to its logical conclusion the narrative of male
Bildung that is the focus of Goethe's *Wilhelm Meisters Lehrjahre.* In that
classic *Bildungsroman,* we witness in the opening chapters the soporific
effects on a female listener of the hero's life history, as the actress Mariane
falls asleep to the sound of Wilhelm's voice. Heine's *Florentinische Nächte,* I
suggest, deliberately mirrors this scene of male storytelling and foregrounds
the female petrification that would seem to be its inevitable by-product.
Although Goethe's novel, unlike Heine's *Florentinische Nächte,* does not
explicitly stage Wilhelm's relationships with women in terms of the struggle
between Perseus and the Gorgon, it does contain hints of those mythical
structures of desire. Philine, the anarchic coquette of Goethe's novel, after
attempting, in what might be read as an ironic Medusean gesture, to pin
down a reluctant Wilhelm Meister in an amorous embrace, concludes in
mock disappointment that he is "ein steinerner Mann" (a stone man).[70] Yet
by the end of Wilhelm's journey of *Bildung,* the sexually assertive Philine has
been banished from the world of the novel, and Mignon, another principal
object of Wilhelm's erotic desires, has been elaborately embalmed, exhibited

in mummified form, by the *Turmgesellschaft,* purveyors of pedagogy. The woman to whom Wilhelm is finally betrothed, the ethereal and asexual Natalie, receives no physical description in the novel and exists as a dream apparition in Wilhelm's mind, thus anticipating the statuesque phantom woman considered by Heine's narrator Maximilian to be the greatest love of his life.

In Eichendorff's works, as I began to suggest earlier, the Medusa/Perseus trope is already more clearly elaborated. Significantly, several of the seductive females who populate his narratives display the petrifying powers that characterize the Medusa. Florio's first vision of Venus, for example, dwells on the statue's deadly stone gaze: "das Venusbild, so fürchterlich weiß und regungslos, sah ihn fast schreckhaft mit den steinernen Augenhöhlen aus der grenzenlosen Stille an. Ein nie gefühltes Grausen überfiel da den Jüngling" (from out of an endless calm the Venus statue, so dreadfully white and motionless, fixed an almost startling stare upon him with its stony eye-sockets. The youth was overcome by a horror he had never before experienced [*Das Marmorbild,* vol. 2: 318]). When Florio is lured back to the "Lustgarten" (pleasure garden) for a return visit, he is confronted with more sinister evidence of Venus's relationship of sisterhood with the Gorgon, this time in the petrified shape of a male admirer:

> Unter der Mauer auf zerschlagenen Marmorsteinen und Säulenknäufen, zwischen denen hohes Gras und Blumen üppig hervorschossen, lag ein schlafender Mann ausgestreckt. Erstaunt erkannte Florio den Ritter Donati. Aber seine Mienen schienen im Schlafe sonderbar verändert, er sah fast wie ein Toter aus. Ein heimlicher Schauer überlief Florio bei diesem Anblick.

> Under the wall, in amidst broken marble slabs and columns where tall grasses and flowers had shot up in proliferation, lay a sleeping man. Florio was amazed when he recognized him as the knight Donati. But his facial expression seemed so strangely altered by sleep that he looked almost corpse-like. At this sight, a quiet shudder ran down Florio's spine. (323)

Still later, when Florio himself is on the verge of succumbing to Venus's fatal charms, he glimpses a snake, mark of the Medusa (338), and moments later witnesses a horrible serpentine proliferation. Unsurprisingly, with Venus's gaze suddenly stony, the phenomenon coincides with the predatory advances of grotesquely animated statues:

> Florio hatte indes, im Schreck zurücktaumelnd, eines von den steinernen Bildern, die and der Wand herumstanden, angestoßen. In demselben Augenblicke begann dasselbe sich zu rühren, die Regung teilte sich schnell den andern mit, und bald erhoben sich alle die Bilder mit furchtbarem Schweigen . . .

auch die hohen Blumen in den Gefäßen fingen an, sich wie buntgefleckte Schlangen gräßlich durcheinander zu winden.

Recoiling in horror, Florio had bumped into one of the marble statues that stood along the wall. It instantly began to move, and quickly its movement spread to the other statues, so that soon they all stirred to life, in a ghastly silence . . . even the tall-stemmed flowers in the vases began to writhe around horribly, like mottled snakes. (339)

The ultimate triumph of Christianity, as transmitted by a male artwork, Fortunato's song, lies in the Virgin Mary's ability to bring about Venus's final metamorphosis, into stone: "Die Augen untergehen, / Der schöne Leib wird Stein." ("Her eyes perish, / Her beautiful body turns to stone" [343].) Similar mythical patterns involving animation and petrification undercut *Ahnung und Gegenwart.* One of Leontin's songs, for example, powerfully conveys the realization that art can spell death, rather than a kiss of life: "Doch wolle nie dir halten / Der Bilder Wunder fest, / Tot wird ihr freies Walten, / Hältst du es wirklich fest." (But may the wonder of images / Never hold you fast, / Dead will be its free dominion, / If you seize hold of it. [vol. 2: 91].) As noted above, Romana casts herself as a *femme fatale,* taking on the roles both of the sorceress Armida and of the Lorelei;[71] her complexion is repeatedly described as marmoreal; and the novel dwells on her ferocious, magnetic gaze (135). In death, however, she displays the stasis of the vanquished Venus statue in *Das Marmorbild,* thus fulfilling her role as "griechische Figur, die lebenslustige, vor dem Glanze des Christentums zu Stein gewordene Religion der Phantasie" (a Greek figure, the vital religion of fantasy, which has turned to stone before the radiant light of Christianity [130]). Rudolf, himself in disguise, turns the Medusa trope against the subversive transvestite Angelina, thus, the novel suggests, precipitating her deathly faint: "Ich bitte dich um Gottes willen, unterbrach mich hier Angelina dringend, nimm die Larve ab, ich fürchte mich vor dir.—Laß das, sagte ich abwehrend, es gibt fürchterliche Gesichter, die das Herz in Stein verwandeln, wie das Haupt der Medusa." ("I beg you, for God's sake," Angelina interrupted me urgently, "take your mask off, I'm afraid of you." "Stop that," I retaliated, "there are horrible physiognomies that turn the heart to stone, like the head of the Medusa" [281].) Rudolf's response to her plea is to continue with his song, which tells of a ghostly knight "mit steinern'n Armen" (with arms of stone) whose icy embrace kills a beautiful young bride (281). The final scene of the novel, of course, involves Rosa falling into a dramatic faint at the sight of Friedrich in monk's habit. This in itself may constitute a strange kind of Perseus-like retaliation on the hero's part:

as Marjorie Garber points out, "the sartorial fantasy of Catholic crossover goes in both gender directions, male to female as well as female to male. Underneath the cowl and flowing robes the body of the celibate is itself an object of suspicion."[72] In Goethe's *Wilhelm Meisters Lehrjahre,* Philine's transvestite charade with Friedrich renders Wilhelm petrified. Is Friedrich's garb, then, perhaps a way of inverting the perilous effects of transvestism, of turning it back against the female cross-dresser, just as Perseus turns the gaze of the Gorgon back upon herself?

Keller's novel *Der grüne Heinrich* also identifies its hero with the victim of a Medusean gaze. Among his dead mother's papers, Heinrich Lee discovers a poem that tells of an old sailor who seems "wie ein Medusen-schild / Der erstarrten Unruh Bild" (Like Medusa's shield that day / Numbed the turbulent waters lay),[73] and parallels Heinrich's own self-identification as "gefrorner Christ" (frozen Christian [1067; Holt, 651]). Freud's "Das Medusenhaupt" reads the mother as the original Medusa; Heinrich Lee's *Bildung,* I would argue, is predicated on the ultimate death of the mother, and on the hero's adoption of the Perseus persona: "Ich nahm den leblosen Kopf [der Mutter] in die Hände und hielt dies Haupt vielleicht zum ersten Male in meinem Leben so in der Hand." (I took the lifeless head in my hands and held it thus for perhaps the first time in my life [1103; Holt, 685]).

After this glance at the process of female petrification that seems to characterize that master text of the *Kunstperiode, Wilhelm Meisters Lehr-jahre,* Eichendorff's narratives, and also Keller's *Der grüne Heinrich,* I turn now to Maximilian's second evening of storytelling in the *Florentinische Nächte.* The scene opens with Maria's remonstrances to the doctor about the bitter medicine she is being forced to swallow; the "medicine," of course, might plausibly be interpreted as Maximilian's supposedly therapeutic narra-tive. It is Maximilian, not the doctor, who coaxes the invalid into swallowing the draft. With her ambivalent reaction—she begs Maximilian to continue his story, while shuddering at the prospect—Maria herself is caught up in the dynamics of dread and desire generated by narrative.

The second evening of narrative is dominated by the profoundly enig-matic and troubling figure of the dancer Mademoiselle Laurence. Like the androgynous Mignon who haunts the pages of *Wilhelm Meisters Lehrjahre,* Laurence belongs to the theatrical world, more specifically to the prebour-geois theater of circus, of freak show. In rational, mechanistic England, she is as much a foreign body ("Fremdkörper") as Goethe's Mignon in the world of the *Turmgesellschaft.* Like Mignon, Laurence displays the liminal and indeterminate sexuality of an adolescent; her name suggests something of the linguistic indeterminacy of Mignon's masculine name; she, too, wears boy's clothing; she has the penetrating dark sidelong glance, the "Seitenblick" of Mignon. Like Mignon in her maenad-like frenzies, Laurence dances "in der frevelhaft kühnen Weise jener Bacchantinnen, die wir auf den Reliefs der antiken Vasen mit Erstaunen betrachten. Ihr Tanz hatte dann etwas trunken Willenloses, etwas finster Unabwendbares, etwas Fatalistisches, sie tanzte dann wie das Schicksal" ("like the wilful and daring bacchantes whom we see with amazement on the reliefs of antique vases. . . . Then her dancing had an involuntary and intoxicated quality—something darkly inevitable, something fatalistic, she danced like fate" [594; Carter, 72]). Once again, the transvestite female body is the locus of political and aesthetic crisis. Critics have convincingly read Laurence's spasmodic and anguished dance, which Maximilian deliberately contrasts with the stiff classical ballet of the *ancien régime,* as an allegory of political revolution,[74] though it is important to point out that this is a dance performed in utter isolation, in the stultifying atmosphere of political restoration, and against the background of Türlütü's crowing reminiscences of the good old aristocratic days.

Significantly for Maximilian's narrative of desire, in the figure of the dancing Laurence he once again encounters a petrifying Medusean power. He recalls in his bedside narrative her deathly white face, her eerily blank and staring eyes, her lips trembling with desire and pain, her black tresses flying in the air. The link with the Medusa is underlined by two references to Laurence's eel-like characteristics (602, 614; Carter, 84, 103): her gaze produces an electric shock in Maximilian, and at the end of the narrative she slithers out of his embrace, sinuous as an eel, to begin her dance. His story, then, reflects back to Maria what is intended as a fatal mirror image of herself. Laurence's gaze, too, is hypnotic, driving Maximilian to abandon his dull touristic distractions in London in order to follow the peregrinations of the troupe. (Tellingly, one of the few high points in his London visit is viewing the ax with which Anne Boleyn was beheaded.) Maximilian's narrative repeatedly circles around Laurence's gaze: from his aimless wanderings around the city, Maximilian is drawn by this female "Seitenblick" into a frozen state of stasis and fascination, and her gaze, having singled him out in the crowd, deliberately turns him into a passive spectator. Paradoxically, while this gaze is precisely what Maximilian seeks out, he does so in order to deflect it, finally, back upon Laurence. As these examples indicate, the threat presented by the Medusa is to Maximilian's vision; and her power consists in her luring of the male gaze into what is perceived as the enigma of femininity. Bram Dijkstra has shown in his work on later, fin-de-siècle representations of femininity that Medusas are frequently depicted as viraginous monsters, their autoerotic self-sufficiency represented by the uroboric snakes coiling on their heads, serpentine symbols of androgyny.[75] Precisely the sexual indeterminacy of the Medusean Laurence, turned into spectacle by her theatrical transvestite dress, serves both to fuel and to frustrate one of Maximilian's deepest urges: to pin down, to fix his female love objects with his gaze: "Ich der sonst die Signatur aller Erscheinungen so leicht begreift, ich konnte dennoch dieses getanzte Rätsel nicht lösen." ("I, who as a rule divine the significance of all appearances so easily, could not resolve this danced riddle" [593; Carter, 72].) Significantly, in their second encounter Maximilian transforms Laurence through his interpretative gaze from kinetic transvestite to inert statue; where she was previously only "griechisch schön" ("Grecian in [her] loveliness" [590; Carter, 65]), she now possesses all the attributes of a marble sculpture, and, what is more, she has relinquished both her bacchic dance and her transvestite costume:

> Es war dasselbe Gesicht, das an Form und sonniger Färbung einer Antike gleich; nur war es nicht mehr so marmorrein und marmorglatt wie ehemals. Dem geschärften Blicke waren auf Stirn und Wange einige kleine Brüche, vielleicht Pockennarben, bemerkbar, die hier ganz an jene feinen Witterungs- flecken mahnten, wie man sie auf dem Gesichte von Statuen, die einige Zeit dem Regen ausgesetzt standen, zu finden pflegt.

> "It was the same face, resembling an antique in shape and sunny colouring, but it was not so marble-pure and smooth as once upon a time. For the acute observer there were to be seen on the forehead and cheeks small flaws, marks that reminded one of the delicate weathering found on the faces of statues which have been subjected to rain for a time." (602; Carter, 84)

As the reader probably already suspects from Maximilian's own narrative, interpretation, like storytelling itself, may reveal killer instincts. Laurence now resembles not only a statue but a statue bearing the marks of disease and decay. What, then, is one to make of Maximilian's apparently frivolous but perhaps self-exonerating comparison between Parisian women and butterflies? "Es gibt Leute, welche glauben, sie könnten den Schmetter- ling ganz genau betrachten, wenn sie ihn mit einer Nadel aufs Papier festgestochen haben. Das ist eben so töricht wie grausam. Der angeheftete, ruhige Schmetterling ist kein Schmetterling mehr." ("There are people who think they can observe a butterfly more accurately when they have pinned it down to a piece of paper. That is as foolish as it is cruel. The motionless and transfixed butterfly is a butterfly no longer" [600; Carter, 82].) Is this a statement of monumental self-delusion, since, after all, Maximilian has been engaged in acts of female petrification since the beginning of his storytelling? Or is there a shift in the male structures of desire presented in this "second night" of the *Florentinische Nächte,* written by Heine after a break in composition of more than five years? Rather than the serene and already petrified marble beauties of the "Erste Nacht," this second evening of narrative presents women caught up in spasmodic, feverish dance. Significantly, it is in this portion of the narrative that Maximilian tells the story of the Willis. According to legend, these are young brides who have died before their wedding day, and who emerge from their graves under cover of night to dance wild, orgiastic dances. Bearing in mind that Heine inscribes both the aesthetics and politics of the *Kunstperiode* and of *Das Junge Deutschland* on the female body, does Maximilian's obsession with the frenetic dancer Laurence, a corporeal cipher for political engagement, or his interest in the legend of the Willis signal a break from the stagnation of the *Kunstperiode?* Maximilian omits one key detail in his story of these dancing virginal corpses, but it is a significant one, and it is present in Heine's account of the Willis in his *Elementargeister* (Elemental Spirits). Heine warns, "wehe dem jungen Menschen, der ihnen da begegnet! Er muß mit ihnen tanzen, sie umschlingen ihn mit ungezügelter Tobsucht, und er tanzt mit ihnen, ohne Ruh und Rast, bis er tot niederfällt" (woe betide the young man who strays across their path! He is forced to dance with them, they embrace him with maniacal energy, and there is no rest until he drops dead [vol. 3: 654]). Once again, contact with women, posited as sexually rapacious beings, is presented as a life-and-death struggle, but in this "Zweite Nacht" of Maximilian's narrative, it is the final paroxysms of female life, rather than the passivity of the eternally dead marble statue, that become the focus of male desire. The convulsive Willis, doomed to return to their graves, the last flutterings of an impaled butterfly, and of course the final breaths of a moribund female invalid: it is precisely this liminal stage between life and death over which Maximilian's narrative lingers. And it is this never-ending process of female mortification that the narrative sustains. While Maximilian mounts a critique of the sadistic voyeurism so dominant in bourgeois male society, he cynically indulges in just this scopophilia.

The enigmatic Mademoiselle Laurence, too, ultimately falls prey to Maximilian's narrative; her fate and that of Maria begin to converge. At this point in Maximilian's reminiscences, significantly, Maria no longer seems able to resist the deathly grip of his narrative; drained of all Medusean force now, her movements are languid, and she can scarcely yawn a question about Laurence's history. In Maximilian's third encounter with Laurence, which Maximilian now relates, the dancer reveals the macabre circumstances of her birth, in a scene that formally echoes Maximilian's own *Urszene.* Laurence's mother, the victim of repeated abuse at the hands of her husband, was buried alive while pregnant, and a band of graverobbers miraculously delivered Laurence from the grave. Given over to a manipulative ventriloquist and his mistress, Laurence spent her childhood being tortured by this ventriloquist's subversive male voice, by words that seemed to rise in ghostly fashion from beneath the earth, as if from her dead mother. While Türlütü denounced her as "ein verfluchtes Gespenst, ein Vampir, ein Totenkind" ("an accursed ghost, a vampire, a child of death" [610; Carter, 99]), Maximilian's obsession with this woman hovering precariously between life and death is but a logical outcome of his necrophilic desires: "sie war so schlank, so jung, so schön, diese Lilje die aus dem Grabe gewachsen, diese Tochter des Todes, dieses Gespenst mit dem Gesichte eines Engels und dem Leib einer Bajadere!" ("she was so slim, so young, so lovely, this lily that had grown from the tomb, the daughter of death, the phantom with the face of an angel and the body of a dancing-girl!" [612; Carter, 100]). Furthermore, Laurence is marked here as an androgyne by the association with the lily, with the angel, and with death. What happens next shows Maximilian as a virtuoso of manipulation: whether it is the influence of the chair he is sitting in, usually occupied by Laurence's ravaged Bonapartist husband, or pure instinct, Maximilian displays his own mastery of ventriloquism, embarking on the same war story her husband had been narrating just a few nights previously. It is a seductive strategy, and also a deadly one, uniting ventriloquism, vampirism, and a deflection of the female gaze. This creative manipulation of narrative is what enables Maximilian to make his sexual conquest. More than this, the moment of erotic contact between Laurence and Maximilian in the inset narrative is also the moment of Maria's final words.

The fatal association of male voyeurism, sculpture, androgyny, and death comes to its logical conclusion at the end of the *Florentinische Nächte*.[76] Maria drifts away into a deathly sleep, with barely enough strength left for one more climactic outburst. She begs to hear a description of the bed in which Maximilian finally took possession of the "Totenkind," the child of death. Now, in the final act of the *Florentinische Nächte*, Maximilian stages one more mythological drama, casting himself this time in the role of Pluto, the god of the underworld, with the sleeping Proserpina, the woman who oscillates between life and death, in his arms. Unlike the perilous stone Medusas of the "Erste Nacht," Laurence presents the seductive possibility of a fully aestheticized woman, of an artwork eternally poised between life and petrification. Once again Laurence dances the convulsive dance she had performed on the London streets, so reminiscent of the dances of the Willis, but there is one important change. Her eyes are now closed, blank; she has lost the Medusean power to transfix Maximilian with her gaze. Whatever transgressive potential her performance may contain, then, is completely at the disposal of the vampiric male narrator. If Laurence was interred by her own father, Maximilian's narrative has the sadistic potential to repeat over and over again similarly murderous acts. The head of the blinded Medusa, pinned up on the narrative frame, continues its deadly effects on the still living, as Maximilian narrates Maria into death. Maximilian ends his story and slips away from the sickroom, with no backward glance, leaving Maria's fate unknown, and thus also implicating the reader in the life-or-death powers of legibility or "Lesbarkeit." If this woman does die, it is the reader who seals her death.

Heine's *Florentinische Nächte,* finally, is a work that comments explicitly on the late romantic desire to reimpose order both on the female body, terrifying in its polymorphousness, and on an aesthetic that has itself, through the influence of Friedrich Schlegel, become predicated on androgynous chaos. The doctor (representative of Heine himself?), can do no more than diagnose the malaise and abandon the scene of a sadistic sexual/textual crime. The marble statue that takes the place of the kinetic female transvestite will, however, go on to play a central role in the program of realist education that is my focus in the next chapter.

4

Collecting Statues

Androgyny and Narrative Petrification:
Stifter's *Der Nachsommer*

One of the most prominent features of criticism on Stifter's *Der Nachsommer* (Indian Summer), from Hebbel to Lukács and onward, is its obsessive need to account for the universally acknowledged tedium of the novel. Thomas Mann, himself no stranger to exquisitely drawn-out narratives, famously commented on the "Sensationellwerden der Langeweile" (sensationalism of boredom) in Stifter's works.[1] Rudolf Wildbolz, one of many who has addressed this problem, goes so far as to describe "die Stifterische Langeweile" (Stifterian boredom) as the central aesthetic experience generated by *Der Nachsommer.*[2] But where Wildbolz resorts to a rather vague notion of fascination as an antidote to boredom—describing how the reader gets caught up in the repetitive rhythms of the novel—I want to emphasize instead the aesthetic and psychological structures that are set up by this work precisely to obstruct and resist narrative progress. Repetition, after all, is that element of narrative that seems to block temporal forward movement. The retardation of Stifter's narrative, I propose, is linked with incestuous gender constellations on the one hand and, on the other hand, with an aesthetic of petrification embodied in Heinrich's relationship with the marble statue.

Adorno, reflecting on Stifter's *Der Nachsommer,* perceptively uncovers the dynamic tensions between the novel's hyper-objectivist form and the restorative idyll that forms its thematic focus. Precisely this friction, writes Adorno, makes Stifter's version of the *Bildungsroman* more than a reactionary novel of quiescence: "Ideologische Überspannung verleiht dem Werk mittelbar seinen unideologischen Wahrheitsgehalt, seine Überlegenheit über alle Literatur tröstenden Zuspruchs und beflissen landschaftlicher Geborgenheit und erwirbt ihm die authentische Qualität, die Nietzsche bewunderte." (The ideological eccentricity of his work mediately imparts truth content to it and establishes Stifter's superiority over the average edification literature of his time, giving him that authentic quality which Nietzsche admired).[3] The novel paradoxically *insists* too much on restraint, Adorno suggests: "Objektivität erstarrt zur Maske, beschworenes Leben wird zum abweisenden Ritual" (objectivity is reduced to a lifeless mask . . . and the alleged evocation of life reads more like a ritual to keep life at a distance). Adorno's final, and astute, judgment is that it is this fixedly affirmative quality of *Der Nachsommer* that ultimately renders the work a cipher of despair.

My focus here is the relationship between the gender constellations presented by Stifter and the implicitly repressive aesthetics of petrification suggested by Adorno in his discussion of *Der Nachsommer.* More specifically, I will be concentrating on what I see as two pivotal elements in Heinrich Drendorf's progress toward maturity: first, the obsessive brother-sister dyads of the novel, posited in terms of an androgynous union, and second, the role of woman-as-statue. Like the *Bildungsromane* considered in the previous chapters—Goethe's *Wilhelm Meisters Lehrjahre,* Friedrich Schlegel's *Lucinde,* and Eichendorff's *Ahnung und Gegenwart*—Stifter's novel consciously situates androgyny as a point of departure for *Bildung.*[4] Very soon after Heinrich's initial arrival at the Asperhof, the young hero is confronted with a relationship that immediately relegates him to the alienated role of outsider. This relationship, one of complete, narcissistic exclusivity, is that between the siblings Gustav and Natalie: "Auf dem Sandwege aber gingen Natalie und Gustav herauf. Ich sah in die schönen jugendlichen Angesichter, sie aber konnten mich nicht sehen, weil sie ihre Augen nicht erhoben." (Natalie and Gustav were walking up the sandy path. I looked at their youthful faces; however, they couldn't see me since they didn't raise their eyes.)[5] That Heinrich's experience here is an echo of his host Risach's own life story becomes clear to Heinrich only after he has himself intruded upon the hermetic relationship between Gustav and Natalie. During Risach's confessional account, Heinrich learns of the intimacy that existed between the young Mathilde and her brother Alfred, and of the devastating rupture caused by Risach's erotically charged relationship with Mathilde. Significantly, Risach turns to flower symbolism when he describes Mathilde's beauty as a young girl: " 'sie war wie der Stengel einer himmlischen Lilie zaubervoll anmutsvoll unbegreiflich' " ("she was like the stalk of a divine lily—magic, graceful, incomprehensible" [653; Frye, 427]). What is expressed in the image of the white lily, as in *Wilhelm Meisters Lehrjahre,* is the alluring, impenetrable mystery of the androgyne. Yet the brother-sister relationship, in the incestuous form that dominates *Der Nachsommer,* proves to be disastrously sterile. Mathilde's brother Alfred, we read, is fated to remain single and childless. Not only do the brother-sister dyads seem to deny the generative impulses of the bourgeois family, whose construction is the work of the *Bildungsroman;* in a related move, they also function as structural impediments to narrative progress. Peter Brooks has intriguingly read incest as a narrative device, based on what he regards as the Freudian masterplot, *Jenseits des Lustprinzips.* The fraternal-sororal version of incest, Brooks suggests, "hovers as the sign of a passion interdicted because its fulfillment would be too perfect, a discharge indistinguishable from death, the very cessation of narrative movement."[6] Once again we have the association of androgyny, death, and aesthetic stasis.

Returning to Heinrich Drendorf's formative experiences at the Asperhof, the first sexually indeterminate character he encounters there is, in fact, a radiantly attractive boy. Gustav, poised on the threshold between boyhood and manhood and thus occupying the liminal space characteristic of the androgyne, appears in Heinrich's eyes a figure of sexual polymorphousness: "Ein sanftes Rot war auf seinen Wangen braune Haarfülle um die Stirne, und die großen schwarzen Augen waren wie bei einem Mädchen." (A gentle red was in his cheeks, a brown abundance of curls encircled his brow, and his large dark eyes were like those of a girl [186; Frye, 124]) This description of the beautiful youth, early in the novel, resonates throughout the work, as Heinrich returns repeatedly to the captivating androgynous softness of the boy's features: "so war Gustavs Antlitz so kräftig, daß es vor Gesundheit zu schwellen schien, es war so einfach, daß es gleichsam keinen Wunsch keine Sorge kein Leiden keine Bewegung aussprach, und doch war es wieder so weich und gütig, daß man, wenn der feurige Blick nicht gewesen wäre, in das Angesicht eines Mädchens zu blicken geglaubt haben würde." (Gustav's face was so powerful that it seemed fairly bursting with health, it was so uncomplicated, seemingly expressing no desire, worry, suffering or agitation, and was so soft and kind that if it weren't for his fiery gaze, you would have thought you were looking at a maiden's face [406; Frye, 266].) If anything, Gustav's femininity is intensified as the novel progresses to its conclusion, when Heinrich offers this final assessment of the young man's development:

> "Er ist ein vollkommner Jüngling geworden, . . . ich habe auf meinen Reisen keinen gesehen, der ihm gleich wäre. Er war ein sehr kraftvoller Knabe, und ist auch ein solcher Jüngling geworden, aber, wie ich glaube, gemilderter und sanfter. Ja sogar in seinen Augen, die noch glänzender geworden sind, erscheint mir etwas, das beinahe wie das Schmachten bei einem Mädchen ist."

> "He has developed into a splendid youth, . . . in all my travels I haven't seen anyone who could compare with him. He was a very strong boy and has also developed into a robust youth, but he is, I believe, milder, even gentler. His eyes have even gotten an added luster but there is something almost languishing about them, such as you would find in a maiden." (711; Frye, 465)

That Gustav and his sister share the sexual fluidity of an androgynous ideal is further emphasized by the impressions recorded by Heinrich of Natalie's appearance. Not only is the brother-sister relationship one of perfect complementarity, but any distinct contours of gender are repeatedly blurred under Heinrich's gaze. At times, indeed, Heinrich seems thoroughly mystified about who is boy and who is girl in this dyadic constellation. If Gustav reminds Heinrich of a ravishing young girl, recalling the beautiful hermaphrodite sculptures of Winckelmann's writings, Natalie shares the severe and rather mannish beauty of antique female forms such as those admired by Friedrich Schlegel.[7] Inspecting for the first time his father's collection of carved gemstones, Heinrich is struck by the peculiar beauty of the female heads that the classical artists chose to depict: "Allgemein . . . waren diese Köpfe kräftiger, und erinnerten mehr an die Männlichkeit als die unserer heutigen Frauen. Sie erschienen dadurch reizender und ehrfurchterweckender." (In general these heads were more powerful, reminding me more of the heads of men than today's women [399; Frye, 262].) He notices the similarity only later, observing that Natalie's head is quite "antique" in its remarkable combination of "das Zarte und doch das Kräftige" (tender yet powerful [431; Frye, 283]). Tellingly, Heinrich's gaze, in this scene of aesthetic recognition, passes from sister to brother and then to sister again, apparently unable to disentangle the dual objects of desire. Heinrich predicts that in later years Gustav will perfectly resemble the youths carved in the gemstones. This does not mean, as one might expect, and according to the logic of Winckelmann's notion of *Bildung,* that Gustav will progress from the fluid condition of adolescence to a more clearly defined gender identity, that of manhood. Instead, Heinrich believes "daß er dann Natalien noch mehr gleichen würde" (he would be even more like Natalie [432; Frye, 283]).

The self-absorbed, solipsistic relationship between Gustav and Natalie seems the perfect reflection of the aesthetics of containment at work in Stifter's novel, which contrasts the controlled idyll of the Asperhof with the chaos and fragmentation of the external world. (One thinks, for example, of Heinrich's almost obsessive and inevitably fruitless expeditions in search of the missing wood carvings that would complete his father's collection.) The natural physical similarity between brother and sister is aestheticized by the novel into a relationship of perfect identity. Raising his eyes to meet Natalie's, Heinrich is met instead by the ultimate symbol of narcissism, the reflection of both siblings unified in a mirror: "[Ich] wagte es, den Blick zu dem Spiegel zu erheben, in dem ich sie sehen mußte. Ich sah aber fast nichts mehr als die vier ganz gleichen schwarzen Augen sich in dem Spiegel umwenden." (I did venture to raise my glance to the mirror to be able to catch a glimpse of brother and sister turning to go out the door. However, in the mirror I saw almost nothing more than four dark eyes, each like the others, in the act of turning around [218; Frye, 146].) Heinrich notes that "[sie] freuten sich des gegenseitigen Lebens, das sich an einander schmiegte, und dessen sie sich kaum als eines gesonderten bewußt wurden" ([they] were] enjoying . . . each other's lives which . . . united them, though they scarcely seemed aware that they were separate [222]).[8] We hear him repeat his mournful observation that "sie schienen sich sehr zu lieben" (the two must have loved each other very much [219, 222; Frye, 147, 148]), and the sight of the couple's intimacy casts the voyeuristic hero into a strange melancholy. The hermetic self-absorption of Natalie and Gustav is easily convertible into an incestuous sexual act, the novel would seem to suggest.[9] One revealing passage describes the siblings as Siamese twins, who "sehr nahe an einander gingen, so war es von ferne, als sähe man eine einzige braune glänzende Haarfülle, und *als teilen sich nur unten die Gestalte*" (if the two . . . bent close, it looked from a distance like one single shiny brown luxuriance of hair and *only beneath were the figures separate* [219; Frye, 147; my emphasis]).

If Natalie and Gustav share an erotically charged and exclusive relationship, the same may also be said of the bond between Heinrich Drendorf and his sister Klotilde. The novel describes Klotilde's complete indifference to the numerous young men who visit her father's house seeking her favors; and on his visits home Heinrich slowly awakens to the realization that his sister is blossoming into sexual maturity "wie eine prachtvolle Rose" (like a splendid rose [277; Frye, 183]):

> Die Schwester kam dazu, und da die Mutter fortgegangen war, schlang sie
> beide Arme um meinen Hals, küßte mich, und sagte, daß ich so gut sei, und

daß sie mich nach Vater und Mutter unter allen Dingen, die auf der Welt sein
können, am meisten und am außerordentlichsten liebe. Mir wären bei dieser
Rede bald die Tränen in die Augen getreten.

My sister came in to join us; when Mother had gone she embraced me, kissed
me, saying I was so good, and after Father and Mother she loved me most
in the world. When she said this, tears almost came into my eyes. (277;
Frye, 184)

The love between this brother and sister is indeed, like that of Gustav
and Natalie, truly extraordinary or "außerordentlich," outside the "Ordnung"
superimposed by the bourgeois family on sexuality in general; and it is
"außerordentlich," I stress, precisely because it is androgynous. (We should
recall, too, that Heinrich uses just this word, "außerordentlich," of the love
between Gustav and Natalie: "Die Geschwister mußten sich außerordentlich
lieben" [222].) What the novel does with this disquieting androgynous desire
is to redirect it in the familiar oedipal channels of the bourgeois family.[10]
More specifically, it is the oedipal version of incest, here, that becomes a
way of making androgyny legible, and thus containable. Within the idyllic
nuclear Drendorf family, we read, Klotilde, quite literally, has eyes only for
her father and brother: "die Schwester, deren glänzende Augen bald auf mich
bald auf den Vater schaute, zeigte, daß sie mit mir zufrieden sei" (my sister,
whose shining eyes kept looking first at me and then my father, showed that
she too was pleased with me [276; Frye, 183]). And when Heinrich attempts
to conceive of the inconceivable—of a future husband for his sister—his
unconscious permits him to think only in terms of an incestuous union
between sister and father: "dies [könne] kein anderer Mann sein, als der
so wäre wie der Vater" (her husband had to be the same type of man as
Father [164; Frye, 110]).

Yet the destabilizing force of the love between brother and sister continues to ripple throughout the text. A rose given by Klotilde to her brother
symbolizes the forbidden eroticism that dominates their relationship—but
instead of thanking her for the flower, Heinrich remarks that cutting roses is
strictly forbidden in the controlled, passionless sphere of the Asperhof.[11] For
Klotilde, Heinrich's engagement to Natalie is deeply traumatic. Stifter carefully builds up the picture of a family idyll thrown into distressing disarray by
Heinrich's news of his marriage plans: the family, quite uncharacteristically,
do not linger in one another's company after their evening meal, the flame
of the candle trembles, the night is sultry, a thunderstorm is approaching.
Frau Drendorf, warning her son that the announcement of his betrothal will
require Klotilde to alter " 'die Art ihrer Neigung' " ("her type of affection"),

cloaks her fears—fears that are perhaps no longer surprising to the reader—
in language that surely seems hyperbolically doom-laden and religious in
tone: " 'möge das alles mit gelindem Kelche vorübergehen' " ("I hope all
that passes with a mild cup" [518; Frye, 340]). Indeed, the knowledge of her
brother's impending marriage does provoke veritable torrents of tears, and
Klotilde confesses that she is experiencing a mixture of joy and pain at his
news (520; Frye, 341). Heinrich's response—that she, too, will eventually
find a marriage partner—is emphatically rebuffed by Klotilde: " 'Nie, nie
werde ich das tun,' rief sie beinahe heftig, 'nein, ich könnte ihm zürnen, ihm,
der mein Herz hier wegführen würde. Ich liebe nur den Vater die Mutter und
dich.' " ("I'll never do that, never," she exclaimed almost violently, "no, I
would be very angry with whoever tried to take my heart away from here. I
only love Father, Mother, and you" [522; Frye, 342].) Somewhat ominous,
too, are her words of congratulation to Heinrich: " 'bereue nie, auch nicht im
geringsten, den Schritt, den du getan hast' " ("be happy, . . . never regretting
the step you have taken even in the slightest" [521; Frye, 341]).

Klotilde's feelings, as Heinrich's narrative indicates, are not one-sided.
But if Klotilde's erotic relationship with Heinrich has been made legible by
critics as a variant on father-daughter oedipal structures, the same move has
been staged for Heinrich. Critical literature on Stifter repeatedly claims that
Heinrich's love for Klotilde is a symptom of a deeper-seated desire, that
for the mother. Along these interpretative lines, Heinrich's dedication to the
earth sciences is yet another displacement of his desire for his mother.[12]
(Gerhard Kaiser has also read Keller's *Der grüne Heinrich* along these
lines, stressing the oedipal mother-son fixation that dominates the novel.[13] It
would be tempting, however, to regard Keller's exclusion of his adored sister
Regula from the autobiographically oriented novel as an example of this
urge to repress androgynous desire, and to redirect it instead along oedipal
channels.) For critics to read Heinrich Drendorf's truly extraordinary love of
his sister as a straightforward displacement of oedipal desire for his mother
is, quite simply, to repeat the repression of androgyny enacted by the novel
itself. Collapsing mother into daughter serves as an attempt to ward off the
perils of androgyny by rendering desire "safely" oedipal.

"Ich hatte nicht geglaubt," observes Heinrich, "daß ich von diesem
meinen innersten Wesen zu irgend jemanden sprechen könnte; aber Klotil-
dens Seele war der einzige liebe Schrein, in welchem ich das Teure nieder-
legen konnte." (I had never dreamed I could talk with anyone from the very
depths of my heart; but Klotilde's soul was the only beloved shrine where I
could offer up what was most precious to me [523; Frye, 343].) Heinrich's
description of Klotilde's soul as a "Schrein" conjures up the female body,

open to penetration by "das Teure." That this is the symbolic content of this image is strongly reinforced by the nature of Natalie's wedding gift from Heinrich's father—appropriately, of course, an oedipalized *paternal* token—a sealed casket that may be opened only after the marriage rites have been completed. This casket is merely the translation into materiality of the "Schrein" image. Freud, it should be noted, identified boxlike containers in general, and particularly jewelry boxes, as symbols for the female sexual organs.[14] As if to underline this connection still further, Natalie's casket contains fetish objects—precious jewels—placed there by the two "fathers," thus directly echoing Heinrich's metaphorical deposit of "das Teure" into Klotilde's "Schrein." There is more than one moment in the narrative, indeed, when the images of the two beloved women in Heinrich's mind seem to coincide, or even to interfere with each other (e.g., 175; Frye, 117).

The marriage is preceded by a journey by Klotilde and Heinrich into the mountains, Heinrich's most sacred realm. Like Natalie and Gustav, they are able in this intimate situation to exchange confidences, in conversations whose content is deliberately hidden from the reader. (This in a novel that otherwise dwells relentlessly on detail.) What is more, we read that Heinrich, even outdoing Wilhelm's decidedly chaste relationship with Natalie in the *Wilhelm Meister* novels, does not engage in a correspondence with his fiancée during their separation.[15] Ironically, indeed, the announcement of Heinrich's engagement to Natalie is followed by what seems like a series of deliberate delaying tactics that serve to spin out, almost interminably, the wedding, the one discernible "goal" or even "event" of the novel: first the journey with Klotilde, and then a hiatus of two whole years before the wedding, during which Heinrich undertakes his grand tour of Europe. It would not be too far-fetched to view the journey with Klotilde as the real "honeymoon" of the novel, a privileged time during which brother and sister are permitted to enter into a relationship of new and deeper intimacy. As Heinrich confesses: "Es war mir äußerst lieblich, die Gestalt der Schwester neben mir in dem Wagen zu wissen, ihr schönes Angesicht zu sehen, und ihren Atem zu empfinden." (I enjoyed knowing that my sister was sitting beside me in the carriage, seeing her lovely face, feeling her breath [563; Frye, 368].) That the journey also contains strong sexual undercurrents is underlined by eroticized descriptions of mountain landscapes. The couple penetrates into regions of thawing ice and snow, and the last natural image encountered in this landscape is a waterfall, a symbol of elemental sexuality, only mentioned by Heinrich in one brief sentence before he abruptly changes the subject and begins to think of the return to society and to the disciplined family: "Auch einen Wassersturz von einer steilrechten Wand zeigte ich Klotilden. Hierauf aber begann ich, auf unsere Rückreise zu den Eltern zu denken." (I also showed Klotilde a waterfall plunging over a sheer precipice. But then I began to think about the trip back to our parents [568; Frye, 372].)[16] The all-consuming, perilous nature of this erotic journey is powerfully conveyed: "Wir kamen unter Wiegen und Ächzen unseres Wägleins immer tiefer und tiefer" (Amidst the rocking and groaning of our buggy we descended more and more [569; Frye, 372]); "Wir glitten mit unserem Fuhrwerke sehr schnell abwärts, wilde Gründe umgaben uns" (We descended very quickly with our buggy, wild terrain surrounded us [569; Frye, 372]); "Als wir zurückgekehrt waren, sank mir Klotilde fast erschöpft an das Herz" (When we had reached our quarters, Klotilde sank onto my bosom, near total exhaustion [568; Frye, 372]). What is at the heart of Heinrich's *Bildung* is the transition from the dark recesses of androgyny to a socially permissible union, marriage to Natalie.

The pattern recurs throughout Stifter's works. The novella *Bergkristall* (Rock Crystal) focuses on a comparably hazardous journey into the mountains by a brother-sister couple. In the case of this narrative, however, the unspeakable nature of androgynous desire is defused by confining incest to the presexual realm of childhood. The contrast between the eroticized, nomadic space of the mountains and the confined, disciplined paternal realm emerges again clearly in *Der Hagestolz* (The Recluse) (1844).[17] There, a young man trapped at the country estate of an embittered bachelor uncle finds an escape route by swimming in the waters surrounding the island estate; he later journeys through the mountains, away from the prisonlike home of his uncle, to his beloved foster mother. Water and mountains, I argue, represent in Stifter's works natural spaces in which desires roam free. (This is in stark contrast to the compulsive—and repressive—concern with keys and locks at the Asperhof estate. Creating impermeable boundaries is of paramount concern in Stifter's narratives.) Like *Der Nachsommer,* the novella *Der Hagestolz* presents the reader with a strange lacuna of several years before the hero's wedding—and in this case, the incest motif is blindingly obvious, since Victor's bride is also his foster sister. Victor insists upon expressing his love in brother-sister terms: " 'wir werden leben, wie zwei Geschwister, die sich über alles, alles lieben, was nur immer diese Erde tragen kann, und die sich ewig, ewig treu bleiben werden' " ("we shall live like a brother and sister who love each other more than anything in the whole world, and are faithful to each other for ever and ever" [825; Luke, 50]).

If theater provides Goethe's Wilhelm Meister with an education about sexuality, gender, and desire, and more precisely about oedipal socialization, the drama at the center of Stifter's *Der Nachsommer,* Shakespeare's *King Lear,* explicitly foregrounds incestuous desire in the relationship between

Lear and his daughter Cordelia.[18] In fact, the performance of *King Lear*
forces Heinrich to *see* incest for the first time. Significantly, Heinrich's
father disapproves of the theater especially because it can arouse forbidden
sexual appetites: "Der Vater hatte, so lange wir Kinder waren, nie erlaubt,
daß wir ein Schauspiel zu sehen bekämen. Er sagte, es würde dadurch die
Einbildungskraft der Kinder überreizt und überstürzt, sie behingen sich mit
allerlei willkürlichen Gefühlen, und gerieten dann in Begierden oder gar Lei-
denschaften." (When we were children Father had never permitted us to see
a play. He felt that because of a child's great power of imagination we could
easily become overwrought; children are subject to a variety of emotions
which the excitement could turn into unhealthy desires, even uncontrollable
passions [167; Frye, 112].) Nevertheless, despite these potentially pernicious
effects, Herr Drendorf *is* prepared to use the theater to pedagogical effect,
carefully monitoring the performances his son and daughter may attend. It is
probably safe to assume, then, that it is with his father's express permission
that Heinrich attends *King Lear.* At the performance of Shakespeare's play,
Heinrich is forced to confront, in symbolic form, the incestuous love between his sister and father, that is, strictly oedipal structures of desire. This
point of emotional trauma, of course, also marks a second encounter with
Natalie, the woman who will eventually facilitate Heinrich's repression of
his own androgynous desires for his sister and thus gain him the approval of
both fathers.

   Walter Benjamin harshly criticized Stifter for what he thought of as
an addiction to the visual, which, according to Benjamin, is closely related
to an abject failure on Stifter's part to convey trauma, or "Erschütterung."[19]
I would argue, however, that in Stifter's writing it is precisely such visual
detours that are used to convey psychological trauma. The performance of
King Lear, just to take one clear example, forces Heinrich to become a spectator of incest for the first time. If the consummation of the wedding between
Heinrich and Natalie is the point of rupture for the solipsistic, nongenerative
brother-sister couplings of the novel, then what could better convey its
violent intrusion than the narrative's visual insistence on implicitly violent
acts of uncovering and penetration? I am thinking here, for example, of how
the novel circles obsessively around one specific, protracted, and apparently
trivial project of architectural restoration at the Sternenhof, Mathilde and
Natalie's home, the stripping of the whitewash from the external walls in
order to lay bare the underlying stonework. Tellingly, the completion of this
work coincides with the marriage of Heinrich and Natalie (787; Frye, 475).

   This is a union sanctioned, indeed required by the bourgeois family,
whose continued success demands an escape route from nongenerative

androgynous relationships, and of course also a closing off of homoerotic desire, hinted at in the unusually powerful bond between Heinrich and Gustav, or indeed between Risach and Mathilde's brother Alfred.[20] (Heinrich, whose relationship with Natalie is described in remarkably chaste terms, notes that he and Gustav routinely exchange kisses on meeting or parting [514; Frye, 337].) Androgyny, in this novel manifest in both homoerotic and heterosexual forms, is suspect *because* it is so sexual. The solution is to contain androgyny by colonizing childhood as an androgynous, *pre*sexual space which must be left behind as an individual matures physically and psychologically. As a genre, the *Bildungsroman* delineates and inscribes the education of desire. Simply put, *Der Nachsommer* seeks to restage *Bildung* without desire.

Marriage, too, comes at the expense of eroticism, which, as revealed in the story of Risach and Mathilde, may erupt tragically as a force of fragmentation. Heinrich's hyperbolically asexual bride Natalie is surely, in terms of her literary genealogy, the most extreme version of Wilhelm Meister's Natalie. In fact, Natalie Tarona is scarcely even a physical presence, far less a sexual one: "Sie legte ihren Arm in den meinigen, aber so leicht, daß ich ihn kaum empfand." (I offered her my arm, she put hers on mine, but so lightly that I could scarcely feel it [440; Frye, 288].) Indeed, it can convincingly be argued that it is the beautiful marble statue at the Asperhof with which Heinrich falls in love, rather than the living woman, Natalie.[21] Early on in the narrative, Heinrich is captivated by the play of light on the surface of the white marble—from the rosy shimmer of candlelight to the gleaming purity of sunlight, effects only later duplicated in Natalie's marmoreal complexion. From the scene in which Heinrich first views the sculpture, the narrative circles around his encounters with marble women, both with the classical statue at the museumlike Asperhof and with the delicate nymph in the carefully tended garden of the Sternenhof. But if Heinrich finds himself attracted to these statues, his feelings are decidedly ambivalent. On the one hand, there is the sensuality of the marble, inviting the touch, on the other hand the inviolability of the frigid stone. Natalie herself discerns the paradox, the tension between resistance and penetration: " 'Mir ist immer, wenn ich ihn [den Stein] lange betrachte, . . . als hätte er eine sehr große Tiefe, als sollte man in ihn eindringen können, und als wäre er durchsichtig, was er nicht ist. Er hält eine reine Fläche den Augen entgegen, die so zart ist, daß sie kaum Widerstand leistet.' " ("It always seems whenever I gaze at it for a longer time, as if there is a very great depth there, as if you should be able to penetrate into it, but also as if it were transparent, which it isn't. Your eyes feast upon its pure surface . . . so delicate you can scarcely resist it" [482; Frye, 316].) It is no accident that Heinrich may only enter the statue's domain at the Asperhof with protective felt shoes on his feet, that he never seems to touch her seductive marble surface. The semantic field surrounding the marble women stresses "Weiße" (whiteness), "Reinheit" (purity), "Fleckenlosigkeit" (spotlessness). Risach's account of his discovery of the marble statue in Italy also dwells on this tension between surface and interior. The statue, as Risach first sees it, appears to be a plaster bust, a cheap reproduction of an antique sculpture whose tall pedestal is covered in protective wooden boards, but as Risach peeps through a gap between the planks of wood, he discerns that this is in fact a lifesize and complete female form. Having stripped away the wood, Risach brings the statue back to his estate, where he is astonished to discover, during the work of restoration and "Reinigung," that the plaster, too, is a protective shell, covering over an authentic Greek marble statue, an "edler Kern" (noble core, 335; Frye, 219). The lengthy description of this conservation process, reminiscent of the technique of subtractive sculpture, turns around repeated references to "Messer" (knife) and "Feile" (file)—in a single page, the word "Messer" appears four times—a project curiously at odds with the nonviolent aesthetic of "Ruhe" (tranquility) presented by Risach in the same chapter. The statue woman can only be loved as resistance, by virtue of her impenetrability, and as the embodiment of absolute otherness: yet this is precisely what is most alluring in Stifter's fictional world.[22] The novel stresses, for example, the petrified state of the "Wasserbecken," or pool, at the nymph's grotto, a symbol that speaks of frozen sexual desires. What is more, the novel places these statues, emblems of petrified eroticism and of absolute difference, within the carefully cultivated, passionless spheres of museum and garden.

It is an encounter with the marble muse at the Asperhof—doubly distanced by the antique provenance of the statue—that forms the very center of *Der Nachsommer.* This passage oscillates in symptomatic fashion between stasis and movement (325–27; Frye, 214–15). Heinrich begins by marveling at the lifelike quality of the female figure, suggesting that she could spring into motion at will—the pedestal on which she stands "[schien] eher eine Stufe, auf die sie gestiegen war, um herumblicken zu können" (seemed more a step in a set of stairs which she had ascended to be able to survey the scene [326; Frye, 214f.).[23] As he contemplates her beautiful marble brow, the distinctions between statue and living woman become decidedly blurred: "Die Stirne war rein, und es ist begreiflich, daß man *nur aus Marmor* so etwas machen kann. Ich habe nicht gewußt, daß *eine menschliche Stirne* so schön ist." (The brow was pure; it was quite understandable that you could make something like that *only from marble.* I hadn't realized *a human brow* could be so beautiful [my emphasis] [326; Frye, 215].) If anything, the statue seems to come ever closer to animation as the passage progresses: "Daß sich die Gestalt nicht regte, schien bloß in dem strengen bedeutungsvollen Himmel zu liegen, der mit den fernen stehenden Gewittern über das Glasdach gespannt war, und zur Betrachtung einlud." (That the figure didn't move seemed merely due to the heavy ominous skies stretching over the skylight with thunderstorms in the distance; the whole was an invitation to gaze in wonder [326; Frye, 215].) Yet for Heinrich Drendorf the enactment of the Pygmalion myth, the crossing of boundaries between dead matter and living flesh, is fraught with peril: "Ich hatte eine Empfindung, als ob ich bei einem lebenden schweigenden Wesen stände, und hatte fast einen Schauer, als ob sich das Mädchen in jedem Augenblicke regen würde. Ich blickte die Gestalt an, und sah mehrere Male die rötlichen Blitze und die graulich weiße Farbe auf ihr wechseln." (I had a feeling as if I were standing beside a silent living human being and almost shuddered to think that the maiden might move at any moment. I gazed enraptured at the figure, watching the reddish flashes and the grayish white color alternating several times [326; Frye, 215].) (Note here the sinister turn taken by light conditions previously described as charming.) At this point, significantly, Heinrich chooses to leave the hall, departing as quietly as possible, as if still fearful that he might arouse the statue. It is this awesome version of Schiller's aesthetic icon the Juno Ludovisi, then, that takes center stage in Stifter's *Bildungsroman,* rather than the beautiful hermaphroditic statues that figure in Winckelmann's writings and find their faint echo in the androgynous boy Gustav.[24] Indeed, it is precisely the mobility of Winckelmann's androgynous aesthetics that is here perceived as risky, just as it was in Eichendorff's restorative narratives of containment. Winckelmann's connoisseurship of hermaphroditic sculptures stresses the liberating aesthetic fluidity of multiperspectival viewing, the power of desire and of unfettered subjectivity. Of a Telephus statue, Winckelmann exclaims: "Das Gesicht dieses jungen Helden ist völlig *weiblich,* wenn man es von *unten herauf* betrachtet, und es scheinet sich etwas *Männliches* in dasselbe zu mischen, wenn man es von *oben herunter* ansiehet." (The face of this young hero is completely feminine when one looks at it from below, and it seems that something masculine is mixed in with it when one looks at it from above.)[25] In a similar vein, Schlegel's hero Julius praises the aesthetic/erotic effects generated by indeterminate lighting: "die Beleuchtung wird so viel reizender. Wie schön glänzt diese weiße Hüfte in dem roten Schein" (the light is so much more enticing that way. How beautifully this white hip gleams in the red light!)[26] In the 1780s, it had become a modish activity to visit the Italian sculpture galleries at night, by torchlight, in order to experience the

pleasurable illusion that the statues were moving. But Heinrich Drendorf, in
sharp contrast, emphasizes the necessity of containment for the female form,
and also—like so many of Eichendorff's heroes—displays considerable
anxiety at the subversive, volatile effects of "verworrenes" light on marble;
what this hero yearns for is the certainty afforded by one fixed, hierarchical
perspective on the statue, by the gaze from above.[27] (During the restoration
process, Risach transfers the statue to a revolving pedestal, thus achieving
total visual mastery over the female form.) Furthermore, the statue is safest
when placed in a purpose-made, artificially lit, institutional space—the
museum:

> Mir dünkte es gut, daß man diese Gestalt nicht in ein Zimmer gestellt hatte,
> in welchem Fenster sind, durch die alltägliche Gegenstände herein schauen,
> und durch die *verworrene Lichter* einströmen, sondern daß man sie in einen
> Raum getan hat, der ihr allein gehört, der sein Licht von oben bekömmt, und
> sie mit einer dämmerigen Helle wie mit einem Tempel umfängt.

> It seemed appropriate that they had not put this figure in a room where there
> were windows, where ordinary things could gaze in, where a *confusion of light*
> would be streaming in; rather, they had put it in a space all its own, lighted
> from above, surrounding it with the light of a temple. (327; Frye, 215; my
> emphasis)

Where the female statue is unsettling because it threatens to come to
life, Natalie is a reassuring presence because of her statuesque fixity, even
morbidity. On several occasions, Heinrich comes accidentally upon Natalie
as she sits in a posture of absolute speechlessness and immobility: "Sie regte
sich nicht, und wendete sich nicht." (She neither moved nor turned around
[435; Frye, 285].) Sitting close to her twin, the marble nymph, Natalie adopts
a sculptural pose:

> Als ich schon nahe an der Grotte war, und schief in dieselbe blicken konnte,
> sah ich, daß Natalie auf dem Marmorbänklein sitze, welches sich seitwärts von
> der Nymphengestalt befand. Sie saß an dem innersten Ende des Bänkleins. Ihr
> blaßgraues Seidenkleid schimmerte aus der dunkeln Höhlung heraus. Einen
> Arm ließ sie an ihrer Gestalt ruhen, den andern hatte sie auf die Lehne des
> Bänkleins gestützt, und barg die Stirn in ihrer Hand.

> As I approached the grotto and could see it from an angle, I spied Natalie
> sitting on the marble bench which was off to the side of the marble statue.
> She was sitting on the innermost end of the bench. Her pale gray silk dress
> gleamed in the dark hollow. One arm was resting on her lap, the other was
> propped on the back of the bench, and she was holding her forehead with her
> hand. (455; Frye, 298)

Yet it seems to be precisely the possibility that he might cause Natalie, the statue-woman, to stir into life that Heinrich fears: "Daß ich nicht in die Grotte gehen wolle, war mir klar; allein die kleinste Wendung, die ich machte, konnte ein Geräusch erregen, und sie stören." (It was clear that I didn't want to enter the grotto; but even the slightest turn could make a noise and startle her [455; Frye, 298].) In the case of both woman and statue, animation and mobility seem ghastly eventualities for Heinrich. Following this logic, the aestheticizing of woman, the act of conversion into a static, fetishized artwork, is a reassuring move. In the microcosm of the Asperhof, the only approximation of wholeness is gained through the artwork, an object holding up the promise of (impossible) totality. Erotic desire is sublimated fully in Heinrich's ever-intensifying relationship with art, his "Kunsttrieb."[28] "Lust," as erotic desire, is more disciplined and controllable by the subject in the form of the aesthetic gaze, "die Lust des Schauens" (482; Frye, 316). Thus, from the first glimpse of Natalie, as she and her mother accidentally cross his path, Heinrich seems impelled to render this unknown living woman into aesthetic form: "Ich dachte mir, da der Wagen immer tiefer über den Berg hinabging, ob denn nicht eigentlich das menschliche Angesicht der schönste Gegenstand zum Zeichnen wäre." (I thought, as the carriage was going driving down the hill, that perhaps the human countenance was the most beautiful object to draw [156; Frye, 105].) Similarly, it is his encounter with the same mysterious young woman at the theater in Vienna that finally inspires Heinrich to take up drawing—with the subject of his first sketches, predictably enough, being female faces. Natalie's form, I should stress, provides more than harmless artistic inspiration; something more is at work in the narrative than a peaceable merger of art and reality.[29] The novel urgently stresses the need for her actual conversion into an artwork: so, for instance, Klotilde declares emphatically that " 'ein Bild muß doch ausgeführt werden' " ("a painting must be done"), thus already anticipating (or even rehearsing) Natalie's death in her wish for a commemorative reproduction of the young bride (694; Frye, 453). In this aestheticizing move, Heinrich is, of course, repeating the act of sublimation and substitution undertaken by Risach, who places the marble muse at the center of the Asperhof as a replacement object following the loss of the real woman, Mathilde. Thus, the statue functions fetishistically again, an epitaph or monument to erotic desire that has been renounced and presumably also mastered. Almost as important as the transformation of the living woman into an artwork, however, is the act of framing, which serves both to contain the aesthetic object (so often posited as female) and to subject it to the public gaze. We are told, for example, that the inhabitants of the Asperhof gather to celebrate the restoration of a beautiful Madonna and Child only when the painting has been set ritualistically within an ornate gilt frame (356; Frye, 234). And, in one of the final images in *Der Nachsommer,* the newlyweds present themselves to their families in the static form of a tableau, disciplined and de-eroticized, one more precious, and commodified, object in their parents' already extensive art collection.[30]

The conversion of woman to artwork is explicable as a method of restoring lost totality in a world perceived as hopelessly fragmented. For this reason, then, the marble muse at the Asperhof is defined, in classical terms, by her wholeness and plenitude: "Was ist der Mensch, und wie hoch wird er, wenn er in solcher Umgebung und zwar in solcher Umgebung von größerer Fülle weilen darf." (What must a man be, how high could he strive if he could abide in such surroundings, in such an abundance! [599; Frye, 392].) The paradox is in the violence that implicitly underlies this totalizing, aestheticizing move. It is a violence of containment and a violence of appropriation. What I mean by this is that the narrative insists on the woman as artwork, and more precisely as an artwork *acquired,* for a collection, for a family. Thus, Heinrich refers to his bride Natalie as a reified, fetishized collector's item, " 'mein Kleinod und mein höchstes Gut' " ("my jewel, my most treasured possession in the world" [714; Frye, 467]). This urge of Heinrich's to take possession of the woman/artwork simply echoes, of course, the paternal discourse on art. Von Risach describes how aesthetic *Bildung* enables the individual to arrive independently at " 'den Besitz der Schönheit' " ("the *possession* of beauty") without having to rely on outside intervention (328; Frye, 216; my emphasis). This is a society of curators and inventory-takers, not artists. Furthermore, if we read the marble statue at the Asperhof as a self-conscious allusion to Schiller's Juno Ludovisi, the incarnation of the aesthetic state, then the utopia being proposed here is itself a kind of historical artifact, a monument to classical idealism carefully framed and preserved in Stifter's museumlike narrative.[31] Even the "Schauer" (shudder) experienced by Heinrich in his encounter with the statue might be interpreted as a nostalgic, ritualistic gesture toward an antiquated aesthetic response. (If Stifter's literary response to an age of commodification resides in such citationality, Gottfried Keller's strategy, as I show below, is radically different, depending as it does on parody.) What is perhaps most significant in the citation of Schiller's aesthetic icon is the way Schiller's dialectical model of *Bildung* uniting sensuality and reason, and perfectly incarnated in an androgynous marble statue, is displaced by an aesthetic repressive of the body, of erotic passion, and of sexual mobility. While *Der Nachsommer* might appear to initiate a classicist/humanist model of integration, in effect it preaches the impossibility of this ideal.[32] It is no accident that von Risach delivers a lengthy curatorial account of the classical statue acquired in Italy in a sober tone far removed from Winckelmann's, or for that matter from Schiller's, often rapturous—and "unscientific"—descriptions of indeterminacy and fluidity. In the meantime, von Risach repeatedly expresses anxieties about Roland's overly subjective approach to his paintings—artworks that, we are told, are monstrous and incomprehensible precisely because they do not adhere to a standard of rational verisimilitude. (Indeed, the novel's happy ending will necessarily exclude Roland, who leaves to pursue his artistic career in Rome.) The subjective animating powers of a Pygmalion yield in this novel to the scientific techniques of modern art conservation. That this is a decidedly antiquarian Juno is a point highlighted by the chronological location of Stifter's novel: the narrative, published in 1857, is pointedly set retrospectively, a whole generation earlier, in the Biedermeier 1820s, a period of restoration.[33] If Eichendorff insists upon converting Schlegel's aesthetic of androgynous chaos into fixed binaries, Stifter completely de-eroticizes and drains androgyny, placing an antique marble statue before the passive viewer as one more in a historical—and thus doubly dead—collection of *natures mortes.* Russell Berman's remarks on the ossification effected by this realist text resonate with particular force if applied to the particular case of the androgyne: "In Stifter's frozen world, the sole meaning of the various semantic systems . . . is the exigency of subordination and the command to submit."[34]

Robert Holub has proposed a (re)definition of realism as "a normed discourse that excludes otherness."[35] Following the lead of his compellingly presented argument, it is worth taking a closer look at two novellas by Stifter that rehearse the fate of androgyny, what I have been describing here as the repetitively enacted move from subjectivity to repression, from sexual mobility to the de-eroticized bourgeois family: *Brigitta* (1844) and *Katzensilber* (1853).[36] In the case of the female child who surfaces so mysteriously in *Katzensilber,* the repressive refashioning undertaken in the name of *Bildung* proves once more to be utterly inimical to the androgyne, that most extreme embodiment of alterity and mobility. From the outset, the child provokes wildly subjective responses; we read, for example, that the foresters and pitch burners who inhabit the woodlands all have radically divergent descriptions to offer of the androgynous girl. The child's initial appearance is another citation of Mignon in *Wilhelm Meisters Lehrjahre;* all the conventional attributes of the German literary androgyne are present: exotic male costume; a dark, penetrating gaze; a stubborn insistence on concealing wounds for fear of drawing attention to her true biological

gender; an affinity with the natural world; speechlessness; and a reluctance,
or inability, to respond to questions concerning her origins:[37]

> aus dem Gebüsche [kam] ein fremdes, braunes Kind heraus. Es war ein
> Mädchen, es war fast so groß und noch schlanker als Blondköpfchen, hatte
> nackte Arme, die es an der Seite herab hängen ließ, hatte einen nackten
> Hals, und hatte ein grünes Wams und grüne Höschen an, an welchem viele
> rote Bänder waren. In dem Angesichte hatte es schwarze Augen. . . . Die
> Großmutter sagte nichts, und fuhr fort, zu reden. . . . Als die Großmutter
> geendet hatte, redete sie das Mädchen an, und sagte: "Wer bist du denn?"
>   Das Mädchen aber antwortete nicht, es sprang in die Büsche und lief davon,
> daß man die Zweige sich rühren sah.

> a strange, dark child came out from the bushes. It was a girl, almost as tall as
> and even more slender than Goldilocks, with bare arms hanging by her side,
> a bare neck, and wearing a green jerkin and green trousers festooned with red
> ribbons. She had black eyes. . . . Grandmother said nothing, and carried on
> talking. . . . When she had finished, she addressed the child, asking: "Who are
> you then?"
>   But the girl didn't reply; with a rustle of twigs, she jumped into the bushes
> and made off. (vol. 1: 226)

Following her adoption by an idealized bourgeois family—whose
stereotypical function is highlighted by the elision of its members' proper
names—the child is gradually, step by step, coaxed into conventional female
dress. The unstated function of this clothing is to inhibit the free movement
characteristic of the androgyne and to facilitate "correct," that is, strictly
gendered, behavior: "Da es weibliche Kleider trug, war es scheuer, und
machte kürzere Schritte." (Now that she was wearing feminine clothing,
she was more timid, and her steps were daintier [273].) Indeed, the whole
education of the androgynous child is predicated on this costume change into
appropriate feminine clothing. The aggressive psychological deformation
that must result from this version of *Bildung*—a companion piece to the
strange violence of the "sanftes Gesetz" (gentle law) heralded by Stifter's
foreword—is clearly visible in the novella. One of the male servants, for
example, expresses his desire to reify the volatile, androgynous creature:
" 'Ich fange das Ding,' sagte ein Knecht." ("I'll catch the thing," said one
servant [240].) But the words of the enlightened paterfamilias display a
similar, if more subtly worded, urge to contain the threatening instability
incarnated by the child, and to divert its energies into more acceptable and
socially useful forms. Of particular note is the father's emphasis on the uses
to which the child may be put by him and his family, rather than concern for
a waif who has, after all, just saved his only son from a fiery death:

"Lasse das," sagte der Vater, "das Mädchen hat meiner Mutter und meinen Kindern heute den größten Dienst erwiesen. Darf man es überhaupt nicht rauh behandeln, so darf man es jetzt um so weniger, *so lange es sich nicht schädlich erweist.* Wir werden es schon *auszukundschaften* und zu *finden* wissen, dann muß es gut behandelt werden, daß es Zutrauen gewinnt, und wir werden die Art schon finden, wie wir das Kind belohnen, und *ihm sein Leben vielleicht nützlicher machen können, als es jetzt ahnt.*"

"Stop it," said the father, "the girl has performed the greatest service to my mother and my children today. She shouldn't be handled roughly at all, and especially not now, *as long as she doesn't harm anyone.* We're sure to be able *to get to the bottom of her story,* and then she should be treated well, so that we win her confidence, and we'll find a way of repaying the child, and perhaps of *making her life more useful than she can suspect at the moment.* (240; my emphasis)

The biographical grounding of this repressive plot is revealing. Stifter had in 1847 become the foster parent of a girl named Juliana Mohaupt, a gypsy-like child of a peculiarly wild and exotic beauty, the orphaned niece of his wife Amalia.[38] In 1853, Stifter dedicated a copy of the collection *Bunte Steine* (Colored Stones) to his wayward foster daughter with the strangely premonitory inscription: "Wenn du einst von dem Guten weichen wolltest, so lasse dich durch diese Blätter bitten, es nicht zu tun" (Should you ever wish to err from the right path, hear the prayer of these pages not do so [*Sämtliche Werke,* vol. 1: 762].) In 1859, at the age of eighteen, Juliana ran away from home; four weeks later, her body was retrieved from the Danube. *Katzensilber,* published six years before Juliana's suicide, may have served as part of a (dramatically unsuccessful) pedagogical containment strategy within Stifter's own home.

The plot of the novella *Brigitta* may in its turn be viewed as a prototype for *Der Nachsommer.* One critic at least has also seen a connection here with Plato's discussion of love in the *Symposium,* a link that I, too, see as highly significant, particularly as it relates to my point of departure in this study, the interconnectedness of androgyny and *Bildung.*[39] *Brigitta* is famously prefaced with the narrator's comments on the mysterious, labyrinthine dimensions of human existence, often experienced in connection with the aesthetic sphere:

Es gibt oft Dinge und Beziehungen in dem menschlichen Leben, die uns nicht sogleich klar sind, und deren Grund wir nicht in Schnelligkeit hervor zu ziehen vermögen. Sie wirken dann meistens mit einem gewissen schönen und sanften Reize des Geheimnisvollen auf unsere Seele. . . . Die Seelenkunde hat manches beleuchtet und erklärt, aber vieles ist ihr dunkel und in großer Entfernung geblieben.

There are often things and relationships in human life which are not at once
clear to us and whose basis we are unable speedily to lay bare. These then affect
our souls with the soft and beautiful charm of the mysterious. . . . Psychology
has illuminated and explained many things, but there is much that it still finds
dark and impenetrable.[40]

But, as we have observed so often in fictions of androgyny, the chaos
of aesthetic subjectivity is inextricably linked with a bewildering, perilous
experience of gender illegibility. Against the alienating, blank backdrop of
the Hungarian steppes, with their curious "Fieberluft" (malarial air [751;
Watanabe-O'Kelly, 110]), the narrator encounters a figure who resists all
easy definition. The text wrestles to pin the enigma down: first, Brigitta is
identifiable only in the most imprecise fashion, as "eine Gestalt" (a figure);
then the narrator, basing his assumptions on the crowd of workers gathering
around, decides that this must be the local landowner; moments later, the
figure is a "Reiter" (rider), but the narrator is now able to read her as a
transvestite, middle-aged woman; finally, by this point in a state of utter
confusion, he misreads her social class, addressing her in the form suitable
only for a peasant woman, "Guten Abend, Mutter" ("Good evening, Mother"
[741; Watanabe-O'Kelly, 102]). Significantly, however, and for the first time
in the literature we have considered, the androgynous female is read in this
work as physically undesirable, if not monstrous, with the narrator choosing
finally to cast her in the sexless role of an old peasant woman.[41] At the same
time, we do read of one strikingly attractive feature, her "Reihe sehr schöner
Zähne" (set of beautiful teeth [743; Watanabe-O'Kelly, 103]). That this,
along with Brigitta's penetrating dark gaze[42] and the "rabenschwarze Locke,
die sich um die Stirne schlang" (raven-black hair encircling [her forehead]
[770; Watanabe-O'Kelly, 126]), may be part of the familiar Medusean
repertoire of attributes is strongly supported by the narrator's nightmare
vision of petrification, related to us shortly after their first encounter:

Dann träumte mir allerlei von ihr, vorzüglich kam ich von dem Traume nicht
los, daß ich auf der Haide vor der seltsamen Reiterin stehe, die mir damals
die Pferde mitgegeben hatte, daß sie mich mit schönen Augen banne, daß
ich immer stehen müsse, daß ich keinen Fuß heben könne, und daß ich alle
Tage meines Lebens nicht mehr von dem Flecke der Haide weg zu kommen
vermöge.

Then I had all sorts of dreams about her, above all I could not shake off the
dream in which I was standing on the heath in front of the strange female rider
who had given me the horses that time, who was putting a spell on me with
her beautiful eyes, so that I must always stand there, unable to move a foot,

unable all the days of my life to move away from that spot on the heath. (765; Watanabe-O'Kelly, 121)

This young narrator, however, is confronted not only with the transvestite Brigitta but with an enigmatic and charismatic hero, Stephan Murai, whose taste for exotic, flowing silk robes brands him, like his estranged wife, Brigitta, as a kind of cross-dresser.[43] Where the narrator's nocturnal fantasies about Brigitta conjure up the terrifying gaze of the Medusa, his dream about Stephan Murai, decidedly more seductive in nature, dwells on the older man's mercurial costume changes, his delight in the performance of alterity. Stephan's softness, even effeminacy, conjures up the contours of Winckelmann's hermaphroditic Antinous.[44] But if Brigitta's sexual indeterminacy is simultaneously hideous, sterile, and life-threatening, Murai's physical ambiguity is endlessly seductive. Tellingly, the young man first encounters Murai in Italy,[45] and his spellbound descriptions of Murai evoke superbly the androgynous, bisexual fluidity of Winckelmann's aesthetics:

> Ich möchte sagen, es war eine sanfte Hoheit, die um alle seine Bewegungen floß, so einfach und siegend, daß er mehr als einmal auch Männer betörte. Auf Frauenherzen aber, ging die Sage, soll er einst wahrhaft sinnverwirrend gewirkt haben. . . . Aber ein Fehler, sagte man, hänge ihm an, der ihn erst recht gefährlich mache; nämlich, es sei noch niemanden, selbst der größten Schönheit, die diese Erde trage, gelungen, ihn länger zu fesseln, als es ihm eben beliebte.

> There was, I should say, a soft majesty that surrounded all his movements, so simple and so winning that more than once he bewitched men too. But, so legend had it, his influence over women's hearts had once been truly disturbing. . . . But he had one fault, so it was said, which made him really dangerous, which was that no one, not even the greatest beauty on earth, had succeeded in captivating him for longer than it suited him. (737; Watanabe-O'Kelly, 99)

Furthermore, although we are told that Murai, like Brigitta, has already advanced well into middle age, he appears to be fixed in the eternal adolescence of Winckelmann's androgynes. His soul, the narrator recalls, "[hatte an sich] das Kindliche, Unbewußte, Einfache, Einsame, ja oft Einfältige" ([had] childlike, unconscious, simple, even naive qualities [738; Watanabe-O'Kelly, 100]). What is more, it is this primally androgynous aspect of Murai's personality that makes him, in the narrator's eyes, the embodiment of the aesthetic realm. Murai's soul, he writes, was "das Glühendste und Dichterischste, was mir bis dahin vorgekommen ist" (the most ardent and poetic soul I had ever encountered [738; Watanabe-O'Kelly, 100]). Once again, the aesthetic is related to undifferentiation, preconsciousness, and an inability to function in the social sphere. Brigitta, too, it should be noted, is defined by her relationship to the aesthetic sphere. The "Papiere, auf denen seltsame wilde Dinge gezeichnet waren, die von ihr sein mußten" (pages . . . with strange wild drawings on them, which must have been by her), the "Laute, die sie von niemandem gehört hatte" (sounds that she had heard from no one), the "halbe Reden und Ausrufungen" (half-finished speeches and exclamations [767; Watanabe-O'Kelly, 122]), all indicate a rich and poetic inner world. But as an androgyne, Brigitta is also speechless; and, as a female androgyne, the version of *Bildung* imposed upon her further interiorizes her experience: "Sie mochte eine phantastische verstümmelte Welt in ihr Herz hinein brüten." (She must have been hatching a fantastic and deformed world within her heart [767; Watanabe-O'Kelly, 123].) That the relationship between Murai and the narrator is defined by its homoeroticism is a point at the very least hinted at by the text: Murai repeatedly pays extended visits to the young man's bedroom early in the morning, with remarkable disregard for his guest's dishabille.[46] Yet by the end of Stifter's novella, we are presented with a radically different picture. Now the narrator has veered away from the seductive aesthetic realm of (homoerotic) androgyny, from a nomadic way of life, and acquired all the trappings of bourgeois respectability: a solid mercantile career, a home, and a wife. In other words, what *Brigitta* stages—and stages with obvious pedagogical intent—is the shift from sexual mobility, indeed from homosexuality, in the persons of both Murai and his wife Brigitta, as well as of the narrator, to a legible world of heterosexual relationships. By the end of this gender plot, as one critic has observed, Stephan Murai has shaken off his excessive femininity, just as Brigitta has laid aside the trappings of her mannishness.[47] It is important to stress the shift here from a nongenerative and perhaps homosexual form of androgyny, a possibility delineated already in Plato's *Symposium,* to the image of the heterosexual Brigitta and Stephan united, and de-eroticized, by their role as parents. At the same time, however, and as the culminating tableau of Gabriele's marble tombstone underscores, the restorative reunion of husband and wife also has everything to do with a negation of eroticism. The wolf at the door of Stephan Murai's estate is sexuality.

In all of Stifter's works, we have observed the perils of nomadic androgynous desire, indeed of desire itself. Gail Finney has finely drawn the distinction between the eroticized pleasure gardens of the nineteenth-century French novel, derived from the classical *locus amoenus,* and the cultivated spaces that are yoked in the service of self-cultivation in the German *Bildungsroman.*[48] These fictional German gardens, Finney argues, are characteristically exclusive of passions that might imperil social or individual stability. Stifter's narratives are exemplary of a tendency to evacuate desire from the hermetic and artificial setting of the museum and the garden. Androgynous desire, meanwhile, roams in the wild mountain margins of *Der Nachsommer;* it erupts in a conflagration that destroys the perfectly tended bourgeois home in *Katzensilber;* and in *Brigitta* the land separating the estates of Stephan and his estranged wife contains no human point of reference but a gallows, and this barren steppe is populated by roaming wolves.

Mirror Effects: Sexual/Textual Refractions in the Narratives of Gottfried Keller

> Eine Spiegelwelt ist die Welt der Kellerschen Schriften—freilich auch darin, daß irgend etwas in ihr von Grund auf verkehrt, rechts und links darinnen vertauscht ist. Während das Tätige, Gewichtige in ihr scheinbar unangetastet seine Ordnung wahrt, wechselt das Männliche ins Weibliche, das Weibliche ins Männliche unmerklich über.

> The world of Keller's writings is a world of mirrors—certainly insofar as things as are always completely back to front, with left and right transposed. While the active and important elements in Keller's world appear to remain untouched by disorder, the masculine imperceptibly becomes feminine, and the feminine masculine.

WALTER BENJAMIN, "Gottfried Keller"[49]

Benjamin was one of the first critics to recognize the importance of androgyny in the works of Gottfried Keller, memorably characterizing the Swiss writer as an androgyne-poet, an individual who brought into harmony psychological qualities of masculinity and femininity. If Keller's own personality could, in Benjamin's eyes at least, be described as sexually fluid, Benjamin perceived similar qualities in his writing, and defined in androgynous terms what he saw as the remarkable product of Keller's literary realism: a reflection of reality that reveals itself as apparently identical with reality, as its mirror image, yet that may also, like a mirror image, be simultaneously the inverse of reality.

To take up the androgynous image deployed by Benjamin in his literary critique, what we find reflected in Keller's realist texts is, however, a uniquely distorted, often kaleidoscopic, mirror image of the androgynous myth, and in particular of the tradition of female androgyny that plays such a central aesthetic and pedagogical role in German narratives of *Bildung*. The second version of *Der grüne Heinrich* (Green Henry) contains, for instance, a dazzling example of Keller's literary/transvestite play.[50] Heinrich Lee finds

himself in a playful carnivalesque scene in which a group of craftsmen is
taking turns at storytelling, at narrative dressing up. Tales of female cross-
dressers are laughingly circulated, and the theme of female transvestism is
initiated by folk reports that tell of multiple sightings of the Virgin Mary. (The
cross-dressing Virgin is, of course, also the focus of Keller's *Sieben Legenden*
[Seven Legends], a work considered in more detail below.) Significantly,
these fantastic occurrences are explained by the "Bergkönig" (the Mountain
King) in essentialist terms, as examples of the univeral polymorphousness of
woman, rather than as the exclusive mystical domain of the divine mother:

> "Die Sache bedeutet nach meiner Ansicht die ungeheure Allgemeinheit, All-
> gegenwart, Teilbarkeit und Wandlungsfähigkeit der Himmelskönigin; sie ist
> alles in allem, wie die Natur selbst, und steht dieser schon als Frau am
> nächsten auch in Hinsicht der unaufhörlichen Veränderlichkeit, wie sie denn
> auch außerdem in allen möglichen Gestalten aufzutreten liebt und sogar als
> streitbarer Soldat gesehen worden ist. Hierin gerade mag sie einen Zug ihres
> Geschlechtes bewähren, wenigstens der vorzüglicheren Mitglieder desselben,
> nämlich einen gewissen Hang, Mannskleider anzuziehen."

> "In my opinion, the affair signifies the Queen of Heaven's immense univer-
> sality, omnipresence, divisibility, and power to transform herself; she is all in
> all, like Nature itself, and stands, as a woman, next to Nature, in respect to
> perpetual mutability, as she loves to be seen in all possible shapes and has
> even been seen as a combatant soldier. And in this respect, she may display
> as true a characteristic of her sex, or at least of the more eminent members of
> it, namely a certain inclination to don masculine clothes."[51]

But over the course of these chronicles of female cross-dressing,
several shifts in perspective occur. From this initial description as a harmless
if not alluring pastime, transvestism acquires a dizzying and rather sinister
array of connotations. The next anecdote, related by a stained-glass painter
and introduced as " 'ein drolliges Beispiel' " ("an amusing example") of
" 'Verkleidungs*kunst*' " ("ability to disguise oneself" [883; Holt, 477; my
emphasis]), foregrounds the aesthetic dimension of transvestism, associated
here with the notion of gender as performance. The craftsman tells of his boyhood history as a street urchin, and of the unknown, prankish child who often
accompanied him and his companions on their escapades. The tale is replete
with category confusion. This "boy" turned out to be not only of the opposite
sex but also of the wrong age. A desperately poor widow, the " 'künstlicher
Gassenjunge' " ("make-believe street urchin") donned the clothing of her
dead son, cut off her hair, and foraged the streets with the town guttersnipes.
The story turns around the artifice and artfulness of transvestism, and thus the
constructedness of gender, referring to the widow's masquerading strategy

as " 'ihre Kunst' " and " 'ihr Genie' " ("ingenuity," "cleverness" [884; Holt, 478]). But this, since we find ourselves in Keller's literary world, is as much an economic strategy as an aesthetic one; in order to gain access to the male-controlled circulation of comestibles in the town, the widow found herself compelled to circulate in the appropriate clothing. The final tale of female transvestism pushes these economic aspects to their extreme. Set in the distant sixteenth century, it tells of a hangman's wife who, when her husband has been taken ill, is so eager to profit financially from an offer of work in a neighboring town that she disguises herself in her husband's clothing and presents herself there in the role of executioner. The revelation of her correct gender occurs at the climactic moment when one of the condemned criminals is ready to be hanged. The reaction of the local citizenry is telling. A hang-man's assistant—who has just completed the task of shaving the condemned man's head before the execution—is ordered to cut open the woman's clothing for the assembled townspeople in order to display the "correct" sex of the executioner, in a move that equates gender transgression with capital offense. The blood lust of the townswomen is now turned upon the female transvestite, while the condemned man returns safely to his prison cell: " 'Dennoch stürzten die Frauen und Mägde aus den Häusern, verfolgten die fliehende Scharfrichterin mit Kunkeln und Besenstielen bis vor die Stadt und zerbläuten ihr den glänzend weißen Rücken. So nahm diese Verkleidung ein schlechtes Ende für die verwegene Amazone.' " ("Nevertheless, the women and girls rushed out of the houses, pursued the fleeing female executioner with distaffs and broomsticks until she was outside the town and thrashed her gleaming white back. Thus the disguise ended badly for the daring Amazon" [886; Holt, 479].) But what is especially important to note in this increasingly violent sequence of male narratives about female transvestism is the intended audience: the naive young girl Agnes, who, we were told before the stories commenced, has been sitting happily with the men "wie ein Kamerad" (like a comrade [883; Holt, 476]). By the end, however, the situation is very different: "Mit dieser derben Geschichte hatte unser Geplauder die Grenze fast überschritten, die wir dem anwesenden Mädchen schuldig waren. Sie schüttelte schauernd den Kopf." (With this blunt story, our talk had almost overstepped the bounds that we owed to the girl who was with us. She shook her head, shuddering [886; Holt, 480].) Again, circulating transvestite tales are being used strategically, to pedagogical effect. What they do here, quite literally, is to engender correct female behavior, while placing the female listener in a passive (here, indeed, insensible) role within the narrative circulation. By the end of the festivities, Agnes is in fact so inebriated that she loses consciousness: "sie sank uns aus den Händen und zu Boden, wo

sie leichenblaß mit zitternden Lippen und Händen ausgestreckt lag und bald
gänzlich leblos schien, so daß jetzt eine ängstliche Stille eintrat" (she slipped
from our hands and sank to the floor, where she lay prone, deathly pale, with
trembling lips and hands, and by and by appeared absolutely lifeless, so that
now there was an anxious silence [887; Holt, 481]).

Much of Keller's satirical invective against the "Mannweib" or androgyne, the nineteenth-century symbol of the emancipated intellectual
woman, must by now sound relentlessly familiar. In this vein, Keller ridicules
the writing couple Fanny Lewald and Adolf Stahr—parodically deforming
the language of Plato's *Symposium*—as "das vierbeinige-zweigeschlecht-
liche Tintentier" (the four-legged, dual-sexed octopus).[52] The androgynous
female artist of the novella *Regine*, in Keller's late work *Das Sinngedicht*
(The Epigram), is, unlike her classical and romantic precursors, depicted as
entirely demonic but also as laughably demonic. Reinhart, the narrator of
this story, describes her in scathingly unfavorable terms, as a "weibliche[r]
Schmierteufel" (devilish female dauber [vol. 2: 1000]), "der Unhold" (the
monster [1001]), "die dämonische Malerin" (the demonic female artist
[1014]). Here we find a catalog of classical and romantic attributes for the androgyne, a figure now overdetermined to the point of parody. Where Goethe's
or Eichendorff's female cross-dressers possessed an undeniable, if perilous,
erotic allure, this woman's drab transvestite garb is downright shabby and
unappealing. Keller even ironizes the pronominal uncertainty initiated in
Goethe's descriptions of Mignon: *"er* hatte noch nicht gefrühstückt, wie *er*
sagte, und *er* genoß immer nur rohes Obst und Brot des Morgens, weil es das
Billigste war. . . . Beim Erwerbe aber wußte *sie, um ihrem Geschlecht jetzt
wieder die Ehre zu geben,* sich sehr unschüchtern überall vorzudrängen, und
hier nahm *sie* urplötzlich die Rücksichten auf das Geschlecht von jedermann
in Anspruch." (*He* had not yet eaten breakfast, *he* said, and *he* only ever
partook of raw fruit and bread in the morning, as that was cheapest. . . .
When it came to making a living, however, *she—and I give her sex the honor
due to it now*—was the opposite of shy, pushing *herself* forward everywhere,
and suddenly taking into account everyone's sex [1000; my emphasis].) The
artist—whose first name, we read, she has shortened so that it is impossible
to detect whether it designates a man or a woman—has acquired a certain
notoriety. Significantly, this stems from her unhealthy influence on the
innocent young bride Regine: Regine's husband is no longer able to proceed,
without interference, with the Pygmalion-like forming and fashioning of his
impressionable wife, whom he refers to as his "Bildungswerk" (educational
work [994]). From passive object of contemplation, in Stifter's museumlike
fictional edifice, to active artist figure and pedagogue, the androgyne has

obtained new and frighteningly subversive powers. The narrator's reaction, meanwhile, is to turn his gaze nostalgically to a lost aesthetic state. Staring in horror and disgust at the androgyne, as she inelegantly spits out apple pips, Reinhart shifts the conversation to the "ideal woman" of the past, in this case of the eighteenth century, and alludes to a contemporary of Winckelmann in Rome, the ethereal Angelika Kauffmann, herself an artist of some repute. Kauffmann, we should note, was famed for her delicate renderings of androgynous adolescents—but these were androgynous creatures who safely occupied their place on canvas as harmless aesthetic constructions.[53]

The female androgyne presented in *Regine,* far from acting as a stage on the path to male completion as does Goethe's Natalie or Schlegel's Lucinde, threatens to take over an exclusively male role as sculptor and modeler of an infinitely malleable female protagonist. The anxiety she provokes among the male inhabitants of the town seems precisely to be an anxiety about replicating androgynes; she coaxes several respectable middle-class wives into nocturnal transvestite adventures, and Erwin Altenauer returns from his journey to find his bride transformed into a monster through the influence of the androgyne. Regine has become not only a monster but a monstrous artwork.[54] Reinhart, expressing his revulsion at the butch artist's transsexual fantasies, trots out the scurrilous story of Nero's obsession with obtaining a sex change, which culminates in the Roman emperor "giving birth" to a toad. This tale illustrates, then, precisely Reinhart's fear at the generative powers of the supposedly sterile androgyne, even though this anxiety is cloaked in a broader moral message about the dangers of sexual fluidity: "In der Tat hat die Wut, sich die Attribute des andern Geschlechtes anzueignen, immer etwas Neronisches; möge jedes Mal die Kröte in den Sumpf springen!" (Indeed, the insane compulsion to acquire the attributes of the opposite sex always smacks of Nero; may the toad always jump into the swamp! [997]). The irony is that Erwin Altenauer himself, who stages his relationship with his bride entirely in terms of the love affair between Pygmalion and his statue, ultimately loses his creation, just as Pygmalion and Nero do. Altenauer is confronted with the madness of his pedagogical enterprise in a crushing scene of revelation. First, he stumbles upon the artist's portrait of Regine on the art market in New York; his wife has been commodified as an image or "Bild," but only as he himself has already commodified her. Then, entering his home for the first time after his return from America, he is faced with a tawdry plaster replica of the most celebrated classical statue, an oversized and obviously parodic statement about his pedagogical enterprise: "Verwundert fand er im Gesellschaftssaale eine große Neuigkeit: auf eigenem Postamente stand ein mehr als vier

Fuß hoher Gipsabguß der Venus von Milo. . . . Erwin betrachtete einige
Sekunden die edle Gestalt, die übrigens in ihrem trockenen Gipsweiß die
Farbenharmonie des Saales störte." (To his surprise, he found a new item
in the parlor: standing on its own pedestal was a plaster cast of the Venus
de Milo, over four feet tall. . . . Erwin spent a few moments gazing at the
noble figure, whose dry white plaster, however, spoiled the harmonious color
combination in the room [1011–12].) But Altenauer is still more shocked
when, moments later, he sees his wife gazing at herself in a mirror. Her
narcissism is linked to the solipsism that characterizes her androgynous
"creator"; according to Ovid's version of the story of the hermaphrodite,
Hermaphroditus, like Narcissus fleeing the amorous advances of a nymph, is
fused with the seductress Salmacis by the gods, against his will. If Narcissus
perishes gazing at his reflection in a pool, the hermaphrodite's fate is to infect
others with his sterility:[55]

> Aber wie überrascht stand er [Altenauer] eine Minute später unter der Türe
> des Schlafzimmers, das er leise geöffnet, als er eine durchaus verwandte,
> jedoch vom farbigen Leben pulsierende Erscheinung sah. . . . Welch ein An-
> blick! . . . . Aber auch welche Gewohnheiten! Wie kommt die einfache Seele
> dazu, auf solche Weise die Schönheit zu spiegeln und die Venus im Saale
> nachzuäffen?

> But how astonished he [Altenauer] was a moment later, when, having quietly
> opened the bedroom door he stood there and saw a figure that was intimately
> related to the first, though pulsating and vibrant with life. . . . What a sight!
> . . . . But what behavior, too! How had that simple spirit hit upon the idea of
> mirroring beauty and aping the Venus in the salon? (1012)

Excluded from this tableau of narcissistic self-indulgence, Altenauer
is profoundly troubled by the fact that the artwork he has created may
have come to life and acquired her own independent existence. Worse,
she has stirred into life not in the unique form of a superb classical artwork but as a cheap, mass-producible imitation of the statuesque ideal.[56]
Keller's literary response to an age of commodification is always parody, and his *Sinngedicht* is indeed, in its entirety, a work preoccupied
with parodic literary redressings of the Pygmalion myth. At the beginning of the novella cycle stands the enigmatic epigram by baroque author
Friedrich von Logau, itself embedded in an edition of the long-dead Enlightenment thinker Lessing: "Wie willst du weiße Lilien zu roten Rosen
machen? Küß eine weiße Galathee: sie wird errötend lachen." (How will
you transform white lilies into red roses? Kiss a white Galatea; she will
laugh, blushing [938].)[57] We also know that Keller originally planned to

entitle his work after Pygmalion's beloved, unnamed in the Greek myth but in later versions of the story known as Galatea.[58] *Regine* illustrates in parable form the danger inherent in compulsively acting out the myth of Pygmalion and Galatea; the only scene of physical tenderness between Altenauer and his wife occurs when Regine is dead and Altenauer takes her lifeless body in his arms. Yet what we find at the end of the cycle of tales, as Kaiser has suggested, is a neutralized bourgeois adaptation of the mythical story, a redressing of the myth in nineteenth-century terms.[59] In Lucie's story *Die Berlocken* (The Charms) the culminating novella in the cycle, we glimpse a tiny sea-nymph, Amphitrite, decorating an enameled watch, perceptively identified by Kaiser as "Galatea im Taschenformat" (a pocket-sized Galatea).[60] This miniaturized, decorative version of Galatea is accompanied by a delicate engraving of a harbor—perhaps an allusion to the safe haven of marriage—and can be safely contained within a man's pocket. Here "woman as artwork" has been yoked into the service of bourgeois industry.

If the female androgyne surfaces in the novella *Regine* as a grotesque specter of the emancipated woman, and if she poses an external threat to the social stability provided by the institution of marriage, androgyny also serves Keller repeatedly as an image for bourgeois marriage itself. But where romantics such as Friedrich Schlegel or integrational classical thinkers such as Goethe embraced a heterosexual version of androgynous union in marriage, a restoration of lost totality in an age of difference, Keller's reading of the Platonic myth is decidedly more ambivalent. It could hardly be otherwise, in an age of capitalism and atomization where love is perceived as inextricably bound with economy. As noted above, Keller lampooned husband and wife Fanny Lewald and Adolf Stahr as a kind of grotesque hermaphroditic polypod, with a nod to Aristophanes' already playful descriptions of the primal androgyne in the *Symposium*. Benjamin, however, reminds us of the bitter sting in Keller's humor: "So ist auch Kellers Humor nicht goldne Politur der Oberfläche, sondern der unberechenbare Anlageplan seines melancholisch-cholerischen Wesens." (Thus Keller's humor, too, is not just a gilded surface, but rather the unpredictable system deriving from his melancholic and choleric disposition.)[61] The classical androgyne, viewed through his own inimitable distorting lens, provides Keller with a grotesque metaphor for bourgeois marriage. Thus, in *Die mißbrauchten Liebesbriefe* (The Misused Love Letters), we read of Viggi Störteler's comically disastrous attempts to "educate" his wife, Gritli, in the refinements of high-brow culture. But, much to Viggi's displeasure, reading out loud from his latest literary dabblings merely sends the prospective muse to sleep:[62]

"Das kann so nicht gehen, liebe Frau! Du siehst, wie ich mir alle Mühe gebe, dich zu mir heranzubilden, und du kommst mir dennoch nicht entgegen! Du weißt, daß ich die dornenvolle Laufbahn eines Dichters betreten habe, daß ich des Verständnisses, der begeisternden Anregung, des liebevollen Mitempfindens eines weiblichen Wesens, einer gleichgestimmten Gattin bedarf, und du lässest mich im Stich, du schläfst ein!"

"Things can't go on like this, my dear wife. You can see all the effort I'm making to educate you up to my level, but you don't meet me halfway. You know I have embarked upon the thorny career of a poet, that I need the understanding, the inspiring stimulus, the loving sympathy of a female being, a spouse who shares my ideas, and yet you leave me in the lurch, you fall asleep!" (vol. 2: 335)[63]

Viggi's first attempt at a love letter of literary note is hilariously *recherché,* not least because of its hyperbolic repertoire of androgynous terms. Its opening lines read, " 'Wenn sich zwei Sterne küssen, so gehen zwei Welten unter!' " ("When two stars kiss two worlds perish" [337; Bullock, 29].) Here androgyny has descended into hackneyed literary commodification, in a move analogous to Keller's parodic recycling of the Pygmalion and Galatea myth. Viggi's proposed title for the sentimental correspondence between himself and his wife is a further hint in this direction. He has the inspired idea of twinning their pompous literary aliases, in a thoroughly androgynous fusion, and publishing the letters as "Kurtalwino, Briefe zweier Zeitgenossen" (Kurtalwino, Letters of Two Contemporaries [348; Bullock, 41]).[64] Moments later, however, on discovering the cunning gender switch in letter-writing roles undertaken by Gritli, Viggi is forced to confront the hopeless fictionality of his androgynous ideal: " 'Kurtalwino! Kurtalwino! fahre wohl, du schöner Traum!' " ("Kurtalwino, Kurtalwino, now the lovely dream is ended" [349; Bullock, 44].) However, it is precisely Gritli's destabilization of gender through the male medium of writing that seems most to disturb her husband, rather than the amorous contents of her correspondence with the young schoolmaster. Tellingly, this overturning of the rule of difference is experienced by Viggi as an act of physical aggression, even as a form of murder: " '[Gritli] verrenkt das Geschlecht und verdreht die Namen. . . . Sie dreht dem Geschlechte abermals das Genick um.' " ("She . . . twists the sex and juggles the names . . . she twists the neck of the sexes again" [350; Bullock, 44].) There are obvious parallels here with the transvestite female executioner who makes such a scandalous narrative appearance in *Der grüne Heinrich* (vol. 1: 885–86). Female transvestism is troped repeatedly in Keller's works, then, as a most obvious form of the castration threat. The ultimate irony, to return to *Die mißbrauchten Liebesbriefe,* is in Viggi's choice of replacement muse, Kätter Ambach, a comically hideous hag. Kätter is depicted in graphic detail as a globular, monstrously malformed creature—a kind of voracious, lascivious, and misshapen Platonic androgyne? "Denn was ihre Gestalt betraf, so besaß sie einen sehr langen hohen Rumpf, der auf zwei der allerkürzesten Beinen einherging, so daß ihre Taille nur um ein Drittel der ganzen Gestalt über der Erde schwebte." (As to her figure, she had a very tall trunk that moved on the shortest of legs, so that her torso floated only a third of the total figure above the ground [vol. 2: 353; Bullock, 49].) While Wilhelm and Gritli, finally united in a loving marriage, prosper financially and go on to have many healthy children and grandchildren, Viggi and Kätter succeed only in reproducing more and more of the laughable love letters, in an image that links aesthetic sterility with the picture of a monstrously androgynous union of man and wife.[65] Viggi has fallen victim to his own literary cliché of androgynous perfection, culled from German novels of the late eighteenth and early nineteenth centuries.

In the late novella *Der Landvogt von Greifensee* (The Landvogt of Greifensee), we find a similar undercutting of the bourgeois myth of "androgynous" union in marriage. Set retrospectively in the year 1783, and thus at the height of the intellectual obsession with the ideal figure of the androgyne, the narrative has as its protagonist a middle-aged bachelor, Salomon Landolt, who convokes five old girlfriends to decide upon a wife for him, in an ironic "symposium" on the nature of love. I am consciously invoking Plato's *Symposium* here, since this novella rehearses the full repertoire of androgynous possibilities, ultimately revealing the untenability of the myth in an age of atomization. Within the novella are the stories of the five failed romances, the first of which already hints at the impossibility of androgynous union. It is a love story strategically couched in androgynous terms, more precisely in terms of an androgynous heterosexual union. The first name of Salomon's beloved, Salome, is a mirror image of his own, their families are related, and they bear an almost uncanny resemblance to each other:

> Außerdem wurden sie wegen ihrer ähnlich lautenden Namen der Gegenstand heiterer Betrachtungen, und es gab manchen Scherz, der ihnen nicht zuwider war, wenn sie auf einen Ruf gleichzeitig sich umsahen und errötend wahrnahmen, daß vom andern die Rede sei. Beide gleich hübsch, gleich munter und lebenslustig, schienen sie wohlgesinnten Freunden für einander schicklich und eine Vereinigung nicht von vornherein untunlich zu sein.

> They also became the object of humorous remarks because of their similar-sounding names, and they were not annoyed at the laughter that ensued whenever one's name was called and they simultaneously turned around, only to realize, with a blush, that the other had been intended. Both equally

attractive, bright, and energetic, they seemed to their well-meaning friends a good match, and their union did not at the outset appear imprudent. (vol. 2: 728)

But with the failure of this relationship, in which the two lovers play out what might be termed a fraudulent—since fictive—androgynous idyll, Salomon enters into a train of fractured romances, in a decidedly Aristophanic quest for a soul-mate. (The name Salome, associated as it is with castration, is itself strangely premonitory.) The second woman with whom Salomon falls in love also can be read as a parodic version of the androgynous ideal. Figura Leu's very name is redolent with hermaphroditic hints: first there is the masculine form of "Leu," and then the comic phallic associations of Salomon's pet name for her, "Hanswurstel" (clown or, literally, Hans sausage).[66] She is described as "einem Engel des Himmels gleich, der ein Mysterium feiert" (like an angel from heaven celebrating a mystery [744]), as "ein elementares Wesen" (an elemental spirit) who lives for "Tanzen und Springen" (dancing and leaping [735]), attributes that, like her first name "Figura," with its connotations of a purely aesthetic construction, place her, like the solipsistic Mignon, in the realm of the fictive primal androgyne. That this relationship, too, is impossible is revealed in the practical joke played by Figura Leu on her suitor. In what is ostensibly an ironic commentary on the vanity of the writer Bodmer, in whose company the young people find themselves, Leu secretly pins a mirror to the back of Landolt's head and revels in the narcissistic mirror images of herself afforded by the arrangement:

> Sogleich aber schritt sie, auf dem Moosboden unhörbar für ihn, mit pantomimischen Tanzschritten hinter ihm her, auf und nieder, so leicht und zierlich wie eine Grazie, und führte ein allerliebstes Spiel auf, indem sie sich fortwährend in dem Spiegel auf Landolts Rücken und in dem Handspiegel abwechselnd beschaute und zuweilen den Handspiegel und ihren Oberkörper, immer tanzend, so wendete, daß man sah, sie bespiegele sich von allen Seiten zugleich.

> At once she began striding up and down behind him on the mossy ground, inaudible for him: her pantomimic dance steps made her as light and dainty as one of the Graces, and she presented the most delightful spectacle as, alternately looking at her reflection in the mirror on Landolt's back and her reflection in her hand mirror, and all the time dancing, she occasionally turned the hand mirror and her upper body so that one could see she was mirroring herself from all sides simultaneously. (750)

Leu cannot break out of her own self-involvement, the truth of which is pointedly revealed by the poet Geßner's witty response. He drapes himself in a shawl belonging to one of the ladies and, brandishing Leu's mirror, climbs up on a stone in order to present the assembled company with a hilarious tableau: an allegorical statue of a cross-dressed Veritas (751). The whole tradition of the hermaphroditic classical statue is placed on a pedestal, but for comic effect. Finally, the sterility of the relationship between Leu and Landolt is devastatingly summed up in the grandmother's ivory skeleton figurine, a cautionary reminder about the futility of bourgeois marriage, the impossibility of a fusion of two human beings; the totem migrates in the narrative from Landolt's grandmother to Landolt, who in turn bequeaths it to Leu.[67] For one last example of the perilous nature of androgyne love, we can turn to Landolt's final attempt to find love, in the person of the enticing Aglaja. This union is also fated to nonresolution, but precisely because Aglaja has already been beguiled by another narcissistic androgyne figure, a dreamy, pietistic preacher:[68]

> Es war ein junger Mann in schwarzer Tracht, mit ziemlich regelmäßigen Gesichtszügen und allerdings großen, dunklen Augen, mit welchen manche Maler Jesum von Nazareth darstellen. Man konnte sie auch schwarze Junoaugen nennen. Landolt aber dachte, indem er das Bild mit bitteren Gefühlen, aber starren Blicken betrachtete: es sind die Augen einer Kuh!

> It was a young man in somber garb, with fairly regular features but with the large dark eyes used by some artists in their depictions of Jesus of Nazareth. They could also be termed black and Junoesque. Landolt, however, staring fixedly and bitterly at the picture, thought: those are the eyes of a cow! (781)

Landolt appears destined, by the time of his curious invitation to the old girlfriends, to lead a solitary existence. (Ironically, though, his professional duties require him to sit in judgment over marital disputes.) The five aging beauties are greeted at Landolt's castle by the grotesque spectacle of an animal cross-dressing both as a human being and as a female of the species, Salomon's pet monkey Cocco, "für diesen Tag besonders abgerichtet, als eisgraues Mütterchen bekleidet" (specially trained for the occasion, and dressed up as a hoary old woman [783]).[69] What is more, the transvestite Cocco, the "kleiner Landvogt" (little landvogt [784]), is a strategically placed mirror image of Salomon himself. This is only a taste of what is to come, for the choice of bride that confronts the five women is between a mustached, hussar-like woman and an androgynous boy dressed up seductively as a maid. (Both, it should be noted, are also crossing class boundaries, since the Amazonian Marianne is in fact Salomon's housekeeper, and the boy maid or "Knabenzofe" is a respectable middle-class pastor's son.) With the choice of the cross-dressing boy, the impossibility of heterosexual androgynous union is sealed, and at the end of the novella, many years later, both Landolt and Marianne die in solitude.

I identified in Stifter's *Der Nachsommer* and *Brigitta* what I see as a resurgent mid-nineteenth century anxiety about the peculiarly male version of androgyny that had first gained literary currency in Germany with the homoerotic writings of Winckelmann. This anxiety stands in sharp contrast to the fascination of classical and romantic writers with the category of female androgyny. For Stifter, as I showed, the solution to the disquieting spectacle of homoerotic fluidity seems to lie in repressing male androgyny, the figure of the "beautiful boy," in favor of the stability of de-eroticized, heterosexual marriage. A possible explanation of this radical nineteenth-century shift in perspective is offered by Foucault in his *History of Sexuality*. Commenting on the medicalization of homosexuality that occurred in the 1870s, Foucault makes the argument that homosexuality came to be defined "less by a type of sexual relations than by a certain quality of sexual sensibility, *a certain way of inverting the masculine and the feminine in oneself.*" According to Foucault, nineteenth-century medical science attributed a "singular nature" to the *male* homosexual. He continues: "Homosexuality appeared as one of the forms of sexuality when it was transposed from the practice of sodomy onto a kind of *interior androgyny, a hermaphrodism of the soul*. The sodomite had been a temporary aberration; the homosexual was now a species."[70] Perhaps, following Foucault's bold line of thought, we might say that androgyny at this point in history becomes the exclusive psychological and medical preserve of the male homosexual.

In Keller's works, we often see male bodies becoming unglued, destabilized, and effeminate. Most strikingly, this phenomenon seems to come about through the contagious effect of contact with female protagonists, and all of this in a society that places the law of heterosexual marriage at its center.[71] As noted earlier, in the discussion of *Das Sinngedicht*, the female androgynes who appear throughout Keller's works have the same infectiously emasculating effect on male protagonists as Ovid's Hermaphroditus. One of the most revealing examples of such anxiety vis-à-vis the androgynous male body is contained in the novella *Frau Regel Amrain und ihr Jüngster* (Regula Amrain and Her Youngest Son), from the Seldwyla cycle. Frau Regel Amrain, having been abandoned by a feckless husband, is left to bring up three small children, the youngest of whom, the sensitive and cherubic Fritz, is especially dear to her. In charge of her husband's stone quarry and also of the domestic sphere, Frau Amrain is what I would call the model of a capitalist androgyne: she controls both economic production (predicated as male) and the production of children. Even her liberal political tendencies are identified by the narrator as highly compatible with "wahre Männlichkeit" (real manliness [vol. 2: 149; Fremantle, 120]). What, then, are we to make of the curious scene in which Fritz, by now on the brink of manhood, dresses up in his mother's best silk frock to attend a wedding party?[72] His external "look" having been perfected by an immaculate hairdo and prosthetic breasts, Fritz's psychological gender identification is also affected:

> Als er daher mit seiner Gesellschaft dem Rathause zuzog, ein Körbchen mit den Geschenken tragend, sah er so verschämt und verwirrt aus wie ein wirkliches Mädchen und schlug die Augen nieder, und als er so auf der Hochzeit erschien, erregte er den allgemeinen Beifall, besonders der versammelten Frauen.

> When, therefore, he marched off with his gang toward the Town Hall, carrying a little basketful of gifts, he looked so bashful and confused, casting down his eyes, like a real girl, that when he appeared thus at the wedding he aroused general applause, especially from the women present. (142; Fremantle, 112)

The lengthy description of Fritz's metamorphosis dwells on the erotic, sexual elements of his cross-dressing.[73] Thus, having donned "die besten und buntesten Toilettenstücke" (her finest and most colorful outfits [141; Fremantle, 111]) from his mother's wardrobe, Fritz's next impulse is to burrow among her boxes: "[er] wühlte dazu aus den reichlichen Schachteln Krausen, Bänder und sonstigen Putz hervor. Zum Überfluß hing er sich noch die Halskette der Mutter um" (in addition he dug out of the numerous boxes all kinds of ruffles, ribbons and other finery. On top of it all, he put on his mother's necklace [141; Fremantle, 111]). If the "Schmuckkästchen" or jewelry box may be read, according to Freud, as symbolic of the female sexual organs, Frau Amrain's ransacked trinket box casts further light on the psychological importance of the scene.[74] To compound matters still further, Frau Amrain, after her initial dismayed conviction that nothing is more likely to lead her beloved son into a dissolute "Lotterleben" (sluttish life [142; Fremantle, 112]) than this transvestite adventure, finds her own aesthetic— and perhaps erotic—curiosity piqued:

> Je länger sie ihn aber nicht fand, desto mehr wünschte sie ihn zu sehen, nicht allein mehr aus Besorgnis, sondern auch um wirklich zu schauen, wie er sich wirklich ausnähme und ob er in seiner Dummheit nicht noch die Lächerlichkeit zum Leichtsinn hinzugefügt habe, indem er als eine ungeschickt angezogene schlottrige Weibsperson sich weiß Gott wo herumtreibe.

> The longer, however, she failed to find him the more she wanted to see him, now not only because of her anxiety, but also in order to see what he really looked

like, and whether he had not added foolishness to frivolity in bustling about, God knew where, clumsily disguised as a sluttish wife. (143; Fremantle, 113)

Frau Amrain finds herself inspecting a giddy and flirtatious group of Seldwyla women, and is initially quite unable to distinguish her own son from among them. As Gerhard Kaiser has pointed out, the novella seems to dwell strangely on the names of these rather insignificant characters—Anderau, Haider, Ackerstein, Aufdermauer, Amhag.[75] Anagrammatic splinters of the name Amrain, they indicate, perhaps, the seductive dangers of mother fixation and mother identification.[76] (Tellingly, the novella identifies Frau Amrain's strategy of *Bildung* in androgynous terms, speaking of the "Liebe, mit welcher sich das Wesen ihrer Person dem seinigen einprägte und sie ihre Instinkte die seinigen werden ließ" (the love which she bestowed on him, and by which she caused her instincts to become his [139; Fremantle, 108]). If Fritz's transvestite escapade is influenced by the sexual fluidity of his mother, it is significant that other women, too, play an activist role in his metamorphosis: we read of a "lachendes Dienstmädchen" (laughing maid [141; Fremantle, 111]), of "muntere Schwestern" and "wenig schüchterne Mädchen" (jolly sisters and not too bashful girls [142; Fremantle, 112]), and the dubious Seldwyla women with whom Fritz associates, described as having a "geheimnisvoller Ruf" (their good name was somewhat in doubt [144; Fremantle, 114]), also seem to be incarnations of the polymorphously perverse. Fritz plays an increasingly passive role in his own transformation at female hands: "[er ließ] diese Bemühungen der wenig schüchternen Mädchen um sich geschehen" (enduring the efforts made by the not too bashful girls upon his person [142; Fremantle, 112]). And, indeed, it is in frivolous female company that Regel Amrain finally discerns her son, a strange mirror image of herself:

Nachdem Frau Amrain die Beschaffenheit dieses weiblichen Kreises erkannt, wollte sie eben Gott danken, daß ihr Sohn wenigstens auch da nicht zu erblicken sei, als sie noch eine weibliche Gestalt zwischen ihnen entdeckte, die sie im ersten Augenblicke nicht kannte, obgleich sie dieselbe schon gesehen zu haben glaubte. Es war ein großes prächtig gewachsenes Wesen von amazonenhafter Haltung und mit einem kecken blonden Lockenkopfe, das aber hold verschämt und verliebt unter den lustigen Frauen saß und von ihnen sehr aufmerksam behandelt wurde. Beim zweiten Blick erkannte sie jedoch ihren Sohn und ihr violettes Seidenkleid zugleich und sah, wie trefflich ihm dasselbe saß, und mußte sich auch gestehen, daß er ganz geschickt und reizend ausgesputzt sei.

Mrs. Amrain at once recognized the nature of this group of ladies, and she was just about to thank God that her son was not at least visibly there, when she discovered among them a feminine figure whom at first glance she did not recognize, yet thought she had seen before. She was tall, magnificently built, a creature made like an Amazon, with a shock of blond curls, who was seated bashfully, fascinated by the gay women, and who was the subject of much attention from them. At second glance, however, she recognized her son, and in the same instant her indigo silk dress; noticing how excellently it fitted him, she had to admit that he was got up with skill and charm. (145; Fremantle, 115)

This moment of uncanny doubleness, however, provides a powerful impetus for Frau Amrain's efforts to provide her son with an effective form of *Bildung,* one that will push him from his infantile polymorphousness and mother fixation into a successful societal role.[77] Frau Amrain's first step, after she has literally torn to pieces the infectiously seductive violet dress, is to find Fritz a wife in her own image, a nameless, blank "Frauchen" (little wife) who, needless to say, will come from Frau Amrain's hometown and correspond perfectly to her "Vorspiegelungen" (wildest fancies [148; Fremantle, 120]). The hurdle of bourgeois marriage having successfully been overcome, Regula Amrain's next task is to encourage her son to become actively—and thoughtfully—engaged in the public sphere, in the man's world of politics. The crowning moment in this process of *Bildung* occurs when Frau Amrain's husband returns unexpectedly to the family fold, and finds in Fritz "sein junges Ebenbild" (image of himself [170; Fremantle, 148]). Successful socialization for Fritz involves divesting himself of any hint of sexual fluidity—the perturbing compulsion to mimic his mother—and slipping into something more comfortable, the role of the father.

Another example of the contagious influence on male sexual identity of female gender shifting occurs in the novella *Eugenia,* from Keller's late work *Sieben Legenden* (Seven Legends) published in 1872.[78] The transvestite Roman noblewoman Eugenia, cast so often by critics in the role of an unnatural monster as a consequence of her gender camouflage,[79] surrounds herself with two youths of increasingly doubtful sexuality. If Eugenia is "eine liebliche Rose" (a lovely rose), her two companions are "zwei zierliche Jünglingsblumen" (two graceful flowers of youth), and the three adolescents, all of whom occupy the androgynous territory between childhood and adulthood, are almost indistinguishable: "Der eine trug ein azurblaues Gewand, der andere ein rosenfärbiges und sie selbst ein blendend weißes, und ein Fremdling wäre ungewiß gewesen, ob er drei schöne zarte Knaben oder drei frisch blühende Jungfrauen vor sich sehe." (The one wore an azure-blue, the other a rose-red robe, and she herself one of a dazzling white. A stranger would have been uncertain whether he saw three fair, tender boys,

or three fresh, blooming maidens before him [vol. 2: 534; Wyness, 334].)
The narrator ironically points out the "curious" fact that both boys share the
name Hyazinthus, a reference worth pursuing further. As Herbert Anton has
shown, an earlier Latin version of the Eugenia legend describes the boys
quite explicitly as "eunuchi," whereas Kosegarten, Keller's source for the
legends, names one Prothus and the other Hyazinthus.[80] If Keller selects
the second of these names for both of Eugenia's famuli, he is undoubtedly overlaying these boyish androgynes with homosexual connotations.
Hyacinthus, in Ovid's *Metamorphoses,* is a young lover of Apollo. When
he is accidentally struck and killed by Apollo's discus, a hyacinth flower
springs up from the boy's blood.[81] What is more, the juice of the hyacinth
was also thought to inhibit male sexual development, a belief alluded to by
Winckelmann in his discussion of hermaphrodite beauty in the *Geschichte
der Kunst des Altertums:* "Ja, männlichen Knaben suchete man, auch unter
den Römern, die Bekleidung der Männlichkeit zurückzuhalten, durch den
Saft von Hyacinthenwurzeln, die in süßem Wein abgekocht wurden, um das
Kinn und andere Theile damit zu bestreichen." (The Romans too attempted
to delay the onset of manhood in boys, using the juice of hyacinth roots
which had been boiled in sweet wine and with which they anointed the chin,
and other parts.)[82] Thus, the boy companions of Eugenia seem to be forever
excluded from "normal" (i.e., heterosexual) maturation and *Bildung* through
their contact with the transgressive Roman woman. (It is no accident that
Aquilinus—who is pointedly described as "männlich" or manly—when he
first proposes marriage to Eugenia begs her to return the impressionable
children to the care of their parents.) If it is the homosexual version of the
androgynous myth that initially prevails in the figures of the two Hyazinthen,
the same appears to be true for Eugenia herself. Not only is Eugenia's statue
placed in the temple of Minerva, a goddess who, as discussed above in
chapter 2 on Goethe's *Wilhelm Meister,* is associated with androgyny,[83] but
in an ironic twist on the Pygmalion myth, she falls in love with her own
marble image and shortly afterward, still in monastic robes, succumbs to the
charms of a beautiful pagan. Where Kosegarten's pious Eugenia does not
yield for an instant to homosexual temptation,[84] Keller's heroine responds
with unholy ambivalence:

> Eugenia, welche, von ihren anderweitigen Gedanken eingenommen, nicht auf
> das unheilige Aussehen des Weibes geachtet hatte und ihr Gebaren für Demut
> und geistliche Hingebung hielt, ließ sie gewähren, und dadurch aufgemuntert
> schlang die Heidin ihre Arme um Eugenias Hals, den schönsten jungen Mönch
> zu umarmen wähnend. Kurz, ehe der sichs versah, fand er sich von der
> leidenschaferfüllten Person umklammert und fühlte seinen Mund von einem

Regen der heftigsten Küsse getroffen. Ganz betäubt erwachte endlich Eugenia aus ihrer Zerstreuung; doch dauerte es Minuten, bis sie sich aus der wilden Umhalsung losmachen und aufrichten konnte.

Eugenia, who, absorbed in far other thoughts, had not observed the woman's unsaintly appearance, and had taken her behavior for humility and pious devotion, let her have her way; and the heathen, thus encouraged, flung her arms about Eugenia's neck, imagining that she was embracing the handsomest of young monks. In short, before he was aware, he found himself clasped tight by the amorous creature, and felt his mouth the target for a storm of passionate kisses. Completely dumbfounded, Eugenia awoke at last from her reverie; and even then it was some minutes before she could disengage herself from the wild embrace and rise to her feet. (541; Wyness, 340)

Even more scandalously, in the legend *Die Jungfrau als Ritter* (The Virgin as Knight), the Virgin Mary herself puts on male dress in order to help her protégé, the sluggish Zendelwald, win success with the opposite sex—her own—but not before placing herself in a tender tête-à-tête with the fair Bertrade.[85] Over the course of this useful intervention, of course, she succeeds in displacing a dormant and decidedly unmanly Zendelwald. The Virgin also triumphantly cuts off the mustache belonging to the knight Guhl and the grotesquely coiffed nose hairs of the knight "Maus der Zahllose" (Mouse the Numberless), trophies of virility. Yet the purpose of the mission is finally to engender correct—that is, properly masculine—behavior in the hapless Zendelwald. The happy outcome of Eugenia's story occurs when, on trial before Aquilinus for the alleged assault of the heathen woman, she tears away her monk's habit in order to expose her "authentic" gender and identity (a thoroughly Eichendorffian moment): "[Eugenia] riß ihr Mönchsgewand entzwei, bleich wie eine weiße Rose und in Scham und Verzweiflung zusammenbrechend" (ripping her monk's robe in two, pale as a white rose, she collapsed in shame and despair [545, Wyness; 344]). Having received appropriate female clothing from the hands of her husband and modified her unfeminine scholarly behavior, in the final irony of Eugenia's socialization she becomes the patron saint of recalcitrant schoolgirls (547; Wyness, 346).

The paradox in this seemingly unequivocal moral lesson about the dangers of gender transgression lies in Keller's own aesthetic appropriation of what might be called "transvestite" narrative strategies. On the one hand, scholars have pointed out the constant play in the narratives between "Schein" and "Sein," appearance and reality, dichotomies that are fittingly given symbolic form in the problem of transvestism. Critics have also been assiduous in their unraveling and analysis of the textual sources for the

Sieben Legenden, the Christian legends collected by the Protestant pastor Kosegarten in 1804, and have often remarked on the many textual strata interwoven in this late work by Keller—from the moralistic language of Catholic hagiography to that of fairy tale, from a flavor of Greco-Roman paganism to the contemporary piquancy of the deliberately anachronistic epithet "Blaustrümpfchen" (bluestocking) for Eugenia.[86] These circulating literary discourses, aptly described by one reader as "eine artistisch-virtuose Gratwanderung sich gegenseitig irritierender und spiegelnder Erzählhaltungen" (a virtuoso artistic tightrope walk of mutually bewildering and reflective narrative perspectives),[87] may be termed the aesthetic counterpoint to the literal cross-dressing that occurs on the novella stage, an interpretative possibility that is opened up by Keller himself in the preface to the *Sieben Legenden.* Remarking on the different literary strands at work in the Christian legends that are his source, Keller identifies both "die kirchliche Fabulierkunst" (the religious art of storytelling) and, lurking beneath this, "die Spuren einer ehemaligen mehr profanen Erzählungslust oder Novellistik" (the traces of what was once a more profane pleasure in narrative or novellas [532]). His own work, in the growing genre of the nineteenth-century realist novella, and perhaps inevitably, involves a kind of literary historical cross-dressing, just as the *Bildungsroman* was initiated by a slippage of genres and genders, as argued in chapter 2, above.[88] (Indeed, the genre that is Keller's source here inherently demands emulation, the obvious moral goal of the legend being *imitatio.)* What is more, we know that Keller originally intended to weave these legends into the novella cycle that was eventually published separately as *Das Sinngedicht.* Remarkably, the reason for Keller's final decision to withhold Kosegarten's material from the Galatea cycle appears to have been a concern that he had been unable successfully to graft the older genre of legend onto that of the novella. Although he wrote to Heyse in 1871 that he was still considering placing the legends within the structure of the *Sinngedicht,*[89] and had even eliminated the miracle episodes from the stories of Vitalis and Eugenia so as to make them more suitable for inclusion, he was in fact by now planning to publish the legends separately, as legends. But even then, his publisher, Theodor Vischer, talked him into giving the work the title "Sieben Legenden," precisely because this would strike readers as "recht ironisch" (altogether ironic), and Keller himself referred to his latest publication as "jene ironisch reproduzierten 7 Legenden" (those ironically reproduced seven legends).[90] In a final generic twist, contained in a letter of 1872 to Ferdinand Weibert, Keller insists that these are "völlig frei geschriebene kleine *Novellen"* (quite freely written little novellas).[91] The metaphor of literary cross-dressing is sustained by

the final sentence of the preface to the *Sieben Legenden,* which stresses
the materiality of Keller's sources, in the neatly polysemous German word
Stoff (material): "Der ungeheure Vorrat des Stoffes ließe ein Ausspinnen
der Sache in breitestem Betriebe zu." (The immense supply of material
would permit the most expensive spinning out of the matter [532].) Thus,
I would argue, the biblical interdiction from Deuteronomy against cross-
dressing that stands at the opening of *Eugenia* serves as a kind of ironic
camouflage device for a set of narratives that actually revels in transvestite
possibilities, in both a literal and a hermeneutic sense. Departing from
the traditional depiction of saints and martyrs as rather one-dimensional
exemplary figures,[92] Keller presents them—predominantly female, it should
be noted—as volatile shape-shifters. Not only might an icon of the Virgin
Mary spring into life here at any moment in order to intercede on behalf of
earthly lovers, even donning male garb like "eine kühne Brunhilde" (a bold
Brunhilde) in *Die Jungfrau als Ritter* (559; Browning, 358), but her image
also dissolves into that of the pagan goddess Juno. In *Der schlimm-heilige
Vitalis* (Unholy-Holy Vitalis), for example, we read that the lovelorn Vitalis
finds himself in a shrine in which an antique marble statue of Juno has been
erected. Bedecked with a golden halo, the "cross-dressed" pagan goddess
poses as the Virgin Mary. As he prays before the icon, Vitalis finds himself
unable to determine the identity of the female deity before him, or even
whether she is divine or human:

> Nur als ein rötlicher Schein vorüberziehender Frühwolken über den Mar-
> mor flog, schien das Gesicht auf das holdeste zu lächeln, mochte es nun
> sein, daß die alte Göttin, die Beschützerin ehelicher Zucht und Sitte, sich
> bemerklich machte, oder daß die neue über die Not ihres Verehrers lachen
> mußte; denn im Grunde waren beides Frauen und diese lächert es immer,
> wenn ein Liebeshandel im Anzug ist. Aber Vitalis wurde davon nicht klüger;
> im Gegenteil machte ihm die Schönheit des Anblicks noch wunderlicher
> zu Mut, ja merkwürdigerweise schien das Bild die Züge der errötenden Jole
> anzunehmen, welche ihn aufforderte, ihr die Liebe zu ihm aus dem Sinne zu
> treiben. (588)

> Only when a rosy glow of fleeting morning clouds sped over the marble did
> the face appear to smile in the most delightful way; whether it was the ancient
> goddess, protectress of nuptial morals and duty, who was making her presence
> felt, or whether it was the new goddess laughing at the predicament of her
> admirer—for after all, both were women, and love affairs in the offing are
> always amusing to women. But Vitalis was none the wiser. On the contrary,
> the beauty of this sight made him feel quite peculiar, and strangely enough, in
> fact, the statue seemed to take on the characteristics of a blushing Jole, who
> was challenging him to banish her love for him from her mind.

Foremost among the shape-shifters, then, is the Virgin herself, her polymorphousness announced in the poem by Angelus Silesius with which the legend *Die Jungfrau als Ritter* is prefaced: "Wie kann sie alles sein? sie ist ein' andre Welt." (How can she be all this? She is another world [555; Browning, 354].) Indeed, she is the ultimate cross-dresser, migrating between heaven and earth, between Christianity and paganism, between chastity and eroticism, yet possible only as a poetic fiction.

On the one hand, we find Keller repeatedly launching scathing attacks on the polymorphous possibilities presented by the related phenomena of androgyny and transvestism. Yet still these motifs circulate throughout his narratives, particularly in late works such as the *Sinngedicht* and the *Sieben Legenden,* perfectly mirroring the endless literary proliferation that operates in these texts. If transvestism serves as the ideal metaphor for a literary strategy privileging citation, it is no accident that scholars such as Herbert Anton have exhausted themselves in tracking down Keller's precise textual and mythological sources. The truth is that Keller appears consciously to destabilize such hermeneutic efforts. The sheer weight of their literariness increases the artificiality—and laughability—of his androgynous creations. As Iris Denneler shows in her article on *Der Schlimm-heilige Vitalis,* Keller is capable of setting us up in a situation that seems to demand a precise identification of mythological allusions, only to withhold any possibility of success. Denneler offers the tantalizing example of the carved gemstones belonging to Jole's father: a deep violet amethyst shows Luna, unwittingly transporting Amor in her chariot; an onyx is carved with a pensive Minerva in full armor, holding Amor in her lap; and on a carnelian a dismayed vestal virgin watches Amor, in the form of a salamander, tumbling in the sacred flames.[93] Keller's narrative, however, omits the father's explanation of his gems, as well as the content of the distichs to which the allegorical scenes have inspired him. All we have is a dazzling display of polymorphous femininity. Perhaps this is the irritating mirror game to which Benjamin alludes in his essay on Keller. It is a mirror game that returns repetitively to the scene of androgyny, while declaring the desire to eradicate androgynous effects. Where Stifter contains androgyny within the fixity of the marble statue and the safely de-eroticized oedipal family, in Keller's works it returns as a seismic parodic force rippling throughout the oeuvre. Keller provides a striking postscript to this discussion, in the form of a love poem:

> Gestern eine Aventür
> Hatt ich, die mir weh getan;
> Allerliebste, denke dir!

Einen Burschen traf ich an,
Jung und fein und glatt gestrichen,
Der dir auf ein Haar geglichen,
Wie der Tulp' die Tulipan!

Ja, dein Antlitz trug er dreist,
Deine Züge frech zur Schau;
Doch, was mich noch allermeist
Ärgerte, o zarte Frau!
War das dunkle Gold der Haare
Und dein Rot, das wunderbare,
War der Augen süßes Blau.

Aber was mir stets an dir
War von unschätzbarem Wert,
Ward mir unerträglich hier
In das Gegenteil verkehrt.
Jede Zierde deiner Züge
Schien hier eine schnöde Lüge,
Ja verspottet und entehrt!

Weibisch war der Haare Licht;
Deine Linien, zart und fein,
Sind zum Schneiderangesicht
Worden, unbedeutend, klein.
Deiner Augen Sternenschimmer
Ward zum wässerigen Flimmer,
Blöden Geistes Widerschein.

Seines Mundes Freundlichkeit
War beleidigend für mich:
Was mich freute jederzeit,
Gestern wars mir widerlich;
Schier hätt ich dein Bild geschlagen,
Ja! ihn aus der Welt zu jagen,
Wünscht ich angelegentlich.

Yesterday I had an adventure
That hurt me to the core;
My dear, imagine this!
I met a youth, smooth-haired,
Young and fine,
And you looked like birds of a feather,
Like two peas in a pod.

Yes, it was your face he was wearing so audaciously,
It was your features he was showing off so brazenly;

But what made me angriest of all,
My dearly beloved,
Was the dark gold of his hair
And your marvelous rosiness
And the sweet blue of his eyes.

But what had always been to me
Of incomparable value in you,
Here became intolerable,
Transformed into its opposite.
Every graceful feature of yours
Seemed here a contemptible lie,
Degraded and worthy only of derision!

The sheen of the hair was effeminate;
Your lines, delicate and fine,
Became a tailor's face,
Mediocre and puny.
The sparkling starshine of your eyes
Became a watery glaze,
The reflection of an imbecilic mind.

The friendly expression of his mouth
Was an insult to me;
What had always been a delight
Was repulsive to me yesterday;
I would almost have smashed your image,
Indeed, my most pressing desire
Was to hunt him out of this world. (vol. 3: 103–4)

Coda

With the realist reworkings of androgyny, the reader arrives at a point of rupture, signaled by Stifter's obsessive use of androgyny as a retardation device and by Keller's parodic recycling of a myth promising perfect heterosexual union. Since their works appear to mark a turning point in literary constructions of androgyny, I conclude my investigation in the late nineteenth century. But I am left with many questions about the evolving fate of literary androgyny, some of which I will articulate here, in closing. Throughout this study, I have been showing how crises of meaning concerning both aesthetics and gender have been viewed through the myth of the androgyne. During the period around 1900, marked by the birth of psychoanalysis, as well as of literary modernity, it might be said that the myth becomes associated with the dissolution of apparently immutable gender oppositions and with a resultant, and dizzying, loss of sexual identity. It would be logical if the literary embodiments of androgyny were to reflect this explosion of categories. At the same time, as Foucault has argued, the body of the (male) androgyne becomes the privileged territory for medical and psychological investigations of homosexuality and bisexuality: in journals such as Magnus Hirschfeld's *Jahrbuch für sexuelle Zwischenstufen* (Journal for Intermediate Sexualities) (founded in 1899), which redefined homosexuals as belonging to a "third sex," as well as in the writings of Wilhelm Fließ, who popularized a notion of "psychic hermaphroditism" that would be influential on Freud's theory of bisexuality, and in Otto Weininger's enormously successful *Geschlecht und Charakter* (Sex and Character) of 1903.[1]

If literature of the late eighteenth and nineteenth centuries is preoccupied with predominantly female and/or childish incarnations of the androgyne, and with a heterosexual reading of the Platonic myth, it would be intriguing to investigate the form taken by literary androgynes at the close of the nineteenth century. Do they mirror what Elaine Showalter has termed the

"sexual anarchy" of the fin-de-siècle?[2] What becomes of the liminal phase
of androgynous adolescence?[3] Does the male androgynous body become,
once again, the locus of fascination?[4] Kafka, for one, presents himself in
his diaries as a uroboric snake, or in one fragment as a self-sufficient, self-
enclosed bachelor.[5] At the same time, his works deny the possibility of
satisfying erotic union with the opposite sex. The sexual partners depicted
in the 1926 novel *Das Schloß* (The Castle) find themselves engaged in a
desperate struggle for physical unity that grotesquely echoes Aristophanes'
narrative on androgyny:

> Dort lagen sie, aber nicht so hingegeben wie damals in der Nacht. Sie suchte
> etwas, und er suchte etwas, wütend, Grimassen schneidend, sich mit dem Kopf
> einbohrend in der Brust des anderen, suchten sie, und ihre Umarmungen und
> ihre sich aufwerfenden Körper machten sie nicht vergessen, sondern erinnerten
> sie an die Pflicht, zu suchen; wie Hunde verzweifelt im Boden scharren, so
> scharrten sie an ihren Körpern.

> There they lay, but not in the forgetfulness of the previous night. She was
> seeking and he was seeking, they raged and contorted their faces and bored
> their heads into each other's bosom in the urgency of seeking something, and
> their embraces and their tossing limbs did not avail to make them forget, but
> only reminded them of what they sought; like dogs desperately tearing up the
> ground, they tore at each other's body.[6]

In Stefan George's cycle *Algabal,* by contrast, a narcissistic male hero
seeks erotic union with the dual-sexed god Zeus. This obsession with the
hermaphroditic male body is of course especially apparent in the works
of Thomas Mann.[7] The malleable Hans Castorp, with his polymorphous
erotic desires; the biblical figure Joseph, with his delicate androgynous
beauty; Felix Krull, the pan-erotic eternal adolescent—the list of sexually
indeterminate youths goes on. With the novella *Der Tod in Venedig* (Death
in Venice), it might seem that we have returned full circle to Winckelmann's
seductive hermaphroditic sculptures. The beautiful adolescent Tadzio, whom
we often glimpse poised at the water's edge, the element of androgynous
indeterminacy, is repeatedly described in statuesque terms:

> Sein honigfarbenes Haar schmiegte sich in Ringeln an die Schläfen und in
> den Nacken, die Sonne erleuchtete den Flaum des oberen Rückgrats, die feine
> Zeichnung der Rippen, das Gleichmaß der Brust traten durch die knappe
> Umhüllung des Rumpfes hervor, seine Achselhöhlen waren noch glatt wie
> bei einer Statue, seine Kniekehlen glänzten, und ihr bläuliches Geäder ließ
> seinen Körper wie aus klarerem Stoffe gebildet erscheinen.

The ringlets of honey-coloured hair clung to his temples and neck, the fine down along the upper vertebrae was yellow in the sunlight; the thin envelope of flesh covering the torso betrayed the delicate outline of the ribs and the symmetry of the breast-structure. His armpits were still as smooth as a statue's, smooth the glistening hollows behind the knees, where the blue network of veins suggested that the body was formed of some stuff more transparent than mere flesh.[8]

But androgyny, in this work, has taken another fatal turn. Aschenbach, himself tinged with morbidity, comes to associate the beautiful adolescent Tadzio with Hyacinth, the doomed lover of Apollo, as well as with the impervious, self-absorbed Narcissus. Where Winckelmann's marble statue seems eternally receptive to the gaze of the male viewer, the erotic web of pedagogy, announced in the identification of the protagonists with Socrates and his pupil Phaedrus, become more perilous in this novella. A myth promising plenitude and progress once again highlights human alienation and mortification: Aschenbach, by the end of the narrative, has been reduced to a solitary Everyman, "der Einsame."

Notes

Introduction

1. Roland Barthes, "Myth Today," in *Mythologies,* trans. Annette Lavers (New York: Hill and Wang, 1986), 110.
2. Plato, *Symposium,* trans. Alexander Nehamas and Paul Woodruff (Indianapolis: Hackett, 1989), 191B. All further references are to this edition.
3. On the death-tinged nature of heterosexual union—one might say, after Freud, the collapsing of *eros* and *thanatos*—see Maurice de Gandillac's article comparing Aristophanes' account of the lapse from primal androgyny with the biblical account of the Fall: "Approches platoniciennes et platonisantes du mythe de l'androgyne originel," in *L'Androgyne dans la littérature,* ed. Frédéric Monneyron (Paris: Albin Michel, 1990), 13–23. I will return to Freud's *Beyond the Pleasure Principle,* itself a reading of Aristophanes' narrative, in the conclusion to chapter 1, below.
4. See M. H. Abrams *Natural Supernaturalism: Tradition and Revolution in Romantic Literature* (New York: Norton, 1971), esp. 154–63, for an outline of the philosophical traditions that have appropriated this androgynous myth, from the Kabbala to Christian hermeticism to romanticism. See also A. J. L. Busst's extensive essay "The Image of the Androgyne in the Nineteenth Century," in *Romantic Mythologies,* ed. Ian Fletcher (London: Routledge and Kegan Paul, 1967), 1–95. On German romanticism, see Albert Béguin's important study, which isolated androgyny as the foundational myth of the romantic era, *L'Âme romantique et le rêve: Essai sur le romantisme allemand et la poésie française* (Marseille: Éditions des cahiers du sud, 1937), esp. vol. 1, "Le Rêve, la nature et la réintégration," 93–160; Fritz Giese, *Die Entwicklung des Androgynenproblems in der Frühromantik* (Langensalza: Wendt und Klauwell, 1919); and Ricarda Huch, *Die Romantik, Gesammelte Werke,* ed. Wilhelm Emrich (Cologne: Kiepenhauer und Witsch, 1969), vol. 6. (Huch's book on romanticism was first published in two parts in 1899 and 1902.) Diane Long Hoeveler has more recently provided a useful historical account of the critical reception of the androgynous myth in English romanticism in the introduction to her study *Romantic Androgyny: The Women Within* (University Park: Pennsylvania State University Press, 1990).

5. For a recent approach situated firmly within this tradition, see Wendy Lesser's *His Other Half: Men Looking at Women through Art* (Cambridge: Harvard University Press, 1991). Lesser's study, despite her assertion that gender prejudice is wholly absent from her model of androgynous complementarity, is unidirectional in perspective, presenting women only as passive objects of a male poetic gaze narcissistically desirous for reintegration.

6. See Lou Andreas-Salomé, *Die Erotik* (Frankfurt am Main: Rütten und Loening, 1910); Luce Irigaray, *An Ethics of Sexual Difference,* trans. Carolyn Burke and Gillian C. Gill (Ithaca: Cornell University Press, 1993); and Julia Kristeva, "Manic Eros, Sublime Eros: On Male Sexuality," in *Tales of Love,* trans. Leon S. Roudiez (New York: Columbia University Press, 1987), 59–82. Interestingly, Irigaray is concerned only with androgyny as it relates to the heterosexual couple, while Kristeva views the *Symposium* as a foundational text of male homosexual eroticism. My reading of the *Symposium* explores the mobility of sexualities in Aristophanes' narrative.

7. Carolyn G. Heilbrun, *Toward a Recognition of Androgyny* (New York: Knopf, 1964). For a helpful mapping out of feminist debates about androgyny during the past thirty years, see Kari Weil, *Androgyny and the Denial of Difference* (Charlottesville: University Press of Virginia, 1992), 145–69. Weil, drawing on Kristeva's notion of the three "generations" of women, sheds new light on how the dialogue about androgyny has been a focal point for American and French feminisms, and I am indebted to her work for the broad outline of the analysis that follows. I hope to broaden her perspective by taking into account what I see as parallel developments in German criticism. For Weil's apt formulation of the tripartite movement of signification discernible in theories of androgyny, quoted above, see p. 13. Weil is well aware of the seductive allure of tripartite schemes such as her own: they are at the heart of the success of the androgynous myth itself, premised as it is on antitheses and synthesis, on a desire for the seamless whole. Thus, Weil quite rightly cautions her readers against reading this "third position"—*différance*—as a moment of (theoretical) transcendence or *Aufhebung* (145). Nevertheless, Weil, too, however delicately, expresses a desire for a form of synthesis. Her concern is to allow for the play of differences, while recognizing the importance of historical, materially grounded, experience. For a lucid analysis of the ideological debate over the fluidity of gender constructions versus essentialism, see Diana Fuss, *Essentially Speaking: Feminism, Nature and Difference* (New York: Routledge, 1989). See also the collection of essays edited by Julia Epstein and Kristina Straub, *Body Guards: The Cultural Politics of Gender Ambiguity* (New York: Routledge, 1991); and Rosi Braidotti, *Nomadic Subjects: Embodiment and Sexual Difference in Contemporary Feminist Theory* (New York: Columbia University Press, 1994).

8. Virginia Woolf, *A Room of One's Own; Three Guineas,* ed. Morag Shiach (Oxford: Oxford University Press, 1992), 128. See also Woolf's later discussion of the "nuptials" of the creative mind, in which "the whole of the mind must lie wide open" for fertilization, with the curtains "close drawn" (136). A particularly intriguing feature of this passage from *A Room of One's Own* is its rehearsal of classically inscribed patterns of domination and submission

in the creative process. I will return in chapter 1, below, to the gendered and eroticized rhetoric of genius, initiated in the eighteenth century. On this important subject, see also Christine Battersby, *Gender and Genius: Towards a Feminist Aesthetics* (London: The Women's Press, 1989). For a critical reevaluation of Woolf and her impact on contemporary feminism, see Toril Moi, "Who's Afraid of Virginia Woolf? Feminist Readings of Woolf," in *Sexual/Textual Politics: Feminist Literary Theory,* (London: Methuen, 1985), 1–18. Moi initiates a critique both of Heilbrun's androgynous model of equality and of the essentialism of other feminist readers of Woolf who followed her, in particular Elaine Showalter.

9. "Die Beurteilung der Frauendichtung," vol. 11: 506.

10. "Einleitung zu 'Annette von Droste-Hülshoff: Ausgewählte Werke,'" vol. 6: 881. Huch apparently also understood herself as an incarnation of such an artist-androgyne. Inge Stephan notes that Huch often expressed her misfortune at having been born a woman and that friends and critics singled out for praise her quality of "masculine" strength. See Stephan's essay "Ricarda Huch" in *Ricarda Huch: Studien zu ihrem Leben und Werk,* ed. Hans-Werner Peter (Braunschweig: pp-Verlag, 1985), 25–33.

11. Richard Exner, "Die Heldin als Held und der Held als Heldin: Androgynie als Umgehung oder Lösung eines Konfliktes," in *Die Frau als Heldin und Autorin: Neue kritische Ansätze zur deutschen Literatur,* ed. Wolfgang Paulsen (Bern: Francke, 1979), 17–54. (The volume contains papers delivered at the Amherst Germanists' conference of 1977.) Interestingly, the discussions following Exner's talk already express the disenchantment of many feminists with androgyny as a static, undialectical discourse that also constitutes escapism from the corporeal realm (see 267–82). As recently as the late 1980s, however, the German feminist movement was assessed positively for its adoption of an androgynous utopian ideal inaugurated by romantic literature. See Ulla Bock's study *Androgynie und Feminismus: Frauenbewegung zwischen Institution und Utopie* (Weinheim: Beltz, 1988). For a recent collection of essays announcing itself as an "androgynous manifesto," see Hartmut Meesmann and Bernhard Sill, eds., *Androgyn: "Jeder Mensch in sich ein Paar!?" Androgynie als Ideal geschlechtlicher Identität* (Weinheim: Deutscher Studien Verlag, 1994). For a positive evaluation of androgynous thought in contemporary German fiction, see Armin Züger, *Männerbilder—Frauenbilder: Androgyne Utopie in der deutschen Gegenwartsliteratur* (Bern: Peter Lang, 1992).

12. Another indication of the centrality of androgyny to the theoretical debates, this time in Germany, was the special day-long session on "Androgynität" held at the Bielefeld feminists' conference "Frauen—Weiblichkeit—Schrift" of 1984. The program and several of the talks presented are reprinted in the volume of the same title edited by Renate Berger et al., *Argument* 134 (1985). (See 173 for the program.)

13. See *Women's Studies* 2 (1974), especially Barbara Charlesworth Gelpi, "The Politics of Androgyny," 151–60; Cynthia Secor, "Androgyny: An Early Reappraisal," 161–69; Daniel A. Harris, "Androgyny: The Sexist Myth in Disguise," 171–84; Catherine R. Stimpson, "The Androgyne and the Homosexual," 237–48.

14. Elaine Showalter, *A Literature of Their Own* (Princeton: Princeton University Press, 1977); see 264.

15. See the contributions by Marie Luise Kaschnitz, Ilse Langner, and Oda Schaefer collected under the title "Das Besondere der Frauendichtung" and published in the *Jahrbuch der Deutschen Akademie für Sprache und Dichtung 1957* (Heidelberg: Lambert Schneider, 1958), 59–76.

16. Mary Daly, *Beyond God the Father: Toward a Philosophy of Women's Liberation* (Boston: Beacon Press, 1973), 26; and *Gyn/Ecology: The Metaethics of Radical Feminism* (Boston: Beacon Press, 1978), xii, 387. Cited in Weil, *Androgyny and the Denial of Difference,* 152.

17. Kristeva, *Tales of Love,* 71.

18. Ingeborg Bachmann, *Malina* (Frankfurt am Main: Suhrkamp, 1971), 19. Translation by Philip Boehm (New York: Holmes and Meier, 1990), 8–9.

19. Where Kari Weil focuses on American responses to French theory, Inge Stephan has assessed the impact of poststructuralism on German feminist conceptions of androgyny. See her essay (whose title, significantly, is a quotation from Huch) " 'Die Musen gehören zu den himmlischen Gestalten, die Mann und Weib nicht kennen': Zur Androgynitätsauffassung in Kunst und Wissenschaft," in *Frauensprache—Frauenliteratur? Für und Wider einer Psychoanalyse literarischer Texte,* ed. Inge Stephan and Carl Pietzcker (Tübingen: Max Niemeyer, 1986), 119–26. Stephan notes the particular significance for certain trends in German literary criticism of Kristeva's distinction between semiotic and symbolic poetic modes, with its claims to transcend the barriers of biological sex. See Julia Kristeva, *The Revolution in Poetic Language,* trans. Margaret Waller (New York: Columbia University Press, 1984).

20. Jacques Derrida and Christie V. McDonald, "Choreographies," *Diacritics* 12 (1982): 75; Roland Barthes, *Roland Barthes by Roland Barthes,* trans. Richard Howard (New York: Hill and Wang, 1977), 132, 69.

21. Hélène Cixous, "The Laugh of the Medusa," trans. Keith Cohen and Paula Cohen, *Signs* 1 (1976): 884. See also, in a later text, the description of a dizzying dance between two individuals of mutable and undecidable gender; "Tancrède continue," *Etudes Freudiennes* 21–22 (1983): 115–32.

22. Susan R. Suleiman, ed., *The Female Body in Western Culture* (Cambridge: Harvard University Press, 1986), 4. Quoted in Weil, *Androgyny and the Denial of Difference,* 157.

23. First published in *Socialist Review* 80 (1985): 65–107.

24. See Geoffrey Galt Harpham, *On the Grotesque: Strategies of Contradiction in Art and Literature* (Princeton: Princeton University Press, 1982). In chapter 1 I consider Winckelmann's ideal of the composite, but seamless whole, which should be contrasted with Winckelmann's aesthetic repulsion at grotesque figures. On eighteenth-century distaste for grotesques, see Barbara Maria Stafford, *Body Criticism: Imaging the Unseen in Enlightenment Art and Medicine* (Cambridge: MIT Press, 1993), especially 266–79. On hermaphroditism, see Julia Epstein, "Either/Or—Neither/Both: Sexual Ambiguity and the Ideology of Gender," *Genders* 7 (1990): 99–142. Epstein refers to Ludmilla Jordanova's study of representations of sexual anatomy in the Enlightenment,

which notes that in some of the plates of hermaphrodites in the *Encyclopédie,* the hermaphrodites are depicted scrutinizing their own sexual organs. See Ludmilla Jordanova, *Sexual Visions: Images of Gender in Science and Medicine between the Eighteenth and Twentieth Centuries* (Madison: University of Wisconsin Press, 1989), 61. Cited in Epstein, 135, note 42.

25. Jean Baudrillard, *The Transparency of Evil: Essays on Extreme Phenomena,* trans. James Benedict (New York: Verso, 1993). Note that for Baudrillard this postmodern "transsexual" condition is problematic, signaling for him (political) indifference, a loss of radicality.

26. See, for example, Fausto-Sterling's essay "The Five Sexes: Why Male and Female Are Not Enough," *The Sciences,* March–April 1993, 20–25.

27. Christa Wolf, *Kein Ort. Nirgends* (Berlin: Aufbau, 1991). Translation by Jan van Heurck, *No Place on Earth* (New York: Farrar, Straus and Giroux, 1982).

28. Christa Wolf, "Projektionsraum Romantik," Gespräch mit Frauke Meyer-Gosau (Conversation with Frauke Meyer-Gosau), in *Die Dimension des Autors: Essays und Aufsätze, Reden und Gespräche 1959–1985,* ed. Angela Drescher, (Frankfurt am Main: Luchterhand, 1990), 895.

29. Secor, "Androgyny: An Early Reappraisal," 164.

30. Barthes, "Myth Today," 145.

31. Jacques Lacan, "The Mirror Stage," in *Ecrits: A Selection,* trans. Alan Sheridan (New York: Norton, 1977), 2. Cf. Goethe's description of statue viewing in the *Italienische Reise:* "Umgeben von antiken Statuen empfindet man sich in einem bewegten Naturleben, man wird die Mannigfaltigkeit der Menschengestaltung gewahr und durchaus auf den Menschen in seinem reinsten Zustande zurückgeführt, wodurch denn der Beschauer selbst lebendig und rein menschlich wird" (Surrounded by ancient statues, we feel ourselves in the midst of a vigorous natural life, we become aware of the diverseness of human forms and are led directly back to the human being in his purest state, with the result that the observer himself becomes alive and purely human). *Artemis-Gedenkausgabe,* ed. Ernst Beutler (Munich: Deutscher Taschenbuch Verlag, 1977), vol. 11: 601; *Italian Journey,* ed. Thomas P. Saine and Jeffrey L. Sammons, trans. Robert R. Heitner (New York: Suhrkamp, 1983), 441.

32. Alice Jardine, *Gynesis: Configurations of Woman and Modernity* (Ithaca: Cornell University Press, 1985), 72.

33. Dorothea von Mücke elaborates on this important connection in her study *Virtue and the Veil of Illusion: Generic Innovation and the Pedagogical Project in Eighteenth-Century Literature* (Stanford: Stanford University Press, 1991), 161–62.

34. Peter Brooks makes a related observation about the role of the body in novels of the eighteenth and nineteenth centuries: "The eighteenth-century novel often seems to take pleasure in creating a polymorphous sexuality, whereas the nineteenth-century novel will tend to enforce the law of gender, and its attendant repressions, with more censorious force." See his book *Body Work: Objects of Desire in Modern Narrative* (Cambridge: Harvard University Press, 1993), 53.

Chapter 1

1. Michel Foucault, *The Order of Things: An Archaeology of the Human Sciences* (London: Routledge, 1974), 66.

2. Richard Dellamora uses this epithet for Winckelmann in his book *Masculine Desire: The Sexual Politics of Victorian Aestheticism* (Chapel Hill: University of North Carolina Press, 1990), 110.

3. For a fuller discussion of the Antinous relief, see Ellen Spickernagel, " 'Helden wie zarte Knaben oder verkleidete Mädchen': Zum Begriff der Androgynität bei Johann Joachim Winckelmann und Angelika Kauffmann," *Frauen. Weiblichkeit. Schrift,* ed. Renate Berger et al., spec. issue of *Argument* 134 (1985): 99–118. G. S. Rousseau has presented a paradigm with important implications for Winckelmann studies: "Eros and neoclassical retrieval." The Villa Albani in Rome, which attracted, among others, Winckelmann, Mengs, and the Comte Caylus, is described by Rousseau as an "aesthetic nerve centre for antiquarian and homosocial behaviour," in which the cult of Antinous flourished. See his essay "Love and Antiquities: Gray and Walpole on the Grand Tour," in *Perilous Enlightenment* (Manchester: Manchester University Press, 1990), 172–199.

4. Spickernagel, " 'Helden wie zarte Knaben,' " 100.

5. Walter Bosshard, *Winckelmann: Ästhetik der Mitte* (Zurich: Artemis, 1968).

6. Johann Joachim Winckelmann, *Sämtliche Werke,* ed. Joseph Eiselein (Donauöschingen: Verlag Deutscher Classiker, 1825–29), vol. 12: xliii. (All subsequent references, except the Belvedere Apollo passages, are to this edition.)

7. Friedrich Schiller, *Über die ästhetische Erziehung des Menschen in einer Reihe von Briefen,* in *Nationalausgabe,* ed. Julius Petersen and Gerhard Fricke (Weimar: Hermann Böhlaus Nachfolger, 1943–), vol. 20: 359. All subsequent references will be to this edition. I follow the excellent translation of Elizabeth M. Wilkinson and L. A. Willoughby, *On the Aesthetic Education of Man* (Oxford: Oxford University Press, 1982), 109.

8. "Idee zu einem Katechismus der Vernunft für edle Frauen," *Athenäum,* ed. August Wilhelm Schlegel and Friedrich Schlegel (Stuttgart: Cotta, 1960), 285–87.

9. For a fuller discussion of the polarization taking place in the gender debate at the end of the eighteenth century, see Karin Hausen's important article "Die Polarisierung der 'Geschlechtskaraktere'—Eine Spiegelung der Dissoziation von Erwerbs- und Familienleben," *Sozialgeschichte der Familie in der Neuzeit Europas,* ed. Werner Conze (Stuttgart: Ernst Klett, 1976), 363–93. See also Volker Hoffmann, "Elisa und Robert oder das Weib und der Mann, wie sie sein sollten: Anmerkungen zur Geschlechtercharakteristik der Goethezeit," in *Klassik und Moderne: Die Weimarer Klassik als historisches Ereignis und Herausforderung im kulturgeschichtlichen Prozeß,* ed. Karl Richter and Jörg Schönert (Stuttgart: Metzler, 1983), 80–97. For a brilliant account of the shifting ground in medical thought between "one-sex" and "two-sex" models, see Thomas Laqueur's *Making Sex: Body and Gender from the Greeks to Freud* (Cambridge: Harvard University Press, 1990). Laqueur argues that in the late eighteenth century, the old Galenic model, which presupposed a metaphysics of

hierarchy in the relationship between male and female, yielded to an anatomy of radical dimorphism and incommensurability, "opposite" sexes. For Laqueur, this means that sex replaces gender as a primary interpretive category.

10. Giese, *Die Entwicklung des Androgynenproblems,* 89.

11. Ibid., 53.

12. Other critics have offered their own definitions. Kari Weil proposes androgyny as the fiction of origin and plenitude, hermaphroditism as the fiction of displaced origins and generative play. Contrasting Plato's treatment of the primal androgyne in the *Symposium* with Ovid's account of Hermaphroditus in the *Metamorphoses,* Weil identifies the former as the model for classical integrational aesthetics, the latter as the model for a postclassical critique and deconstruction of binaries. My study aims to show that both emancipatory gender confusion and rigid binarism are modes contained within fictions of androgyny.

13. Giese, *Die Entwicklung des Androgynenproblems,* 57.

14. Hannelore Gauster, "Zu Hermaphroditen-Darstellungen in der Antike," spec. issue of *Argument* 134 (1985): 79–98.

15. Sigmund Freud, "The Antithetical Meaning of Primal Words," *The Standard Edition of the Complete Psychological Works,* ed. and trans. James Strachey (London: Hogarth Press, 1953), vol. 11: 153–61. In German, "Über den Gegensinn der Urworte," *Studienausgabe,* ed. Alexander Mitscherlich, Angela Richards, and James Strachey (Frankfurt am Main: Fischer, 1982), vol. 4: 227–34.

16. Susanne Amrain makes this observation in her essay "Der Androgyn: Das poetische Geschlecht und sein Aktus," spec. issue of *Argument* 134 (1985): 119–29.

17. It is intriguing that Derrida describes his (non)concept *différance* in terms that echo late-eighteenth-century aesthetics. Stressing the neutrality of *différance,* he writes that it is "neither simply active nor simply passive, announcing or rather recalling something like the middle voice." Jacques Derrida, "Différance," trans. Alan Bass, in *Critical Theory since 1965,* ed. Hazard Adams and Leroy Searle (Tallahassee: University of Florida Press, 1986), 124.

18. Joel Black, "The Aesthetics of Gender: Zeuxis' Maidens and the Hermaphroditic Ideal," *New York Literary Forum* 8–9 (1981): 189–209.

19. Ibid., 190–93.

20. In Goethe's novel *Die Wahlverwandtschaften* (Elective Affinities) the infant Otto is a dramatic product of such an *ars combinatoria.* Otto's name itself suggests a specular doubleness, and it is also a prismatic reflection of the names of the four lovers in the novel who "create" the child (Eduard, whose real name is Otto; Charlotte; the Hauptmann, whose first name is also revealed to be Otto; and Ottilie.) Significantly, the child Otto, as a result of his very artifactuality, is doomed to a watery death.

21. Mircea Eliade, *The Two and the One,* trans. J. M. Cohen (London: Harvill Press, 1965).

22. Black, "The Aesthetics of Gender," 201.

23. Ibid., 204.

24. Hans Zeller, *Winckelmanns Beschreibung des Apollo im Belvedere* (Zurich: Atlantis, 1955). Zeller's work includes an appendix containing all of the manuscript versions of the Belvedere Apollo text, from which I cite here (Paris manuscript).
25. Ibid., 152.
26. Ibid., 184.
27. Ibid., "Die Beschreibung des Apollo in der *Geschichte der Kunst.*"
28. Achim Aurnhammer argues that Winckelmann's androgyne can only be nostalgic, since it is an unattainable artistic projection of perfection. *Androgynie: Studien zu einem Motiv in der europäischen Literatur* (Cologne: Böhlau, 1986), 164.
29. Bosshard, *Winckelmann,* 73.
30. Ibid., 77.
31. Klaus Theweleit, *Male Fantasies,* trans. Stephen Conway (Minneapolis: University of Minnesota Press, 1987), vol. 1, *Women. Floods. Bodies. History.,* see 272.
32. Jean Baudrillard, *Seduction,* trans. Brian Singer (New York: St. Martin's Press, 1990), 74.
33. See Aurnhammer, *Androgynie,* 162.
34. This polyperspectival aesthetic experience might be compared with Lacan's analysis of anamorphosis, in which he discusses the erotic effects generated by the interaction between artwork and gaze, the "pulsatile, dazzling and spread out function" of the gaze. (The artwork in question is Holbein's *The Ambassadors,* which tantalizes the viewer with an oblique, deformed, and almost unreadable image of a skull. For Lacan, however, the effect of this perspectival technique is to annihilate the viewing subject.) Jacques Lacan, *The Four Fundamental Concepts of Psycho-Analysis,* ed. Jacques-Alain Miller, trans. Alan Sheridan (New York: Norton, 1981), 79–90.
35. Marjorie Garber has described such moments of transvestite fascination and indeterminacy as primal scenes of narrativized cross-dressing in her book *Vested Interests: Cross-Dressing and Cultural Anxiety* (New York: Routledge, 1992).
36. See Ovid, *Metamorphoses,* ed. G. P. Goold, trans. Frank Justus Miller (Cambridge: Harvard University Press, 1984), 8.159–68: "Daedalus ingenio fabrae celeberrimus artis / ponit opus turbatque notas et lumina flexum / ducit in errorem variarum ambage viarum. / non secus ac liquidus Phrygiis Maeandros in arvis / ludit et ambiguo lapsu refluitque fluitque / occurrensque sibi venturas aspicit undas / et nunc ad fontes, nunc ad mare versus apertum / incertas exercet aquas: ita Daedalus implet / innumeras errore vias vixque ipse reverti / ad limen potuit: tanta est fallacia tecti." (Daedalus, a man famous for his skill in the builder's art, planned and performed the work. He confused the usual passages and deceived the eye by a conflicting maze of divers winding paths. Just as the watery Maeander plays in the Phrygian fields, flows back and forth in doubtful course and, turning back on itself, beholds its own waves coming on their way, and sends its uncertain waters now towards their source and now towards the open sea: so Daedalus made those innumerable winding passages, and was himself scarce able to find his way back to the place of entry, so deceptive was the entry he had built.)

37. See Bernhard Böschenstein, "Apoll und seine Schatten: Winckelmann in der deutschen Dichtung der beiden Jahrhundertwenden," in *Johann Joachim Winckelmann 1717–1768,* ed. Thomas W. Gaehtgens (Hamburg: Felix Meiner, 1986), 327–42. Böschenstein traces the literary influence of Winckelmann's aesthetic writings on statuary, from Goethe's *Die natürliche Tochter* to Jean Paul's *Titan* to Stifter's *Der Nachsommer* (and onward to George and Rilke), but his discussion does not address the shift toward female statuary.

38. Zeller, among others, has remarked upon the eroticism of Winckelmann's aesthetic experience, and specifically on this mutual inspiration of viewer and statue. See *Winckelmanns Beschreibung des Apollo,* 224. For an elucidation of the reference to Branchos, see p. 125. On Winckelmann's sexuality, a question that has received much critical attention in the past decade, see the chapter "Das Leben und die Wunder Johann Winckelmanns" in Paul Derks, *Die Schande der heiligen Päderastie: Homosexualität und Öffentlichkeit in der deutschen Literatur 1750–1850* (Berlin: rosa Winkel, 1990), 174–231; Denis M. Sweet, "The Personal, the Political and the Aesthetic: Johann Joachim Winckelmann's Enlightenment Life," *Journal of Homosexuality* 16 (1988): 146–62; Simon J. Richter and Patrick McGrath, "Representing Homosexuality: Winckelmann and the Aesthetics of Friendship," *Monatshefte* 86 (1994): 45–58.

39. As Zeller proposes *(Winckelmanns Beschreibung des Apollo,* 225). Idris Parry describes Winckelmann's writing as "a ritual incantation," expressing "the ecstasy of a seer." "Belvedere Hercules," *PN Review* 20 (1981): 19.

40. Bosshard, *Winckelmann,* 189.

41. Parry stresses the interconnectedness in Winckelmann's aesthetics between the haptic and the optic, making the link between Winckelmann's "feeling eye" and the "fühlendes Aug' " and "sehende Hand" (seeing hand) of Goethe's fifth Roman elegy. See Parry, "Belvedere Hercules," 19. Yet critics have traditionally played down the eroticism of the relationship with the androgynous statue. Black, for example, contrasts what he sees as the repose of the Hellenistic androgyne with the "erotic frenzy" of later representations of the androgyne. See Black, "The Aesthetics of Gender," 202. Mario Praz, while calling Winckelmann's androgynes "wanton images of budding voluptuousness," argues that their eroticism is only "liminal" and stresses the "fixity," "rigidity," and "serenity" of Winckelmann's aesthetic ideal. Mario Praz, *On Neoclassicism,* trans. Angus Davidson (London: Thames and Hudson, 1969), 49–54. In an article that focuses on the dual questions of Winckelmann's homosexuality and historical difference, Kevin Parker argues that beauty, for Winckelmann, is anything but an object of carnal lust. Instead, Parker suggests that mastering the problem of historical difference becomes a way of mastering homoerotic desire: "The seductive spell of the other's lived body, the body that invites the caress, and whose presence is excessive in the most overwhelming way, has been broken. The absence of the Greek body, guaranteed by Winckelmann's institution of historical difference as a relation of presence to absence, is now the unapproachable object of our gaze. . . . What has been lost by the positing of the death of this boy is made up for by the fact that he can now return safely as an object of a chaste, timeless, placeless knowledge." Kevin Parker, "Winckelmann, Historical Difference, and the Problem of the

Boy," *Eighteenth-Century Studies* 25 (1992): 543. The problem with this argument, as I see it, is that it simplifies what is actually a powerful dialectic in the viewer-statue relationship between presence and absence, eroticism and repression, pleasure and pain. On the association in Winckelmann between aesthetic experience and violence, see Simon J. Richter, *Laocoon's Body and the Aesthetics of Pain: Winckelmann, Lessing, Herder, Moritz, Goethe* (Detroit: Wayne State University Press, 1992), which compares the application of chisel to marble with the surgical interventions that produce castrati and eunuchs, for Winckelmann the embodiments of neoclassical beauty. This reading of sculpture and violence is also relevant to a consideration of Stifter's aesthetics, discussed below.

42. See Parker, "Winckelmann," 540.
43. Bosshard, *Winckelmann*, 133.
44. Spickernagel, " 'Helden wie zarte Knaben,' " 101.
45. This shift also may be linked with the nineteenth-century focus on the female nude as the object of the eroticized gaze, as opposed to the continued dominance of the male nude, with its homoerotic suggestions of Greek ideal beauty, throughout the neoclassical eighteenth century. Until the nineteenth century, female models were absent from studios and academies, exclusively male domains. See Kenneth Clark, *The Nude: A Study in Ideal Form* (Garden City, N.Y.: Doubleday, 1959), 457; Margaret Walters, *The Nude Male: A New Perspective* (Harmondsworth: Penguin, 1978), 228–45; Gill Saunders, *The Nude: A New Perspective* (London: Herbert Press, 1989), 17–18.
46. See Silvia Bovenschen's important study, *Die imaginierte Weiblichkeit: Exemplarische Untersuchungen zu kulturgeschichtlichen und literarischen Präsentationsformen des Weiblichen* (Frankfurt am Main: Suhrkamp, 1979); and Hannelore Schlaffer, "Frauen als Einlösung der romantischen Kunsttheorie," *Jahrbuch der deutschen Schillergesellschaft* 21 (1977): 274–96.
47. Bovenschen, *Die imaginierte Weiblichkeit*, 37.
48. Bosshard also makes this argument. *Winckelmann*, 34.
49. Simon Richter remarks suggestively that the "living death" of the eunuch anticipates the danger of mortification latent within the classical ideal of the "schöner Schein" that would emerge a generation later. See *Laocoon's Body and the Aesthetics of Pain*, 59.
50. See Spickernagel, " 'Helden wie zarte Knaben,' " 102–3; Winckelmann vol. 7: 102–14.
51. Michel Foucault, *The Use of Pleasure*, vol. 2 of *The History of Sexuality*, trans. Robert Hurley (New York: Vintage, 1990). Parker provides an insightful analysis of Winckelmann's appropriation of Greek philosophical discourse on love between men in "Winckelmann," 537.
52. Richter and McGrath make this important point on art and homoeroticism in their essay on Winckelmann and friendship. See "Representing Homosexuality," 50.
53. Giese, *Die Entwicklung des Androgynenproblems*, 43.
54. On the significance of polarized sexual categories for Humboldt's philosophy of language, see Helmut Müller-Sievers, *Epigenesis: Naturphilosophie im Sprachdenken Wilhelm von Humboldts* (Paderborn: Ferdinand Schöningh,

1993). Of course, the establishment of "scientific" gender classifications is not the work of Humboldt alone. For example, Fichte's *Deduction der Ehe,* of 1796, establishes a similar binary scheme. For a useful and concise overview, see Barbara Duden, "Das schöne Eigentum: Zur Herausbildung des bürgerlichen Frauenbildes an der Wende vom 18. zum 19. Jahrhundert," *Kursbuch* 47 (1977): 125–40. What interests me about Humboldt's essays in particular is their recourse to the androgynous fiction of wholeness.

55. Wilhelm von Humboldt, "Über den Geschlechtsunterschied und dessen Einfluß auf die organische Natur," *Werke,* ed. Andreas Flitner and Klaus Giel (Stuttgart: Cotta, 1960), vol. 1, *Schriften zur Anthropologie und Geschichte,* 268. Both essays on sexual difference are contained in this volume.

56. Giese, *Die Entwicklung des Androgynenproblems,* 78.

57. Here Humboldt echoes Hamann's emphasis on the generative powers of the imagination. Tellingly prefacing his comment with a reference to the sensual experience of viewing statuary, Hamann writes in a 1768 letter to Herder: "ich [habe] mehr die *inferna* eines Torso als die *superna* einer Büste zu erkennen und zu unterscheiden gesucht. Und meine grobe Einbildungskraft ist niemals im Stande gewesen, sich einen schöpferischen Geist ohne *genitalia* vorzustellen." (I have always sought to identify and pick out the *inferna* of a torso, rather than the *superna* of a bust. My coarse imagination has never been able to picture a creative spirit without *genitalia*.) Johann Georg Hamann, *Briefwechsel,* ed. Walther Ziesemer and Arthur Henkel (Wiesbaden: Insel, 1955–79), vol. 2: 415. Elsewhere, Hamann, whose work is central for theories of genius, uses the startling image of artistic creativity as an incestuous act: "Ich . . . liebe die Natur, unsere alte Großmutter, wie ein Magus. . . . Die Blutschande mit der Großmutter ist das größte Gebot, das in dem Koran der schönen Künste verkündigt und nicht erfüllt wird." (I love nature, our old grandmother, like a magus. To commit incest with this grandmother is the most important commandment of the Koran of the arts, and it is not obeyed.) *Sämtliche Werke,* ed. Joseph Nadler (Vienna: Herder, 1949–57), vol. 2: 342.

58. Humboldt provides no example of female geniuses, even under the rubric of "feminine" creativity. This gendering of genius persists into nineteenth-century aesthetics, for example in Jean Paul's categories of "passive" (i.e., feminine, receptive) and "active" (i.e., masculine, creative) genius. (Jean Paul names Novalis as a genial androgyne or "Mannweib.") See Jean Paul, *Vorschule der Ästhetik* (Hamburg: Felix Meiner, 1990), 47–55.

59. Sara Friedrichsmeyer, in an essay exploring the ideological implications of the romantic androgyne, identifies what she sees as the roots of the problem: the androgynous ideal, which seems to offer free play and fluidity, continues nevertheless to purvey ossified binaries. "The Subversive Androgyne," *Women in German Yearbook* 3 (1986): 63–74.

60. On the significance of classical sculpture for Schiller, see Johannes Haupt, "Geschichtsperspektive und Griechenverständnis im ästhetischen Programm Schillers," *Jahrbuch der deutschen Schillergesellschaft* 18 (1974): 406–30.

61. See also Ludwig Uhlig, "Schiller und Winckelmann," *Jahrbuch für internationale Germanistik* 17 (1985): 131–46.

62. Elizabeth M. Wilkinson and L. A. Willoughby, in their introduction to Schiller's *On the Aesthetic Education of Man,* remark aptly that this enormously complex, elliptical treatise "has the shape of a torso"; lix.

63. Rose Riecke-Niklewski cites numerous instances of such erotic metaphorical language, in *Die Metaphorik des Schönen: Eine kritische Lektüre der Versöhnung in Schillers "Über die ästhetische Erziehung des Menschen in einer Reihe von Briefen,"* (Tübingen: Max Niemeyer, 1986), 127. Schiller describes the Romans, for example, as "durch morgenländische Üppigkeit entmannt" (unmanned by Oriental luxury), while the Greeks are "Nebenbuhler" (rivals in love), and so on.

64. Despite Riecke-Niklewski's otherwise exhaustive analysis of Schiller's metaphorical language in *Über die ästhetische Erziehung des Menschen,* she mentions the central Juno Ludovisi passage only in passing. It is also worth mentioning that if Schiller here chooses Juno Ludovisi as the summation and embodiment of his aesthetic ideal, rather than any of the numerous other sculptures in the Mannheim collection, this almost certainly reflects the influence of Goethe, who was captivated by the colossal bust while in Rome and had installed in his rooms a cast of Juno, his "erste Liebschaft in Rom" (his first Roman love). Johann Wolfgang von Goethe, *Italienische Reise,* in *Artemis-Gedenkausgabe,* vol. 11: 168. The link between Goethe's admiration of the Juno Ludovisi and Schiller's subsequent description of her in letter XV is made by Wilkinson and Willoughby in their commentary to *On the Aesthetic Education of Man,* 254–55.

65. Riecke-Niklewski also makes the case that metaphor does not function in a one-dimensional way. *Die Metaphorik des Schönen,* 82.

66. Wilkinson and Willoughby, *On the Aesthetic Education of Man,* lxxxv–lxxxvi.

67. Aurnhammer discusses this poem in some detail as part of a chapter on botany and androgyny in Goethe, Novalis, Schiller, and Friedrich Schlegel. *Androgynie,* 194–96.

68. Claudette Sartiliot, *Herbarium Verbarium: The Discourse of Flowers* (Lincoln: University of Nebraska Press, 1993), 17. See also the remarks by Derrida on the flower's incessantly instantaneous reversal: penis/vagina, castration/virginity, erection/relapse, natural organism/disarticulated artifact, total body proper/fetishized morsel, and so on. Jacques Derrida, *Glas,* trans. John P. Leavey, Jr., and Richard Rand (Lincoln: University of Nebraska Press, 1986), 126b.

69. *Nationalausgabe,* part 2, vol. 1: 308. All citations of Schiller's poetry, unless otherwise indicated, are from this source.

70. *Standard Edition,* vol. 7: 136; "Drei Abhandlungen zur Sexualtheorie," *Studienausgabe,* vol. 5: 48. For an insightful analysis of Freud's "rehabilitation" of heterosexuality vis-à-vis the (destabilizing) homosexuality present in the Platonic myth, see Monique Schneider, "L'androgyne, un mythe critique," in Monneyron, ed., *L'Androgyne,* 114–25.

71. *Standard Edition,* vol. 19: 145; "Die infantile Genitalorganisation," *Studienausgabe,* vol. 5: 241.

72. *Standard Edition,* vol. 7: 191; "Drei Abhandlungen zur Sexualtheorie," *Studienausgabe,* vol. 5: 97.

73. *Der Briefwechsel zwischen Schiller und Goethe,* ed. Emil Staiger (Frankfurt am Main: Insel, 1977), vol. 1: 43.

74. "Die Künstler," *Nationalausgabe,* part 2, vol. 1: 383.

75. See her chapters "Die Ohnmacht des 'schönen Verstandes' und die Vermögen der ästhetischen Urteilskraft" and "Poetologische Begründungen poetischer Inkompetenz," both of which have been valuable sources for my study. *Die imaginierte Weiblichkeit,* 220–56. Bovenschen, who also discusses Kant's systematic exclusion of women from the realm of art, does give Schiller credit for making his study of the feminine a central element of his aesthetic program, rather than a peripheral issue, and sees this as another aspect of his enterprise of "Versöhnung" or reconciliation.

76. Letter to Goethe, June 30, 1797, *Briefwechsel,* vol. 1: 412.

77. Bovenschen, *Die imaginierte Weiblichkeit,* 224.

78. Johann Peter Eckermann, *Gespräche mit Goethe in den letzten Jahren seines Lebens,* ed. Fritz Bergemann (Frankfurt am Main: Insel, 1981), 236.

79. See Riecke-Niklewski, *Die Metaphorik des Schönen,* 144.

80. Sander L. Gilman, *Difference and Pathology: Stereotypes of Sexuality and Madness* (Ithaca: Cornell University Press, 1985).

81. See Aurnhammer, *Androgynie,* 113. Laqueur discusses the cultural attribution of sexual ambiguity to animals; *Making Sex,* 19. For the cultural tradition of the hermaphroditism of hyenas, see also Ovid's *Metamorphoses,* 15.408–10: " 'Si tamen est aliquid mirae novitatis in istis, / alternare vices et, quae modo femina tergo / passa marem est, nunc esse marem miremur hyaenam.' " ("But if there is anything to wonder at in such novelties as these, we might wonder that the hyena changes her nature and that a creature which was but now a female and mated with a male is now a male herself.")

82. Joan B. Landes, *Women and the Public Sphere in the Age of the French Revolution* (Ithaca: Cornell University Press, 1988), 146.

83. See Aurnhammer, *Androgynie,* 197, who criticizes earlier studies of androgyny in Schlegel, such as Giese's, for failing to recognize the aesthetic dimensions of the model.

84. Friedrich Schlegel, "Nachricht von den Gemälden in Paris," *Kritische Ausgabe,* ed. Ernst Behler (Paderborn: Ferdinand Schöningh, 1958–1991), vol. 4: 31. (All subsequent references, unless otherwise noted, are to this edition.) "Description of Paintings in Paris and the Netherlands in the Years 1802–1804," in *The Aesthetic and Miscellaneous Works of Friedrich von Schlegel,* trans. E. J. Millington (London: Henry G. Bohn, 1849), 26.

85. As Ernst Behler notes in his essay "Friedrich Schlegel: *Lucinde* (1799)" contained in *Romane und Erzählungen der deutschen Romantik,* ed. Paul Michael Lützeler (Stuttgart: Reclam, 1981), 115.

86. Friedrich Schlegel, *Lucinde and the Fragments,* trans. Peter Firchow (Minneapolis: University of Minnesota Press, 1971), 45.

87. See Sara Friedrichsmeyer, *The Androgyne in Early German Romanticism: Friedrich Schlegel, Novalis and the Metaphysics of Love* (Bern: Peter Lang, 1983), 149.

88. See Behler, "Friedrich Schlegel: *Lucinde* (1799)," 116.

89. I follow the translation of Ernst Behler and Roman Struc, *Dialogue on Poetry and Literary Aphorisms* (University Park: Pennsylvania State University Press, 1968), 86.

90. In the first edition of the novel, however, I found the variant "erste," which does help to disentangle the four different allegorical figures in this labyrinthine passage. See Friedrich Schlegel, *Lucinde* (Berlin: Heinrich Frölich, 1799), 45.

91. See *Caroline: Briefe aus der Frühromantik,* ed. Erich Schmidt (Leipzig: Insel, 1913), vol. 1: 514. Hans Eichner refers to this letter in his brief discussion of the "Allegorie der Frechheit," *Kritische Ausgabe,* vol. 5: xxxix. Curiously, however, there seems to have been little critical response to this important manifestation of the androgyne as an aesthetic principle in *Lucinde,* despite the fact that several scholars have explored the theme of androgyny in Schlegel's work. See Giese, *Die Entwicklung des Androgynenproblems,* esp. 198–214 on *Lucinde.* Giese's study is valuable particularly for its extensive documentation of androgynous fictions in romanticism. See also Aurnhammer, *Androgynie,* 196–200; Friedrichsmeyer, *The Androgyne,* 109–67. Conversely, those scholars who do devote some attention to the "Allegorie der Frechheit" fail to make the connection with the novel's androgynous thematics. See Cornelia Hotz-Steinmeyer, *Friedrich Schlegels* Lucinde *als "Neue Mythologie": Geschichtsphilosophischer Versuch einer Rückgewinnung gesellschaftlicher Totalität durch das Individuum* (Frankfurt am Main: Peter Lang, 1985), esp. 31–36.

92. Karl Konrad Polheim points to the virtuosity of this narrative strategy in "Friedrich Schlegels *Lucinde,*" *Zeitschrift für deutsche Philologie* 88 (1969): 77.

93. See Karl Konrad Polheim, *Die Arabeske: Ansichten und Ideen aus Friedrich Schlegels Poetik* (Munich: Ferdinand Schöningh, 1966), 348, where *Lucinde* itself is characterized as an arabesque, 348.

94. See Black, "The Aesthetics of Gender," 94.

95. Ibid., 194.

96. Ibid., 196.

97. Indeed, Schlegel expressed his ambition to become "der Winckelmann der griechischen Poesie" (the Winckelmann of Greek literature). Cited in Rudolf Haym, *Die romantische Schule: Ein Beitrag zur Geschichte des deutschen Geistes* (Berlin: Rudolph Gaertner, 1870), 193.

98. See Black, "The Aesthetics of Gender," 198.

99. Friedrichsmeyer also presents biographical evidence of Schlegel's attraction, in real life, to women perceived as androgynous. Caroline Böhmer, one of the greatest influences on Schlegel's life, was described by the philosopher Schelling as a woman "of masculine greatness of soul, of the sharpest intellect combined with the gentleness of the most feminine, most tender, most loving heart." Friedrichsmeyer, *The Androgyne,* 111. Tieck wrote, too, but in scathing vein, that being with Böhmer or with Dorothea Schlegel was like being with an androgyne or even a hermaphrodite. It is important to stress the ambivalence of the emotions aroused by such androgynous beings. Tieck also laments in the novel *William Lovell* the degeneration of the virile Romans and Greeks into "unnatural" hermaphrodites; Brentano, in his novel *Godwi,* identifies

Protestantism as "Religionen für Eunuchen, Amphibien und Hermaphroditen" (religions for eunuchs, amphibians und hermaphrodites); and A. W. Schlegel describes the hermaphrodite as the "Abweg der Wollust" (aberration of desire). Cited by Paul Kluckhohn in his rich collection of sources on romanticism and love, *Die Auffassung der Liebe in der Literatur des 18. Jahrhunderts und in der deutschen Romantik,* 3rd ed. (Tübingen: Max Niemeyer, 1966), 567.

100. Georges Bataille, *Erotism: Death and Sensuality,* trans. Mary Dalwood (San Francisco: City Lights, 1986), 211.

101. See the afterword by Winfried Menninghaus to his edition of Friedrich Schlegel, *Theorie der Weiblichkeit* (Frankfurt am Main: Insel, 1983), 197. Menninghaus points to Schlegel's deliberate departure from Humboldt's polarizing mode, also citing Schlegel's scathing review of Schiller's poem "Würde der Frauen."

102. Aurnhammer, *Androgynie,* 196.

103. This is undoubtedly an allusion to Winckelmann's aesthetic ideal of "edle Einfalt" (noble simplicity) and "stille Größe" (calm grandeur).

104. Cited by Martha B. Helfer, "Confessions of an Improper Man: Friedrich Schlegel's *Lucinde,*" in *Outing Goethe and His Age,* ed. Alice A. Kuzniar (Stanford: Stanford University Press, 1996), 176. Helfer does groundbreaking work in examining the homoerotic subtext of the novel. She reads what she sees as the homoerotic aesthetic of the "Lehrjahre der Männlichkeit" as an instantiation of romantic literary theory. To my knowledge, Paul Derks is the first critic to have acknowledged this aspect of the novel, although he rather understates what he views as its vaguely homoerotic suggestiveness. See Derks, *Die Schande der heiligen Päderastie,* 218–21.

105. It would be possible to compare this move in Schlegel's novel with Hölderlin's *Bildungsroman Hyperion,* which arguably delineates the passage from failed specular reciprocity with a male friend to perfect specular reciprocity with a female (the latter, however, being premised on the muteness of the female muse, Diotima).

106. See *Kritische Ausgabe,* vol. 24: 244, cited in Helfer, "Confessions," 179f.

107. See Aurnhammer, *Androgynie,* 109. Aurnhammer sees evidence of this shift in passages on heterosexual love that take up the botanical metaphor of androgyny: "Wir beide werden noch einst in Einem Geiste anschauen, daß wir Blüten Einer Pflanze oder Blätter Einer Blume sind, und mit Lächeln werden wir dann wissen, daß was wir jetzt nur Hoffnung nennen, eigentlich Erinnerung war." (There will come a time when the two of us will perceive in a single spirit that we are blossoms of a single plant or petals of a single flower, and then we will know with a smile that what we now call merely hope is really remembrance [Schlegel, *Lucinde,* vol. 5: 12; Firchow, 48].) For Baader's conception of androgyny, see, for example, his "Sätze aus der erotischen Philosophie," in *Schriften,* ed. Max Pulver (Leipzig: Insel, 1921), 243–57. See also Bernhard Sill, *Androgynie und Geschlechtsdifferenz nach Franz von Baader: Eine anthropologisch-ethische Studie* (Regensburg: Friedrich Pustet, 1986). Kluckhohn, in an early consideration of the role of androgyny in Schlegel's works, seems to want to overlook any allusions to the Platonic myth. He argues that since Schlegel maintains the dichotomous poles of male

and female, the concept of androgyny has in fact no application in his works, thus overlooking the developmental aspects of Aristophanes' account. See Kluckhohn, *Die Auffassung der Liebe,* 354–55.

108. See Friedrichsmeyer, *The Androgyne,* 139. It is worth noting, too, that Schlegel in this essay engages in a potentially problematic act of ventriloquism, inserting in the text Dorothea's voice, what he conceives of as Dorothea's reactions and objections to his arguments. Furthermore, he sees his own (androgynous?) mediating role of "Mittelsperson" as indispensable, if Dorothea is to acquire a grasp of philosophy.

109. Friedrichsmeyer, "The Subversive Androgyne," 67. Kurt Lüthi too hastily conflates the myth of the bisexual, sexually mobile androgyne with that of the heterosexual, complementary model of androgyny, in his analysis of Schlegel and the romantic concept of polarity. He concludes optimistically— with recourse to C. J. Jung—that the romantic androgynous ideal relativizes the sharp division between the sexes while valorizing notions of "partnership" and that it should be adopted as a model by modern feminists. See his *Feminismus und Romantik: Sprache, Gesellschaft, Symbole, Religion* (Vienna: Böhlau, 1985), esp. 138.

110. Cited in Schlegel, *Theorie der Weiblichkeit,* 151. The analogy between women and flowers is taken up again by Hegel in a section on marriage in his *Grundlinien der Philosophie des Rechts* (1821): "Der Unterschied zwischen Mann und Frau ist der des Tieres und der Pflanze: das Tier entspricht mehr dem Charakter des Mannes, die Pflanze mehr dem der Frau, denn sie ist mehr ruhiges Entfalten, das die unbestimmtere Einigkeit der Empfindung zu seinem Prinzip erhält." (The difference between men and women is like that between animals and plants. Men correspond to animals, while women correspond to plants because their development is more placid and the principle that underlies it is the rather vague unity of feeling.) Georg Wilhelm Friedrich Hegel, *Werke* (Frankfurt am Main: Suhrkamp, 1969–71), vol. 7: 319–20; *The Philosophy of Right,* trans. T. M. Knox (Oxford: Oxford University Press, 1942), 263. Hegel, like Schlegel, stresses the notion that women do not experience a dynamic, teleological process of *Bildung,* but rather passive, vegetative growth.

111. Friedrich Nietzsche, *Sämtliche Werke, Kritische Studienausgabe,* ed. Giorgio Colli and Mazzino Montinari (Munich: Deutscher Taschenbuch Verlag, 1980), vol. 3: 424; *The Gay Science,* trans. Walter Kaufmann (New York: Random House, 1974), 123.

112. For the inherent problems of the model of femininity being presented in *Lucinde*—in which "the feminine" becomes the metaphor for all that is antithetical to Western logic, the illogical, decentered, polyvalent, ambiguous, inaccessible—see Sigrid Weigel, " 'Das Weibliche als Metapher des Metonymischen': Kritische Überlegungen zur Konstitution des Weiblichen als Verfahren oder Schreibweise," in Stephan and Pietzcker, eds., *Frauensprache—Frauenliteratur?,* 108–18. See also Barbara Becker-Cantarino, "Priesterin und Lichtbringerin: Zur Ideologie des weiblichen Charakters in der Frühromantik," in Paulsen, ed., *Die Frau als Heldin und Autorin,* 111–24; and Sigrid Weigel, "Wider die romantische Mode: Zur ästhetischen Funktion des Weiblichen in Friedrich Schlegels *Lucinde,*" *Die verborgene Frau: Sechs*

Beiträge zu einer feministischen Literaturwissenschaft, ed. Inge Stephan and Sigrid Weigel, spec. issue of *Argument* 96 (1983): 67–82. Weigel cautions here against the uncritically enthusiastic reception of Schlegel's novel by a post-1968 student generation and lucidly reads the work from the perspective of both gender and genre. She shows the irresolvable tension in Schlegel's aesthetic between utopia (domestic bliss, mystical union) and irony (aesthetic reflexivity). These distinctions also correspond to the two forms of androgyny I have delineated.

113. Friedrichsmeyer, "The Subversive Androgyne," 68.
114. Sigrid Weigel, *Topographien der Geschlechter: Kulturgeschichtliche Studien zur Literatur* (Hamburg: Rowohlt, 1990), 242.
115. See Weigel's persuasive reading, "Wider die romantische Mode," 72.
116. *Standard Edition,* vol. 18: 57; *Jenseits des Lustprinzips, Studienausgabe,* vol. 3: 266. On desire as the force leading to the total merging of each separate organ and cell of the body and to the recollection of human origins as a single-celled amoeba, see Andreas-Salomé, *Die Erotik,* 16–21.
117. *Standard Edition,* vol. 18: 22; *Studienausgabe,* vol. 3: 232.
118. Lacan, too, provides a fascinating commentary on Plato's *Symposium,* or, more accurately, on Freud's own rereading of the myth. For Lacan, the crucial aspect of Aristophanes' narrative is that it presents sexuality as a lack, as an empty space signifying death. He argues further that human beings are questing not so much for their sexual complements, as Aristophanes suggests, but rather for the fiction that there is indeed a lost part of the self. All adult myths of primal unity depend, Lacan argues, on an original experience of loss and the discovery of difference. See Lacan, *The Four Fundamental Concepts,* esp. 196–97, 205, 231–32. For a lucid analysis of Lacan's reworking of Plato's narrative, see John Brenkman, "The Other and the One: Psychoanalysis, Reading, the *Symposium," Yale French Studies* 55–56 (1977): 396–450.
119. Barbara Johnson, *The Critical Difference* (Baltimore: Johns Hopkins University Press, 1981), 31.

Chapter 2

1. *Artemis-Gedenkausgabe,* vol. 7: 126. All subsequent references to the novel will be to this edition. Most Goethe translations, unless otherwise indicated, will be from the Suhrkamp *Collected Works* (New York: Suhrkamp, 1983): vol. 1, *Selected Poems,* ed. Christopher Middleton, trans. Michael Hamburger, David Luke, Christopher Middleton, John Frederick Nims, and Vernon Watkins; vol. 2, *Faust I & II,* ed. and trans. Stuart Atkins; vol. 3, *Essays on Art and Literature,* ed. John Gearey, trans. Ellen von Nardroff and Ernest H. von Nardroff; vol. 6, *Italian Journey,* ed. Thomas P. Saine and Jeffrey L. Sammons, trans. Robert R. Heitner; vol. 7, *Early Verse Drama and Prose Plays,* ed. Cyrus Hamlin and Frank Ryder, trans. Robert M. Browning, Michael Hamburger, Cyrus Hamlin, and Frank Ryder; vol. 9, *Wilhelm Meister's Apprenticeship,* ed. and trans. Eric A. Blackall; vol. 10, *Conversations of German Refugees, Wilhelm Meister's Journeyman Years or the Renunciants,* ed. Jane

K. Brown, trans. Jan van Heurck and Krishna Winston. Translations from the *Venetian Epigrams* are from *Johann Wolfgang von Goethe's Roman Elegies and Venetian Epigrams,* ed. and trans. L. R. Lind (Lawrence: University Press of Kansas, 1974). Translations of "Frauenrollen auf dem römischen Theater durch Männer gespielt," *Artemis-Gedenkausgabe,* vol. 14: 9–13, are from Isa Ragusa, "Goethe's 'Women's Parts Played by Men in the Roman Theatre,' " *Medieval English Theatre* 6 (1984): 96–100.

2. *Kritische Ausgabe,* vol. 2: 144.

3. Karl August Varnhagen von Ense, "Frauen in Mannskleidern," *Denkwürdigkeiten und Vermischte Schriften* (Leipzig: F. A. Brockhaus, 1843), vol. 6: 66–68. Even Anneliese Dick's study devoted to the female characters in the novel, *Weiblichkeit als natürliche Dienstbarkeit: Eine Studie zum klassischen Frauenbild in Goethes* Wilhelm Meister (Frankfurt am Main: Peter Lang, 1986), omits a consideration of the transvestism that occurs throughout the text.

4. Sigmund Freud, "Die Weiblichkeit," *Studienausgabe,* vol. 1: 545; *Standard Edition,* vol. 22: 113.

5. See Max von Boehn, *Die Mode: Menschen und Moden im neunzehnten Jahrhundert nach Bildern und Kupfern der Zeit* (Munich: F. Bruckmann, 1908), vol. 1: facing p. 4.

6. Cited in Andreas Ley, ed., *Anziehungskräfte: Variété de la Mode 1786–1986,* (Munich: Hanser, 1986), 18.

7. Cited by Erika Thiel, *Geschichte des Kostüms: Die europäische Mode von den Anfängen bis zur Gegenwart* (Wilhelmshaven: Heinrichshofen, 1980), 273.

8. William Larrett notes that the novel would have been published in the journal *Die Horen,* had Goethe not just promised it to Unger in Berlin. Significantly, its companion pieces in *Die Horen* would have been Schiller's *Über die ästhetische Erziehung des Menschen,* as well as Humboldt's pivotal and programmatic essays "Über den Geschlechtsunterschied und dessen Einfluß auf die organische Natur" and "Über die männliche und weibliche Form." William Larrett, "Wilhelm Meister and the Amazons: The Quest for Wholeness," *Publications of the English Goethe Society* 39 (1968–69), 32.

9. See M. M. Bakhtin's essay "Epic and Novel" for a discussion of the multiple generic layers self-consciously incorporated within the novel. Trans. Caryl Emerson and Michael Holquist, in *The Dialogic Imagination,* ed. Michael Holquist (Austin: University of Texas Press, 1981), 3–40.

10. Frederick Amrine, "Comic Configurations and Types in *Wilhelm Meisters Lehrjahre,*" *Seminar* 19 (1983): 6–19. Amrine makes the case for a comic reading of the novel, based on Northrop Frye's definition of the term. See also Hans Reiss, "Lustspielhaftes in *Wilhelm Meisters Lehrjahre,*" in *Goethezeit: Studien zur Erkenntnis und Rezeption Goethes und seiner Zeitgenossen,* ed. Gerhart Hoffmeister (Bern: Francke, 1981), 129–44. For an anthropological reading of theatrical chaos or "Unordnung" as an initiation or rite of passage nevertheless culminating in Wilhelm's ultimate reintegration within bourgeois society, see Michael Neumann, *Roman und Ritus:* Wilhelm Meisters Lehrjahre (Frankfurt am Main: Vittorio Klostermann, 1992).

11. I distinguish them from other characters in the novel who fit more easily into the stock roles of comedy, such as the procuress Barbara, who, as Reiss argues, belongs to the comic repertoire. Reiss, "Lustspielhaftes," 130.

12. See Inge Stephan, " 'Daß ich Eins und doppelt bin . . .': Geschlechtertausch als literarisches Thema," spec. issue of *Argument* 96 (1983): 153–75. Garber provides a much fuller analysis of this phenomenon, showing that cross-dressing in literature functions as a marker or emblem of dissonance, and that it is thrown up by category conflicts, for example between East and West, between classes, between races. See her book *Vested Interests.* Terry Castle has provided illuminating insights into the semiotics of masquerade, based primarily on English literature of the eighteenth century. See her study *Masquerade and Civilization: The Carnivalesque in Eighteenth-Century English Culture and Fiction* (Stanford: Stanford University Press, 1986), and her essay "The Culture of Travesty: Sexuality and Masquerade in Eighteenth-Century England," in *Sexual Underworlds of the Enlightenment,* ed. G. S. Rousseau and Roy Porter (Manchester: Manchester University Press, 1987), 156–80.

13. Castle, *Masquerade and Civilization,* 55.

14. Judith Butler, *Gender Trouble: Feminism and the Subversion of Identity* (New York: Routledge, 1990), 137–38.

15. Garber, *Vested Interests,* 11–13, 40.

16. This is the central argument proposed by Larrett in "Wilhelm Meister and the Amazons." Larrett sees this novel as a fictional counterpart to Schiller's *Über die ästhetische Erziehung des Menschen.* Raymond Furness, in an essay that provides a concise survey of the androgyne and its role in German literature, similarly proposes androgyny as "a state of perfection . . . in which all dissonances are resolved." Raymond Furness, "The Androgynous Ideal: Its Significance in German Literature," *Modern Language Review* 60 (1965): 58–64.

17. See Francette Pacteau's reading of androgyny, "The Impossible Referent: Representations of the Androgyne," in *Formations of Fantasy,* ed. Victor Burgin (New York: Methuen, 1986), 62–84. Pacteau relates androgyny to the pre-oedipal phase of development, in which sexual difference is not yet acknowledged, and to the realm of the imaginary, where desire is unobstructed.

18. See, for example, Schiller's description of the "schöne Seele" in the essay "Anmut und Würde," *Nationalausgabe,* vol. 20: 287–88.

19. As mentioned in chapter 1, above, Freud, in *Beyond the Pleasure Principle,* refers both to the Platonic myth and to Tasso's epic (via Goethe) in order to illustrate his theory that the goal of the sexual instinct is to restore a primal state of nondifferentiation—androgynous plenitude, or death.

20. Freud, "Fetishism," *Standard Edition,* vol. 21: 147–57; "Fetischismus," *Studienausgabe,* vol. 3: 379–88. Jacques Lacan and Wladimir Granoff, "Fetishism: The Symbolic, the Imaginary and the Real," in *Perversions: Psychodynamics and Therapy,* ed. Sandor Lorand (New York: Gramercy Books, 1956), 273. See also Marcia Ian, *Remembering the Phallic Mother: Psychoanalysis, Modernism, and the Fetish* (Ithaca: Cornell University Press, 1993). Interestingly, the word *Fetisch* appears in the *Wanderjahre* (*Artemis-Gedenkausgabe,* vol.

8: 47), in an early German usage of the term. The word is not included, for
example, in the Grimms' dictionary.

21. Jochen Hörisch provides a convincing and exhaustive Lacanian analysis of
    "Lücken" (lacunae) in the novel, characterizing Wilhelm as a virtuoso of
    repetition whose path toward *Bildung* is paved with a horrifying number
    of female victims. See *Gott, Geld und Glück: Zur Logik der Liebe in den
    Bildungsromanen Goethes, Kellers und Thomas Manns* (Frankfurt am Main:
    Suhrkamp, 1983), 30–99.

22. Luce Irigaray, "Women on the Market," in *This Sex Which Is Not One,* trans.
    Catherine Porter with Carolyn Burke (Ithaca: Cornell University Press, 1985),
    170–91.

23. For a useful collection of recent scholarship on Mignon, see Gerhart Hoffmeis-
    ter, ed., *Goethes Mignon und ihre Schwestern: Interpretationen und Rezeption,*
    (New York: Peter Lang, 1993). The volume also contains an extensive bibli-
    ography on Mignon, 253–55.

24. See Johanna Lienhard, *Mignon und ihre Lieder, gespiegelt in den Wilhelm-
    Meister-Romanen* (Zurich: Artemis, 1978), 57, on the mythological signifi-
    cance of the pearls.

25. This name also has distinct erotic overtones: the French *mignon* signifies
    "sexual favorite" both in male homosexual circles and in female prostitution.

26. Amrine, "Comic Configurations," 18.

27. See Furness, "The Androgynous Ideal," 61; and Hellmut Ammerlahn, "Mig-
    nons nachgetragene Vorgeschichte und das Inzestmotiv: Zur Genese und
    Symbolik der Goetheschen Geniusgestalten," *Monatshefte* 64 (1972): 15–24.

28. Botanically speaking, the lily is classified as "hermaphroditic," or monocli-
    nous, in that both male and female reproductive organs are present in the same
    flower.

29. It is also worth pointing out that Mignon is repeatedly associated with water
    and drowning, which is symptomatic of the androgynous condition of fluidity
    and nondifferentiation. For example, the gymnasts, on hearing that the child
    is missing, immediately assume that she has drowned (112; Blackall, 58).
    We later learn from the Marchese that Mignon's family had also believed
    her to have suffered this watery fate (618, 629; Blackall, 354, 359). Finally,
    in *Wilhelm Meisters Wanderjahre,* Mignon is no more than a succession of
    artistic images inspired by the view of the Lago Maggiore: "Und so sah man das
    Knaben-Mädchen in mannigfaltiger Stellung und Bedeutung aufgeführt. Unter
    dem hohen Säulenportale des herrlichen Landhauses stand sie, nachdenklich
    die Statuen der Vorhalle betrachtend. Hier schaukelte sie sich plätschernd auf
    dem angebundenen Kahn, dort erkletterte sie den Mast und erzeigte sich als ein
    kühner Matrose." (And so one saw the boyish girl portrayed in various settings
    and significations. Beneath the columned portal she stood, gazing thoughtfully
    at the statues in the entry hall. In one sketch she was rocking and splashing
    in the moored skiff, in another climbing the mast like a bold sailor.) *Artemis-
    Gedenkausgabe,* vol. 8: 247; Winston, 255. Despite her association with water,
    Mignon seems uncannily drawn to statuary, as if in anticipation of her own
    fate. (See also her song "Kennst du das Land?")

30. Aurnhammer develops this comparison more fully in his chapter "Idolatrie zweideutiger Schönheit," in *Androgynie,* esp. 166–72. The androgynous aesthetic ideal forms, as I have shown, a central focus in the works of classical and romantic theorists such as Winckelmann, Schiller, and Schlegel. For Goethe, too, it is a recurring motif, from the dual-sexed Euphorion and the homunculus of *Faust II* to the ginkgo biloba tree of the *West-Östlicher Divan,* a botanical image of duality within unity, both "eins und doppelt" (one and double). "Gingo Biloba," *Artemis-Gedenkausgabe,* vol. 3: 348; Hamburger et al., 209. The association of androgyny with genius figures in Goethe's *Faust* has been extensively documented by Wilhelm Emrich in *Die Symbolik von* Faust II*: Sinn und Vorformen* (Frankfurt am Main: Athenäum, 1957).

31. Letter of July 2, 1796. *Der Briefwechsel zwischen Schiller und Goethe,* vol. 1: 221.

32. Ibid., 222.

33. For an illuminating discussion of this fatal inversion of the Pygmalion myth, see Mathias Mayer, "Midas statt Pygmalion: Die Tödlichkeit der Kunst bei Goethe, Schnitzler, Hofmannsthal und Georg Kaiser," *Deutsche Vierteljahrsschrift für Literaturwissenschaft und Geistesgeschichte* 64 (1990): 278–310. Mayer argues persuasively that Goethe adopts the Midas topos—perhaps implicitly in opposition to that of Pygmalion—in order to uncover the paradoxically lethal effects of art. Just as Midas transforms organic matter into immutable gold, so the living person immortalized in a work of art may be killed by it. (See Goethe's Venetian Epigram 100 for an articulation of this problem.) Mayer's argument obviously has wide-reaching implications for the heroines of Goethe's novels, who are so often the victims of the aesthetic realm with which they are identified—I am thinking, for example, of Ottilie in *Die Wahlverwandtschaften.* On the fatal connection between "Fixierung" (fixation), collecting, and the passion for mimesis, see Goethe's essay "Der Sammler und die Seinigen," *Artemis-Gedenkausgabe,* vol. 13: 263 (The Collector and His Circle, *Suhrkamp Collected Works,* vol. 3: 124). Ludwig Börne already addressed this problem in his 1835 review of *Goethes Briefwechsel mit einem Kinde:* "Goethe schlug Mignon tot mit seiner Leier und begrub sie tief, und verherrlichte ihr Andenken mit den schönsten Liedern." (Goethe struck Mignon dead with his lyre, buried her deep in the ground, and hallowed her memory with the most beautiful songs.) Börne further argues that Goethe's writings are like medical dissections: "Goethe hat nur verstanden was tot war, und darum tötete er jedes Leben, um es zu verstehen. . . . Er zerstückelte das Leben in seine Glieder, in seine einzelne Organe." (Goethe only understood what was dead, and so he killed what was living in order to understand it. . . . He dissected life into its individal limbs and organs). Ludwig Börne, *Kritische Schriften,* ed. Edgar Schumacher (Zurich: Artemis, 1964), 281, 292. Heinrich Heine, in *Die Romantische Schule,* also memorably characterized Goethe's works as lifeless marble statues, "unglückliche Mischlinge von Gottheit und Stein" (unhappy hybrids of divinity and stone). Heinrich Heine, *Sämtliche Schriften,* ed. Klaus Briegleb (Munich: Hanser, 1971), vol. 3: 396.

34. See Freud's comments in his lecture "Die Wunscherfüllung" on the role of theater in the sexual maturation and initiation of bourgeois women. Watching

theatrical performances is connected with learning about difference: "Naive
Mädchen sollen häufig nach ihrer Verlobung ihre Freude darüber verraten
haben, daß sie nun bald zu allen bisher verbotenen Stücken ins Theater gehen,
alles mitansehen dürfen." (Simple-minded girls, after becoming engaged, are
reputed often to express their joy that they will soon be able to go to the theatre,
to all the plays which have hitherto been prohibited, and will be allowed to see
everything.) *Studienausgabe,* vol. 1: 224; "Wish-fulfilment," *Standard Edition,*
vol. 15: 220. On the instrumental role of theater in oedipal socialization, see
Friedrich A. Kittler, "Über die Sozialisation Wilhelm Meisters," in Gerhard
Kaiser and Friedrich A. Kittler, *Dichtung als Sozialisationsspiel: Studien zu
Goethe und Gottfried Keller* (Göttingen: Vandenhoeck und Ruprecht, 1978),
13–124. See also David Roberts's psychoanalytic reading, *The Indirections of
Desire: Hamlet in Goethe's* Wilhelm Meister (Heidelberg: Carl Winter, 1980);
and Rolf Selbmann's historically oriented genre study, *Theater im Roman:
Studien zum Strukturwandel des deutschen Bildungsromans* (Munich: Wilhelm
Fink, 1981).

35. On the religious tradition of the sexlessness of angels, see Stuart Schneiderman,
An Angel Passes: How the Sexes Became Undivided (New York: New York
University Press, 1988). German mystical tradition is rich in androgynous
models that may have influenced Goethe. Mystics such as Jakob Böhme,
drawing on cabbalistic and gnostic thought, viewed God as an androgynous
unity, as well as the first human creation, Adam before the Fall. The fusion of
male and female, then, the restoration of lost unity, became Böhme's vision
of redemption. This is a view well known in the late eighteenth century, a
period marked by a revival of interest in mysticism. The German Pietist Graf
von Zinzendorf, who plays an important role in the *Lehrjahre,* also believed in
the androgyny of Christ. On androgyny in the writings of Böhme, Zinzendorf,
and Swedenborg, see Lüthi, *Feminismus und Romantik.* A second tradition,
perhaps even more central to Goethe's thoughts, is the Hermetic Androgyne
of alchemy, the union of two complementary principles: sulphur, the "King,"
regarded as "male" and fixed in essence; and mercury, the "Queen," "female"
and volatile. Both Böhme's and Zinzendorf's concepts of androgyny, as well as
the alchemical tradition, are the expression of a longing for the overcoming of
dualities and for the restoration of an original idyllic state of sexual harmony.
For a comprehensive discussion of the influence of alchemical thought on
Goethe, see Ronald D. Gray, *Goethe the Alchemist: A Study of Alchemical
Symbolism in Goethe's Literary and Scientific Works* (Cambridge: Cambridge
University Press, 1952), 229, where the author identifies Natalie with a Pietist-
alchemical ideal of androgyny. In Thomas Mann's *Bildungsroman Der Zauberberg,* the obscurantist Naphta links alchemy with a kind of mystical pedagogy: " 'der lapis philosophorum, das mann-weibliche Produkt aus Sulfur und
Merkur, die res bina, die zweigeschlechtige prima materia war nichts weiter,
nichts Geringeres als das Prinzip der Steigerung, der Hinauftreibung durch
äußere Einwirkungen,—magische Pädagogik, wenn Sie wollen' " ("the *lapis
philosophorum,* the male-female product of sulphur and mercury, the *res bina,*
the double-sexed prima materia, was no more, and no less, than the principle
of levitation, of the upward impulse due to the working of influences from

without. Instruction in magic, if you like"). *Der Zauberberg,* (Frankfurt am Main: Fischer, 1982), 538; *The Magic Mountain,* trans. H. T. Lowe-Porter (New York: Vintage, 1992), 510.

36. An interesting analogy may be drawn between Mignon and the autoerotic acrobat Bettina of the *Venetian Epigrams,* a sexually and morphologically ambiguous figure. Epigrams 36 and 37 list her kaleidoscopic array of forms: cherub, mollusk, bird, fish, reptile, angel. *Artemis-Gedenkausgabe,* vol. 1: 229–30. In Epigram 38, Bettina attracts the gaze of Jupiter and the envy of Ganymede, and is thus the object of homoerotic desire (230). Like Mignon, Bettina plunges the viewer into an aesthetics of indeterminacy: "So beweget ein Traum den Sorglichen, wenn er zu greifen, / Vorwärts glaubet zu gehn, alles veränderlich schwebt: / So verwirrt uns Bettine, die holden Glieder verwechselnd." (So a dream moves the anxious, who thinks he is grasping it, forwards, / As everything hovers in space in an unstable form. / So Bettina confuses us, twisting her beautiful limbs.) Epigram 41, vol. 1: 231–42; Lind, 103. The incarnation of the polymorphously perverse, the gymnast provokes anxiety in the male spectator: "Was ich am meisten besorge: Bettina wird immer geschickter, / Immer beweglicher wird jegliches Gliedchen an ihr; / Endlich bringt sie das Züngelchen noch ins zierliche F . . . , / Spielt mit dem artigen Selbst, achtet die Männer nicht viel." (What worries me most is that Bettina grows always more skilful, / Always more supple becomes every joint in her frame; / At last she'll bring even her little tongue into her dainty . . . ; / She'll play with her charming self, lose all interest in men.) Withheld Epigram 34, vol. 2: 181; Lind, 149.

37. For details of the cultural significance of the Amazon figure, especially for the history and iconography of the French Revolution, see Inge Stephan, " 'Da werden Weiber zu Hyänen . . .': Amazonen und Amazonenmythen bei Schiller und Kleist," in *Feministische Literaturwissenschaft,* ed. Inge Stephan and Sigrid Weigel, spec. issue of *Argument* 120 (1984): 23–42; Susanne Petersen, *Marktweiber und Amazonen: Frauen in der französischen Revolution* (Cologne: Pahl-Rugenstein, 1987); Nicole Pellegrin, *Les vêtements de la liberté* (Aix-en-Provence: Alinea, 1989); Marc de Villiers, *Histoire des clubs de femmes es des légions d'amazones: 1793–1848—1871* (Paris: Plon, 1910); Marina Warner, *Monuments and Maidens: The Allegory of the Female Form* (New York: Atheneum, 1985).

38. For a meticulous analysis of the correspondences between Tasso's epic and Goethe's novel, see Hans-Jürgen Schings, "Wilhelm Meisters Schöne Amazone," *Jahrbuch der deutschen Schillergesellschaft* 29 (1985): 141–206.

39. The *Goethe-Handbuch* suggests that the Amazon, while apparently unrelated to an androgynous ideal of harmony between the sexes, in fact exhibits similar characteristics: "Doch die gelegentlich geäußerte Vermutung, durch die Verbindung der flachen Mannesbrust und der vollen, hervortretenden Weibesbrust an einem und demselben Leibe hätte man die Vereinigung der beiden Geschlechter, bzw. die noch nicht eingetretene Trennung, ihren (fast hermaphroditischen) Ausgleich in *einer* Person andeuten wollen, weist in eine Richtung, die sich zumindest enfernt mit goetheschem Denken berührt." (The theory occasionally advanced that the combination in one body of flat

masculine chest and full, rounded feminine breast was intended to suggest either the union of both sexes or the [almost hermaphroditic] restoration of a pre-differentiated state indicates, however remotely, a Goethean train of thought.) Alfred Zastrau, ed., *Goethe-Handbuch,* (Stuttgart: Metzler, 1961), vol. 1: 204.

40. *Der Briefwechsel zwischen Schiller und Goethe,* vol. 1: 221.

41. See Schings, "Wilhelm Meisters Schöne Amazone," 168. This is not the only occasion when Wilhelm is physically "marked" by a female character; Mignon also inflicts bite wounds on him (351; Blackall, 198).

42. Marianne Hirsch, "Spiritual Bildung: The Beautiful Soul as Paradigm," in *The Voyage In: Fictions of Female Development,* ed. Elizabeth Abel, Marianne Hirsch, and Elizabeth Langland (Hanover: University Press of New England, 1983), 26. Hirsch argues that in the "schöne Seele's" life we can find a positive paradigm for female development that questions the valorization of progress and social involvement central to the *Bildungsroman.* See also Barbara Becker-Cantarino, "Die 'Bekenntnisse einer schönen Seele': Zur Ausgrenzung und Vereinnahmung des Weiblichen in der patriarchalen Utopie von *Wilhelm Meisters Lehrjahren,"* in *Verantwortung und Utopie,* ed. Wolfgang Wittkowski (Tübingen: Max Niemeyer, 1988), 70–86. Becker-Cantarino points to the repeated pedagogical experiments by the men in the "schöne Seele's" life, culminating in those of her uncle, who stresses social engagement. Indeed, he excludes the spiritual "schöne Seele" from any role in the education of her four nephews and nieces. Becker-Cantarino regards the "schöne Seele" as profoundly uneducable or "bildungsunfähig."

43. I am grateful to Emily Dougherty for pointing out to me this structural supplementarity.

44. Cited in Larrett, "Wilhelm Meister and the Amazons," 35–36.

45. *Briefwechsel,* vol. 1: 225.

46. Ibid., 244.

47. Ibid., 221.

48. Warner discusses the polymorphousness of Minerva and Athena and their frequent incarnations as allegorical figures in the eighteenth and nineteenth centuries, in *Monuments and Maidens,* 88–103. See also Lutz S. Malke on the androgynous aspects of Minerva/Athena, "Weibmann und Mannweib in der Kunst der Renaissance," in *Androgyn: Sehnsucht nach Vollkommenheit,* ed. Ursula Prinz (Berlin: Dietrich Reimer, 1986), 33–56.

49. *Briefwechsel,* vol. 1: 221.

50. See Aristophanes' account of the third phase of androgyny, in which Zeus, having rendered the human beings he had divided infertile by placing their genitals at the back of their bodies, altered their anatomy once more to permit internal reproduction: "Before then, you see, they used to have their genitals outside, like their faces, and they cast seed and made children, not in one another, but in the ground, like cicadas. So Zeus brought about this relocation of genitals, and in doing so he invented interior reproduction, *by* the man *in* the woman. . . . This, then, is the source of our desire to love each other. Love is born into every human being; it calls back the halves of our original nature

together; it tries to make one out of two and heal the wound of human nature." *Symposium,* 191B–191D.

51. Friedrich Schlegel, "Über Goethes Meister," *Kritische Ausgabe,* vol. 2: 144.
52. Jacques Derrida, *Of Grammatology,* trans. Gayatri Chakravorty Spivak (Baltimore: Johns Hopkins University Press, 1976), 141–64. Jonathan Culler, in *On Deconstruction: Theory and Criticism after Structuralism* (Ithaca: Cornell University Press, 1982), 165, notes that the opposition man/woman is multiply marked as supplemental, from the biblical narrative that tells of woman's creation as "helpmeet" or supplement to man. Supplementarity, then, is a condition of heterosexuality.
53. In a sense, the novel punishes Philine, who has often commented on her indifference toward children, by channeling her hypersexuality, contrary to her desires, into reproduction: "Pfui Teufel! sagte sie . . . das garstige Bild! Man sieht doch ganz niederträchtig aus!" ("Oh, my god! . . . How hideous, how vulgar one looks!" [599; Blackall, 342].) Philine, the incarnation of pure sexuality, is as uneducable as the androgyne Mignon, and as unacceptable to the *Turmgesellschaft.*
54. In the Bible, see 2 Samuel I:26, in which David memorably characterizes the intimacy of his relationship with his friend Jonathan: "Your love was wonderful to me, passing the love of women." Robert Tobin alerted me to some of these points at a panel entitled "Outing Goethe" at the MLA conference in 1993.
55. On the pathologizing of Mignon's aberrant sexuality by the *Turmgesellschaft,* see Robert Tobin, "The Medicinalisation of Mignon," in Hoffmeister, ed., *Goethes Mignon und ihre Schwestern,* 43–60. See also Thomas W. Kniesche's essay in the same collection, "Die psychoanalytische Rezeption von Mignon," 61–81, which reads Mignon's (bi)sexual desire as a threat to the heterosexual couples on which *Bildung* is premised.
56. *Artemis-Gedenkausgabe,* vol. 8: 294–99; Winston, 286–89. On homosexuality in the *Wanderjahre,* see Yahya A. Elsaghe, "Wilhelm Meisters letzter Brief: Homosexualität und Nekrophilie bei Goethe," *Forum Homosexualität und Literatur* 24 (1995): 6–24.
57. John H. Smith argues that *Bildung* serves primarily to propagate a triangular codification of Self-Other, male-female relations. Differentiating *Entwicklungsromane* from *Bildungsromane,* Smith maintains that "the latter display as a motor of their narration specific forces of desire, control, and representation that propel the hero from Imaginary oscillation to Symbolic grounding and repression." Note that he assumes the subject to be male, positing *Bildung* as a gender-coded concept. See "Cultivating Gender: Sexual Difference, *Bildung,* and the *Bildungsroman,*" *Michigan Germanic Studies* 13 (1987): 206–25. A possible countermodel to Schlegel's and Goethe's textual inscription of heterosexuality is provided by Novalis's *Bildungsroman Heinrich von Ofterdingen.* Novalis's preoccupation with *Bildung* and androgyny has been amply documented, for example in Friedrichsmeyer's *The Androgyne.* While it is true that Novalis generally attributes to heterosexual/androgynous union a redemptive function, some recent scholarship has emphasized the gender lability that occurs throughout his work, particularly in *Heinrich von Ofterdingen,* a work intended as a critique of Goethe's *Wilhelm Meister.* See Alice A. Kuzniar's

NOTES TO PAGES 139–143

excellent article "Hearing Woman's Voices in *Heinrich von Ofterdingen*," *PMLA* 107 (1992): 1196–1207, which concludes that "Novalisian *Bildung* is both ventriloquistic and transsexual."

58. Larrett, "Wilhelm Meister and the Amazons," 56. This has been a traditional view. See also Ivar Sagmo, *Bildungsroman und Geschichtsphilosophie: Eine Studie zu Goethes Roman* Wilhelm Meisters Lehrjahre (Bonn: Bouvier, 1982), in which, while noting the deathly fate of the "dissonant" female androgynes in the novel, Sagmo concurs with Larrett's proposition that Natalie is the incarnation of Schiller's integrational ideal.

Chapter 3

1. Joseph Freiherr von Eichendorff, *Neue Gesamtausgabe der Werke und Schriften,* ed. Gerhart Baumann (Stuttgart: Cotta, 1958), vol. 2, *Romane, Novellen, Märchen, Erlebtes:* 202. All further references, unless otherwise indicated, will be to this edition. I have also referred to the extensive critical apparatus of the *Historisch-Kritische Ausgabe,* ed. Wilhelm Kosch and August Sauer, reissued and expanded by Hermann Kunisch and Helmut Koopmann (Regensburg: J. Habbel, 1962–).

2. *Neue Gesamtausgabe,* vol. 2: 1024.

3. For an exhaustive study of this recurring feature of Arnim's works, see Christof Wingertszahn, *Ambiguität und Ambivalenz im erzählerischen Werk Achims von Arnim* (St. Ingbert: Röhrig, 1990).

4. See Elisabeth Stopp, "Eichendorff und Shakespeare," *Aurora* 32 (1972): 20.

5. This title is untranslatable into English. See the discussion by Egon Schwarz, *Joseph von Eichendorff* (New York: Twayne, 1972), 24. The German *Gegenwart* may be rendered as "the present," while the word *Ahnung* signifies "intituition," "vision," "presentiment"; perhaps the closest approximation to the German would be "Foreshadowing and the Present."

6. Two critical studies have focused on the theme of masquerade in Eichendorff's works. See John C. Fisher, "Das Verkleidungsmotiv in den Prosawerken von Joseph Freiherrn von Eichendorff," dissertation, Princeton University, 1976; and Otto Eberhardt, *Verkleidung und Verwechslung in der erzählenden Dichtung Eichendorffs* (Heidelberg: Carl Winter, 1987).

7. For such studies of literary cross-dressing, see Dorothea Flashar, "Bedeutung, Entwicklung und literarische Nachwirkung von Goethes Mignongestalt," *Germanische Studien* 65 (1929); Stopp, "Eichendorff und Shakespeare"; and Marianne Thalmann, "Der Trivialroman des 18. Jahrhunderts und der romantische Roman," *Germanische Studien* 24 (1923): 103, 273. Significantly for this discussion, Thalmann notes that while romantic interest in the androgyne begins to wane, authors become increasingly fascinated by the phenomenon of female cross-dressing. See also Eberhardt, *Verkleidung und Verwechslung,* 13–25. (Eberhardt strangely underemphasizes the role of transvestism in Goethe's novel, asserting that with the sole exception of Mignon's male dress, cross-dressing appears only seldom or coincidentally and is then always practically motivated.)

8. See Eberhardt, *Verkleidung und Verwechslung,* 25, which points to several key diary entries by Eichendorff. In February 1802, Eichendorff noted that he had dressed in women's clothing to play a female role in Schröder's drama *Der Fähndrich* (The Sergeant). *Neue Gesamtausgabe,* vol. 3, *Tagebücher:* 23. In 1804, he played the part of Babette in Kotzebue's farce *Wirrwarr* (Hubbub), with another man, Baron Zedlitz, in the role of Doris, thus, we can assume, adding to the mayhem suggested by the title (vol. 3: 63, 64).

9. See Stopp, "Eichendorff und Shakespeare," 18. Her discussion of transvestism is, however, restricted to Eichendorff's comedy *Die Freier.*

10. See Garber, *Vested Interests,* 16–17, arguing that the presence of a transvestite figure in a text that does not seem primarily concerned with gender difference indicates another category conflict, for example between races, classes, religions.

11. See Eberhardt, *Verkleidung und Verwechslung,* 64; and Fisher, "Das Verkleidungsmotiv," 96, 133, on the tropes of hunting costume, hunter, and hunted.

12. Stoller acknowledged that certain women may have "transvestic tendencies"; however, even for these rare female cross-dressers, he argued, "men's clothes have no erotic value whatsoever." For Stoller, such apparently transvestite women are in fact transsexuals exhibiting a ("natural") desire to be men. See *Sex and Gender,* vol. 1, *The Development of Masculinity and Femininity* (London: Hogarth Press and the Institute of Psycho-Analysis, 1968), 195. Later in his career, Stoller did revise his theories to admit the—slim—possibility of female fetishistic cross-dressing. See *Observing the Erotic Imagination* (New York: Oxford University Press, 1985).

13. While Eberhardt notes the seductive effects of cross-dressing, he disregards the gender fluidity suggested by such transvestite scenes, and argues that they serve instead to intensify a purely *female* eroticism. See *Verkleidung und Verwechslung,* 72.

14. Letter, October 20, 1814, in Eichendorff, *Briefe und Dichtungen,* ed. Wilhelm Kosch (Cologne: Kommissions-Verlag, 1906), 41. Loeben himself seems to be entangled in the gender indeterminacy exhibited by Mignon and Erwin, as evidenced by his use of the masculine "dieser" after the feminine pronoun "eine."

15. See Horst Hüseler, "Erwin: Eine 'poetische Gestalt,' " *Aurora* 28 (1968): 70–79. Hüseler, like so many Eichendorff scholars, imposes a strictly Christian reading on the text, going so far as to argue that Erwin functions symbolically as an angelic mediator between God and man. This interpretation, however, represses the powerful eroticism of the relationship between Erwin and Friedrich.

16. Significantly, Eichendorff himself represents poetry allegorically in the form of the androgynous Florentin/Aurora in *Viel Lärmen um Nichts.* See also Alexander von Bormann, "Joseph von Eichendorff: *Aus dem Leben eines Taugenichts* (1826)," in *Romane und Erzählungen zwischen Romantik und Realismus,* ed. Paul Michael Lützeler (Stuttgart: Reclam, 1983), 94–116. Bormann characterizes the essence of Eichendorff's aesthetic as "Bewegtheit" (mobility), a statement that might be linked with Eichendorff's predilection for transvestite and androgynous characters.

17. Richard Exner readily associates the two phenomena of transvestism and androgyny in Eichendorff's works, in "Androgynie und preußischer Staat: Themen, Probleme und das Beispiel Heinrich von Kleist," *Aurora* 39 (1979): 51–78, esp. 57.

18. Similarly, the "schöne Gräfin" in *Aus dem Leben eines Taugenichts* is presented under the dual androgynous signs of lily and angel (vol. 2: 356). Later, we are told that the snow-white lily is the mirror image of the woman (363) and, again, that in her white dress she looks like "eine Lilie in der Nacht" (a lily in the night [366]). For a fuller discussion of the flower symbolism in the *Taugenichts,* see Robert Mühlher, "Der Poetenmantel: Wandlungen eines Sinnbildes bei Eichendorff," in *Eichendorff heute: Stimmen der Forschung mit einer Bibliographie,* ed. Paul Stöcklein (Darmstadt: Wissenschaftliche Buchgesellschaft, 1966), 180–203, esp. 188.

19. Thomas A. Riley, "An Allegorical Interpretation of Eichendorff's *Ahnung und Gegenwart,*" *Modern Language Review* 54 (1959): 210. For a fuller discussion of the romantic "blaue Blume," see Aurnhammer's chapter "Botanische Beglaubigung der Androgynie" in *Androgynie,* 177–200, particularly the section on Novalis's *Heinrich von Ofterdingen,* 183–90.

20. "In dem Kelche lag Eros selbst, über ein schönes schlummerndes Mädchen hergebeugt, die ihn fest umschlungen hielt. Eine kleinere Blüthe schloß sich um beyde her, so daß sie von den Hüften an in Eine Blume verwandelt zu seyn schienen." (In the flower cup lay Eros himself leaning over a beautiful, slumbering maiden with her arms tightly clasped around him. A smaller flower closed around them so that from the hips down they appeared to be changed into one flower.) Novalis, *Heinrich von Ofterdingen,* in *Werke,* ed. Hans-Joachim Mähl and Richard Samuel (Munich: Carl Hanser, 1981), 348; *Henry von Ofterdingen,* trans. Palmer Hilty (New York: Frederick Ungar, 1964), 131.

21. Garber, *Vested Interests,* 9–11. The works to which she is referring are: Sandra M. Gilbert and Susan Gubar, *No Man's Land,* vol. 2, *Sexchanges* (New Haven: Yale University Press, 1988); and Stephen Greenblatt, *Shakespearean Negotiations: The Circulation of Social Energy in Renaissance England* (Berkeley: University of California Press, 1988).

22. *Erlebtes, Halle und Heidelberg,* in *Neue Gesamtausgabe,* vol. 2: 1062.

23. Ibid., 1063. See also *Ahnung und Gegenwart,* vol. 2: 131.

24. See *Das Herkunftswörterbuch: Eine Etymologie der deutschen Sprache* (Mannheim: Duden, 1963), 118.

25. The novel explicitly refers to Romana as an Amazon: "Romana teilte die Menge rasch zu Pferde wie eine Amazone. Friedrich hatte sie nie so schön und wild gesehen." (Romana rode through the crowd like an Amazon. Friedrich had never seen her so beautiful and wild [175].)

26. Theweleit notes the popular associations of the word with *penis* in a section on images of communist women entitled "Rifle-Women (Flintenweiber): The Castrating Woman," in *Male Fantasies,* vol. 1: 70.

27. See Theresa Sauter Bailliet, *Die Frauen im Werk Eichendorffs: Verkörperungen heidnischen und christlichen Geistes* (Bonn: Bouvier, 1972), 189. Bailliet sees Romana's "masculine" poetic endeavors as the cause of her ultimately

catastrophic "Verwilderung." (I will return later to this notion of calamitous organic proliferation.)

28. Adorno saw in this poetic declaration by Romana an apt motto for Eichendorff's entire oeuvre. Theodor W. Adorno, "Zum Gedächtnis Eichendorffs," *Akzente* 5 (1958): 82.

29. "Die deutsche Salonpoesie der Frauen," *Neue Gesamtausgabe,* vol. 4: 927.

30. Ibid., 928.

31. Ibid., 929.

32. Ibid., 930.

33. *Historisch-Kritische Ausgabe,* vol. 3: 416. Eichendorff uses the same construction, "ins Männliche hineinpfuschen," of Romana, as noted above.

34. See Bailliet, *Die Frauen,* 188, in which the following two quotations from Eichendorff are placed side by side. In the essay "Über die ethische und religiöse Bedeutung der neueren romantischen Poesie in Deutschland" (On the Ethical and Religious Significance of Modern Romantic Poetry in Germany), Eichendorff likens the romantic movement to "eine prächtige Rakete, [die] funkelnd zum Himmel emporstieg, und nach kurzer wunderbarer Beleuchtung der nächtlichen Gegend, oben in tausend bunte Sterne spurlos zerplatzte" (a magnificent rocket that sparkled as it soared into the heavens, then briefly and wonderfully lit up the night sky, only to burst into a thousand bright stars and disappear without a trace). *Neue Gesamtausgabe,* vol. 4: 428. The image is strikingly similar to one applied to Romana in *Ahnung und Gegenwart.* Romana's "rasches Leben" (fast life) is compared with "eine Rakete . . . , die sich mit schimmerndem Geprassel zum Himmel aufreißt und oben unter dem Beifallsklatschen der staunenden Menge in tausend funkelnde Sterne ohne Licht und Wärme prächtig zerplatzt" (a rocket that soars shimmering and crackling into the heavens and then, accompanied by the applause of amazed spectators, explodes magnificently into a thousand glittering stars without light or warmth). *Neue Gesamtausgabe,* vol. 2: 188.

35. F. Schlegel, *Kritische Ausgabe,* vol. 5: 9; Firchow, 45.

36. Raimar Stefan Zons contrasts the poetic "Schweifen" (hovering) of Eichendorff's heroes, always rooted in Christian morality, with the danger of "Ausschweifen" (dissipation) embodied in his sensual, pagan female characters, in " 'Schweifen': Eichendorffs *Ahnung und Gegenwart,*" in *Eichendorff und die Spätromantik,* ed. Hans-Georg Pott (Paderborn: Ferdinand Schöningh, 1985), 39–68. See also Peter von Matt, "Der irrende Leib: Die Momente des Unwissens in Eichendorffs Lyrik," *Aurora* 49 (1989): 47–57.

37. Fisher recognizes the ethical dangers presented to Eichendorff's heroes in their encounters with transvestite women, and sees in this threat to *Bildung* the reason for Eichendorff's negative view of cross-dressing. See Fisher, "Das Verkleidungsmotiv," 151, 181.

38. See Jochen Hörisch's illuminating essay " 'Larven und Charaktermasken': Zum elften Kapitel von *Ahnung und Gegenwart,*" in Pott, ed., *Eichendorff und die Spätromantik,* 27–38. Hörisch's reading distinguishes sharply between what he sees as Friedrich's organic, unitary experience of nature and the fragmenting effects of his encounter with society, encapsulated in the masquerade scene. While I agree that the masquerade provokes a dizzying breakdown of

meaning, I see a similar blurring of categories dominating the liminal setting of the forest.

39. See Foucault, *The History of Sexuality,* vol. 1: 55.

40. On the first point, see Hans Eichner, "Zur Auffassung der Sexualität in Eichendorffs erzählender Prosa," in *Eichendorffs Modernität,* ed. Michael Kessler and Helmut Koopmann (Tübingen: Stauffenburg, 1989), 44. On the significance of such episodes in both erasing and signaling lesbian desire, see Terry Castle, *The Apparitional Lesbian: Female Homosexuality and Modern Culture* (New York: Columbia University Press, 1993), 36.

41. See Friedrich Heer, "Die Botschaft eines Lebenden: Zur einhundertjährigen Wiederkehr seines Todestages," in Stöcklein, ed., *Eichendorff heute,* 66–105, esp. 100.

42. Garber stresses the dual impact of social regulation of dress on gender and on class, noting that sumptuary legislation has, historically, often been more concerned with status than with gender. See her discussion of Renaissance sumptuary laws in *Vested Interests,* 25–32.

43. For the foundational mythological approach to the novella, see Lothar Pikulik, "Die Mythisierung des Geschlechtstriebes in Eichendorffs *Marmorbild,*" in *Mythos und Mythologie in der Literatur des 19. Jahrhunderts,* ed. Helmut Koopmann (Frankfurt am Main: Vittorio Klostermann, 1979), 159–72. An example of a binaristic structuralist approach is Winfried Woesler, "Frau Venus und das schöne Mädchen mit dem Blumenkranze," *Aurora* 45 (1985): 33–48.

44. See, for example, Waltraud Wiethölter's Foucauldian study "Die Schule der Venus: Ein diskursanalytischer Versuch zu Eichendorffs *Marmorbild,*" in Kessler and Koopmann, eds., *Eichendorffs Modernität,* 171–201.

45. Wiethölter explores the interconnected history of artistic representations of the Madonna and of the goddess Venus. She argues that by the time of the romantics, the heavenly Venus had become associated with the Virgin Mary, while conversely the image of the Virgin had become eroticized, citing Eichendorff's own highly sensual "Marien-Lyrik" as exemplary of this iconic fluidity. See ibid., 176–77.

46. Foucault, *The History of Sexuality,* vol. 1: 45.

47. Details of the publication history may be found in *Eichendorff Chronik: Daten zu Leben und Werk,* ed. Wolfgang Frühwald (Munich: Carl Hanser, 1977). *Das Marmorbild* appeared in the *Frauentaschenbuch* of 1819. That the sensibilities of the female readership were being taken into account is reflected in Fouqué's editorial efforts "zwei Stellen zu mildern, wo die Farben allzu dreist erglühten, um nach [seiner] Überzeugung vor Jungfrauen treten zu können" (to tone down two passages where the colors burn all too passionately to be set down before virgins). Cited by Frühwald, 82.

48. Lacan connects voyeurism with a desire for mastery or power over one's libidinal objects: the gaze enacts sadistic, phallic power over its passive, masochistic "feminine" objects. See Lacan, "Of the Gaze as Objet Petit a," *The Four Fundamental Concepts,* 67–78.

49. Bailliet, in *Die Frauen,* neatly breaks the repertoire up into Venus/Diana figures on the one hand and Virgin Mary figures on the other, but without problematizing the repetitive structural use of such binarisms.

50. See Mario Praz, *The Romantic Agony,* 2nd ed., trans. Angus Davidson (London: Oxford University Press, 1951), 121–22.

51. "Je l'ai apporté ici, dans un tombeau qui est dans l'enceinte même de ma maison, de façon que Mrs. Parker et moi, nous avons la triste satisfaction de l'orner de fleurs et d'entrenir ce lieu comme une chambre plutôt que comme un sépulcre." (All translations from French are my own.) Praz, *The Romantic Agony,* 172, n. 80.

52. "Pâle, maigre, osseuse, les yeux flamboyants, elle jouait aux effets de spectre ou de fantôme. Volontiers elle accréditait certains bruits qui, pour plus d'*effet,* lui mettaient à la main la coupe ou le poignard des trahisons italiennes à la cour des Borgia." Cited in Praz, *The Romantic Agony,* 122.

53. Heinrich Heine, *Florentinische Nächte, Sämtliche Schriften,* vol. 1, 559. I follow the English translation, *Florentine Nights,* by Frederick Carter (London: Gerald Howe, 1933), 12.

54. Barbara Johnson, in a Lacanian analysis of the Parnassian obsession with marble muses, argues that love of a statue represents "the equation between desire and impossible satisfaction," concluding that "the statue can be loved only *as* resistance." "The Dream of Stone," in *A New History of French Literature,* ed. Denis Hollier et al. (Cambridge: Harvard University Press, 1989): 743–48.

55. Sigmund Freud, "Das Medusenhaupt," *Gesammelte Werke,* ed. Anna Freud (London: Imago, 1940–1968), vol. 17: 47–48; "Medusa's Head," *Standard Edition,* vol. 18: 273–74.

56. Teresa de Lauretis similarly emphasizes the combination of dread and arousal in her reading of Freud's essay, "Desire in Narrative," in *Alice Doesn't: Feminism, Semiotics, Cinema* (Bloomington: Indiana University Press, 1984), 135. Freud, "Das Medusenhaupt," 47; "Medusa's Head," 273.

57. Praz, *The Romantic Agony,* 271.

58. Barbara Johnson, "The Lady in the Lake," in Hollier, ed., *A New History,* 631. On the conjunction of beauty, morbidity, and the feminine, see Elisabeth Bronfen, *Over Her Dead Body: Death, Femininity and the Aesthetic* (Manchester: Manchester University Press, 1992).

59. Rolf Hosfeld has worked out the parallels between the *Florentinische Nächte* and Eichendorff's *Das Marmorbild* in "Nachtgedanken: Heinrich Heines *Florentinische Nächte,*" *Heinrich Heine und das neunzehnte Jahrhundert: Signaturen,* ed. Rolf Hosfeld, spec. issue of *Argument* 124 (1986): 74–79.

60. See Gonthier-Louis Fink, "Pygmalion und das belebte Marmorbild: Wandlungen eines Märchenmotivs von der Frühaufklärung bis zur Spätromantik," *Aurora* 43 (1983): 92–123. Fink explains that the popularity of the Pygmalion motif in early Enlightenment literature derives from its didactic potential, while later writers use it to illustrate the problematic relationship between art and artist. On the deathly implications of the Pygmalion myth for Heine's protagonists, see Hans von Hentig, "Der nekrotrope Mensch: Vom Totenglauben zur morbiden Totennähe," *Beiträge zur Sexualforschung* 30 (1964): 37–48. See also Mayer, "Midas statt Pygmalion." Mayer makes the case that Goethe adopts the Midas topos implicitly, at least, as a substitution for the Pygmalion myth. Midas's transformation of organic matter into beautiful, but dead, gold signals

a paradigmatic shift from the life-giving power of art in the Pygmalion myth. (See Venetian Epigram 100, *Artemis-Gendenkausgabe,* vol. 1: 241.) I would suggest, however, that the figure of Perseus is still more central to classical, romantic, and postromantic discourse on the relationship between artist and artwork, in works by authors ranging from Goethe, Eichendorff, Heine, and Keller to Huysmans and Sacher-Masoch. The Medusa image appears in several of Goethe's works. In the *Italienische Reise,* Goethe expresses his fascination with the tensions revealed in a cast of the Medusa Rondanini between "Tod und Leben, . . . Schmerz und Wollust" (death and life, grief and sensual pleasure). *Artemis-Gedenkausgabe,* vol. 11: 601; Heitner, 441. Faust experiences an uncanny encounter with a Medusean figure who bears an eery resemblance to his dead lover Gretchen. Mephistopheles: "Laß das nur stehn! dabei wird's niemand wohl. / Es ist ein Zauberbild, ist leblos, ein Idol. / Ihm zu begegnen, ist nicht gut; / Vom starren Blick erstarrt des Menschen Bild, / Und er wird fast in Stein verkehrt, / Von der Meduse hast du ja gehört." Faust: "Fürwahr, es sind die Augen eines Toten, / Die eine liebende Hand nicht schloß." (Mephistopheles: "Leave that alone—it can only do harm! / It is a magic image, a phantom without life. / It's dangerous to meet up with; / its stare congeals a person's blood / and almost turns him into stone— / you've surely heard about Medusa!" Faust: "I know those are the eyes of someone dead, / eyes that no loving hand has closed." *Faust* I, *Artemis-Gedenkausgabe,* vol. 5: 274, lines 4189–96; Atkins, 107.

61. For a translation of this poem, see *The Complete Poems of Heinrich Heine,* trans. Hal Draper (Boston: Suhrkamp, 1982), 7–8.

62. De Lauretis, *Alice Doesn't,* 103.

63. Poe famously asserted that "the death of a beautiful woman is, unquestionably, the most poetical topic in the world." Edgar Allan Poe, "The Philosophy of Composition," in *Works,* ed. James A. Harrison (New York: AMS Press, 1965), vol. 14: 1084.

64. Adorno refers to the birth of Pegasus as an allegory for the inherent barbarity of all art: "Grausamkeit des Formens ist Mimesis an den Mythos, mit dem sie umspringt. Der griechische Genius hat das bewußtlos allegorisiert: ein frühdorisches Relief des Palermitanischen archäologischen Museums, aus Selinunt, stellt den Pegasus dar als entsprungen aus dem Blut der Medusa." (The cruelty of artistic shaping is mimetic abandonment to myth as well as manipulation of myth. The genius of the Greeks unknowingly expressed this idea in allegorical form: an early Doric relief from Selinunte, on display at the archaeological museum in Palermo, portrays Pegasus as having sprung from the blood of Medusa.) Theodor W. Adorno, *Ästhetische Theorie,* ed. Gretel Adorno and Rolf Tiedemann (Frankfurt am Main: Suhrkamp, 1973), 80; *Aesthetic Theory,* trans. C. Lenhardt, ed. Gretel Adorno and Rolf Tiedemann (London: Routledge and Kegan Paul, 1984), 74.

65. See Hosfeld, "Nachtgedanken," 87.

66. Robert C. Holub argues that Maximilian's ambivalent relationship with the marble statue is analogous to Heine's relationship with Goethe. See his book *Heinrich Heine's Reception of German Grecophilia: The Function and Application of the Hellenic Tradition in the First Half of the Nineteenth Century*

(Heidelberg: Carl Winter, 1981), 59–86. E. M. Butler states categorically that it was Heine "who gave the coup de grâce to Winckelmann's Greece." See *The Tyranny of Greece over Germany: A Study of the Influence Exercised by Greek Art and Poetry over the Great German Writers of the Eighteenth, Nineteenth and Twentieth Centuries* (Cambridge: Cambridge University Press, 1935), 7.

67. Hinrich C. Seeba also has explored Heine's problematization of the Pygmalion story, arguing that Heine appropriates the myth of the allegedly childless Pygmalion in order to demonstrate the aesthetic impotence of the "Kunstperiode" dominated by Winckelmann, A. W. Schlegel, Fichte, and Goethe. See his article "Die Kinder des Pygmalion: Die Bildlichkeit des Kunstbegriffs bei Heine. Beobachtungen zur Tendenzwende der Ästhetik," *Deutsche Vierteljahrsschrift für Literaturwissenschaft und Geistesgeschichte* 50 (1976): 158–202.

68. I follow the translation by Helen Mustard contained in vol. 33 of the German Library. Heinrich Heine, *The Romantic School and Other Essays,* ed. Jost Hermand and Robert C. Holub (New York: Continuum, 1985), 36.

69. Afterword to the late poem cycle *Romanzero,* vol. 6, part 1: 184; Draper, *The Complete Poems,* 696. See Manfred Schneider, *Die kranke schöne Seele der Revolution: Heine, Börne, das "Junge Deutschland," Marx und Engels* (Frankfurt am Main: Syndikat, 1980), 28–30, for a fuller analysis of this scene.

70. "Bleibe ja, damit ich den steinernen Mann auf der steinernen Bank wieder finde." ("Stay here, and let me find the stone man sitting on the same stone bench when I return.") *Artemis-Gedenkausgabe,* vol. 7: 143; Blackall, 76.

71. The name "Lorelei" is itself suggestive of predatory ocular powers, deriving as it does from the Middle High German *lûren* or *lauern.* Marlies Janz makes this point in her book on literary uses of female statuary, *Marmorbilder: Weiblichkeit und Tod bei Clemens Brentano und Hugo von Hofmannsthal* (Königstein am Taunus: Athenäum, 1986), 80.

72. Garber, *Vested Interests,* 220.

73. Gottfried Keller, *Der grüne Heinrich,* second version, in *Sämtliche Werke und ausgewählte Briefe,* ed. Clemens Heselhaus (Munich: Carl Hanser, 1956–58), vol. 1: 1107. I follow the English translation, *Green Henry,* by A. M. Holt (London: John Calder, 1960), 689. See also Gerhard Kaiser, *Gottfried Keller: Das gedichtete Leben* (Frankfurt am Main: Insel, 1981), 53, for an analysis of the correspondence between mother and Medusa.

74. See Schneider's chapter "Heinrich Heine: Die Angst des Revolutionärs vor der Revolution," *Die kranke schöne Seele,* 27–86.

75. Bram Dijkstra, *Idols of Perversity: Fantasies of Feminine Evil in Fin-de-Siècle Culture* (New York: Oxford University Press, 1986), 310. See also Malke's discussion of both Medusa and Sphinx as incarnations of the androgyne, "Weibmann und Mannweib," 36. In Eichendorff's novella *Die Entführung,* there is a clear association between the mannish Diana and a deadly sphinx statue: "Es war ihm [Gaston] wie eine prachtige Nacht, vor der eine marmorkalte Sphinx lag, er mußte ihr Rätsel lösen oder sie tötete ihn." (It seemed to him like a splendid night, with a marmoreal, cold sphinx lying before it— he had to solve her riddle, or she would kill him.) *Neue Gesamtausgabe,* vol. 2: 867.

76. Positioning herself strategically in the role of smiling Gorgon, Hélène Cixous, in a polemic against theories of "woman as lack," is obviously parodying Freud's "Medusenhaupt" essay when she writes: "You only have to look at the Medusa straight on to see her. And she's not deadly. She's beautiful and she's laughing. Men say that there are two unrepresentable things: death and the feminine sex. That's because they need femininity to be associated with death; it's the jitters that gives them a hard-on!" "The Laugh of the Medusa," 885. For a rigorous reading of the paradoxes and complexities of Freud's essay, see Sarah Kofman, *The Enigma of Woman: Woman in Freud's Writings,* trans. Catherine Porter (Ithaca: Cornell University Press, 1987), especially "Penis Envier, Prostitute, Homosexual, Fetishist," 82–89.

Chapter 4

1. Thomas Mann, *Briefe 1937–1947* (Frankfurt am Main: Fischer, 1963), 458.

2. Noting that Stifter himself had planned to shorten the work, Wildbolz, standing in for most readers, confesses that hardly any of Stifter's public would oppose such a plan; yet even he is forced to admit that the novel, with the most judicious pruning, would still have remained "monoton." Rudolf Wildbolz, *Adalbert Stifter: Langeweile und Faszination* (Stuttgart: Kohlhammer, 1976), 142. On boredom as an aesthetic strategy in *Der Nachsommer,* see also Marina van Zuylen, *Difficulty as an Aesthetic Principle: Realism and Unreadability in Stifter, Melville, and Flaubert* (Tübingen: Gunter Narr, 1994).

3. Adorno, *Ästhetische Theorie,* 346; Lenhardt, 331. For Nietzsche's admiration of Stifter's novel, see, for example, *Kritische Studienausgabe,* vol. 2: 599 and vol. 13: 634.

4. On Stifter's concept of androgyny, see Christine Oertel Sjögren, "Ein Muster-beispiel der Liebestheorie in Stifters *Nachsommer,*" *Vierteljahresschrift des Adalbert Stifter-Instituts des Landes Oberösterreich* 26 (1977): 111–15. While Sjögren remarks on the similarities between the relationship of the lovers, Heinrich and Natalie, and that of Natalie and Gustav, she fails to notice the powerful sexual attraction between brother and sister. Describing the relationship between the siblings with the curious formulation "keusche[r] Sinnlichkeit" (chaste sensuality), she still misses the contradiction between the lack of passion displayed by the lovers and the corresponding eroticism in the brother-sister dyad.

5. Adalbert Stifter, *Der Nachsommer, Sämtliche Werke* (Munich: Winkler, 1979), vol. 2: 252. All further Stifter references will be to this edition. I follow the English translation by Wendell Frye, *Indian Summer* (New York: Peter Lang, 1985), 168.

6. Peter Brooks, *Reading for the Plot: Design and Intention in Narrative* (New York: Knopf, 1984), 109.

7. Sjögren suggests that Stifter was also influenced by Wilhelm von Humboldt's androgynous ideal. See "Ein Musterbeispiel," 113, and also chapter 1, above.

8. Frye translates *gesondert* as "out of the ordinary."

9. For a perceptive reading of the incest drama in *Der Nachsommer,* see Jürgen Manthey, *Wenn Blicke zeugen könnten: Eine psychohistorische Studie über das Sehen in Literatur und Philosophie* (Munich: Carl Hanser, 1983), 261–86.

10. The narrative quickly establishes the parental bedroom as forbidden territory to Heinrich and Klotilde: "Dieser Zug strenger Genauigkeit prägte sich uns ein, und ließ uns auf die Befehle der Eltern achten, wenn wir sie auch nicht verstanden. So zum Beispiele durften nicht einmal wir Kinder das Schlafzimmer der Eltern betreten." (We were quite impressed by this quality of strict preciseness and obeyed our parents' instructions even if we didn't understand them. For example, we children were not even allowed to enter our parents' bedroom [9; Frye, 11].)

11. See Christine Oertel Sjögren, "Klotildes Reise in die Tiefe: Psychoanalytische Betrachtungen zu einer Episode in Stifters *Nachsommer,*" *Vierteljahresschrift des Adalbert Stifter-Instituts des Landes Oberösterreich* 24 (1975): 107–11. While Sjögren identifies Klotilde's incestuous desires for her brother, her argument seems to suppose Heinrich immune to such powerful drives.

12. This is the approach taken, for example, by Manthey, *Wenn Blicke zeugen könnten,* 270.

13. See his important study *Gottfried Keller.*

14. Freud, "Die Symbolik im Traum," *Studienausgabe,* vol. 1: 165–66; "Symbolism in Dreams," *Standard Edition,* vol. 15: 156.

15. "Ich hatte mit Natalien keinen Briefwechsel verabredet, ich hatte nicht daran gedacht, sie wahrscheinlich auch nicht." (I hadn't arranged any correspondence with Natalie; I just hadn't thought of it and apparently neither had she [572; Frye, 375].)

16. Sjögren notes the eroticism of this image in her essay "Klotildes Reise," 110.

17. *Sämtliche Werke,* vol. 5; *The Recluse,* trans. David Luke (London: Jonathan Cape, 1968).

18. On this point, I take issue with Russell A. Berman's ideological critique of *Der Nachsommer,* which represses the psychological trauma that underlies the novel. Berman asserts that "unlike Wilhelm Meister, the paradigmatic Bildungsroman hero with whom he begs to be compared, Heinrich merely meets this literature and loves it immediately. There are no interpretive difficulties, no fruitful misreadings, and no important literary critical passages associated with these textual encounters. The *King Lear* episode in *Der Nachsommer* has none of the weighty significance of the Hamlet problem for Goethe's novel. The canon is merely established as such, cultural material arbitrarily declared worthy of preservation." See *The Rise of the Modern German Novel: Crisis and Charisma* (Cambridge: Harvard University Press, 1986), 119.

19. Walter Benjamin, "Stifter," in *Gesammelte Schriften,* vol. 2, bk. 2, ed. Rolf Tiedemann and Hermann Schweppenhäuser (Frankfurt am Main: Suhrkamp, 1980), 608–10. See also Marianne Schuller's argument that conflict is deliberately excluded from Stifter's fictional world in "Das Gewitter findet nicht statt oder die Abdankung der Kunst: Zu Adalbert Stifters Roman *Der Nachsommer,*" *Poetica* 10 (1978): 25–52.

20. Heinrich comments on his relationship with Natalie's brother: "Ich weiß nicht, welcher innre Zug von Neigung mich zu dem Jünglinge hinwendete,

der in seinem Geiste zuletzt doch nur ein Knabe war, den ich über die einfachsten Dinge täglicher Erfahrung belehren mußte, namentlich, wenn es Wanderungsangelegenheiten waren, und der mir in seiner Seele nichts bieten konnte, wodurch ich erweitert und gehoben werden mußte, es müßte nur das Bild der vollkommensten Güte und Reinheit gewesen sein, das ich täglich mehr an ihm sehen lieben und verehren lernte." (I don't know what subconscious affection drew me to this youth who, after all, intellectually was still a boy and whom I had to teach the simplest things of everyday life, particularly concerning hiking, and who could offer me nothing intellectually through which my horizons could be broadened and elevated; it must have been simply the image of complete goodness and purity which I daily learned to love and revere all the more in him [324; Frye, 213].)

21. See G. Joyce Hallamore, "The Symbolism of the Marble Muse in Stifter's *Nachsommer,*" *PMLA* 74 (1959): 398–405. Hallamore's essay does not address the problematic nature of this configuration of woman and statue, petrification and animation, concluding that "art and nature merge; the ideal is not lost but vitalized in the process." It is important to bear in mind that Stifter's aesthetic strategy of containment is premised on female petrification.

22. See W. G. Sebald's perceptive comments on the related obsessions of Stifter with female virginity and morbidity in "Bis an den Rand der Natur: Versuch über Stifter," in *Die Beschreibung des Unglücks: Zur österreichischen Literatur von Stifter bis Handke* (Salzburg: Residenz, 1985), 15–37.

23. As he reads the *Odyssey,* in a later passage, Heinrich returns to this theme of animation, though what is interesting here is that the marble statue comes to "life" in the form of another artistic creation—the antique literary figure Nausicaa—rather than as a living woman: "Als Nausikae kam, war es mir wieder, wie es mir bei der ersten richtigen Betrachtung der Marmorgestalt gewesen war, die Gewänder des harten Stoffes löseten sich zu leichter Milde, die Glieder bewegten sich, das Angesicht erhielt wandelbares Leben, und die Gestalt trat als Nausikae zu mir." (When Nausica came, I felt just as I had the first time I had really looked at and understood the marble statue, the garments made of the hard material dissolved into lighter mildness, the limbs began to move, the countenance assumed living expressions, and the statue seemed like Nausica [600; Frye, 393].) Significantly, the story of Nausicaa has to do with Odysseus's averting of an undesired marriage.

24. Peter Uwe Hohendahl has discussed the influence of Schiller's conception of "aesthetic education" on Stifter's novel, but without making the specific connection between the Juno Ludovisi of Schiller's work and the marble muse at the Asperhof. See his informative essay "Die gebildete Gemeinschaft: Stifters *Nachsommer* als Utopie der ästhetischen Erziehung," in *Utopieforschung: Interdisziplinäre Studien zur neuzeitlichen Utopie,* ed. Wilhelm Voßkamp (Stuttgart: Metzler, 1982), vol. 3: 333–56.

25. Winckelmann, *Sämtliche Werke,* vol. 4: 141.

26. F. Schlegel, *Kritische Ausgabe,* vol. 5: 30; Firchow, 70.

27. Berman argues that the linguistic structures of the novel themselves impose a process of ossification on the reader, in their deliberate negation of subjective response. See *The Rise of the Modern German Novel,* 133.

28. See Manthey's point that the artwork's suggestion of totality is what makes it into a fetish object; *Wenn Blicke zeugen könnten,* 259. This reading derives from Lacan's notion of the "object-a," an object used to deflect the subject's attention from the traumatic absence of a beloved other, such as the mother. See Lacan, "Of the Gaze as Objet Petit a."

29. In this respect, my reading, stressing the mortification implicit in the close relationship between woman and statue, diverges from Robert C. Holub's otherwise persuasive account of the "realist education." See his book *Reflections of Realism: Paradox, Norm, and Ideology in Nineteenth-Century German Prose* (Detroit: Wayne State University Press, 1991).

30. See Manthey, *Wenn Blicke zeugen könnten,* 280.

31. Schuller, aptly drawing on Benjamin's ideas on the changing nature of art in an age of mechanical reproducibility, similarly terms Goethe's presence in the novel an auratic "Denkmal" or monument to lost totality; "Das Gewitter findet nicht statt," 39.

32. See Holub's comparison of Stifter's concept of *Bildung* with those of his predecessors in the *Goethezeit,* in *Reflections of Realism,* 92–93.

33. Hohendahl, in "Die gebildete Gemeinschaft," makes the case that *Der Nachsommer* is an attempt by the author to work through the shock of the 1848 revolution, which Stifter entered as a moderate liberal, by stabilizing his worldview in a deliberately nostalgic fictional universe. Berman, questioning the assertion that *Der Nachsommer* is a fundamentally nostalgic and thus reactionary work, characterizes Stifter's utopian novel as the seismographic "guilty conscience" of nineteenth-century capitalism, and argues persuasively that the aesthetic of order at work here serves as a doomed attempt to ward off what he calls the "entropy of decay." See *The Rise of the Modern German Novel,* 105.

34. Berman, *The Rise of the Modern German Novel,* 122.

35. Holub, *Reflections of Realism,* 17. Interestingly, Holub discusses Keller's novella *Romeo und Julia auf dem Dorfe* (A Village Romeo and Juliet) from the point of view of repressed incestuous desires. If we shift the emphasis from the (oedipal) notion of incest to androgyny, this line of thought might be even more applicable to Stifter's works. See Holub's chapter "The Desires of Realism: Repetition and Repression in Keller's *Romeo und Julia auf dem Dorfe,*" 101–31.

36. The mineral referred to in the title of the second novella is muscovite.

37. The androgyne's exclusion from language is foregrounded by the novella: "Darauf machte es ein Zeichen, weil es die Sache nicht mit Worten sagen konnte." (Thereupon she made a sign, because she could not express the matter in words.) Stifter, *Sämtliche Werke,* vol. 1: 230. For a Lacanian analysis of the connection between androgyny and speechlessness, see Andrea Kuhn, "Sprachlosigkeit—das Geheimnis des Hermaphroditen," in Prinz, ed., *Androgyn: Sehnsucht nach Vollkommenheit,* 120–26. Kuhn suggests that in Plato's account of androgyny, we must assume that language postdates the traumatic separation of halves. Significantly, we are told in *Katzensilber* that it is the children, perhaps because they themselves are not yet fully integrated into the symbolic realm, who are the only ones to understand the androgyne's

words (247). On the one occasion when we hear the child speak, she has been pressed again, by the children's parents, for information on her family, and the bizarre words that she blurts out in response—"Sture Mure ist tot, und der hohe Felsen ist tot" (Sture Mure is dead, and the tall crag is dead [274])—provoke her traumatic final departure from her foster family. These words appear to be an echo of Mignon's monosyllabic answer to Wilhelm Meister's question concerning her father's identity: "Der große Teufel ist tot." ("The big devil is dead" [105; Blackall, 54].) On repeated configurations of childhood, androgyny, and speechlessness in Stifter's works, see Eva Geulen, *Worthörig wider Willen: Darstellungsproblematik und Sprachreflexion in der Prosa Adalbert Stifters* (Munich: iudicium, 1992), 123–50.

38. For biographical details of Stifter's relationship with his foster child, see Urban Roedl, *Adalbert Stifter in Selbstzeugnissen und Bilddokumenten* (Hamburg: Rowohlt, 1965).

39. Walter Haußmann, "Adalbert Stifter: *Brigitta,*" *Der Deutschunterricht* 3 (1951): 30.

40. Stifter, vol. 5: 735. I follow Helen Watanabe-O'Kelly's translation (London: Angel, 1990), 97.

41. A different perspective is offered by Christine Oertel Sjögren in "The Allure of Beauty in Stifter's *Brigitta,*" *Journal of English and Germanic Philology* 81 (1982): 47–54. Sjögren describes Brigitta as a "dual-sexed fertility goddess" who stands out against the barren steppe and whose potent creativity is aptly expressed by Stifter in a fusion of male and female imagery.

42. Rosemarie Hunter-Lougheed suggestively connects Brigitta's "heiße trockene Augen" (hot, dry eyes [768; Watanabe-O'Kelly, 124]) with the stony plain that surrounds Maroshely "und das jetzt in der Abendluft draußen lag und in den rötlich spinnenden Strahlen heiß und trocken herein sah zu dieser kühlen grünen Frische" (and which lay now behind us in the evening air and, hot and dry in the red shimmering rays, looked across to this cool green freshness [742; Watanabe-O'Kelly, 103]). See "Adalbert Stifter: *Brigitta* (1844–47)," in *Romane und Erzählungen zwischen Romantik und Realismus: Neue Interpretationen,* ed. Paul Michael Lützeler (Stuttgart: Reclam, 1983), 354–85, esp. 366.

43. "Außer den Waffen hingen auch Kleider da [an den Wänden], ungarische, die man aus früheren Zeiten aufgehoben hatte, und dann jene schlotternden seidenen, die entweder Türken oder gar Tartaren angehört haben mochten." (Apart from the weapons there were also garments there too, Hungarian ones, which had been preserved from earlier days, and also loose silk ones, which might have belonged to Turks or Tatars [747; Watanabe-O'Kelly, 107].) "Auf der Oberlippe hatte er den gebräuchlichen Bart, der die Augen noch funkelnder machte, das Haupt deckte ein breiter runder Hut und von den Lenden fiel das weite weiße Beinkleid hinab. Es war ganz natürlich, daß es so sein mußte, ich konnte plötzlich nicht mehr denken, wie ihm der Frack stehe, seine Tracht schien mir reizend, daß mir mein deutscher Flaus, der bestaubt und herabgeschunden auf einer Bank unter dem verschossenen Seidenkleide eines Tartaren lag, fast erbärmlich vorkam." (On his top lip he wore the usual moustache which made his eyes seem even more sparkling, his head was

covered with a broad round hat and from his hips fell the wide white trousers. It was quite natural that he should be like this, I suddenly could not even think how he looked in a tail-coat, his costume appeared charming to me, so that my German coat of coarse wool, which lay dusty and battered on a bench under the faded silk garment of a Tatar, seemed almost pitiful to me [749; Watanabe-O'Kelly, 108].)

44. Haußmann remarks on the sexual polymorphousness characterizing both protagonists. See "Adalbert Stifter: *Brigitta,*" 43. For a reading of repressed homosexuality in the novella, see Claude Owen, "Zur Erotik in Stifters *Brigitta,*" *Österreich in Geschichte und Literatur* 15 (1971): 106–14.

45. Italy, of course, is the home of Winckelmann's androgynes, of Goethe's Mignon, and of Eichendorff's Amazonian Romana.

46. See Owen, "Zur Erotik," 109.

47. Haußmann, "Adalbert Stifter: *Brigitta,*" 43.

48. Gail Finney, *The Counterfeit Idyll: The Garden Ideal and Social Reality in Nineteenth-Century Fiction* (Tübingen: Max Niemeyer, 1984).

49. Walter Benjamin, "Gottfried Keller: Zu Ehren einer kritischen Gesamtausgabe seiner Werke," *Gesammelte Schriften,* vol. 2, bk. 2, 291.

50. On transvestism as a disruptive force in Keller's work, see Antje Harnisch, " 'Die Sucht, den Mann zu spielen' in Gottfried Kellers Realismus," *German Quarterly* 68 (1995): 147–59.

51. Keller, *Sämtliche Werke,* vol. 1: 883; Holt, 477.

52. Cited in Emil Ermatinger, *Gottfried Kellers Leben,* 8th rev. ed. (Zurich: Artemis, 1950), 405. See also Keller's parodic poem "Tagelied" (Dawn Song), vol. 3: 102.

53. See Spickernagel, " 'Helden wie zarte Knaben,' " which reproduces several of Kauffmann's paintings.

54. For a Freudian analysis of such "uncanny" moments in the love story of Erwin and Regine, see Hanns-Josef Ortheil, "Stille Heimlichkeit: Zur *Regine*-Erzählung in Gottfried Kellers *Sinngedicht,*" *Jahrbuch der deutschen Schillergesellschaft* 30 (1986): 453–71. Taking his cue from Gerhard Kaiser's ground-breaking Freudian-oriented study of Keller's life and works, *Gottfried Keller: Das gedichtete Leben,* Ortheil explains the generative Pygmalion/statue thematics of the novella in terms of an infantile mother fixation.

55. See Ovid, *Metamorphoses,* 4.285–388, esp. lines 383–86: "Hermaphroditus ait: 'nato date munera vestro, / et pater et genetrix, amborum nomen habenti: / quisquis in hos fontes vir venerit, exeat inde / semivir et tactis subito mollescat in undis!' " (Hermaphroditus cried. "Oh, grant this boon, my father and my mother, to your son who bears the name of both: whoever comes into this pool as man may he go forth half-man, and may he weaken at touch of the water" [Miller, vol. 1: 205].)

56. She awakens, writes Gerhard Kaiser, in the guise of a gigantic mass-produced ornament, or boudoir bric-a-brac. See *Gottfried Keller,* 521. On the lethal combination of woman and artwork, see Adolf Muschg's biographical *Gottfried Keller* (Munich: Kindler, 1977), esp. 85. See also Keller's satirical poem on the commodification of art, which takes as its subject the same classical statue, the "Venus von Milo." The opening verse of the poem describes the

ghastly fate of the modish statue, now serially reproduced in plaster, porcelain, and pewter and placed on desks, mantels, and commodes (vol. 3: 382). On the aesthetic failure of classicism and the principle of commodification that becomes the main focus of the realist novel, see Hörisch, *Gott, Geld und Glück,* esp. 100–115.

57. The fullest investigation of Keller's mythological sources has been undertaken by Herbert Anton, in *Mythologische Erotik in Kellers* Sieben Legenden *und im* Sinngedicht (Stuttgart: Metzler, 1970), esp. "Pygmalion und Galatea," 89–101.

58. See *Dichter über ihre Dichtungen: Gottfried Keller,* ed. Klaus Jeziorkowski (Munich: Ernst Heimeran, 1969), 340. Anton notes that Ovid had already signaled the animation of marble with the statue's blush; *Mythologische Erotik,* 84. See Ovid, *Metamorphoses,* 10.290–94: "tum vero Paphius plenissima concipit heros / verba, quibus Veneri grates agat, oraque tandem / ore suo non falsa premit, dataque oscula virgo / sensit et erubuit timidumque ad lumina lumen / attollens pariter cum caelo vidit amantem." (Then did the Paphian hero pour out copious thanks to Venus, and again pressed with his lips real lips at last. The maiden felt the kisses, blushed and, lifting her timid eyes up to the light, she saw the sky and her lover at the same time [Miller, vol. 2: 85].)

59. Kaiser, *Gottfried Keller,* 505.

60. Galatea, too, was a nereid, or sea-nymph.

61. Benjamin, "Gottfried Keller," 287.

62. This scene is very probably a parodic citation of Goethe's *Wilhelm Meisters Lehrjahre,* where Wilhelm lulls Mariane to sleep with a long-winded account of his childhood. A similar incident occurs in Keller's novella *Pankraz, der Schmoller* (Pankraz the Sulker), when Pankraz's story of his exploits in America sends both his mother and his sister into a deep slumber (vol. 2: 33). For a fuller discussion of such petrification of female characters through male narratives, see chapter 3, above.

63. Gottfried Keller, *The Misused Love Letters and Regula Amrain and Her Youngest Son,* trans. Michael Bullock and Anne Fremantle (New York: Frederick Ungar, 1974), 26.

64. See Anton, *Mythologische Erotik,* 48.

65. Kaiser points out that Viggi and Kätter, as newlyweds, spend their evenings in long and intimate conversations over the pages of an illustrated anatomy textbook! See *Gottfried Keller,* 364.

66. See ibid., 469. Anton, citing Jung's *Psychologie und Alchemie,* interprets the lion, too, as a symbol for hermaphroditism. See *Mythologische Erotik,* 37.

67. See Kaiser, *Gottfried Keller,* 469. Kaiser also notes the text's intriguing conflation of love and death, Cupid's arrow and the Grim Reaper, in Landolt's final words: "Im Spätherbste seines siebenundsiebzigsten Lebensjahres, als das letzte Blatt gefallen, sah er das Ende kommen: 'Der Schütze dort hat gut gezielt!' sagte er, auf das elfenbeinerne Tödlein zeigend, das er von der Großmutter geerbt hatte." (In the late autumn of his seventy-seventh year, when the last leaf had fallen from the trees, he saw the end was near. "That archer has aimed well," he said, pointing to the ivory death figurine that he had inherited from his grandmother [801].)

68. Anton, in *Mythologische Erotik,* 50, sees this androgynous Christlike figure as an ironic commentary on the aesthetic fads of the Nazarenes, whose ideal of sexual fluidity may itself hark back to Friedrich Schlegel's famous commentary on a Leonardo Madonna, which I quote in my first chaper. As a further example of Keller's parodic treatment of a tired artistic fashion, Anton cites the marginalia to the Manesse manuscript drawn by the medieval illuminator Hadlaub, in the *Züricher Novellen.* Hadlaub chooses to depict his beloved in the form of an androgynous knight: on the one hand, the narrator tells us, Hadlaub was thus able to portray the woman he loved in hidden form, but he also stresses the ideal aesthetic character of such androgynous creations. Vol. 2: 669.

69. Still more hilarious is the spectacle provided by Cocco of the unsustainability of a transvestite persona: he hops into the room, a pitiful sight, his bonnet dangling into his face and his skirts tangled up in his legs and tail. Returning the sad creature to his natural state also restores the equanimity of the five women, who have been distinctly perturbed by the puzzling appearance of the "Zofenknabe."

70. Foucault, *The History of Sexuality,* vol. 1: 43 (my emphasis).

71. See Thomas Laqueur's observations about pervasive reports of male effeminacy in early modern Europe: "Bodies actually seem to slip from their sexual anchorage in the face of heterosexual sociability; being with women too much or being too devoted to them seems to lead to the blurring of what we call sex." *Making Sex,* 124. Laqueur's remarks, it should be noted, depend on his argument that in the Renaissance "one-sex" model, there is a slippage between categories of sex and gender. In post-Enlightenment thought, on the other hand, according to Laqueur's book, behavior tends to become irrelevant, and the question of sex is posited as purely biological.

72. Anton associates the transvestism in this scene with ancient religious rites surrounding marriage celebrations, and links it also with myths of androgyny. See *Mythologische Erotik,* 43–44. Pia Reinacher interprets Fritz's transvestite staging of self as an attempt to master, or escape from, a threatening new developmental stage, the choice of a love object. Reinacher further argues that this male cross-dressing plays an apotropaic role, in warding off, or neutralizing, the castrating powers of woman. See her semiotic analysis of clothing, *Die Sprache der Kleider im literarischen Text: Untersuchungen zu Gottfried Keller und Robert Walser* (Bern: Peter Lang, 1988), 94.

73. See Reinacher, *Die Sprache der Kleider,* 95.

74. See the related German slang use of *Schachtel* for "woman."

75. Kaiser, *Gottfried Keller,* 318.

76. Ironically, Keller gives Frau Amrain a version of his sister Regula's first name.

77. The novella stresses the oedipal family drama that dominates events in the Amrain household—so, for example, we read of Fritz's childhood "triumph" over the bold journeyman who attempts to seduce Frau Amrain.

78. I follow the English translation of vol. 44 of the German Library, Gottfried Keller, *Stories,* ed. Frank G. Ryder, trans. Robert M. Browning, Paul Bernard Thomas, Harry Steinhauer, Frank G. Ryder, B. Q. Morgan, and Martin Wyness (New York: Continuum, 1982).

79. Kaiser, for example, characterizes her as a deathly muse and sees her monastic career as the pinnacle of her perversity. *Gottfried Keller,* 401. See also Barbara R. Frank, "Irony in Keller's *Sieben Legenden,*" *Germanic Review* 49 (1974): 132, where Frank equates Eugenia's scholarly aspirations with "falsely directed vanity."

80. Anton, *Mythologische Erotik,* 48–49.

81. Ovid, *Metamorphoses,* 10.162–219.

82. Winckelmann, *Sämtliche Werke,* vol. 4: 72.

83. See also Malke, "Weibmann und Mannweib."

84. See Anton, *Mythologische Erotik,* 49.

85. "Die Jungfrau Maria, welche ja als Zendelwald neben ihr saß, las dies Gebet in ihrem Herzen und war so erfreut über die fromme Dankbarkeit ihres Schützlings, daß sie Bertraden zärtlich umfing und einen Kuß auf ihre Lippen drückte, der begreiflicherweise das holde Weib mit himmlischer Seligkeit erfüllte; denn wenn die Himmlischen einmal Zuckerzeug backen, so gerät es zur Süße." (The Virgin Mary, who was of course sitting beside her in the form of Zendelwald, read this prayer in her heart and was so pleased at the pious gratitude of her protégée that she tenderly embraced her and planted a kiss on her lips, which understandably filled the lovely lady with heavenly bliss; for when heaven-dwellers once set about making fancy desserts, they turn out to be pretty sweet [563; Browning, 361].)

86. See, for example, Karl Reichert's account of the complex genesis of the *Sieben Legenden,* "Die Entstehung der *Sieben Legenden* von Gottfried Keller," *Euphorion* 57 (1963): 228–53; Frank, "Irony in Keller's *Sieben Legenden*"; Anya Banasik, "Gottfried Keller's Adaptation of Medieval Legends for the XIXth C. Audience," in *Legenda Aurea: Sept Siècles de Diffusion. Actes du colloque international sur la Legenda aurea: Texte latin et branches vernaculaires,* ed. Brenda Dunn-Lardeau (Montreal: Bellarmin, 1986), 283–88; and Iris Denneler, "Verkehrtes Bekehren, bekehrtes Verkehren, oder Das Martyrium der Schrift: Zur Erzählstruktur von Gottfried Kellers Legende vom 'Schlimm-heiligen Vitalis,' " *Germanisch-Romanische Monatsschrift* N.F. 39 (1989): 196–209.

87. Denneler, "Verkehrtes Bekehren, bekehrtes Verkehren," 197.

88. For a full analysis of transvestism as a literary strategy in the realist novella, see Eric S. Downing's work on the *Sieben Legenden,* which will appear as a chapter in his forthcoming book entitled *Double Exposures: Repetition and Realism.*

89. Keller writes, once again taking up a metaphor related to personal grooming: "Auch habe ich eine Anzahl Novellchen ohne Lokalfärbung liegen, die ich alle 1½ Jahr einmal besehe und ihnen die Nägel beschneide, so daß sie zuletzt ganz putzig aussehen werden." (I also have a number of novellas without local color lying around: I take them out every eighteen months or so to trim their nails, so that in the end they'll look rather cute.) Letter of April 2, 1871, cited in Jeziorkowski, ed., *Dichter über ihre Dichtungen,* 455.

90. Letter of Oct. 1, 1871, ibid., 455. For the debate between Keller and Vischer on the title, see ibid., 455–56, 460.

91. Ibid., 461 (my emphasis).

92. Keller is quick to attack the simple-mindedness of Kosegarten's adaptation: "Ich fand nämlich eine Legendensammlung von Kosegarten in einem läppisch frömmelnden und einfältiglichen Stile erzählt (von einem norddeutschen Protestanten doppelt lächerlich) in Prosa und Versen. Ich nahm 7 oder 8 Stück aus dem vergessenen Schmöker, fing sie mit den süßlichen und heiligen Worten Kosegärtchens an und machte dann eine erotisch-weltliche Historie daraus, in welcher die Jungfrau Maria die Schutzpatronin der Heiratslustigen ist." (I found a collection of legends by Kosegarten, narrated, in prose and verse, in a ridiculously pious and simplistic style [all the more silly for a Northern German Protestant]. I took seven or eight pieces from the forgotten tome, introduced them with old Kosegarten's sugary holy words, and then turned them into erotic secular stories with the Virgin Mary as the patron saint of young lovers.) Tellingly, Keller follows this revelation of his source with an admission that some critics might construe his work as plagiarism—citation, as I have argued, being a literary strategy aptly expressed in transvestite narratives. Letter to Ferdinand Freiligrath of April 22, 1860, ibid., 359.
93. Denneler, "Verkehrtes Bekehren, bekehrtes Verkehren," 196–99. The passage she refers to is contained in the *Sieben Legenden,* 588. It is certainly tempting, in the case of Luna, to make the connection with Aristophanes' speech in the *Symposium,* where he identifies the moon as androgynous (190B).

Coda

1. Achim Aurnhammer presents a concise survey of such intellectual trends in his chapter "Sexualpsychologie um 1900," *Androgynie,* 209–18. See also Jacques Le Rider's outstanding study *Modernity and Crises of Identity,* trans. Rosemary Morris (Cambridge: Polity Press, 1993).
2. Elaine Showalter, *Sexual Anarchy: Gender and Culture at the Fin de Siècle* (New York: Viking, 1990).
3. John Neubauer has investigated adolescence as the privileged life phase of the turn of the century. See his fascinating historical account, *The Fin-de-Siècle Culture of Adolescence* (New Haven: Yale University Press, 1992).
4. Bram Dijkstra's rich study of popular art at the fin-de-siècle, *Idols of Perversity,* citing depictions of androgynous male beauties by such artists as Herbert Draper, Heinrich Friedrich Heyne, and Jean Delville, seems to corroborate this hypothesis as far as the pictorial arts are concerned.
5. Cited by Aurnhammer, *Androgynie,* 218–19.
6. Franz Kafka, *Das Schloß* (Frankfurt am Main: Fischer, 1983), 47; *The Castle,* trans. Willa Muir and Edwin Muir (New York: Knopf, 1968), 60.
7. See Barbara Wedekind-Schwertner, *"Daß ich eins und doppelt bin": Studien zur Idee der Androgynie unter besonderer Berücksichtigung Thomas Manns* (Frankfurt am Main: Peter Lang, 1984). This exhaustive study of mythological sources is, however, problematic, in that it does not address shifting historical constructions of gender and sexuality. Jonathan Dollimore sees the turn to androgyny itself as an evasive response to homosexual otherness: "Put bluntly, to be identified positively, homosexuality usually has to be dissolved into the

androgynous." See his book *Sexual Dissidence: Augustine to Wilde, Freud to Foucault* (Oxford: Oxford University Press, 1991), 332.

8. Thomas Mann, *Der Tod in Venedig* (Frankfurt am Main: Fischer, 1979), 41; *Death in Venice and Seven Other Stories,* trans. H. T. Lowe-Porter (New York: Vintage, 1989), 43.

Bibliography

Primary Literature

Baader, Franz von. "Sätze aus der erotischen Philosophie." In *Schriften,* ed. Max Pulver. Leipzig: Insel, 1921.

Bachmann, Ingeborg. *Malina.* Frankfurt am Main: Suhrkamp, 1971.

———. *Malina,* trans. Philip Boehm. New York: Holmes and Meier, 1990.

Eckermann, Johann Peter. *Gespräche mit Goethe in den letzten Jahren seines Lebens,* ed. Fritz Bergemann. Frankfurt am Main: Insel, 1981.

Eichendorff, Joseph von. *Briefe und Dichtungen,* ed. Wilhelm Kosch. Cologne: Kommissions-Verlag, 1906.

———. *Neue Gesamtausgabe der Werke und Schriften,* 4 vols., ed. Gerhart Baumann. Stuttgart: Cotta, 1958.

———. *Historisch-Kritische Ausgabe,* 16 vols., ed. Wilhelm Kosch and August Sauer, reissued and expanded by Hermann Kunisch and Helmut Koopmann. Regensburg: J. Habbel, 1962–.

Goethe, Johann Wolfgang. *Johann Wolfgang von Goethe's Roman Elegies and Venetian Epigrams,* ed. and trans. L. R. Lind. Lawrence: University Press of Kansas, 1974.

———. *Artemis-Gedenkausgabe,* 18 vols., ed. Ernst Beutler. Munich: Deutscher Taschenbuch Verlag, 1977.

———. *Conversations of German Refugees, Wilhelm Meister's Journeyman Years or the Renunciants,* ed. Jane K. Brown, trans. Jan van Heurck and Krishna Winston. New York: Suhrkamp, 1983.

———. *Early Verse Drama and Prose Plays,* ed. Cyrus Hamlin and Frank Ryder, trans. Robert M. Browning, Michael Hamburger, Cyrus Hamlin, and Frank Ryder. New York: Suhrkamp, 1983.

———. *Essays on Art and Literature,* ed. John Gearey, trans. Ellen von Nardroff and Ernest H. von Nardroff. New York: Suhrkamp, 1983.

———. *Faust I and II,* ed. and trans. Stuart Atkins. New York: Suhrkamp, 1983.

———. *Italian Journey,* ed. Thomas P. Saine and Jeffrey L. Sammons, trans. Robert R. Heitner. New York: Suhrkamp, 1983.

———. *Selected Poems,* ed. Christopher Middleton, trans. Michael Hamburger, David Luke, Christopher Middleton, John Frederick Nims, and Vernon Watkins. (New York: Suhrkamp, 1983.

————. *Wilhelm Meister's Apprenticeship,* ed. and trans. Eric A. Blackall. New York: Suhrkamp, 1983.

Hamann, Johann Georg. *Sämtliche Werke,* 6 vols., ed. Joseph Nadler. Vienna: Herder, 1949–57.

————. *Briefwechsel,* 6 vols., ed. Walther Ziesemer and Arthur Henkel. Wiesbaden: Insel, 1955–79.

Heine, Heinrich. *Florentine Nights,* trans. Frederick Carter. London: Gerald Howe, 1933.

————. *Sämtliche Schriften,* 6 vols., ed. Klaus Briegleb. Munich: Hanser, 1968–76.

————. *The Complete Poems of Heinrich Heine,* trans. Hal Draper. Boston: Suhrkamp, 1982.

————. *The Romantic School and Other Essays,* ed. Jost Hermand and Robert C. Holub. New York: Continuum, 1985.

Humboldt, Wilhelm von. *Werke,* 5 vols., ed. Andreas Flitner and Klaus Giel. Stuttgart: Cotta, 1960.

Jean Paul. *Vorschule der Ästhetik.* Hamburg: Felix Meiner, 1990.

Kafka, Franz. *The Castle,* trans. Willa Muir and Edwin Muir. New York: Knopf, 1968.

————. *Das Schloß.* Frankfurt am Main: Fischer, 1983.

Keller, Gottfried. *Sämtliche Werke und ausgewählte Briefe,* 3 vols., ed. Clemens Heselhaus. Munich: Hanser, 1956–58.

————. *Green Henry,* trans. A. M. Holt. London: John Calder, 1960.

————. *The Misused Love Letters and Regula Amrain and Her Youngest Son,* trans. Michael Bullock and Anne Fremantle. New York: Frederick Ungar, 1974.

————. *Stories,* ed. Frank G. Ryder, trans. Robert M. Browning, Paul Bernard Thomas, Harry Steinhauer, Frank G. Ryder, B. Q. Morgan, and Martin Wyness. New York: Continuum, 1982.

Mann, Thomas. *Briefe 1937–1947.* Frankfurt am Main: Fischer, 1963.

————. *Der Tod in Venedig.* Frankfurt am Main: Fischer, 1979.

————. *Der Zauberberg.* Frankfurt am Main: Fischer, 1982.

————. *Death in Venice and Seven Other Stories,* trans. H. T. Lowe-Porter. New York: Vintage, 1989.

————. *The Magic Mountain,* trans. H. T. Lowe-Porter. New York: Vintage, 1992.

Novalis. *Henry von Ofterdingen,* trans. Palmer Hilty. New York: Frederick Ungar, 1964.

————. *Werke,* ed. Hans-Joachim Mähl and Richard Samuel. Munich: Carl Hanser, 1981.

Ovid. *Metamorphoses,* 2 vols., ed. G. P. Goold, trans. Frank Justus Miller. Cambridge: Harvard University Press, 1984.

Plato. *Symposium,* trans. Alexander Nehamas and Paul Woodruff. Indianapolis: Hackett, 1989.

Poe, Edgar Allan. *Works,* 17 vols., ed. James A. Harrison. New York: AMS Press, 1965.

Schelling, Friedrich Wilhelm Joseph von. *Von der Weltseele: eine Hypothese der höheren Physik zur Erklärung des allgemeinen Organismus.* Hamburg: F. Perthes, 1809.

Schiller, Friedrich. *Nationalausgabe,* 42 vols., ed. Julius Petersen and Gerhard Fricke. Weimar: Hermann Böhlaus Nachfolger, 1943–.

———. *On the Aesthetic Education of Man,* ed. and trans. Elizabeth M. Wilkinson and L. A. Willoughby. Oxford: Oxford University Press, 1982.

Schlegel, Friedrich von. *Lucinde.* Berlin: Heinrich Frölich, 1799.

———. *The Aesthetic and Miscellaneous Works of Friedrich von Schlegel,* trans. E. J. Millington. London: Henry G. Bohn, 1849.

———. *Kritische Ausgabe,* 35 vols., ed. Ernst Behler. Paderborn: Ferdinand Schöningh, 1958–1991.

———. *Dialogue on Poetry and Literary Aphorisms,* trans. Ernst Behler and Roman Struc. University Park: Pennsylvania State University Press, 1968.

———. *Lucinde and the Fragments,* trans. Peter Firchow. Minneapolis: University of Minnesota Press, 1971.

———. *Theorie der Weiblichkeit,* ed. Winfried Menninghaus. Frankfurt am Main: Insel, 1983.

Schleiermacher, Friedrich Daniel Ernst. "Idee zu einem Katechismus der Vernunft für edle Frauen." In *Athenäum,* ed. August Wilhelm Schlegel and Friedrich Schlegel. Stuttgart: Cotta, 1960. 285–87.

Schmidt, Erich, ed. *Caroline: Briefe aus der Frühromantik,* 2 vols. Leipzig: Insel, 1913.

Staiger, Emil, ed. *Der Briefwechsel zwischen Schiller und Goethe,* 2 vols. Frankfurt am Main: Insel, 1977.

Stifter, Adalbert. *The Recluse,* trans. David Luke. London: Jonathan Cape, 1968.

———. *Sämtliche Werke,* 5 vols. Munich: Winkler, 1979.

———. *Indian Summer,* trans. Wendell Frye. New York: Peter Lang, 1985.

———. *Brigitta; with Abdias; Limestone; and The Forest Path,* trans. Helen Watanabe-O'Kelly. London: Angel, 1990.

Winckelmann, Johann Joachim. *Sämtliche Werke,* 12 vols., ed. Joseph Eiselein. Donauöschingen: Verlag Deutscher Classiker, 1825–29.

Wolf, Christa. *Die Dimension des Autors: Essays und Aufsätze, Reden und Gespräche 1959–1985,* ed. Angela Drescher. Frankfurt am Main: Luchterhand, 1990.

———. *Kein Ort. Nirgends.* Berlin: Aufbau, 1991.

———. *No Place on Earth,* trans. Jan van Heurck. New York: Farrar, Straus and Giroux, 1982.

Woolf, Virginia. *A Room of One's Own; Three Guineas,* ed. Morag Shiach. Oxford: Oxford University Press, 1992.

Critical Sources

Abrams, M. H. *Natural Supernaturalism: Tradition and Revolution in Romantic Literature.* New York: Norton, 1971.

Adorno, Theodor W. "Zum Gedächtnis Eichendorffs." *Akzente* 5 (1958): 73–95.

———. *Ästhetische Theorie,* ed. Gretel Adorno and Rolf Tiedemann. Frankfurt am Main: Suhrkamp, 1973.

———. *Aesthetic Theory,* trans. C. Lenhardt, ed. Gretel Adorno and Rolf Tiedemann. London: Routledge and Kegan Paul, 1984.

Ammerlahn, Hellmut. "Mignons nachgetragene Vorgeschichte und das Inzestmotiv: Zur Genese und Symbolik der Goetheschen Geniusgestalten." *Monatshefte* 64 (1972): 15–24.

Amrain, Susanne. "Der Androgyn: Das poetische Geschlecht und sein Aktus." In *Frauen. Weiblichkeit. Schrift,* ed. Renate Beger et al., spec. issue of *Argument* 134 (1985): 119–29.

Amrine, Frederick. "Comic Configurations and Types in *Wilhelm Meisters Lehrjahre," Seminar* 19 (1983): 6–19.

Andreas-Salomé, Lou. *Die Erotik.* Frankfurt am Main: Rütten und Loening, 1910.

Anton, Herbert. *Mythologische Erotik in Kellers* Sieben Legenden *und im* Sinngedicht. Stuttgart: Metzler, 1970.

Aurnhammer, Achim. *Androgynie: Studien zu einem Motiv in der europäischen Literatur.* Cologne: Böhlau, 1986.

Bailliet, Theresa Sauter. *Die Frauen im Werk Eichendorffs: Verkörperungen heidnischen und christlichen Geistes.* Bonn: Bouvier, 1972.

Bakhtin, M. M. "Epic and Novel." In *The Dialogic Imagination,* trans. Caryl Emerson and Michael Holquist, ed. Michael Holquist. Austin: University of Texas Press, 1981. 3–40.

Banasik, Anya. "Gottfried Keller's Adaptation of Medieval Legends for the XIXth C. Audience." In *Legenda Aurea: Sept Siècles de Diffusion. Actes du colloque international sur la Legenda aurea: Texte latin et branches vernaculaires,* ed. Brenda Dunn-Lardeau. Montreal: Bellarmin, 1986. 283–88.

Barthes, Roland. *Roland Barthes by Roland Barthes,* trans. Richard Howard. New York: Hill and Wang, 1977.

———. *Mythologies,* trans. Annette Lavers. New York: Hill and Wang, 1986.

Bataille, Georges. *Erotism: Death and Sensuality,* trans. Mary Dalwood. San Francisco: City Lights, 1986.

Battersby, Christine. *Gender and Genius: Towards a Feminist Aesthetics.* London: The Women's Press, 1989.

Baudrillard, Jean. *Seduction,* trans. Brian Singer. New York: St. Martin's Press, 1990.

———. *The Transparency of Evil: Essays on Extreme Phenomena,* trans. James Benedict. New York: Verso, 1993.

Becker-Cantarino, Barbara. "Priesterin und Lichtbringerin: Zur Ideologie des weiblichen Charakters in der Frühromantik." In *Die Frau als Heldin und Autorin: Neue kritische Ansätze zur deutschen Literatur,* ed. Wolfgang Paulsen. Bern: Francke, 1979. 111–24.

———. "Die 'Bekenntnisse einer schönen Seele': Zur Ausgrenzung und Vereinnahmung des Weiblichen in der patriarchalen Utopie von *Wilhelm Meisters Lehrjahren.* In *Verantwortung und Utopie,* ed. Wolfgang Wittkowski. Tübingen: Max Niemeyer, 1988. 70–86.

Béguin, Albert. *L'Âme romantique et le rêve: Essai sur le romantisme allemand et la poésie française,* 2 vols. Marseille: Éditions des cahiers du sud, 1937.

Behler, Ernst. "Friedrich Schlegel: *Lucinde* (1799)." In *Romane und Erzählungen der deutschen Romantik,* ed. Paul Michael Lützeler. Stuttgart: Reclam, 1981. 98–124.

Benjamin, Walter. *Gesammelte Schriften,* 12 vols., ed. Rolf Tiedemann and Hermann Schweppenhäuser. Frankfurt am Main: Suhrkamp, 1980.

Berger, Renate, et al., eds. *Frauen. Weiblichkeit. Schrift.* Special issue of *Argument* 134 (1985).

Berman, Russell A. *The Rise of the Modern German Novel: Crisis and Charisma.* Cambridge: Harvard University Press, 1986.

Black, Joel. "The Aesthetics of Gender: Zeuxis' Maidens and the Hermaphroditic Ideal." *New York Literary Forum* 8–9 (1981): 189–209.

Bock, Ulla. *Androgynie und Feminismus: Frauenbewegung zwischen Institution und Utopie.* Weinheim: Beltz, 1988.

Boehn, Max von. *Die Mode: Menschen und Moden im neunzehnten Jahrhundert nach Bildern und Kupfern der Zeit,* 3 vols. Vol. 1, *1790–1817.* Munich: F. Bruckmann, 1908.

Bormann, Alexander von. "Joseph von Eichendorff: *Aus dem Leben eines Taugenichts* (1826)." In *Romane und Erzählungen zwischen Romantik und Realismus,* ed. Paul Michael Lützeler. Stuttgart: Reclam, 1983. 94–116.

Börne, Ludwig. *Kritische Schriften,* ed. Edgar Schumacher. Zurich: Artemis, 1964.

Böschenstein, Bernhard. "Apoll und seine Schatten: Winckelmann in der deutschen Dichtung der beiden Jahrhundertwenden." In *Johann Joachim Winckelmann 1717–1768,* ed. Thomas W. Gaehtgens. Hamburg: Felix Meiner, 1986. 327–42.

Bosshard, Walter. *Winckelmann: Ästhetik der Mitte.* Zurich: Artemis, 1968.

Bovenschen, Silvia. *Die imaginierte Weiblichkeit: Exemplarische Untersuchungen zu kulturgeschichtlichen und literarischen Präsentationsformen des Weiblichen.* Frankfurt am Main: Suhrkamp, 1979.

Braidotti, Rosi. *Nomadic Subjects: Embodiment and Sexual Difference in Contemporary Feminist Theory.* New York: Columbia University Press, 1994.

Brenkman, John. "The Other and the One: Psychoanalysis, Reading, the *Symposium.*" *Yale French Studies* 55–56 (1977): 396–450.

Bronfen, Elisabeth. *Over Her Dead Body: Death, Femininity and the Aesthetic.* Manchester: Manchester University Press, 1992.

Brooks, Peter. *Reading for the Plot: Design and Intention in Narrative.* New York: Knopf, 1984.

———. *Body Work: Objects of Desire in Modern Narrative.* Cambridge: Harvard University Press, 1993.

Busst, A. J. L. "The Image of the Androgyne in the Nineteenth Century." In *Romantic Mythologies,* ed. Ian Fletcher. London: Routledge and Kegan Paul, 1967. 1–95.

Butler, E. M. *The Tyranny of Greece over Germany: A Study of the Influence Exercised by Greek Art and Poetry over the Great German Writers of the Eighteenth, Nineteenth and Twentieth Centuries.* Cambridge: Cambridge University Press, 1935.

Butler, Judith. *Gender Trouble: Feminism and the Subversion of Identity.* New York: Routledge, 1990.

Castle, Terry. *Masquerade and Civilization: The Carnivalesque in Eighteenth-Century English Culture and Fiction.* Stanford: Stanford University Press, 1986.

———. "The Culture of Travesty: Sexuality and Masquerade in Eighteenth-Century England." In *Sexual Underworlds of the Enlightenment,* ed. G. S. Rousseau and Roy Porter. Manchester: Manchester University Press, 1987. 156–80.

————. *The Apparitional Lesbian: Female Homosexuality and Modern Culture.* New York: Columbia University Press, 1993.

Cixous, Hélène. "The Laugh of the Medusa," trans. Keith Cohen and Paula Cohen. *Signs* 1 (1976): 875–93.

————. "Tancrède continue." *Etudes Freudiennes* 21–22 (1983): 115–32.

Clark, Kenneth. *The Nude: A Study in Ideal Form.* Garden City, N.Y.: Doubleday, 1959.

Culler, Jonathan. *On Deconstruction: Theory and Criticism after Structuralism.* Ithaca: Cornell University Press, 1982.

Daly, Mary. *Beyond God the Father: Toward a Philosophy of Women's Liberation.* Boston: Beacon Press, 1973.

————. *Gyn/Ecology: The Metaethics of Radical Feminism.* Boston: Beacon Press, 1978.

de Lauretis, Teresa. *Alice Doesn't: Feminism, Semiotics, Cinema.* Bloomington: Indiana University Press, 1984.

Dellamora, Richard. *Masculine Desire: The Sexual Politics of Victorian Aestheticism.* Chapel Hill: University of North Carolina Press, 1990.

Denneler, Iris. "Verkehrtes Bekehren, bekehrtes Verkehren, oder Das Martyrium der Schrift: Zur Erzählstruktur von Gottfried Kellers Legende vom 'Schlimm-heiligen Vitalis.'" *Germanisch-Romanische Monatsschrift* N.F. 39 (1989): 196–209.

Derks, Paul. *Die Schande der heiligen Päderastie: Homosexualität und Öffentlichkeit in der deutschen Literatur 1750–1850.* Berlin: rosa Winkel, 1990.

Derrida, Jacques. *Of Grammatology,* trans. Gayatri Chakravorty Spivak. Baltimore: Johns Hopkins University Press, 1976.

————. "Différance," trans. Alan Bass. In *Critical Theory since 1965,* ed. Hazard Adams and Leroy Searle. Tallahassee: University of Florida Press, 1986. 120–36.

————. *Glas,* trans. John P. Leavey, Jr., and Richard Rand. Lincoln: University of Nebraska Press, 1986.

Derrida, Jacques, and Christie V. McDonald. "Choreographies." *Diacritics* 12 (1982): 66–76.

Dick, Anneliese. *Weiblichkeit als natürliche Dienstbarkeit: Eine Studie zum klassischen Frauenbild in Goethes* Wilhelm Meister. Frankfurt am Main: Peter Lang, 1986.

Dijkstra, Bram. *Idols of Perversity: Fantasies of Feminine Evil in Fin-de-Siècle Culture.* New York: Oxford University Press, 1986.

Dollimore, Jonathan. *Sexual Dissidence: Augustine to Wilde, Freud to Foucault.* Oxford: Oxford University Press, 1991.

Duden, Barbara. "Das schöne Eigentum: Zur Herausbildung des bürgerlichen Frauenbildes an der Wende vom 18. zum 19. Jahrhundert." *Kursbuch* 47 (1977): 125–40.

Eberhardt, Otto. *Verkleidung und Verwechslung in der erzählenden Dichtung Eichendorffs.* Heidelberg: Carl Winter, 1987.

Eichner, Hans. "Zur Auffassung der Sexualität in Eichendorffs erzählender Prosa." In *Eichendorffs Modernität,* ed. Michael Kessler and Helmut Koopmann. Tübingen: Stauffenburg, 1989. 37–52.

Eliade, Mircea. *The Two and the One,* trans. J. M. Cohen. London: Harvill Press, 1965.

Elsaghe, Yahya A. "Wilhelm Meisters letzter Brief: Homosexualität und Nekrophilie bei Goethe." *Forum Homosexualität und Literatur* 24 (1995): 6–24.

Emrich, Wilhelm. *Die Symbolik von* Faust II: *Sinn und Vorformen.* Frankfurt am Main: Athenäum, 1957.

Epstein, Julia. "Either/Or—Neither/Both: Sexual Ambiguity and the Ideology of Gender." *Genders* 7 (1990): 99–142.

Epstein, Julia, and Kristina Straub, eds. *Body Guards: The Cultural Politics of Gender Ambiguity.* New York: Routledge, 1991.

Ermatinger, Emil. *Gottfried Kellers Leben,* 8th rev. ed. Zurich: Artemis, 1950.

Exner, Richard. "Androgynie und preußischer Staat: Themen, Probleme und das Beispiel Heinrich von Kleist." *Aurora* 39 (1979): 51–78.

———. "Die Heldin als Held und der Held als Heldin: Androgynie als Umgehung oder Lösung eines Konfliktes." In *Die Frau als Heldin und Autorin: Neue kritische Ansätze zur deutschen Literatur,* ed. Wolfgang Paulsen. Bern: Francke, 1979. 17–54.

Fausto-Sterling, Anne. "The Five Sexes: Why Male and Female Are Not Enough." *The Sciences,* March–April 1993, 20–25.

Fink, Gonthier-Louis. "Pygmalion und das belebte Marmorbild: Wandlungen eines Märchenmotivs von der Frühaufklärung bis zur Spätromantik." *Aurora* 43 (1983): 92–123.

Finney, Gail. *The Counterfeit Idyll: The Garden Ideal and Social Reality in Nineteenth-Century Fiction.* Tübingen: Max Niemeyer, 1984.

Fisher, John C. "Das Verkleidungsmotiv in den Prosawerken von Joseph Freiherrn von Eichendorff." Dissertation, Princeton University, 1976.

Flashar, Dorothea. "Bedeutung, Entwicklung und literarische Nachwirkung von Goethes Mignongestalt." *Germanische Studien* 65 (1929).

Foucault, Michel. *The Order of Things: An Archaeology of the Human Sciences.* London: Routledge, 1974.

———. *The History of Sexuality,* trans. Robert Hurley. Vol. 1, *An Introduction.* Vol. 2, *The Use of Pleasure.* New York: Vintage, 1990.

Frank, Barbara R. "Irony in Keller's *Sieben Legenden.*" *Germanic Review* 49 (1974): 129–45.

Freud, Sigmund. "Das Medusenhaupt." In *Gesammelte Werke,* 18 vols., ed. Anna Freud. London: Imago, 1940–1968. Vol. 17: 47–48.

———. *The Standard Edition of the Complete Pyschological Works,* 24 vols., ed. and trans. James Strachey. London: Hogarth Press, 1953.

———. *Studienausgabe,* 10 vols. and one supplementary vol., ed. Alexander Mitscherlich, Angela Richards, and James Strachey. Frankfurt am Main: Fischer, 1982.

Friedrichsmeyer, Sara. *The Androgyne in Early German Romanticism: Friedrich Schlegel, Novalis and the Metaphysics of Love.* Bern: Peter Lang, 1983.

———. "The Subversive Androgyne." *Women in German Yearbook* 3 (1986): 63–74.

Frühwald, Wolfgang. *Eichendorff Chronik: Daten zu Leben und Werk.* Munich: Carl Hanser, 1977.

Furness, Raymond. "The Androgynous Ideal: Its Significance in German Literature." *Modern Language Review* 60 (1965): 58–64.

Fuss, Diana. *Essentially Speaking: Feminism, Nature and Difference.* New York: Routledge, 1989.

Gandillac, Maurice de. "Approches platoniciennes et platonisantes du mythe de l'androgyne originel." In *L'Androgyne dans la littérature,* ed. Frédéric Monneyron. Paris: Albin Michel, 1990. 13–23.

Garber, Marjorie. *Vested Interests: Cross-Dressing and Cultural Anxiety.* New York: Routledge, 1992.

Gauster, Hannelore. "Zu Hermaphroditen-Darstellungen in der Antike." In *Frauen. Weiblichkeit. Schrift,* ed. Renate Beger et al., spec. issue of *Argument* 134 (1985): 79–98.

Gelpi, Barbara Charlesworth. "The Politics of Androgyny." *Women's Studies* 2 (1974): 151–60.

Geulen, Eva. *Worthörig wider Willen: Darstellungsproblematik und Sprachreflexion in der Prosa Adalbert Stifters.* Munich: iudicium, 1992.

Giese, Fritz. *Die Entwicklung des Androgynenproblems in der Frühromantik.* Vol. 1 of *Der romantische Charakter.* Langensalza: Wendt und Klauwell, 1919. (No further volumes appeared.)

Gilbert, Sandra M., and Susan Gubar. *No Man's Land,* 2 vols. Vol. 2, *Sexchanges.* New Haven: Yale University Press, 1988.

Gilman, Sander L. *Difference and Pathology: Stereotypes of Sexuality and Madness.* Ithaca: Cornell University Press, 1985.

Gray, Ronald D. *Goethe the Alchemist: A Study of Alchemical Symbolism in Goethe's Literary and Scientific Works.* Cambridge: Cambridge University Press, 1952.

Greenblatt, Stephen. *Shakespearean Negotiations: The Circulation of Social Energy in Renaissance England.* Berkeley: University of California Press, 1988.

Hallamore, G. Joyce. "The Symbolism of the Marble Muse in Stifter's *Nachsommer.*" *PMLA* 74 (1959): 398–405.

Haraway, Donna. "A Manifesto for Cyborgs: Science, Technology, and Socialist Feminism in the 1980's." *Socialist Review* 80 (1985): 65–107.

Harnisch, Antje. " 'Die Sucht, den Mann zu spielen' in Gottfried Kellers Realismus." *German Quarterly* 68 (1995): 147–59.

Harpham, Geoffrey Galt. *On the Grotesque: Strategies of Contradiction in Art and Literature.* Princeton: Princeton University Press, 1982.

Harris, Daniel A. "Androgyny: The Sexist Myth in Disguise." *Women's Studies* 2 (1974): 171–84.

Haupt, Johannes. "Geschichtsperspektive und Griechenverständnis im ästhetischen Programm Schillers." *Jahrbuch der deutschen Schillergesellschaft* 18 (1974): 406–30.

Hausen, Karin. "Die Polarisierung der 'Geschlechtscharaktere'—Eine Spiegelung der Dissoziation von Erwerbs- und Familienleben." In *Sozialgeschichte der Familie in der Neuzeit Europas,* ed. Werner Conze. Stuttgart: Ernst Klett, 1976. 363–93.

Haußmann, Walter. "Adalbert Stifter: *Brigitta.*" *Der Deutschunterricht* 3 (1951): 30–48.

Haym, Rudolf. *Die romantische Schule: Ein Beitrag zur Geschichte des deutschen Geistes.* Berlin: Rudolph Gaertner, 1870.

Heer, Friedrich. "Die Botschaft eines Lebenden: Zur einhundertjährigen Wiederkehr seines Todestages." In *Eichendorff heute: Stimmen der Forschung mit einer Bibliographie,* ed. Paul Stöcklein. Darmstadt: Wissenschaftliche Buchgesellschaft, 1966. 66–105.

Hegel, Georg Wilhelm Friedrich. *The Philosophy of Right,* trans. T. M. Knox. Oxford: Oxford University Press, 1942.

———. *Werke,* 20 vols. Frankfurt am Main: Suhrkamp, 1969–71.

Heilbrun, Carolyn G. *Toward a Recognition of Androgyny.* New York: Knopf, 1964.

Helfer, Martha B. "Confessions of an Improper Man: Friedrich Schlegel's *Lucinde.*" In *Outing Goethe and His Age,* ed. Alice A. Kuzniar. Stanford: Stanford University Press, 1996. 174–93.

Hentig, Hans von. "Der nekrotrope Mensch: Vom Totenglauben zur morbiden Totennähe." *Beiträge zur Sexualforschung* 30 (1964): 37–48.

Das Herkunftstwörterbuch: Eine Etymologie der deutschen Sprache. Mannheim: Duden, 1963.

Hirsch, Marianne. "Spiritual Bildung: The Beautiful Soul as Paradigm." In *The Voyage In: Fictions of Female Development,* ed. Elizabeth Abel, Marianne Hirsch, and Elizabeth Langland. Hanover: University Press of New England, 1983. 23–48.

Hoeveler, Diane Long. *Romantic Androgyny: The Women Within.* University Park: Pennsylvania State University Press, 1990.

Hoffmann, Volker. "Elisa und Robert oder das Weib und der Mann, wie sie sein sollten: Anmerkungen zur Geschlechtercharakteristik der Goethezeit." In *Klassik und Moderne: Die Weimarer Klassik als historisches Ereignis und Herausforderung im kulturgeschichtlichen Prozeß,* ed. Karl Richter and Jörg Schönert. Stuttgart: Metzler, 1983. 80–97.

Hoffmeister, Gerhart, ed. *Goethes Mignon und ihre Schwestern: Interpretationen und Rezeption.* New York: Peter Lang, 1993.

Hohendahl, Peter Uwe. "Die gebildete Gemeinschaft: Stifters *Nachsommer* als Utopie der ästhetischen Erziehung." In *Utopieforschung: Interdisziplinäre Studien zur neuzeitlichen Utopie,* 3 vols., ed. Wilhelm Voßkamp. Stuttgart: Metzler, 1982. Vol. 3: 333–56.

Holub, Robert C. *Heinrich Heine's Reception of German Grecophilia: The Function and Application of the Hellenic Tradition in the First Half of the Nineteenth Century.* Heidelberg: Carl Winter, 1981.

———. *Reflections of Realism: Paradox, Norm, and Ideology in Nineteenth-Century German Prose.* Detroit: Wayne State University Press, 1991.

Hörisch, Jochen. *Gott, Geld und Glück: Zur Logik der Liebe in den Bildungsromanen Goethes, Kellers und Thomas Manns.* Frankfurt am Main: Suhrkamp, 1983.

———. " 'Larven und Charaktermasken': Zum elften Kapitel von *Ahnung und Gegenwart.*" In *Eichendorff und die Spätromantik,* ed. Hans-Georg Pott. Paderborn: Ferdinand Schöningh, 1985. 27–38.

Hosfeld, Rolf. "Nachtgedanken: Heinrich Heines *Florentinische Nächte.*" In *Heinrich Heine und das neunzehnte Jahrhundert:Signaturen,* ed. Rolf Hosfeld, spec. issue of *Argument* 124 (1986): 73–90.

Hotz-Steinmeyer, Cornelia. *Friedrich Schlegels* Lucinde *als "Neue Mythologie": Geschichtsphilosophischer Versuch einer Rückgewinnung gesellschaftlicher Totalität durch das Individuum.* Frankfurt am Main: Peter Lang, 1985.

Huch, Ricarda. *Gesammelte Werke,* 11 vols., ed. Wilhelm Emrich. Cologne: Kiepenhauer und Witsch, 1969.

Hunter-Lougheed, Rosemarie. "Adalbert Stifter: *Brigitta* (1844–47)." In *Romane und Erzählungen zwischen Romantik und Realismus: Neue Interpretationen,* ed. Paul Michael Lützeler. Stuttgart: Reclam, 1983. 354–85.

Hüseler, Horst. "Erwin: Eine 'poetische Gestalt.'" *Aurora* 28 (1968): 70–79.

Ian, Marcia. *Remembering the Phallic Mother: Psychoanalysis, Modernism, and the Fetish.* Ithaca: Cornell University Press, 1993.

Irigaray, Luce. *This Sex Which Is Not One,* trans. Catherine Porter with Carolyn Burke. Ithaca: Cornell University Press, 1985.

———. *An Ethics of Sexual Difference,* trans. Carolyn Burke and Gillian C. Gill. Ithaca: Cornell University Press, 1993.

Janz, Marlies. *Marmorbilder: Weiblichkeit und Tod bei Clemens Brentano und Hugo von Hofmannsthal.* Königstein am Taunus: Athenäum, 1986.

Jardine, Alice. *Gynesis: Configurations of Woman and Modernity.* Ithaca: Cornell University Press, 1985.

Jeziorkowski, Klaus, ed. *Dichter über ihre Dichtungen: Gottfried Keller,* Munich: Ernst Heimeran, 1969.

Johnson, Barbara. *The Critical Difference.* Baltimore: Johns Hopkins University Press, 1981.

———. "The Lady in the Lake." In *A New History of French Literature,* ed. Denis Hollier et al. Cambridge: Harvard University Press, 1989. 627–32.

———. "The Dream of Stone." In *A New History of French Literature,* ed. Denis Hollier et al. Cambridge: Harvard University Press, 1989. 743–48.

Jordanova, Ludmilla. *Sexual Visions: Images of Gender in Science and Medicine between the Eighteenth and Twentieth Centuries.* Madison: University of Wisconsin Press, 1989.

Kaiser, Gerhard. *Gottfried Keller: Das gedichtete Leben.* Frankfurt am Main: Insel, 1981.

Kaiser, Gerhard, and Friedrich A. Kittler. *Dichtung als Sozialisationsspiel: Studien zu Goethe und Gottfried Keller.* Göttingen: Vandenhoeck und Ruprecht, 1978.

Kaschnitz, Marie Luise, Ilse Langner, and Oda Schaefer. "Das Besondere der Frauendichtung." In *Jahrbuch der Deutschen Akademie für Sprache und Dichtung 1957.* Heidelberg: Lambert Schneider, 1958. 59–76.

Kluckhohn, Paul. *Die Auffassung der Liebe in der Literatur des 18. Jahrhunderts und in der deutschen Romantik,* 3rd ed. Tübingen: Max Niemeyer, 1966.

Kniesche, Thomas W. "Die psychoanalytische Rezeption von Mignon." In *Goethes Mignon und ihre Schwestern,* ed. Gerhart Hoffmeister. New York: Peter Lang, 1993. 61–81.

Kofman, Sarah. *The Enigma of Woman: Woman in Freud's Writings,* trans. Catherine Porter. Ithaca: Cornell University Press, 1987.

Kristeva, Julia. *The Revolution in Poetic Language,* trans. Margaret Waller. New York: Columbia University Press, 1984.

————. *Tales of Love,* trans. Leon S. Roudiez. New York: Columbia University Press, 1987.

Kuhn, Andrea. "Sprachlosigkeit—das Geheimnis des Hermaphroditen." In *Androgyn: Sehnsucht nach Vollkommenheit,* ed. Ursula Prinz. Berlin: Dietrich Reimer, 1986. 120–26.

Kuzniar, Alice A. "Hearing Woman's Voices in *Heinrich von Ofterdingen.*" *PMLA* 107 (1992): 1196–1207.

————, ed. *Outing Goethe and His Age.* Stanford: Stanford University Press, 1996.

Lacan, Jacques. *Ecrits: A Selection,* trans. Alan Sheridan. New York: Norton, 1977.

————. *The Four Fundamental Concepts of Psycho-Analysis,* ed. Jacques-Alain Miller, trans. Alan Sheridan. New York: Norton, 1981.

Lacan, Jacques, and Wladimir Granoff. "Fetishism: The Symbolic, the Imaginary and the Real." In *Perversions: Psychodynamics and Therapy,* ed. Sandor Lorand. New York: Gramercy Books, 1956. 265–76.

Landes, Joan B. *Women and the Public Sphere in the Age of the French Revolution.* Ithaca: Cornell University Press, 1988.

Laqueur, Thomas. *Making Sex: Body and Gender from the Greeks to Freud.* Cambridge: Harvard University Press, 1990.

Larrett, William. "Wilhelm Meister and the Amazons: The Quest for Wholeness." *Publications of the English Goethe Society* 39 (1968–69): 31–56.

Le Rider, Jacques. *Modernism and Crises of Identity,* trans. Rosemary Morris. Cambridge: Polity Press, 1993.

Lesser, Wendy. *His Other Half: Men Looking at Women through Art.* Cambridge: Harvard University Press, 1991.

Ley, Andreas, ed. *Anziehungskräfte: Variété de la Mode 1786–1986.* Munich: Hanser, 1986.

Lienhard, Johanna. *Mignon und ihre Lieder, gespiegelt in den Wilhelm-Meister-Romanen.* Zurich: Artemis, 1978.

Lüthi, Kurt. *Feminismus und Romantik: Sprache, Gesellschaft, Symbole, Religion.* Vienna: Böhlau, 1985.

Malke, Lutz S. "Weibmann und Mannweib in der Kunst der Renaissance." In *Androgyn: Sehnsucht nach Vollkommenheit,* ed. Ursula Prinz. Berlin: Dietrich Reimer, 1986. 33–56.

Manthey, Jürgen. *Wenn Blicke zeugen könnten: Eine psychohistorische Studie über das Sehen in Literatur und Philosophie.* Munich: Carl Hanser, 1983.

Matt, Peter von. "Der irrende Leib: Die Momente des Unwissens in Eichendorffs Lyrik." *Aurora* 49 (1989): 47–57.

Mayer, Mathias. "Midas statt Pygmalion: Die Tödlichkeit der Kunst bei Goethe, Schnitzler, Hofmannsthal und Georg Kaiser." *Deutsche Vierteljahrsschrift für Literaturwissenschaft und Geistesgeschichte* 64 (1990): 278–310.

Meesmann, Hartmut, and Bernhard Sill, eds. *Androgyn: "Jeder Mensch in sich ein Paar!?" Androgynie als Ideal geschlechtlicher Identität.* Weinheim: Deutscher Studien Verlag, 1994.

Moi, Toril. *Sexual/Textual Politics: Feminist Literary Theory.* London: Methuen, 1985.

Mücke, Dorothea von. *Virtue and the Veil of Illusion: Generic Innovation and the*

Pedagogical Project in Eighteenth-Century Literature. Stanford: Stanford
    University Press, 1991.

Mühlher, Robert. "Der Poetenmantel: Wandlungen eines Sinnbildes bei Eichen-
    dorff." In *Eichendorff heute: Stimmen der Forschung mit einer Bibliographie,*
    ed. Paul Stöcklein. Darmstadt: Wissenschaftliche Buchgesellschaft, 1966.
    180–203.

Müller-Sievers, Helmut. *Epigenesis: Naturphilosophie im Sprachdenken Wilhelm
    von Humboldts.* Paderborn: Ferdinand Schöningh, 1993.

Muschg, Adolf. *Gottfried Keller.* Munich: Kindler, 1977.

Neubauer, John. *The Fin-de-Siècle Culture of Adolescence.* New Haven: Yale Uni-
    versity Press, 1992.

Neumann, Michael. *Roman und Ritus:* Wilhelm Meisters Lehrjahre. Frankfurt am
    Main: Vittorio Klostermann, 1992.

Nietzsche, Friedrich. *The Gay Science,* trans. Walter Kaufmann. New York: Random
    House, 1974.

———. *Sämtliche Werke, Kritische Studienausgabe,* 15 vols., ed. Giorgio Colli and
    Mazzino Montinari. Munich: Deutscher Taschenbuch Verlag, 1980.

Ortheil, Hanns-Josef. "Stille Heimlichkeit: Zur *Regine*-Erzählung in Gottfried Kel-
    lers *Sinngedicht." Jahrbuch der deutschen Schillergesellschaft* 30 (1986):
    453–71.

Owen, Claude. "Zur Erotik in Stifters *Brigitta." Österreich in Geschichte und
    Literatur* 15 (1971): 106–14.

Pacteau, Francette. "The Impossible Referent: Representations of the Androgyne." In
    Formations of Fantasy, ed. Victor Burgin. New York: Methuen, 1986. 62–84.

Parker, Kevin. "Winckelmann, Historical Difference, and the Problem of the Boy."
    Eighteenth-Century Studies 25 (1992): 523–44.

Parry, Idris. "Belvedere Hercules." *PN Review* 20 (1981): 16–22.

Pellegrin, Nicole. *Les vêtements de la liberté.* Aix-en-Provence: Alinea, 1989.

Petersen, Susanne. *Marktweiber und Amazonen: Frauen in der französischen Revo-
    lution.* Cologne: Pahl-Rugenstein, 1987.

Pikulik, Lothar. "Die Mythisierung des Geschlechtstriebes in Eichendorffs *Marmor-
    bild." In *Mythos und Mythologie in der Literatur des 19. Jahrhunderts,* ed.
    Helmut Koopmann. Frankfurt am Main: Vittorio Klostermann, 1979. 159–72.

Polheim, Karl Konrad. *Die Arabeske: Ansichten und Ideen aus Friedrich Schlegels
    Poetik.* Munich: Ferdinand Schöningh, 1966.

———. "Friedrich Schlegels *Lucinde." Zeitschrift für deutsche Philologie* 88
    (1969): 61–89.

Praz, Mario. *The Romantic Agony,* 2nd. ed., trans. Angus Davidson. London: Oxford
    University Press, 1951.

———. *On Neoclassicism,* trans. Angus Davidson. London: Thames and Hudson,
    1969.

Ragusa, Isa. "Goethe's 'Women's Parts Played by Men in the Roman Theatre.'"
    Medieval English Theatre 1984 (6): 96–100.

Reichert, Karl. "Die Entstehung der *Sieben Legenden* von Gottfried Keller." *Eu-
    phorion* 57 (1963): 228–53.

Reinacher, Pia. *Die Sprache der Kleider im literarischen Text: Untersuchungen zu
    Gottfried Keller und Robert Walser.* Bern: Peter Lang, 1988.

Reiss, Hans. "Lustspielhaftes in *Wilhelm Meisters Lehrjahre.*" In *Goethezeit: Studien zur Erkenntnis und Rezeption Goethes und seiner Zeitgenossen,* ed. Gerhart Hoffmeister. Bern: Francke, 1981. 129–44.

Richter, Simon J. *Laocoon's Body and the Aesthetics of Pain: Winckelmann, Lessing, Herder, Moritz, Goethe.* Detroit: Wayne State University Press, 1992.

Richter, Simon J., and Patrick McGrath. "Representing Homosexuality: Winckelmann and the Aesthetics of Friendship." *Monatshefte* 86 (1994): 45–58.

Riecke-Niklewski, Rose. *Die Metaphorik des Schönen: Eine kritische Lektüre der Versöhnung in Schillers "Über die ästhetische Erziehung des Menschen in einer Reihe von Briefen."* Tübingen: Max Niemeyer, 1986.

Riley, Thomas A. "An Allegorical Interpretation of Eichendorff's *Ahnung und Gegenwart.*" *Modern Language Review* 54 (1959): 204–13.

Roberts, David. *The Indirections of Desire: Hamlet in Goethe's* Wilhelm Meister. Heidelberg: Carl Winter, 1980.

Roedl, Urban. *Adalbert Stifter in Selbstzeugnissen und Bilddokumenten.* Hamburg: Rowohlt, 1965.

Rousseau, G. S. *Perilous Enlightenment.* Manchester: Manchester University Press, 1990.

Sagmo, Ivar. *Bildungsroman und Geschichtsphilosophie: Eine Studie zu Goethes Roman* Wilhelm Meisters Lehrjahre. Bonn: Bouvier, 1982.

Sartiliot, Claudette. *Herbarium Verbarium: The Discourse of Flowers.* Lincoln: University of Nebraska Press, 1993.

Saunders, Gill. *The Nude: A New Perspective.* London: Herbert Press, 1989.

Schings, Hans-Jürgen. "Wilhelm Meisters Schöne Amazone." *Jahrbuch der deutschen Schillergesellschaft* 29 (1985): 141–206.

Schlaffer, Hannelore. "Frauen als Einlösung der romantischen Kunsttheorie." *Jahrbuch der deutschen Schillergesellschaft* 21 (1977): 274–96.

Schneider, Manfred. *Die kranke schöne Seele der Revolution: Heine, Börne, das "Junge Deutschland," Marx und Engels.* Frankfurt am Main: Syndikat, 1980.

Schneider, Monique. "L'androgyne, un mythe critique." In *L'Androgyne dans la littérature,* ed. Frédéric Monneyron. Paris: Albin Michel, 1990. 114–25.

Schneiderman, Stuart. *An Angel Passes: How the Sexes Became Undivided.* New York: New York University Press, 1988.

Schuller, Marianne. "Das Gewitter findet nicht statt oder die Abdankung der Kunst: Zu Adalbert Stifters *Der Nachsommer.*" *Poetica* 10 (1978): 25–52.

Schwarz, Egon. *Joseph von Eichendorff.* New York: Twayne, 1972.

Sebald, W. G. *Die Beschreibung des Unglücks: Zur österreichischen Literatur von Stifter bis Handke.* Salzburg: Residenz, 1985.

Secor, Cynthia. "Androgyny: An Early Reappraisal." *Women's Studies* 2 (1974): 161–69.

Seeba, Hinrich C. "Die Kinder des Pygmalion: Die Bildlichkeit des Kunstbegriffs bei Heine. Beobachtungen zur Tendenzwende der Ästhetik." *Deutsche Vierteljahrsschrift für Literaturwissenschaft und Geistesgeschichte* 50 (1976): 158–202.

Selbmann, Rolf. *Theater im Roman: Studien zum Strukturwandel des deutschen Bildungsromans.* Munich: Wilhelm Fink, 1981.

Showalter, Elaine. *A Literature of Their Own.* Princeton: Princeton University Press, 1977.

———. *Sexual Anarchy: Gender and Culture at the Fin de Siècle.* New York: Viking, 1990.

Sill, Bernhard. *Androgynie und Geschlechtsdifferenz nach Franz von Baader: Eine anthropologisch-ethische Studie.* Regensburg: Friedrich Pustet, 1986.

Sjögren, Christine Oertel. "Klotildes Reise in die Tiefe: Psychoanalytische Betrachtungen zu einer Episode in Stifters *Nachsommer.*" *Vierteljahrsschrift des Adalbert Stifter-Instituts des Landes Oberösterreich* 24 (1975): 107–11.

———. "Ein Musterbeispiel der Liebestheorie in Stifters *Nachsommer.*" *Vierteljahrsschrift des Adalbert Stifter-Instituts des Landes Oberösterreich* 26 (1977): 111–15.

———. "The Allure of Beauty in Stifter's *Brigitta.*" *Journal of English and Germanic Philology* 81 (1982): 47–54.

Smith, John H. "Cultivating Gender: Sexual Difference, *Bildung,* and the *Bildungsroman.*" *Michigan Germanic Studies* 13 (1987): 296–25.

Spickernagel, Ellen. " 'Helden wie zarte Knaben oder verkleidete Mädchen': Zum Begriff der Androgynität bei Johann Joachim Winckelmann und Angelika Kauffmann." In *Frauen. Weiblichkeit. Schrift,* ed. Renate Beger et al., spec. issue of *Argument* 134 (1985): 99–118.

Stafford, Barbara Maria. *Body Criticism: Imaging the Unseen in Enlightenment Art and Medicine.* Cambridge: MIT Press, 1993.

Stephan, Inge. " 'Daß ich Eins und doppelt bin . . .': Geschlechtertausch als literarisches Thema." In *Die verborgene Frau: Sechs Beiträge zu einer feministischen Literaturwissenschaft,* ed. Inge Stephan and Sigrid Weigel, spec. issue of *Argument* 96 (1983): 153–75.

———. " 'Da werden Weiber zu Hyänen . . .': Amazonen und Amazonenmythen bei Schiller und Kleist." In *Feministische Literaturwissenschaft,* ed. Inge Stephen and Sigrid Weigel, spec. issue of *Argument* 120 (1984): 23–42.

———. "Ricarda Huch." In *Ricarda Huch: Studien zu ihrem Leben und Werk,* ed. Hans-Werner Peter. Braunschweig: pp-Verlag, 1985. 25–33.

———. " 'Die Musen gehören zu den himmlischen Gestalten, die Mann und Weib nicht kennen': Zur Androgynitätsauffassung in Kunst und Wissenschaft." In *Frauensprache—Frauenliteratur? Für und Wider einer Psychoanalyse literarischer Werke,* ed. Inge Stephan and Carl Pietzcker. Tübingen: Max Niemeyer, 1986. 119–26.

Stimpson, Catherine R. "The Androgyne and the Homosexual." *Women's Studies* 2 (1974): 237–48.

Stoller, Robert J. *Sex and Gender,* 2 vols. Vol. 1, *The Development of Masculinity and Femininity.* London: Hogarth Press and the Institute of Psycho-Analysis, 1968.

———. *Observing the Erotic Imagination.* New York: Oxford University Press, 1985.

Stopp, Elisabeth. "Eichendorff und Shakespeare." *Aurora* 32 (1972): 7–23.

Suleiman, Susan R., ed. *The Female Body in Western Culture.* Cambridge: Harvard University Press, 1986.

Sweet, Denis M. "The Personal, the Political and the Aesthetic: Johann Joachim

Winckelmann's Enlightenment Life." *Journal of Homosexuality* 16 (1988): 146–62.

Thalmann, Marianne. "Der Trivialroman des 18. Jahrhunderts und der romantische Roman." *Germanische Studien* 24 (1923).

Theweleit, Klaus. *Male Fantasies,* 2 vols., trans. Stephen Conway. Minneapolis: University of Minnesota Press, 1987.

Thiel, Erika. *Geschichte des Kostüms: Die europäische Mode von den Anfängen bis zur Gegenwart.* Wilhelmshaven: Heinrichshofen, 1980.

Tobin, Robert. "The Medicinalisation of Mignon." In *Goethes Mignon und ihre Schwestern,* ed. Gerhart Hoffmeister. New York: Peter Lang, 1993. 43–60.

Uhlig, Ludwig. "Schiller und Winckelmann." *Jahrbuch für internationale Germanistik* 17 (1985): 131–46.

Varnhagen von Ense, Karl August. "Frauen in Mannskleidern." In *Denkwürdigkeiten und Vermischte Schriften,* 9 vols. Leipzig: F. A. Brockhaus, 1843. Vol. 6: 66–68.

Villiers, Marc de. *Histoire des clubs de femmes et des légions d'amazones: 1793–1848—1871.* Paris: Plon, 1910.

Walters, Margaret. *The Nude Male: A New Perspective.* Harmondsworth: Penguin, 1978.

Warner, Marina. *Monuments and Maidens: The Allegory of the Female Form.* New York: Atheneum, 1985.

Wedekind-Schwertner, Barbara. *"Daß ich eins und doppelt bin": Studien zur Idee der Androgynie unter besonderer Berücksichtigung Thomas Manns.* Frankfurt am Main: Peter Lang, 1984.

Weigel, Sigrid. "Wider die romantische Mode: Zur ästhetischen Funktion des Weiblichen in Friedrich Schlegels *Lucinde.*" In *Die verborgene Frau: Sechs Beiträge zu einer feministischen Literaturwissenschaft,* ed. Inge Stephan and Sigrid Weigel, spec. issue of *Argument* 96 (1983): 67–82.

———. "'Das Weibliche als Metapher des Metonymischen': Kritische Überlegungen zur Konstitution des Weiblichen als Verfahren oder Schreibweise." In *Frauensprache—Frauenliteratur? Für und Wider einer Psychoanalyse literarischer Werke,* ed. Inge Stephan and Carl Pietzcker. Tübingen: Max Niemeyer, 1986. 108–18.

———. *Topographien der Geschlechter: Kulturgeschichtliche Studien zur Literatur.* Hamburg: Rowohlt, 1990.

Weil, Kari. *Androgyny and the Denial of Difference.* Charlottesville: University Press of Virginia, 1992.

Wiethölter, Waltraud. "Die Schule der Venus: Ein diskursanalytischer Versuch zu Eichendorffs *Marmorbild.*" In *Eichendorffs Modernität,* ed. Michael Kessler and Helmut Koopmann. Tübingen: Stauffenburg, 1989. 171–201.

Wildbolz, Rudolf. *Adalbert Stifter: Langeweile und Faszination.* Stuttgart: Kohlhammer, 1976.

Wingertszahn, Christof. *Ambiguität und Ambivalenz im erzählerischen Werk Achims von Arnim.* St. Ingbert: Röhrig, 1990.

Woesler, Winfried. "Frau Venus und das schöne Mädchen mit dem Blumenkranze." *Aurora* 45 (1985): 33–48.

Zastrau, Alfred, ed. *Goethe-Handbuch,* 4 vols. Stuttgart: Metzler, 1961.

Zeller, Hans. *Winckelmanns Beschreibung des Apollo im Belvedere.* Zurich: Atlantis, 1955.

Zons, Raimar Stefan. " 'Schweifen': Eichendorffs *Ahnung und Gegenwart."* In *Eichendorff und die Spätromantik,* ed. Hans-Georg Pott. Paderborn: Ferdinand Schöningh, 1985. 39–68.

Züger, Armin. *Männerbilder—Frauenbilder: Androgyne Utopie in der deutschen Gegenwartsliteratur.* Bern: Peter Lang, 1992.

Zuylen, Marina van. *Difficulty as an Aesthetic Principle: Realism and Unreadability in Stifter, Melville, and Flaubert.* Tübingen: Gunter Narr, 1994.

Index

Adorno, Theodor W., 186, 264*n*64

Ahnung und Gegenwart (Eichendorff), 144–48, 149, 150–51; androgyne in, 142, 146–49, 156–57; botanical imagery in, 148–49; female petrification in, 166–67, 178; female transvestism in, 142, 144–55; gender ambiguity and disclosure in, 156–59; imagery of light and dark in, 159–60; masquerade in, 155–56; as narrative of *Bildung,* 151, 155–60; as narrative of epiphany and redemption, 159

Amazon, 45, 255*n*37

Amazon, 44 (ill)

Andreas-Salomé, Lou, 13

Androgyny: in alchemical tradition, 254*n*35; Aristophanes' developmental account of, 11–13, 22, 104, 256*n*50; association with water imagery, 37–38; and *Bildung,* 89, 186, 203, 207; and classical marble statue, 21, 39; and crises of meaning concerning aesthetics and gender, 229; current theoretical debates on, 13–14; difficulty of defining, 28; doubleness in literary treatment of, 32; in Eichendorff's works, 154, 165–66; feminist literary theory on, 16–17, 21–22, 51–52, 234*n*7, 235*n*11; Freud's developmental reading of myth, 58–59; in German aesthetics and literature, 25; in German mystical

tradition, 254*n*35; in Humboldt's works, 48–51; in Keller's works, 210–21, 226–28; as linguistic construction, 29; literary treatment of at end of 19th century, 229–31; myth of, 11–13; in Schiller's works, 55–61; in Schlegel's works, 66–67, 76–77, 81–87; shift to romantic, feminine version of, 13, 22–23, 25, 42, 45–46, 110, 243*n*59; and speechlessness, 269*n*37; in Stifter's works, 206–7; in Winckelmann's works, 23, 25, 28–31, 38–42, 43, 107, 197. *See also specific works*

Antinous, 25–26

Antinous relief, 26–27, 238*n*3

Anton, Herbert, 222, 226, 272*n*68

Apollo Belvedere, 34 (ill)

Arabesque, 75–76

Aristophanes: on dangers of sexual maturity, 104; developmental account of androgyny, 11–13, 22, 46, 256*n*50; on love, 12

Arnim, Ludwig Achim: *Gräfin Dolores,* 142

A Room of One's Own (Woolf), 14, 15, 21, 234*n*8

Ars combinatoria, 29–30, 80, 108, 239*n*20

Athenäum, 27

Aurnhammer, Achim von, 80, 247*n*107